W9-CYV-018

Better Homes and Gardens®

new dieter's cookbook

eat well

feel great

lose weight

Better Homes and Gardens® Books
Des Moines, Iowa

Better Homes and Gardens® Books
An imprint of Meredith® Books

New Dieter's Cookbook
Editor: Kristi Fuller, R.D.
Contributing Editors: Diane Nelson; Janet Pittman; Diane Quagliani, R.D.;
   Donna Shields, R.D.; Marcia Stanley, R.D.; Spectrum Communication Services, Inc.
Associate Art Director: Lynda Haupert
Copy Chief: Angela K. Renkoski
Proofreader: Susan Kling
Test Kitchen Director: Sharon Stilwell
Test Kitchen Home Economist: Marilyn Cornelius
Photographers: Mike Dieter, Scott Little
Food Stylists: Lynn Blanchard, Dianna Nolin, Jennifer Peterson
Electronic Production Coordinator: Paula Forest
Editorial and Design Assistants: Karen Schirm, Judy Bailey, Jennifer Norris
Production Director: Douglas M. Johnston
Production Manager: Pam Kvitne
Prepress Coordinator: Marjorie J. Schenkelberg

Meredith® Books
Editor in Chief: James D. Blume
Design Director: Matt Strelecki
Managing Editor: Gregory H. Kayko
Executive Food Editor: Lisa Holderness

Vice President, General Manager: Jamie L. Martin

Better Homes and Gardens® **Magazine**
Editor in Chief: Jean LemMon
Executive Food Editor: Nancy Byal

Meredith Publishing Group
President, Publishing Group: Christopher M. Little
Vice President and Publishing Director: John P. Loughlin

Meredith Corporation
Chairman of the Board: Jack D. Rehm
President and Chief Executive Officer: William T. Kerr

Chairman of the Executive Committee: E.T. Meredith III

Cover photograph: Pork Lo Mein, recipe on page 207
Photographer: Scott Little

Our seal assures you that every recipe in *New Dieter's Cookbook* has been tested in the Better Homes and Gardens® Test Kitchen. This means that each recipe is practical and reliable, and meets our high standards of taste appeal. We guarantee your satisfaction with this book for as long as you own it.

© Copyright 1997 by Meredith Corporation, Des Moines, Iowa.
All rights reserved. Printed in the United States of America.
Third Edition. Printing Number and Year: 5 4 3 2   01 00 99 98 97
Library of Congress Catalog Card Number: 97-71330
ISBN: 0-696-20714-1

contents

no more dieting!

We're going to help you erase the word diet from your vocabulary. Are you surprised, considering the title of this cookbook? Despite the title, the *New Dieter's Cookbook* can help you ban dieting from your life—forever.

The fact is, diets don't work in the long run. Americans spend $30 billion each year on diet plans, products, and potions, yet most people gain back up to two-thirds of pounds lost within a year, and all of it within five years.

But you can jump off the diet roller coaster, lose weight, and keep it off long term. The following pages are filled with up-to-the-minute advice on healthful eating and physical activity to help you do just that.

And once you reach your goal weight, this is one diet cookbook you won't be tempted to sell at your next garage sale. Why? Because we trimmed the calories, fat, and sodium—but not the flavor— from our recipes. You'll never feel deprived or dissatisfied. Instead, you and your family will continue to enjoy the tasty, reliable, practical, and healthful recipes in this book. So hold on to it and let go of dieting once and for all.

DO YOU NEED TO LOSE?

One in three American adults is overweight. Are you one of them?

The answer to this question is not as clear cut as you might think. Perhaps a better question to ask is are you "overfat"? Extra body weight from fat is what increases your risk for developing health problems such as high blood pressure, heart disease, gallstones, diabetes, and some cancers.

How do you know whether you're carrying too much fat? The number you see on the scale provides only one piece of the puzzle because it doesn't tell you how much of your weight is from fat, muscle, bone, or fluid. Consulting a weight chart offers another clue, but most charts don't account for individual characteristics such as your age, sex, and frame size, and, like the scale, charts can't tell you whether you are carrying an undesirable amount of body fat. Use charts and your bathroom scale as general guides only—not set-in-stone absolutes.

One guideline for determining your weight is the Body Mass Index (BMI). According to the National Center for Health Statistics, a BMI of 27.3 or more for women, and 27.8 or more for men is considered as overweight. A severe weight problem is considered as 32.3 or more for women and 32.1 for men.

To figure your BMI, multiply your weight by 700, then divide by your height (in inches). Divide that number by your height again. For example, a 145 pound woman who stands 5'6" tall has a BMI of 23.

145 pounds × 700 = 101,500 ÷ 66 (5'6") ÷ 66 = 23

Once you calculate your BMI, check the chart, *below,* to see if your weight is putting you at risk for health problems.

Body Mass Index (BMI) Risk for Health Problems	
20 to 25	Very low
26 to 30	Low
31 to 35	Moderate
36 to 40	High
Source: World Health Organization	

SETTING A GOAL WEIGHT

If your BMI suggests you need to lose weight, the next step is to set a healthful goal weight.

The best weight for you is as individual as your fingerprints. To make sure the goal you set is healthful and realistic, ask yourself these questions:

● Am I relying on a weight chart to find the best weight for me? Is it realistic? Remember, weight charts offer general guidelines only. The best weight for you may be higher or lower than the chart indicates.

● Is my goal weight realistic for me? Don't try to look like a tall, willowy fashion model if you are short and big-boned. Instead, set a goal that suits your particular build.

● Can I comfortably maintain my goal weight without constant dieting and exercising? A healthful weight is one you can easily maintain by eating moderate portions of a wide variety of foods, and with moderate amounts of physical activity.

Your doctor or a registered dietitian can help you assess your need to lose weight, and if you do, set the most healthful goal weight for you.

FIGURING YOUR CALORIE NEEDS IS AS EASY AS 1-2-3

How many calories do you need each day to reach your goal weight? It depends on several factors including your age, body size, and activity level. But your needs are easy to figure once you know a little calorie math.

A pound of body fat contains approximately 3,500 calories (about the same number as in a pound of butter or margarine). Figure the calorie math this way: If you eat 3,500 fewer calories than your body uses, you will shed about 1 pound.

Take in 7,000 fewer calories—or, use up 7,000 extra calories—and you will lose about 2 pounds. (Of course, this is over a period of time. Nutrition

experts say losing one-half to 1 pound a week at most is the safest, most effective way to take off pounds and keep them off.)

How does this translate into everyday living? By eating 500 fewer calories each day, you should lose about 1 pound a week. Or cut only 250 calories each day and lose one-half pound a week.

Use the steps below to estimate the calories you need each day to lose about 1 pound per week.

1. Determine the calories you burn per pound each day based on your average level of activity:

13 calories/pound for inactivity (office work/sitting most of the day)

15 calories/pound for moderate activity (office work plus 30 to 60 minutes of aerobic activity, or walking/standing most of the day)

17 calories/pound for extensive activity (strenuous physical work or athletic level of physical activity)

2. Multiply the calories you burn per pound from Step 1 by your current weight in pounds to estimate your daily calorie needs.

3. Subtract 500 calories from your daily calorie needs in Step 2 to determine the number of calories you need to lose 1 pound per week. Create a daily deficit of 500 calories per day by eating fewer calories, burning off extra calories with physical activity, or, best yet, doing both. (See Calories—How Low Can You Go? on page 10.)

So, if you're a moderately active 133-pound woman, you need 15 calories times 133, or about 1,995 calories per day for your weight to stay the same (see example, top of page 6). To lose 1 pound in a week, create a deficit of 500 calories each day. You can do this in different ways. For example, each day you could eat 400 fewer calories and burn off 100 extra calories with physical activity, or eat 300 fewer calories and burn off 200 extra calories. Whatever the combination, the choice is yours.

Sample Calorie Calculation

1,995 maintenance calories per day

-500 calories per day =

1,495 calories per day to lose about 1 pound
per week

Don't cut calories severely! It's difficult to get all the nutrients you need when you eat fewer than 1,200 calories per day. Most dietitians and health experts don't recommend going below this calorie level without the supervision of a doctor.

LOSE WEIGHT AND KEEP IT OFF THE NO-DIET WAY

Now that you're armed with a sensible goal weight and daily calorie level, how do you go about losing weight and keeping it off?

We promised no more dieting, and we're keeping that promise. Diets don't work because they often don't suit your lifestyle, include foods you like best, or teach healthful, new habits.

This section shows you what does work. It begins with the basics you need to develop a healthful plan for eating and physical activity that you can stick with long term. It also includes a lot of strategies and tips to help ensure your success. For further help, a registered dietitian can help you create a customized plan that's right for you. To find a registered dietitian in your area, call The American Dietetic Association at 800/366-1655.

GOOD NUTRITION: BUILD A SOLID FOUNDATION

An eating plan that's high in carbohydrates, moderate in protein, and low in fat provides the best foundation for successful weight control. To build your foundation, follow the Food Guide Pyramid, the U.S. Department of Agriculture's guide to good nutrition for healthy Americans two years of age or more.

Each day, eat at least the lowest number of servings from the Pyramid's five food groups. Choose a variety foods from within each group to ensure that you'll get the carbohydrates, protein, vitamins, and minerals you need for good health. (See sample menus for 1,200 calories, page 12.)

Go easy on foods located in the tip of the Pyramid—fats, oils, and sweets—where there is no suggested serving. The fewer, the better. To trim calories, choose the lowest fat foods from each group, and limit your intake of alcohol.

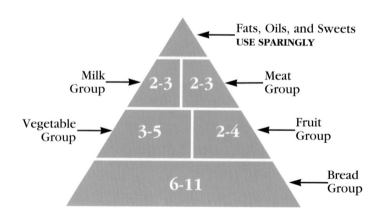

NUTRITION BY THE NUMBERS

Eat less than 30 percent of your calories from fat. Eat more fiber. Don't eat too much sodium. Sound nutrition advice all of it. But how do you apply this advice to your food choices?

Shown below are healthful amounts to consume for several key nutrients, based on daily calorie levels of 1,200, 1,500, 2,000, and 2,500. The guidelines for 2,000 calories are the basis for the Daily Values on the Nutrition Facts food label, so reading labels is an essential tool (along with following the Food Guide Pyramid) for creating a healthful meal plan.

Remember, these are guidelines, not exact targets you must hit each day. Balancing your food choices over time is what's important for good health. (See sample menus, page 12.)

Daily Guidelines				
Calories *	**1,200**	**1,500**	**2,000**	**2,500**
Total Fat	40 g	50 g	65 g	80 g
Saturated Fat	12 g	15 g	20 g	25 g
Cholesterol	300 mg	300 mg	300 mg	300 mg
Sodium	2,400 mg	2,400 mg	2,400 mg	2,400 mg
Total Carbohydrate	180 g	225 g	300 g	375 g
Dietary Fiber	20 g	20 g	25 g	30 g

* If your calorie intake differs, adjust these guidelines accordingly.

ALL CALORIES COUNT— BUT NOT ALL CALORIES ARE EQUAL

Food is a combination of carbohydrates, protein, and/or fat. These nutrients provide the calories found in all foods. But not all calories are created equal. Carbohydrates and protein yield four calories per gram, while fat yields nine calories per gram. Alcohol also contributes calories—about seven calories per gram—but has little nutritional value.

When you compare an equal amount of fat to an equal amount of carbohydrate or protein, fat packs more than twice the calories per gram of either. That's why fatty foods are generally high in calories. But all calories count. Eating more calories than your body needs—whether from carbohydrates, protein, or fat—results in weight gain.

GET ACTIVE: YOU'VE GOT EVERYTHING TO GAIN

To win at weight loss, burning calories through activity is just as important as adopting a healthful eating plan. No matter how you look at it, physical activity comes up a winner. Regular physical activity:

- Burns calories and preserves lean muscle mass while you shed pounds from fat
- Helps maintain your weight once you reach your goal
- Revs up your metabolism so you continue to burn extra calories for up to several hours
- Strengthens bones, muscles, and joints
- Reduces risk of heart disease, high blood pressure, diabetes, and colon cancer
- Just plain makes you feel good by reducing feelings of depression and anxiety, and promoting a sense of well-being

To reap these benefits, health experts recommend striving for a moderate amount of physical activity on a daily basis. What's moderate activity? Any activity that burns about 150 calories a day, or 1,000 calories per week.

Fitness Boom ... or Bust?

- More than 60 percent of American adults aren't physically active on a regular basis.
- One in four adults aren't active at all.
- More women than men aren't active.

The good news is, you don't have to join a gym or invest in expensive equipment to benefit. The chart below shows several options for fitting moderate physical activity into your day. Each activity burns approximately 150 calories in the time indicated. Note that a more strenuous activity, such as running, requires less time than a moderate activity such as walking. For best results, choose a variety of activities you enjoy and that fit easily into your lifestyle.

Washing and waxing a car for 45 to 60 minutes *Less Vigorous, More Time*
Washing windows or floors for 45 to 60 minutes
Playing basketball for 15 to 20 minutes
Playing volleyball for 45 minutes
Playing touch football for 30 to 45 minutes
Gardening for 30 to 45 minutes
Walking 1¾ miles in 35 minutes (20 min./mile)
Basketball (shooting baskets) for 30 minutes
Bicycling 5 miles in 30 minutes
Dancing fast for 30 minutes
Pushing a stroller 1½ miles in 30 minutes
Raking leaves for 30 minutes
Walking 2 miles in 30 minutes (15 min./mile)
Water aerobics for 30 minutes
Swimming laps for 20 minutes
Bicycling 4 miles in 15 minutes
Jumping rope for 15 minutes
Running 1½ miles in 15 minutes (10 min./mile)
Shoveling snow for 15 minutes
Stair climbing for 15 minutes *More Vigorous, Less Time*

Source: U.S. Department of Health and Human Services
(A Report of the Surgeon General, 1996)

Note: If you have health problems or are a man over the age of 40 or a woman over the age of 50, consult your doctor before you begin a new physically active program.

A BAKER'S DOZEN STEPS FOR SUCCESS

Do It for the Right Reasons. Before beginning your weight-loss venture, ask yourself why you want to lose weight. Is it because your class reunion looms on the horizon or your spouse wants you to? The best reason to lose weight is an internal one such as wanting to feel more energetic so you can live life to the fullest.

Take the Slow Road. Make only a change or two at a time to your eating and activity habits, rather than attempting a complete lifestyle overhaul. You're more likely to stick with new habits when you take the slow approach.

Do It Your Way. Many weight loss-diets are one size-fits-all prescriptions that tell you exactly what and when to eat, and seldom take into account your likes, dislikes, and lifestyle. No wonder diets don't work! Plan meals and snacks according to your own preferences. But don't skip meals, which will zap your energy.

Don't Expect Perfection. Use your daily calorie level as a guide, not a rule you must follow. This is true of physical activity, too. Don't feel guilty if you miss a day or two. It's progress made over time that counts.

Look at the Long and Short of It. Establish short-term weight goals as well as a long-term goal. You'll feel good tracking your progress and reaching one weight-loss goal after another.

Raise Your Food IQ. Learning about the calories, fat, vitamins, minerals, and other nutrients in the foods helps you follow your daily calorie level and make informed, healthful food choices. Read food labels to learn how foods fit into your eating plan. Note serving sizes and calories and fat in each serving. Weigh and measure foods a few times to learn what a serving looks like. The recipes and Calorie Tally on page 464 also provide useful information.

Tune In to Your Inner Signals. Listen and trust your body's signals of hunger and fullness. These are keys to achieving your best weight. Tuning in also helps you avoid eating for emotional reasons—boredom, anxiety, anger, or loneliness, for instance—rather than hunger.

Enjoy Favorite Foods. An eating plan you enjoy is an eating plan you'll stick with. Trying to squelch cravings for favorite goodies can backfire into an all-out binge. Allow for an occasional treat in a reasonable portion—and savor every bite!

Put It in Writing. Keep a journal to track your progress, monitor your feelings, plan eating strategies for special occasions, and even log in compliments you receive as you lose weight.

Plan on It. If you're going to a birthday bash or out for a special meal, work in extra physical activity and bank some calories for a few days before and after. That way, you can splurge a little at the event.

Don't Be a Slave to the Scale. Sometimes, despite your best efforts, the needle on the scale won't budge, or may inch upward. Your body may be adjusting to a lower calorie level. Focus on how good you feel—over time your weight will come down.

Celebrate Your Successes. Reward your progress, but not with food. Instead, buy yourself flowers, a new pair of walking shoes, or go to movie when you reach a short-term goal. Splurge on a new outfit or a complete makeover when you reach a long-term goal.

Make It a Family Affair. Enlist your friends, mate, or children as cheerleaders in your weight-loss effort. Involve them in choosing and preparing recipes from this book, then go for a group walk after dinner. It's good for them, too!

KEEPING WEIGHT OFF—YOU'VE GOT WHAT IT TAKES

Congratulations! You've reached your goal weight. But are you worried about keeping those pounds off?

Don't be . . . you've already got what it takes. It's simply a matter of continuing the same healthful eating and activity habits that helped you meet your goal—habits that are second nature by now.

More good news: You can enjoy more calories each day to maintain your weight. Use steps 1 and 2 (omitting Step 3) from the Figuring Your Calorie Needs section on page 5 to calculate the number of calories you need to maintain your new weight. Spend these extra calories wisely by choosing a variety of nutrient-dense foods. Of course an occasional favorite treat is fine, too.

If your weight creeps up a pound or two—say over the holidays or during a vacation—don't fret. Even people who are naturally thin experience weight fluctuations at certain times. Just resume your healthful habits as soon as possible, and the pounds will come off again.

KIDS AND DIETING

Gone are the days when the belief that a fat child was a healthy child. We now know that an overweight preschooler has an increased risk of remaining fat into adulthood and a teenager runs an even greater risk. Obesity contributes to many health problems, such as heart disease, diabetes, high blood pressure, and joint problems.

Because children and teenagers are continually growing until their late teens, it's important NOT to put children on a restrictive diet. The best thing a parent can do for their children is to help them eat moderately and healthfully and encourage physical activity. Keep the cupboards and refrigerator well-stocked with healthful foods and serve meals that are low in fat and moderate in calories. (You can begin by serving the recipes in this book, which are appropriate for the whole family.) Also, to meet a child's high-energy needs, nutritious snacks should be a necessary part of a healthful diet. Although you can't police everything your children eat away from home, you can teach them how to eat right by being a role model for them at home.

Calories—How Low Can You Go?

Severely restricting your calories may seem like the best way to lose weight because the pounds come off quickly. But over time, you'll actually lose *more* total body fat if you follow a plan that is reasonable in calories (more than 1,000). Less than 1,000 and your body starts to lose lean body mass. Lean body mass requires more calories to maintain itself than body fat. That's why men have an advantage over women; men have more muscles or lean body mass and therefore can eat more calories. The best bet for losing fat and maintaining lean body mass is a diet that is at least 1,200 calories *plus* physical activity. Physical activity builds your lean body mass yet burns fat.

DIET MYTHS

Have you heard the one about the fat-burning grapefruit? Or the Chinese magic weight-loss earrings? Have you tried a get-thin-quick scheme or two yourself? Then you've been "myth-taken!" Diet gimmicks waste your money because they don't work. Some are just plain silly and some are downright unsafe. Here are the facts about five popular weight-loss fads.

FAD: Fasting is a quick, effective way to take off pounds.

FACT: Quite the contrary. Fasting for long periods is not only dangerous, but is counterproductive. Any quick weight loss you see is mostly from water and muscle tissue, not body fat. Going without food for long periods deprives you of energy and nutrients. It also slows down your metabolism so you burn fewer calories—not a desirable consequence!

FAD: Try the Cabbage Soup Diet. The more soup you eat, the more weight you'll lose.

FACT: On this seven-day diet you fill up on all the cabbage soup you want, while other foods are strictly limited. There's no magic about cabbage soup. If you lose weight, it's only because you're eating fewer calories. This diet is nutritionally unbalanced, and doesn't teach healthful, new habits, so you'll most likely gain back any weight you lose.

FAD: Chromium supplements stimulate your body to use stored fat so you can eat whatever you want and still lose weight.

FACT: Pills—including chromium supplements—can't stimulate your body to burn fat. Most people get all the chromium they need from food. Taking extra chromium in pill form doesn't appear to offer any benefits, and may cause harm.

FAD: A high-protein, low-carbohydrate diet triggers quick weight loss by causing the body to burn stored fat for fuel.

FACT: Rapid weight loss on this diet is mostly from water, not body fat. Depriving the body of fuel from carbohydrates can cause nausea, weakness, breakdown of muscle, dehydration, and stress on the kidneys, all of which are potentially dangerous. Because this diet forbids almost all grains, fruits, and vegetables, you'll come up short on vitamins, minerals, and fiber.

FAD: Diet pills are an easy way to take off excess pounds.

FACT: Over-the-counter diet pills curb your appetite, but only work for a few weeks. Some pills may cause unpleasant—or even dangerous—side effects. Consult your doctor with questions about over-the-counter or prescription diet aids.

Fat-Free Can Fool You

Some reduced-fat and fat-free foods contain as many or more calories as their regular-fat counterparts. Carefully check the Nutrition Facts panel on food packages for serving size and calorie information.

14-day menu plans

See page 5 to determine your calorie requirements, then use these menus as a guide for a 1,200-calorie-a-day plan (page references tell where to find the recipes). For 1,500 calories, add the foods listed in color. If you need more than 1,500 calories, refer to Calorie Tally on pages 464–469 and choose and add foods from the list to meet your needs.

	Breakfast	**Lunch**	**Dinner**	**Snack***
Day 1	Fruity Oatmeal (page 72) 1 cup skim milk	Tuna-Vegetable Salad (page 139) 1 slice French bread 1 teaspoon margarine 1 cup fresh raspberries mixed with 1 sliced, fresh peach Iced tea	3 ounces grilled, skinless chicken breast half Creamy Spaghetti With Basil (page 376) 1 carrot, cut into sticks 1 cup skim milk Rum-Sauced Bananas (page 442)	Roasted Red Pepper Dip (page 53) 1 carrot 2 whole wheat crackers
For 1,500 calories add:	1 small banana	1 slice French bread 1 teaspoon margarine	1 ounce grilled, skinless chicken breast 2 soft breadsticks	
Day 2	1½ cups cornflakes ½ cup skim milk ½ cup orange juice	Cabbage-Broccoli Salad (page 100) 1 bran raisin muffin 1 teaspoon margarine Lemon-flavored carbonated water (sugar-free)	Curried Pork Chops With Oranges (page 193) 1 cup cooked corn 2 cups tossed salad 2 tablespoons nonfat Italian salad dressing 1 cup skim milk Chocolate-Cinnamon Angel Cake (page 463)	Tropical Banana Milk Shake (page 65)
For 1,500 calories add:	½ English muffin, toasted ½ teaspoon margarine	1 small apple	½ cup cooked corn 1 ounce shredded reduced-fat cheddar cheese to salad	
Day 3	8 ounces raspberry fat-free yogurt 1 2-ounce bagel 1 tablespoon reduced-fat cream cheese Hot coffee	½ turkey sandwich (1 slice whole wheat bread, 1 ounce sliced turkey, 1 ounce Swiss cheese, 1 lettuce leaf, 1 teaspoon mustard) Gazpacho (page 110) 1 cup skim milk	Scallops and Broccoli Pasta (page 310) Hot tea Sweet and Spicy Peaches (page 436)	Carrot Snack Cake (page 62) 1 fresh plum
For 1,500 calories add:	½ cup juice-packed peaches	½ turkey sandwich (same as above)		

*Snacks may be eaten any time during the day.

Note: Unsweetened coffee, tea, and carbonated water are suggested beverages only. Ideally, you should drink 6 to 8 glasses of water throughout the day.

	Breakfast	**Lunch**	**Dinner**	**Snack***
Day 4	Granola (page 71) ½ cup grapefruit juice	Fruited Cottage Cheese Salad (page 92) 2 carrots, cut into sticks 6 whole wheat crackers Iced tea	Veal With Apple-Marsala Sauce (page 186) 1 cup steamed broccoli 1 small whole wheat French roll 1 teaspoon margarine Hot coffee	2 Apricot-Oatmeal Bars (page 61) 1½ cups skim milk
For 1,500 calories add:	½ cup grapefruit juice	½ roast beef sandwich (1 slice whole wheat bread, 2 ounces lean roast beef, 1 lettuce leaf, 1 teaspoon mustard)		1 cup sweet pepper strips Creamy Salad Dressing (page 392)
Day 5	Saucy Prunes and Peaches (page 74) ½ cup cooked oatmeal 1 cup skim milk Hot coffee	Ham and Orzo Salad (page 125) 1 blueberry muffin 1 teaspoon margarine Raspberry-flavored carbonated water (sugar-free)	2 ounces roasted pork tenderloin Lemony Asparagus and New Potatoes (page 359) 3 fresh apricot halves Iced tea Pumpkin Custards (page 450)	Brownie Bites (page 63) 1 cup skim milk
For 1,500 calories add:	½ cup cooked oatmeal	1 medium fresh pear	1 ounce roasted pork tenderloin 1 small sourdough roll	
Day 6	1½ cups toasted oat cereal 1 cup skim milk ½ pink grapefruit with 1½ teaspoons brown sugar	Lentil-Vegetable Salad (page 135) 1 cup skim milk ½ cup watermelon cubes	Vegetable-Barley Pot Pies (page 351) 1 cup skim milk 2 cups tossed salad 2 tablespoons reduced-fat salad dressing Apricot Custards (page 449)	Sugar and Spice Popcorn (page 57)
For 1,500 calories add:	8 ounces cherry fat-free yogurt	1 cup watermelon cubes 5 rye crackers	1 slice French bread	
Day 7	**BRUNCH** Ham and Cheese Frittata (page 81) 2 cups tossed salad 2 tablespoons nonfat salad dressing 2 slices French bread	1 teaspoon margarine 1 cup skim milk Hot coffee Strawberries With Custard Sauce (page 446)	Deep-Dish Vegetable Pizza (page 350) Iced tea (unsweetened) 1 cup fresh pineapple chunks	8 ounces fat-free strawberry yogurt 1 cup fresh blueberries 2 vanilla wafers
For 1,500 calories add:				1½ ounces pretzels 1 ounce reduced-fat cheddar cheese ½ cup orange juice

Snacks may be eaten any time during the day.

	Breakfast	**Lunch**	**Dinner**	**Snack***
Day 8	1 plain waffle 1 teaspoon margarine 2 tablespoons sugar-free syrup 1½ cups skim milk	Minted Pea-Egg Salad (page 96) 3 rye crackers Pineapple sparkler (¾ cup pineapple juice plus 1 cup carbonated water)	Crab Gumbo (page 315) 2 soft breadsticks 2 cups tossed salad 2 tablespoons nonfat salad dressing Carbonated water Cream Puffs (page 34)	Fruit Kabobs With Ginger Dip (page 48)
For 1,500 calories add:	1 plain waffle 1 teaspoon margarine 2 tablespoons sugar-free syrup	3 rye crackers	1 ounce shredded mozzarella cheese to salad 1 soft breadstick	
Day 9	8 ounces fat-free lemon yogurt ½ cup fresh raspberries 1 slice cinnamon bread, toasted Hot tea	Hearty Italian-Style Soup (page 108) 1 cup raw cauliflower pieces 1 cup skim milk	Spiced Pear and Pork Chops (page 191) 1 6-ounce baked potato 2 teaspoons margarine 1 cup steamed, sliced carrots Carbonated water Flan (page 39)	Orange and Spice Tea (page 67)
For 1,500 calories add:	1 slice cinnamon bread, toasted	1 medium apple		5 vanilla wafers
Day 10	1 English muffin, toasted 2 teaspoons margarine 8 ounces fat-free peach yogurt Hot coffee	Clam-Corn Chowder (page 107) 12 oyster crackers Hot herbed tea 1 medium tangerine	Mushroom-Stuffed Beef Roast (page 167) ⅔ cup long-grain and wild rice pilaf 1 cup steamed asparagus Carbonated water Watermelon Sherbet (page 454)	2 Macaroons (page 461) Hot tea
For 1,500 calories add:			⅓ cup long-grain and wild rice pilaf ½ cup steamed, mixed vegetables	3 saltine crackers 2 tablespoons reduced-fat peanut butter ½ cup apple juice
Day 11	Breakfast Rice Cereal (page 70) ½ English muffin, toasted 1 teaspoon margarine 1 cup skim milk	Garbanzo Bean and Vegetable Salad (page 103) Apple and Oat Bran Muffin (page 428) Iced tea	3 ounces grilled salmon Herbed Couscous and Vegetables (page 374) Curried Fruit Salad (page 402) Carbonated water ½ cup raspberry ice	2 Blueberry Gems (page 429) 1 cup skim milk
For 1,500 calories add:	½ English muffin 1 teaspoon margarine	1 cup cubed honeydew melon	1 ounce grilled salmon 1 small mixed-grain roll	

Snacks may be eaten any time during the day.

	Breakfast	**Lunch**	**Dinner**	**Snack***
Day 12	Peach Butter Sweet Rolls (page 431) 1 cup cubed melon 1 cup skim milk	Salmon-and-Pasta-Stuffed Tomatoes (page 137) 2 rice cakes 1 cup skim milk	Baked Chimichangas (page 236) 2 cups tossed salad 2 tablespoons nonfat salad dressing Carbonated water Frozen Cranberry Pie (page 456)	3 cups light microwave popcorn Carbonated water with lime slice
For 1,500 calories add:	8 ounces blueberry fat-free yogurt		1 ounce shredded mozzarella cheese to salad 1 slice French bread	1 medium fresh nectarine
Day 13	1 cup cooked oatmeal with 1 tablespoon dried tart red cherries stirred in ½ cup skim milk	½ ham sandwich (1 slice whole wheat bread, 1 ounce sliced ham, 1 lettuce leaf, 1 slice tomato, 1 teaspoon mustard) Corn Chowder (page 405) 1 carrot, cut into sticks 1 cup skim milk	Chicken With Olives and Leeks (page 247) ½ cup hot cooked linguine Spinach salad (1½ cups spinach, ⅔ cup halved strawberries, ¼ cup sliced mushrooms, and 1 tablespoon sliced green onion) 2 tablespoons reduced-fat honey-dijon salad dressing 1 small sourdough roll 1 teaspoon margarine Iced tea Sweet-Topped Raspberries (page 444)	1 fat-free frozen chocolate sorbet bar
For 1,500 calories add:	1 bran muffin	½ ham sandwich (same as above) 1 medium orange		
Day 14	BRUNCH Pancakes With Orange Sauce (page 76) Turkey and Apple Sausage (page 75) Hot coffee 1 cup skim milk		Spinach-Stuffed Flank Steak (page 185) ⅔ cup cooked brown rice Apple-Cheese Gelatin Salad (page 403) Hot tea Lemon Dessert With Raspberries (page 445)	SNACK 1 Peppy Tomato Sipper (page 66) 2 whole wheat crackers SNACK 2 3 gingersnaps 1 cup skim milk
For 1,500 calories add:	BRUNCH 1 additional serving of Turkey and Apple Sausage (page 75) ½ cup peach nectar		⅓ cup cooked brown rice	2 whole wheat crackers

Snacks may be eaten any time during the day.

CALORIE-TRIMMED

Classi

chapter index

87 calories

Preparation time: 18 minutes ● **Baking time:** 10 minutes

buttermilk biscuits

Biscuits are usually made with shortening, butter, or margarine. Here we've used oil, which is lower in saturated fat, a type of fat that is linked to heart disease. We also cut the calories and total fat per biscuit by half.

1 **cup all-purpose flour***
1 **teaspoon baking powder**
⅛ **teaspoon baking soda**
⅛ **teaspoon salt**
⅓ **cup buttermilk or sour milk**
2 **tablespoons cooking oil**
1 **recipe Orange Spread (optional)**

1 In a medium bowl combine flour, baking powder, baking soda, and salt.

2 In a small bowl stir together the buttermilk or sour milk and oil. Pour over flour mixture; stir until well mixed.

3 On a lightly floured surface, knead dough gently for 10 to 12 strokes. Roll out or pat dough to ½-inch thickness. Cut with a 2-inch biscuit cutter, dipping cutter in flour between cuts. Transfer biscuits to an ungreased baking sheet.

4 Bake in a 450° oven for 10 to 12 minutes or until golden brown. Serve warm. If desired, pass Orange Spread. Makes 8 biscuits.
***Note:** If desired, substitute ¼ cup whole wheat flour or oat bran for ¼ cup of the all-purpose flour.

Nutrition facts per biscuit: 87 calories, 4 g total fat (1 g saturated fat), 0 mg cholesterol, 109 mg sodium, 12 g carbohydrate, 0 g fiber, 2 g protein
Exchanges: 1 Starch

Orange Spread: In a small bowl stir together ½ of an 8-ounce package *reduced-fat cream cheese (Neufchâtel)*, softened, and 2 tablespoons *orange marmalade* or *peach* or *apricot preserves*, until smooth. Makes about ½ cup.

Nutrition facts per 1 tablespoon spread: 50 calories, 3 g total fat (2 g saturated fat), 11 mg cholesterol, 57 mg sodium, 4 g carbohydrate, 0 g fiber, 1 g protein
Exchanges: ½ Fruit, ½ Fat

119 calories

Preparation time: 20 minutes ● **Rising time:** 30 minutes ● **Baking time:** 20 minutes

cinnamon rolls with orange glaze

To easily cut dough, place a long piece of heavy-duty thread under the rolled up dough, about 1 inch from one end. Bring thread up around sides, crisscross it at top, and pull quickly in opposite directions. Repeat for 12 rolls.

1 16-ounce loaf frozen bread dough or
   frozen sweet roll dough, thawed
1 tablespoon margarine or butter, melted
1 tablespoon granulated sugar
1 teaspoon ground cinnamon
   Nonstick spray coating
½ cup sifted powdered sugar
¼ teaspoon finely shredded orange peel
3 to 4 teaspoons orange juice

1 On a floured surface, roll dough into a 12×8-inch rectangle. (If the dough is difficult to roll out, let it rest for a short time and roll again. Repeat as necessary.)

2 Brush dough with melted margarine or butter; sprinkle evenly with the 1 tablespoon granulated sugar and the cinnamon.

3 Roll up dough, beginning from a long side. Seal seam. Slice into twelve 1-inch-thick pieces.

4 Spray a 9×1½- or 8×1½-inch round baking pan with nonstick coating. Place rolls in pan, cut sides down. Cover and let rise in a warm place until nearly double (30 to 60 minutes).

5 Bake in a 375° oven for 20 to 25 minutes or until lightly browned. Cool slightly in pan on wire rack; remove from pan.

6 For glaze, in a small bowl stir together the powdered sugar, orange peel, and enough orange juice to make of drizzling consistency. Drizzle over warm rolls. Serve warm. Makes 12 servings.

Nutrition facts per serving: 119 calories, 1 g total fat (0 g saturated fat), 0 mg cholesterol, 11 mg sodium, 22 g carbohydrate, 0 g fiber, 3 g protein
Exchanges: 1½ Starch

315 calories

Preparation time: 30 minutes ● **Chilling time:** 2 to 24 hours

salad niçoise

This reduced-fat version of the classic French tuna and vegetable salad contains only half the fat of the original. What's the difference? The olives were omitted, and the dressing contains 50 percent less oil.

1 **pound small potatoes, sliced ¼ inch thick**
8 **ounces whole green beans,* halved**
   crosswise
¼ **cup lemon juice**
2 **tablespoons salad oil**
1½ **teaspoons sugar**
4 **teaspoons brown mustard or Dijon-style**
   mustard
1 **teaspoon snipped fresh dill or ¾ teaspoon**
   dried dillweed
   Lettuce leaves
1 **6- or 6½-ounce can tuna (water-packed),**
   drained and broken into chunks
2 **medium tomatoes, seeded and cut into**
   chunks
½ **of a small red onion, thinly sliced and**
   separated into rings
2 **hard-cooked eggs, cut into wedges**

1 In a large saucepan bring 2 inches of *water* to boiling. Add potatoes and green beans. Cover and

simmer 10 minutes or just until tender. Remove beans with a slotted spoon; drain potatoes. Cover and refrigerate for at least 2 or up to 24 hours.

2 Meanwhile, for dressing, in a screw-top jar combine lemon juice, oil, sugar, mustard, dill, 2 tablespoons *water,* ¼ teaspoon *salt,* and ⅛ teaspoon *pepper.* Cover and shake well. Refrigerate for at least 2 or up to 24 hours.

3 To serve, place lettuce leaves on a platter. Arrange potatoes, beans, tuna, tomatoes, onion, and eggs on lettuce. Shake dressing and drizzle over salad. Makes 4 servings.

*Note: If desired, substitute one 9-ounce package frozen cut green beans, thawed, for the fresh beans. Add to potatoes for the last 5 minutes of cooking.

Nutrition facts per serving: 315 calories, 11 g total fat (2 g saturated fat), 120 mg cholesterol, 271 mg sodium, 37 g carbohydrate, 4 g fiber, 20 g protein
Exchanges: 2 Starch, 2 Lean Meat, 2 Vegetable, 1½ Fat

155 calories

Preparation time: 20 minutes ● **Cooking time:** 20 minutes ● **Chilling time:** 4 to 24 hours

creamy potato salad

Who can resist potato salad with a summer barbecue? You won't have to when you make this trimmed-down version. Compared to our classic recipe, we've shaved off 130 calories and 14 grams of fat per serving.

4 medium potatoes* (1¼ pounds total)
1 cup sliced celery
¼ cup finely chopped onion
2 tablespoons dill or sweet pickle relish
½ cup light mayonnaise dressing or salad dressing
½ cup light dairy sour cream
2 tablespoons skim milk
2 teaspoons prepared mustard
½ teaspoon salt
¼ to ½ teaspoon celery seed
1 hard-cooked egg, chopped
Lettuce leaves (optional)

1 Scrub potatoes. In a large covered saucepan cook potatoes in *boiling water* for 20 to 25 minutes or just until tender. Drain well; cool slightly.

2 Peel and cube potatoes. Transfer to a large bowl. Stir in celery, onion, and pickle relish.

3 In a small mixing bowl stir together the mayonnaise dressing or salad dressing, sour cream, milk, mustard, salt, and celery seed. Pour over potatoes. Toss lightly to coat potatoes. Carefully fold in chopped egg.

4 Cover and refrigerate for at least 4 or up to 24 hours. If desired, serve in a lettuce-lined bowl. Makes 8 servings.

*Note: Waxy potatoes, such as long whites and round reds, have a moist, smooth texture and will hold their shape after cooking. Tiny new potatoes are usually just young round reds and will also work well in salads.

Nutrition facts per serving: 155 calories, 7 g total fat (2 g saturated fat), 29 mg cholesterol, 357 mg sodium, 20 g carbohydrate, 1 g fiber, 4 g protein
Exchanges: 1½ Starch, 1 Fat

198 calories

Preparation time: 30 minutes

fried chicken with gravy

Be thrifty with the cooking oil when frying this family favorite. That's the secret to keeping the fat and calories under control. Using evaporated skim milk in the gravy eliminates some of the fat, too.

6 medium skinless, boneless chicken breast halves (about 1½ pounds total)
¼ cup all-purpose flour
½ teaspoon salt
½ teaspoon paprika
1½ teaspoons snipped fresh thyme or
  ½ teaspoon dried thyme, crushed
⅛ to ¼ teaspoon pepper
2 tablespoons cooking oil
½ cup evaporated skim milk
½ cup reduced-sodium chicken broth
  Paprika (optional)
  Fresh thyme (optional)

1 Rinse chicken breast halves; pat dry with paper towels.

2 In a plastic bag combine flour, salt, the ½ teaspoon paprika, the thyme, and pepper. Add chicken breast halves, two at a time, shaking to coat. Remove chicken from bag, shaking off any excess coating into the bag. Reserve the remaining flour mixture.

3 In a 12-inch skillet heat oil. Add chicken and cook, uncovered, over medium heat for 8 to 10 minutes or until chicken is tender and no longer pink, turning once to brown evenly. Drain chicken on paper towels. Keep warm.

4 Pour off drippings in skillet and discard.

5 For gravy, in a small bowl slowly stir evaporated milk into reserved flour mixture. Stir in chicken broth; add mixture to skillet. Cook and stir until thickened and bubbly. Cook and stir 1 minute more. Serve gravy over chicken. If desired, sprinkle with additional paprika and garnish with fresh thyme. Makes 6 servings.

Nutrition facts per serving: 198 calories, 8 g total fat (2 g saturated fat), 60 mg cholesterol, 310 mg sodium, 6 g carbohydrate, 0 g fiber, 24 g protein
Exchanges: ½ Starch, 3 Lean Meat

341 calories

Preparation time: 30 minutes ● **Cooking time:** 50 minutes

chicken and dumplings

You won't have to forfeit Mom's chicken and dumplings again. Skinning the chicken before you cook it keeps the calories and fat in check, making it kinder to your waistline.

 4 **chicken thighs (about 1½ pounds), skinned**
2½ **cups water**
 1 **cup sliced carrots**
 1 **cup sliced celery**
 ½ **cup chopped onion**
 2 **teaspoons instant chicken bouillon granules**
 ¾ **teaspoon snipped fresh sage**
      or ¼ teaspoon dried sage, crushed
 2 **tablespoons cold water**
 4 **teaspoons cornstarch**
 1 **recipe Dumplings**

1 Rinse chicken. In a large saucepan combine chicken, the 2½ cups water, the carrots, celery, onion, bouillon granules, and sage. Bring to boiling; reduce heat. Simmer, covered, for 35 minutes.

2 Remove chicken pieces from saucepan; set aside. Skim fat from broth.

3 Stir together the 2 tablespoons cold water and the cornstarch. Stir into broth in saucepan. Cook and stir until thickened and bubbly. Return chicken to the saucepan.

4 Meanwhile, prepare Dumplings. Drop dough from a tablespoon, making 8 mounds on top of the hot chicken mixture. Cover saucepan tightly; simmer for 10 minutes or until a wooden toothpick inserted into dumplings comes out clean. Makes 4 servings.

Dumplings: In a medium mixing bowl stir together 1 cup *all-purpose flour*, 1 tablespoon snipped *fresh parsley*, 2 teaspoons *baking powder*, and ⅛ teaspoon *salt*. In a small bowl combine 1 beaten *egg*, ¼ cup *skim milk*, and 2 tablespoons *cooking oil*; stir into flour mixture with a fork just until combined.

Nutrition facts per serving: 341 calories, 14 g total fat (3 g saturated fat), 103 mg cholesterol, 808 mg sodium, 33 g carbohydrate, 3 g fiber, 20 g protein
Exchanges: 1½ Starch, 2 Medium-Fat Meat, 2 Vegetable, ½ Fat

256 calories

Preparation time: 15 minutes ● **Baking time:** 30 minutes ● **Standing time:** 2 minutes

individual shepherd's pies

Packaged instant mashed potatoes, a jar of fat-free gravy, and leftover lamb or beef add up to quick-to-fix, family-pleasing casseroles. To save even more time, bake them in your microwave oven.

Packaged instant mashed potatoes (enough for 4 servings) or 2 cups purchased refrigerated mashed potatoes (about ⅔ of a 20-ounce package)

1 **10-ounce package frozen peas and carrots, thawed**

1½ **cups cubed cooked lamb or beef**

1 **12-ounce jar fat-free beef gravy**

1 **tablespoon tomato paste**

½ **teaspoon dried basil, crushed**

1 **tablespoon finely shredded reduced-fat sharp cheddar cheese**

1 If using instant mashed potatoes, prepare according to package directions, except omit butter and substitute skim milk for milk; set potatoes aside.

2 In a mixing bowl stir together peas and carrots, lamb or beef, gravy, tomato paste, and basil. Divide among four 12- to 16-ounce casseroles. Top casseroles with the prepared mashed potatoes.

3 Bake, uncovered, in a 350° oven for 30 to 35 minutes or until heated through. Sprinkle with cheese. Let stand 2 to 3 minutes to melt cheese. Makes 4 servings.

Microwave Directions: If using instant potatoes, prepare as in Step 1; set aside. Place frozen peas and carrots in a microwave-safe 1½-quart casserole. Add 2 tablespoons *water.* Cover and microwave on 100% power (high) for 2 to 4 minutes or until crisp-tender; drain. Stir in lamb or beef, gravy, tomato paste, and basil. Divide among 4 microwave-safe 12- to 16-ounce casseroles. Top with prepared mashed potatoes. Microwave, uncovered, on 100% power (high) for 10 to 12 minutes or until heated through, rearranging dishes once. Sprinkle with cheese. Let stand 2 to 3 minutes.

Nutrition facts per serving: 256 calories, 8 g total fat (3 g saturated fat), 54 mg cholesterol, 648 mg sodium, 26 g carbohydrate, 3 g fiber, 22 g protein
Exchanges: 1½ Starch, 2 Lean Meat, 1 Vegetable

364 calories

Freezing time: 30 minutes ● **Preparation time:** 30 minutes

stroganoff-style beef

This slimmed-down beef Stroganoff contains all the treasured flavors of the original: tender strips of beef, plenty of sliced mushrooms, and a flavorful sour cream sauce.

- 12 **ounces boneless beef round steak**
- 1 **8-ounce carton light dairy sour cream**
- 2 **tablespoons all-purpose flour**
- 1 **tablespoon tomato paste**
- 2 **teaspoons Worcestershire sauce**
- 1 **teaspoon instant beef bouillon granules**
- 1½ **teaspoons snipped fresh thyme or**
     ½ **teaspoon dried thyme, crushed**
- ¼ **teaspoon dry mustard**
- ⅛ **teaspoon pepper**
- 2 **cups sliced fresh mushrooms**
- ½ **cup chopped onion**
- 1 **tablespoon margarine or butter**
- ⅓ **cup water**
- 2 **tablespoons dry white wine or apple juice**
- 2 **cups hot cooked noodles**

1 Partially freeze meat. Trim fat from meat and thinly slice meat across the grain into bite-size strips.

2 In a small bowl stir together sour cream and flour. Stir in tomato paste, Worcestershire sauce, bouillon granules, thyme, dry mustard, and pepper. Set aside.

3 In a large skillet cook mushrooms and onion in hot margarine or butter until tender; remove from skillet.

4 Add beef to skillet. Cook 2 to 4 minutes or until no longer pink. Remove from skillet.

5 Add the water and wine or apple juice to skillet. Bring to boiling. Stir sour cream mixture into skillet. Return meat, mushrooms, and onion to skillet. Cook and stir until thickened and bubbly. Cook 1 minute more. Serve over noodles. Makes 4 servings.

Nutrition facts per serving: 364 calories, 12 g total fat (4 g saturated fat), 86 mg cholesterol, 392 mg sodium, 34 g carbohydrate, 3 g fiber, 29 g protein
Exchanges: 2 Starch, 3 Lean Meat, 1 Vegetable

168 calories

Preparation time: 15 minutes • **Baking time:** 45 minutes

meat loaf

If meat loaf evokes memories of home-cooked meals, you don't have to give it up because you're dieting. The type of meat you use is what makes the difference. Use the leanest beef possible (90 to 95 percent lean).

  1 **egg white or** ¼ **cup refrigerated or
     frozen egg product, thawed**
¼ **cup catsup**
¼ **cup finely chopped onion**
¼ **cup finely chopped celery**
¼ **cup shredded carrot**
¼ **cup fine dry bread crumbs**
¼ **cup skim milk**
¼ **teaspoon pepper**
⅛ **teaspoon salt**
  1 **pound lean ground beef**
  2 **tablespoons catsup**

1 In a large mixing bowl combine egg white or egg product, the ¼ cup catsup, the onion, celery, carrot, bread crumbs, milk, pepper, and salt. Add ground beef and mix well. In a shallow baking pan or dish pat the meat mixture into a 7×3×2-inch loaf.

2 Bake in a 350° oven for 45 to 50 minutes or until no pink remains. Spread the 2 tablespoons catsup over top of meat loaf. If desired, serve with additional catsup. Makes 6 servings.

Mexican-Style Meat Loaf: Prepare as above, except substitute *salsa* for the catsup and add 1 teaspoon *chili powder* with the bread crumbs. If desired, serve with additional salsa.

Nutrition facts per serving: 168 calories, 7 g total fat (3 g saturated fat), 48 mg cholesterol, 329 mg sodium, 10 g carbohydrate, 1 g fiber, 15 g protein
Exchanges: ½ Starch, 2 Lean Meat

281 calories

Preparation time: 45 minutes ● **Baking time:** 30 minutes ● **Standing time:** 10 minutes

lasagna

By using lower-fat cheeses in this recipe, we slashed the fat per serving in half. This slimmer version also has 75 fewer calories than a standard lasagna recipe.

- **8 ounces lean ground beef**
- **1 cup chopped onion**
- **2 cloves garlic, minced**
- **1 16-ounce can low-sodium tomatoes, undrained and cut up**
- **1 6-ounce can low-sodium tomato paste**
- **1½ teaspoons dried basil, crushed**
- **1½ teaspoons dried oregano, crushed**
- **1 teaspoon fennel seed, crushed**
- **9 packaged dried lasagna noodles**
- **1 12-ounce carton low-fat cottage cheese, drained**
- **1½ cups shredded reduced-fat mozzarella cheese (6 ounces)**
- **¼ cup grated Parmesan cheese (1 ounce)**
- **1 egg**
- **2 tablespoons snipped fresh parsley**

1 In a saucepan cook beef, onion, and garlic until meat is brown. Drain off fat. Stir in undrained tomatoes, tomato paste, basil, oregano, fennel seed, and ¼ teaspoon *salt*. Bring to boiling; reduce heat. Simmer, covered, for 15 minutes; stir occasionally.

2 Meanwhile, cook lasagna noodles according to package directions. Drain; rinse with cold water. Drain well.

3 For filling, combine cottage cheese, *1 cup* of the mozzarella cheese, the Parmesan cheese, egg, parsley, and ¼ teaspoon *pepper*.

4 Layer one-third of the cooked noodles in a 2-quart rectangular baking dish, trimming ends to fit. Spread with half of the filling. Top with one-third of sauce. Repeat layers. Top with remaining noodles and sauce. Sprinkle with remaining mozzarella.

5 Bake, uncovered, in a 375° oven for 30 to 35 minutes or until heated through. Let stand 10 minutes before serving. Makes 8 servings.

Nutrition facts per serving: 281 calories, 8 g total fat (5 g saturated fat), 60 mg cholesterol, 491 mg sodium, 27 g carbohydrate, 2 g fiber, 23 g protein
Exchanges: 1½ Starch, 2 Lean Meat, 1 Vegetable

230 calories

Preparation time: 25 minutes ● **Baking time:** 25 minutes

tuna - noodle casserole

To eliminate even more fat from this creamy casserole, replace the cheese with a fat-free cheese product.
Cut the cheese product into cubes instead of shredding it.

> **4** ounces packaged dried medium noodles
> **1** 9¼-ounce can tuna (water-packed)
> **1** tablespoon margarine or butter, melted
> **¼** cup fine dry bread crumbs
> **1** 10-ounce package frozen cut green beans
> **1** cup sliced fresh mushrooms
> **¾** cup chopped green or red sweet pepper
> **½** cup chopped onion
> **½** cup sliced celery
> **1** teaspoon instant chicken bouillon granules
> **1** clove garlic, minced
> **1½** cups skim milk
> **1** tablespoon cornstarch
> **½** teaspoon dry mustard
> **½** cup shredded American or process Swiss
>   cheese (2 ounces)

1 Cook noodles according to package directions; drain and set aside.

2 Meanwhile, drain and flake the tuna. Toss the margarine or butter with bread crumbs. Set aside.

3 In a large saucepan combine green beans, mushrooms, sweet pepper, onion, celery, bouillon granules, garlic, and ½ cup *water*. Bring to boiling; reduce heat. Simmer, covered, 5 minutes or until vegetables are tender.

4 Meanwhile, stir together milk, cornstarch, and dry mustard. Stir into vegetable mixture. Cook and stir until slightly thickened and bubbly. Remove from heat, then stir in cheese until melted. Stir in noodles and tuna.

5 Spoon mixture into a 2-quart casserole. Sprinkle bread crumb mixture around outside edge of casserole. Bake, uncovered, in a 350° oven for 25 to 30 minutes or until bread crumbs are golden brown. Makes 6 servings.

Nutrition facts per serving: 230 calories, 6 g total fat (2 g saturated fat), 35 mg cholesterol, 519 mg sodium, 26 g carbohydrate, 1 g fiber, 19 g protein
Exchanges: 1½ Starch, 2 Lean Meat, 1 Vegetable

223 calories

Preparation time: 20 minutes

lobster newburg

*Milk replaces cream in this lightened version of an easy-to-fix classic. Serve it for a
special brunch with friends or a romantic brunch for two.*

2 teaspoons margarine or butter
1 tablespoon all-purpose flour
¼ teaspoon salt
1½ cups milk
2 beaten egg yolks
8 ounces cubed fresh or frozen cooked
   lobster or refrigerated chunk-style
   lobster-flavored fish pieces
1 tablespoon dry sherry
⅛ teaspoon white or black pepper
   Dash ground red pepper
2 English muffins, split and toasted
   Snipped fresh chives (optional)

1 In a medium saucepan melt margarine or
butter. Stir in flour and salt. Add the milk all at once.
Cook and stir until thickened and bubbly. Cook and
stir 1 minute more.

2 Stir about half of the hot mixture into the
beaten egg yolks. Return all to saucepan. Cook and
stir until mixture is thickened and bubbly.

3 Stir in lobster, dry sherry, white or black
pepper, and ground red pepper.

4 Heat through. Serve over English muffin
halves. If desired, garnish with snipped chives.
Makes 4 servings.

Nutrition facts per serving: 223 calories, 6 g total fat
(1 g saturated fat), 149 mg cholesterol, 629 mg sodium,
22 g carbohydrate, 1 g fiber, 19 g protein
Exchanges: 1 Starch, 2 Lean Meat, ½ Milk

313 calories

Preparation time: 25 minutes ● **Cooking time:** 15 minutes

jambalaya

Jambalaya (juhm-buh-LI-yah) is a Creole dish that usually features ham as one of the main ingredients. Using pork instead helps to lower the sodium content.

4 ounces fully cooked smoked turkey sausage
1½ cups sliced fresh mushrooms
1 cup chopped green or red sweet pepper
¾ cup chopped onion
1 clove garlic, minced
1 teaspoon chili powder
¼ teaspoon ground red pepper (optional)
¼ teaspoon black pepper
2¼ cups water
1 14½-ounce can tomatoes, undrained and
   cut up
2 cups cubed cooked pork or ham
1 9-ounce package frozen cut okra
1 cup long grain rice
2 teaspoons instant chicken bouillon
   granules

1 Halve turkey sausage lengthwise and cut into ¼-inch-thick slices.

2 In a 12-inch skillet cook turkey sausage, mushrooms, sweet pepper, onion, and garlic until onion is tender.

3 Stir in chili powder, ground red pepper (if using), and black pepper. Cook and stir 1 minute.

4 Stir in water, undrained tomatoes, pork or ham, okra, uncooked rice, and bouillon granules. Bring to boiling; reduce heat. Cover and simmer for 15 to 20 minutes or until rice is tender. Makes 6 servings.

Nutrition facts per serving: 313 calories, 9 g total fat (3 g saturated fat), 59 mg cholesterol, 606 mg sodium, 35 g carbohydrate, 2 g fiber, 23 g protein
Exchanges: 1½ Starch, 2 Lean Meat, 3 Vegetable

311 calories

Preparation time: 20 minutes ● **Baking time:** 20 minutes

pork chops with corn bread stuffing

Instead of stuffing extra-thick chops, place thinner boneless chops on top of the stuffing.
The flavor from the pork chops melds into the corn bread mixture.

2 **cups crumbled corn bread**
4 **boneless pork loin chops, cut ¾ inches**
    thick (1 pound total)
    Nonstick spray coating
½ **cup chopped onion**
¼ **cup chopped red and/or green sweet**
    pepper
1 **tablespoon snipped fresh sage**
    or 1 teaspoon dried sage, crushed
1½ **teaspoons snipped fresh thyme**
    or ½ teaspoon dried thyme, crushed
¼ **teaspoon black pepper**
½ **cup frozen whole kernel corn, thawed**
½ **cup finely chopped apple**
½ **cup reduced-sodium chicken broth**
2 **tablespoons apple jelly, melted**
    Fresh thyme or sage sprigs (optional)

1 Spread crumbled corn bread in a shallow baking pan. Bake in a 300° oven for 10 to 15 minutes or until dry, stirring twice. Set aside.

2 Meanwhile, trim fat from pork chops. Spray an unheated 10-inch skillet with nonstick coating. Preheat the skillet over medium-high heat. Add the pork chops and brown on both sides. Remove chops from skillet.

3 Add onion and sweet pepper to skillet. Cook and stir over medium heat for 3 minutes. Stir in sage, thyme, and black pepper. Stir in corn bread, corn, and apple. Drizzle with chicken broth and toss to combine. Spoon into a 2-quart rectangular baking dish. Arrange pork chops on top. Brush tops of chops with apple jelly.

4 Bake in a 375° oven for 20 minutes or until pork is just slightly pink in center and juices run clear. If desired, garnish with fresh herb sprigs. Makes 4 servings.

Nutrition facts per serving: 311 calories, 13 g total fat (3 g saturated fat), 79 mg cholesterol, 274 mg sodium, 30 g carbohydrate, 1 g fiber, 20 g protein
Exchanges: 3 Starch, 2 Lean Meat, ½ Fat

114 calories

Preparation time: 25 minutes ● **Baking time:** 1 hour 10 minutes ● **Standing time:** 10 minutes

cheesy scalloped potatoes

This calorie-trimmed favorite saves 200 calories per serving. For the creamiest results, be sure to use red potatoes. White potatoes have a drier texture and tend to soak up the sauce during baking.

Nonstick spray coating
½ **cup chopped onion**
 1 **clove garlic, minced**
 2 **tablespoons all-purpose flour**
½ **teaspoon seasoned salt or salt**
⅛ **teaspoon pepper**
1½ **cups skim milk**
 4 **medium red potatoes, peeled and thinly**
   sliced
½ **cup shredded reduced-fat cheddar cheese**
   (2 ounces)
   Snipped fresh parsley (optional)

1 For sauce, spray an unheated small saucepan with nonstick coating. Preheat over medium heat. Add the onion and garlic. Cook and stir until the onion is tender.

2 In a small bowl combine flour, salt, and pepper. Gradually stir milk into flour mixture until smooth. Add to saucepan. Cook and stir over medium heat until thickened and bubbly.

3 Spray a 1½-quart casserole with nonstick coating. Place half of the potatoes in the casserole. Top with half of the sauce. Repeat layers with remaining potatoes and sauce.

4 Bake, covered, in a 350° oven for 40 minutes. Uncover and bake about 30 minutes more or until potatoes are tender. Remove from oven and sprinkle with cheese.

5 Let stand for 10 minutes before serving. If desired, garnish with parsley. Makes 8 servings.

Nutrition facts per serving: 114 calories, 2 g total fat (1 g saturated fat), 6 mg cholesterol, 211 mg sodium, 20 g carbohydrate, 1 g fiber, 5 g protein
Exchanges: 1½ Starch

195 calories

Preparation time: 20 minutes

fettuccine alla carbonara

Traditionally, carbonara sauce includes raw eggs, which are not considered safe. Commercial egg product helps update this favorite to make it safe and more healthful.

¼ cup refrigerated or frozen egg product, thawed
2 tablespoons evaporated skim milk or skim milk
4 ounces packaged dried fettuccine or linguine
2 teaspoons margarine or butter
¼ cup grated Parmesan cheese (1 ounce)
2 tablespoons snipped fresh parsley
1 tablespoon cooked bacon pieces

1 In a small mixing bowl stir together the egg product and milk. Set aside.

2 In a large saucepan cook the fettuccine or linguine according to the package directions, except omit any oil or salt. Drain well.

3 Return pasta to the hot saucepan. Immediately pour the egg mixture over pasta. Add margarine or butter. Heat and stir mixture over low heat about 2 minutes or until mixture thickens and pasta is well coated. Add the Parmesan cheese, parsley, and cooked bacon pieces; toss until combined. Serve immediately. Makes 4 servings.

Nutrition facts per serving: 195 calories, 6 g total fat (1 g saturated fat), 6 mg cholesterol, 184 mg sodium, 25 g carbohydrate, 0 g fiber, 9 g protein
Exchanges: 1½ Starch, 1 Lean Meat, ½ Fat

180 calories

Preparation time: 25 minutes ● **Baking time:** 30 minutes ● **Chilling time:** 1 hour

cream puffs

Billows of real whipped cream make cream puffs a dieter's foe. We've filled these with pudding,
which saves you about 50 calories and 12 grams fat over a serving of the classic.

Nonstick spray coating
1 **cup water**
¼ **cup margarine or butter**
1 **cup all-purpose flour**
4 **eggs**
⅔ **cup granulated sugar**
¼ **cup cornstarch**
3 **cups skim milk**
2 **slightly beaten egg yolks**
1 **teaspoon vanilla**
2 **tablespoons sifted powdered sugar**

1 Spray a baking sheet with nonstick coating; set aside. In a medium saucepan bring water, margarine, and ¼ teaspoon *salt* to boiling. Add flour, all at once, stirring vigorously. Cook and stir until mixture forms a ball that doesn't separate. Cool 10 minutes.

2 Add the 4 eggs, 1 at a time, beating until smooth after each addition. Drop batter by heaping tablespoons, 3 inches apart, onto prepared baking sheet, making 12 mounds. Bake in a 400° oven for

30 minutes or until golden brown and puffy. Cool. Split cream puffs; remove any soft dough inside.

3 Meanwhile, for pudding, in a heavy medium saucepan combine granulated sugar, cornstarch, and ⅛ teaspoon *salt*. Stir in milk. Cook and stir over medium heat until bubbly. Cook and stir 2 minutes more. Remove from heat.

4 Gradually stir 1 cup of the hot mixture into the egg yolks. Return all to saucepan; bring to a gentle boil. Reduce heat; cook and stir for 2 minutes more. Remove from heat. Stir in vanilla. Transfer to a bowl; cover surface with plastic wrap. Refrigerate 1 hour or until well chilled. (Do not stir during chilling.)

5 To serve, fill bottoms of cream puffs with pudding; replace tops. Sprinkle with powdered sugar. Makes 12 servings.

Nutrition facts per serving: 180 calories, 7 g total fat (2 g saturated fat), 108 mg cholesterol, 166 mg sodium, 24 g carbohydrate, 0 g fiber, 6 g protein
Exchanges: 1 Starch, ½ Milk, 1 Fat

206 calories

Preparation time: 20 minutes ● **Chilling time:** 1 hour ● **Baking time:** 10 minutes

strawberry shortcake

Another time, use a combination of berries, such as raspberries, blackberries, and blueberries.

  3 cups sliced fresh strawberries
  2 tablespoons sugar
1⅔ cups all-purpose flour
  1 tablespoon sugar
  2 teaspoons baking powder
  ¼ teaspoon baking soda
  3 tablespoons margarine or butter
  1 beaten egg
  ½ cup buttermilk or sour skim milk
    Nonstick spray coating
  2 cups frozen fat-free whipped dessert
    topping, thawed, or 1.3-ounce envelope
    whipped dessert topping mix
    Fresh strawberry fans (optional)

1 Combine sliced berries and the 2 tablespoons sugar. Cover; let stand in refrigerator at least 1 hour.

2 In a mixing bowl stir together flour, the 1 tablespoon sugar, baking powder, and baking soda. Using a pastry blender, cut in margarine or butter until mixture resembles coarse crumbs. Combine egg and buttermilk. Add to flour mixture all at once, stirring until combined.

3 Drop dough from a tablespoon onto an ungreased baking sheet, making 8 mounds.

4 Bake in a 450° oven for 7 to 8 minutes or until golden. Transfer shortcakes to a wire rack and cool about 10 minutes.

5 Meanwhile, if using topping mix, prepare according to package directions using skim milk. To serve, cut shortcakes in half horizontally. Spoon *half* of the strawberries and *one-fourth* of the whipped topping over bottom layers. Replace tops. Spoon remaining topping onto each shortcake. If desired, garnish with strawberry fans. Makes 8 servings.

Nutrition facts per serving: 206 calories, 6 g total fat (1 g saturated fat), 27 mg cholesterol, 215 mg sodium, 34 g carbohydrate, 2 g fiber, 4 g protein
Exchanges: 2 Starch, 1 Fat

163 calories

Preparation time: 25 minutes ● **Baking time:** 35 minutes ● **Cool:** 2 hours ● **Chilling time:** 4 hours

strawberry-topped cheesecake

To test for a perfectly baked, creamy cheesecake, gently shake the pan after the minimum baking time.
The center should appear nearly set. If it still jiggles, bake it 5 minutes longer and test again.

½ **cup graham cracker crumbs**
4 **teaspoons margarine or butter, melted**
2 **8-ounce packages fat-free cream cheese**
1 **cup fat-free cottage cheese**
¼ **cup skim milk**
¾ **cup sugar**
2 **tablespoons all-purpose flour**
1¼ **teaspoons vanilla**
½ **teaspoon finely shredded lemon peel**
3 **eggs or ¾ cup refrigerated or frozen**
  egg product, thawed
¼ **cup fat-free or light dairy sour cream**
1 **teaspoon sugar**
2 **teaspoons skim milk**
1 **cup sliced fresh strawberries**

1 In a small bowl stir together graham cracker crumbs and melted margarine or butter. Press onto the bottom of an 8-inch springform pan. Set aside.

2 Cut up cream cheese. In a large food processor bowl place undrained cottage cheese and the ¼ cup milk; cover and process until smooth. Add the cream cheese, the ¾ cup sugar, the flour, *1 teaspoon* of the vanilla, and the lemon peel; cover and process until smooth. Add eggs or egg product and process just until combined. Do not overprocess. Pour mixture into pan. Place on a baking sheet.

3 Bake in a 375° oven for 35 to 40 minutes or until set. Cool 15 minutes. Using a narrow metal spatula, loosen the side of the cheesecake from pan. Cool 30 minutes more, then remove the side of pan. Cool completely. Cover; refrigerate at least 4 hours.

4 In a bowl combine sour cream, the 1 teaspoon sugar, the 2 teaspoons milk, and the remaining vanilla. To serve, arrange berries on cheesecake and drizzle with sour cream mixture. Makes 12 servings.

Nutrition facts per serving: 163 calories, 3 g total fat (1 g saturated fat), 62 mg cholesterol, 92 mg sodium, 22 g carbohydrate, 0 g fiber, 11 g protein
Exchanges: 1½ Starch, 1 Lean Meat

171 calories

Preparation time: 30 minutes ● **Baking time:** 40 minutes

deep-dish apple pie

*Bite into this all-American dessert and you'll forget you're dieting. Each forkful boasts
a luscious cinnamon-apple filling and flaky pastry.*

**6 cups thinly sliced peeled cooking apples
(2 pounds total)**
¼ cup sugar
1 teaspoon ground cinnamon
1 tablespoon cornstarch
⅛ teaspoon salt
**¾ cup all-purpose flour or ½ cup all-purpose
flour plus ¼ cup whole wheat flour**
Dash ground nutmeg
3 tablespoons margarine or butter
2 to 3 tablespoons cold water
Skim milk

1 Place apples in a 2-quart square baking dish.
2 In a small mixing bowl combine sugar and
cinnamon; set aside 1 teaspoon of the mixture. Stir
cornstarch and salt into remaining sugar mixture and
mix well. Sprinkle evenly over apples in dish.

3 In a medium mixing bowl stir together flour
and nutmeg. Using a pastry blender, cut in
margarine or butter until mixture resembles coarse
crumbs. Sprinkle *1 tablespoon* of the water over part
of the mixture; gently toss with a fork. Push to side
of bowl. Repeat, using 1 tablespoon water at a time,
until all of the dough is moistened. Form into a ball.

4 On a floured surface, roll dough into a 10-inch
square. Cut decorative vents in pastry. Carefully
place pastry over apples. Using the tines of a fork,
press edges to sides of dish. Brush pastry with milk
and sprinkle with the reserved sugar mixture.

5 Bake in a 375° oven about 40 minutes or until
apples are tender and crust is golden brown. Serve
warm. Makes 8 servings.

Nutrition facts per serving: 171 calories, 5 g total fat
(1 g saturated fat), 0 mg cholesterol, 85 mg sodium,
33 g carbohydrate, 2 g fiber, 1 g protein
Exchanges: 2 Fruit, 1 Fat

135 calories

Preparation time: 30 minutes ● **Baking/standing time:** 35 minutes/1 hour ● **Chilling:** 1 hour

pavlova

This dessert was named after the Russian ballerina Anna Pavlova, who performed in Australia and New Zealand in the early 1900s. Lemon yogurt plus whipped topping replaces the traditional whipped cream.

2 egg whites
**1 teaspoon white vinegar or ¼ teaspoon
cream of tartar**
⅛ teaspoon salt
½ cup sugar
½ cup lemon low-fat yogurt
**¼ of an 8-ounce container frozen light or fat-
free whipped dessert topping, thawed**
**2½ cups desired fresh fruit (raspberries;
blueberries; sliced kiwifruit, strawberries,
and/or papaya; and/or cubed pineapple)**

1 Let egg whites stand at room temperature for 30 minutes. Meanwhile, line a baking sheet with foil or clean brown paper. Draw six 3-inch circles on the foil or paper. Set aside.

2 In a small mixing bowl combine egg whites, vinegar or cream of tartar, and salt. Beat with an electric mixer on medium speed until soft peaks form (tips curl).

3 Gradually add the sugar, 1 tablespoon at a time, beating on high speed until very stiff peaks form (tips stand straight) and sugar is almost dissolved (about 4 minutes).

4 Place egg mixture in a pastry bag fitted with a large star tip. Pipe the meringue onto the circles, building the sides up to form shells. (Or, use the back of a spoon to spread the egg white mixture over the circles, building up the sides.)

5 Bake in a 300° oven for 35 minutes. Turn off oven. Let shells dry in oven, with door closed, for at least 1 hour. Remove from foil. Cool completely.

6 Stir together the yogurt and whipped topping. Divide mixture among shells. Cover and refrigerate for 1 to 2 hours. To serve, arrange desired fruit over yogurt mixture. Makes 6 servings.

Nutrition facts per serving: 135 calories, 2 g total fat (1 g saturated fat), 1 mg cholesterol, 82 mg sodium, 29 g carbohydrate, 2 g fiber, 2 g protein
Exchanges: 1 Starch, 1 Fruit

123 calories

Preparation time: 20 minutes ● **Baking time:** 30 minutes ● **Cooling:** 30 minutes ● **Chilling:** 4 hours

flan

Try this caramel-topped custard as a delicious ending to a Spanish meal. Serve it with paella, another traditional favorite from Spain (see recipe, page 267).

¼ **cup sugar**
4 **eggs**
1 **cup skim milk**
1 **cup evaporated skim milk or skim milk**
¼ **cup sugar**
1 **teaspoon vanilla**
   Dash salt
   Edible flowers, such as dianthus, pansies, or violets (optional)

1 To caramelize sugar, in a small heavy skillet cook ¼ cup sugar over medium-high heat until sugar begins to melt, shaking skillet occasionally to heat sugar evenly. Do not stir. Reduce heat to low and cook about 5 minutes more or until all of the sugar is melted and golden.

2 Quickly pour caramelized sugar into an 8×1½-inch round baking pan, tilting pan to coat bottom (use a pot holder if pan becomes too hot).

3 In a mixing bowl beat eggs. Stir in skim milk, evaporated skim milk, ¼ cup sugar, the vanilla, and salt. Pour into sugar-coated pan.

4 Set the round pan in a large baking pan set on an oven rack. Pour *hot water* into the large baking pan around the round pan to a depth of 1 inch.

5 Bake, uncovered, in a 325° oven about 30 minutes or until a knife inserted near the center of the custard comes out clean. Carefully remove from pan of water. Cool in pan on a wire rack for 30 minutes. Cover flan and refrigerate 4 to 8 hours or until thoroughly chilled.

6 Loosen flan from side of pan. Carefully invert onto a serving plate. Cut into wedges; if desired, garnish with edible flowers. Makes 8 servings.

Nutrition facts per serving: 123 calories, 3 g total fat (1 g saturated fat), 108 mg cholesterol, 101 mg sodium, 18 g carbohydrate, 0 g fiber, 7 g protein
Exchanges: 1½ Starch

Appetizers
& SNACKS

chapter index

33 calories

Preparation time: 20 minutes ● **Marinating time:** 8 hours or overnight

marinated zucchini and mushrooms

Lemony and refreshing, the dressing for this appetizer uses just a little olive oil for flavor. All you need is a splash because olive oil packs a lot of flavor in every drop.

**8 ounces small whole fresh mushrooms
(3 cups)**

**2 small zucchini and/or yellow summer
squash, bias-sliced into ½-inch-thick
slices (2 cups)**

**1 small red sweet pepper, cut into square
pieces**

¼ cup lemon juice

2 tablespoons olive oil or salad oil

1 tablespoon sugar

¼ teaspoon salt

**¼ teaspoon dried tarragon or oregano,
crushed, or ¾ teaspoon snipped fresh
tarragon or oregano**

¼ teaspoon pepper

1 clove garlic, minced

1 Place mushrooms, zucchini and/or summer squash, and sweet pepper in a plastic bag set in a deep bowl.

2 For marinade, in a small mixing bowl stir together lemon juice, oil, sugar, salt, tarragon or oregano, pepper, and garlic. Mix well. Pour marinade over vegetables in bag. Seal bag. Marinate the vegetables in the refrigerator for 8 hours or overnight, turning bag occasionally.

3 To serve, pour vegetables and marinade into serving dish. Serve with toothpicks. Makes about 8 (⅔-cup) servings.

Nutrition facts per serving: 33 calories, 2 g total fat (0 g saturated fat), 0 mg cholesterol, 36 mg sodium, 4 g carbohydrate, 1 g fiber, 1 g protein
Exchanges: 1 Vegetable, ½ Fat

31 calories

Preparation time: 30 minutes ● **Chilling:** 2 to 24 hours; 2 hours

Vegetable spring rolls

The long, white, carrot-shaped daikon is a Japanese radish with a mildly spicy, radishlike flavor. If you can't find daikons in your supermarket, substitute shredded radishes or zucchini.

½ **cup shredded daikon (Oriental white radish) or radishes**
2 **green onions, thinly sliced**
2 **tablespoons rice vinegar**
1 **teaspoon sugar**
1 **small fresh jalapeño or serrano chili pepper, seeded and finely chopped**
½ **teaspoon toasted sesame oil**
½ **cup shredded carrot**
½ **cup short thin strips cucumber**
2 **tablespoons snipped fresh cilantro**
1 **tablespoon reduced-sodium soy sauce**
6 **8½-inch-diameter rice papers**
1½ **cups shredded Boston or curly leaf lettuce**
  Fresh cilantro (optional)
  Shredded carrot (optional)

1 Combine daikon, green onions, vinegar, sugar, chili pepper, and sesame oil. In another bowl combine the ½ cup carrot, cucumber, cilantro, and soy sauce. Cover both mixtures; refrigerate at least 2 or up to 24 hours; stir once. Drain both mixtures.

2 Pour 1 cup *warm water* into a pie plate. Carefully dip rice papers into water, 1 at a time. Place papers, not touching, on clean dry kitchen towels. Let soften for a few minutes until pliable.

3 Place ¼ cup shredded lettuce on each rice paper near one edge. Place about 1 rounded tablespoon of each vegetable mixture on the lettuce. Fold in the ends. Beginning at that edge, tightly roll the rice paper. Place seam side down on a plate. Cover with a damp towel. Repeat with remaining filling and papers. Cover and refrigerate for up to 2 hours. Cut each roll in half crosswise on a diagonal to make 12 pieces. If desired, garnish with cilantro and shredded carrot. Makes 12 servings.

Nutrition facts per serving: 31 calories, 0 g total fat, 0 mg cholesterol, 48 mg sodium, 7 g carbohydrate, 0 g fiber, 0 g protein
Exchanges: 1 Vegetable

22 calories

Preparation time: 30 minutes

cheese-stuffed baby vegetables

To stuff the vegetables, place the filling in a plastic sandwich bag. Snip off one corner of the bag and squeeze some filling into each vegetable. Or, put the filling in a decorating bag fitted with a large round tip.

⅓ **cup low-fat ricotta cheese**
2 **tablespoons reduced-fat soft-style cream cheese**
2 **tablespoons finely shredded radish**
1 **tablespoon snipped fresh chives**
2 **teaspoons snipped fresh thyme, basil, dill, or marjoram or ½ teaspoon dried thyme, basil, dillweed, or marjoram, crushed**
⅛ **teaspoon onion salt**
20 **to 24 cherry tomatoes and/or 10 to 12 baby summer squash (such as zucchini or pattypan squash)**

1 For filling, stir together ricotta cheese, cream cheese, radish, chives, desired herb, and onion salt. Mix well. Set aside.

2 Slice a thin layer off the top of each tomato. Using a small spoon, carefully scoop out and discard pulp. Invert tomatoes onto paper towels to drain. (If using squash, cut in half lengthwise for zucchini or horizontally for pattypan; scoop out and invert as for the cherry tomatoes.)

3 Stuff tomatoes or squash with filling. Serve immediately or refrigerate until serving time. Makes 10 to 12 servings.

Nutrition facts per serving: 22 calories, 1 g total fat (0 g saturated fat), 3 mg cholesterol, 45 mg sodium, 3 g carbohydrate, 1 g fiber, 1 g protein
Exchanges: 1 Vegetable

58 calories

Preparation time: 20 minutes ● **Baking time:** 9 minutes

oven-fried vegetables

*Lower the fat and calories in deep-fat fried vegetables by baking them instead.
They're better for you and less messy to make, too.*

Nonstick spray coating
¼ **cup fine dry bread crumbs**
1 **tablespoon grated Parmesan cheese**
⅛ **teaspoon paprika**
2 **cups ¼-inch-thick zucchini slices, onion
    rings, red sweet pepper strips, and/or
    cauliflower flowerets**
2 **tablespoons reduced-calorie Italian salad
    dressing**

1 Spray a baking sheet with nonstick coating.
Set aside.

2 In a 9-inch pie plate stir together bread
crumbs, Parmesan cheese, and paprika until well
mixed. In a medium mixing bowl place the zucchini
slices, onion rings, sweet pepper strips, and/or
cauliflower flowerets. Drizzle vegetables with salad
dressing; toss until coated. Roll vegetables in crumb
mixture until coated. Place the coated vegetables in
a single layer on the prepared baking sheet.

3 Bake vegetables in a 450° oven for 9 to
11 minutes or until golden brown. Makes 4 servings.

Nutrition facts per serving: 58 calories, 2 g total fat
(0 g saturated fat), 2 mg cholesterol, 136 mg sodium,
9 g carbohydrate, 1 g fiber, 2 g protein
Exchanges: 1 Vegetable, ½ Fat

60 calories

Preparation time: 20 minutes ● **Baking time:** 5 minutes

garden quesadillas

Most quesadillas send your calorie budget through the roof because of all of the cheese. This vegetable-stuffed version uses fat-free cream cheese and vegetables, which saves you calories and fat.

2 **small green and/or red sweet peppers, cut into thin strips**
1 **small red onion, cut into thin, 1-inch-long strips**
2 **teaspoons olive oil or cooking oil**
½ **teaspoon ground cumin**
½ **teaspoon chili powder**
2 **tablespoons snipped fresh cilantro or parsley**
⅓ **cup fat-free cream cheese**
5 **6- to 7-inch flour tortillas**
Salsa (optional)

1 In a large nonstick skillet cook sweet peppers and onion in *1 teaspoon* of the oil for 3 to 5 minutes or until crisp-tender. Stir in cumin and chili powder. Cook and stir for 1 minute more. Stir in the cilantro or parsley. Set aside.

2 Spread cream cheese over half of 1 side of each tortilla. Top with pepper mixture. Fold tortilla in half over peppers, pressing gently.

3 Place tortillas on ungreased baking sheet. Brush tortillas with remaining oil. Bake in a 425° oven for 5 minutes. Cut each quesadilla into 4 wedges. Serve warm with salsa, if desired. Makes 10 servings.

Nutrition facts per serving: 60 calories, 2 g total fat (0 g saturated fat), 1 mg cholesterol, 102 mg sodium, 9 g carbohydrate, 1 g fiber, 3 g protein
Exchanges: ½ Starch, 1 Vegetable

53 calories

Preparation time: 12 minutes ● **Baking time:** 7 minutes

nutty chicken fingers

*Include these chicken bites at your next buffet party or feature them as a main dish
(enough for five main-dish servings).*

½ **cup finely chopped pecans**
⅓ **cup cornflake crumbs**
1 **tablespoon dried parsley flakes**
⅛ **teaspoon salt**
⅛ **teaspoon garlic powder**
12 **ounces skinless, boneless chicken breast
    halves, cut into 3×1-inch strips**
2 **tablespoons skim milk**
   **Reduced-calorie ranch-style dressing
   (optional)**

1 In a shallow dish combine pecans, cornflake crumbs, parsley flakes, salt, and garlic powder. Dip chicken strips in milk, then roll in crumb mixture. Place in a 15×10×1-inch baking pan.

2 Bake in a 400° oven for 7 to 9 minutes or until chicken is tender and no longer pink. If desired, serve with ranch-style dressing. Makes 15 pieces.

Nutrition facts per piece: 53 calories, 3 g total fat (0 g saturated fat), 12 mg cholesterol, 42 mg sodium, 2 g carbohydrate, 0 g fiber, 5 g protein
Exchanges: 1 Lean Meat

47 calories

Preparation time: 25 minutes ● **Chilling time:** 2 hours

fruit kabobs with ginger dip

To toast the coconut, spread coconut in a shallow pan and bake in a 350° oven for 5 to 10 minutes or until golden, stirring once or twice during baking.

1 8-ounce carton fat-free dairy sour cream
2 tablespoons chopped toasted coconut
1 tablespoon honey
1 teaspoon finely shredded orange peel
1 teaspoon grated fresh gingerroot
1 small pear and/or apple
1 small orange, peeled and sectioned
1 small papaya, peeled and seeded
2 kiwifruit, peeled
1 cup cubed fresh pineapple
1 cup whole fresh strawberries
   Finely shredded orange peel (optional)

1 For dip, in a small bowl stir together sour cream, the 2 tablespoons coconut, honey, the 1 teaspoon orange peel, and gingerroot. Cover and refrigerate at least 2 hours or until serving time.

2 To prepare fruit kabobs, cut pear and/or apple, orange, and papaya into 1-inch pieces, leaving peel on pear and apple for color. Quarter kiwifruit lengthwise. Thread all fruit on wooden picks or 32 short bamboo skewers. Serve with chilled dip. If desired, sprinkle dip with additional orange peel. Makes about 16 servings.

Nutrition facts per serving: 47 calories, 0 g total fat, 0 mg cholesterol, 10 mg sodium, 10 g carbohydrate, 1 g fiber, 1 g protein
Exchanges: ½ Fruit

114 calories

Preparation time: 25 minutes ● **Chilling time:** up to 2 hours

summer fruit salsa

The refreshing tropical ingredients in this summer salsa pair well with grilled chicken breasts and fish steaks.

1 tablespoon lime juice
1 tablespoon plum or peach jam
½ cup finely chopped fresh peach
   or nectarine
½ cup chopped fresh strawberries
½ cup finely chopped fresh pineapple or
   one 8-ounce can crushed pineapple
   (juice-packed), drained
½ cup finely chopped fresh plums
2 tablespoons finely chopped red onion
1 fresh jalapeño pepper, seeded and finely
   chopped*
   Dash ground cloves
   Jalapeño peppers, cut into thin strips
   (optional)
1 recipe Tortilla Crisps (see recipe, page 52)
   or purchased baked tortilla chips

1 In a medium bowl stir together lime juice and plum or peach jam until smooth. Stir in peach or nectarine, strawberries, pineapple, plums, red onion, jalapeño pepper, and cloves. Cover; refrigerate for up to 2 hours to blend flavors. If desired, garnish with jalapeño strips. Serve with Tortilla Crisps or chips. Makes 8 (¼-cup) servings.

***Note:** Because chili peppers, such as jalapeños, contain volatile oils that can burn your skin and eyes, avoid direct contact with them as much as possible. When working with chili peppers, wear plastic gloves. If your bare hands touch the chili peppers, wash your hands well with soap and water.

Nutrition facts per serving salsa and 6 Tortilla Crisps: 114 calories, 2 g total fat (0 g saturated fat), 0 mg cholesterol, 120 mg sodium, 21 g carbohydrate, 2 g fiber, 2 g protein
Exchanges: 1 Fruit, ½ Starch

83 calories

Preparation time: 15 minutes ● **Chilling time:** 1 hour

cottage cheese – dill dip

A green, yellow, or red sweet pepper shell makes an eye-catching container for this creamy cheese dip. Be sure to remove any sweet pepper seeds before spooning in the dip.

1 **cup fat-free or low-fat cottage cheese**
1 **green onion, cut up**
2 **tablespoons snipped fresh parsley**
1 **tablespoon snipped fresh dill or**
   1 **teaspoon dried dillweed**
½ **teaspoon Worcestershire sauce**
⅛ **teaspoon pepper**
   Dash garlic powder
   Assorted vegetable dippers or crackers

1 In a food processor bowl or blender container place the cottage cheese, green onion, parsley, dill, Worcestershire sauce, pepper, and garlic powder. Cover and process or blend until smooth. Cover and refrigerate for at least 1 hour.

2 Serve with vegetable dippers or crackers. Makes 4 (¼-cup) servings.

Nutrition facts per serving dip and ½ cup assorted vegetables: 83 calories, 0 g total fat, 7 mg cholesterol, 116 mg sodium, 8 g carbohydrate, 2 g fiber, 13 g protein
Exchanges: 1½ Very Lean Meat, 1 Vegetable

133 calories

Preparation time: 45 minutes

roasted garlic-spinach dip

*When garlic is roasted, it becomes sweet and mellow in flavor. Use roasted garlic paste to add flavor without
fat and virtually no calories to soups or salad dressings. Here it updates an all-time favorite dip.*

1 **whole head garlic**
1 **teaspoon olive oil**
1 **10-ounce package frozen chopped spinach**
¼ **cup skim milk**
   Dash bottled hot pepper sauce
1 **8-ounce package reduced-fat cream cheese
   (Neufchâtel), cut up**
   Chopped tomato (optional)
1 **recipe Toasted Pita Wedges**

1 Peel away outer dry leaves from head of garlic,
leaving skin of garlic cloves intact. Cut off pointed
top portion of head (about ¼ inch) with a knife,
leaving the bulb intact. Place on a double-thick,
12-inch square of foil. Drizzle garlic with the oil.
Fold foil to enclose garlic. Bake in a 375° oven for
20 minutes or until garlic is soft. Cool.

2 Cook spinach according to package directions,
except omit salt. Drain well; press out excess liquid.

3 Squeeze pulp from garlic cloves into food
processor bowl, discarding skins. Add the drained
spinach, milk, hot pepper sauce, and ⅛ teaspoon
salt. Cover and process until well combined. Add
cream cheese. Cover; process until nearly smooth.

4 Transfer mixture to saucepan. Cook and stir
over medium-low heat until heated through.

5 To serve, transfer to serving bowl. If desired,
sprinkle with tomato. Serve with Toasted Pita
Wedges. Makes 8 (¼-cup) servings.

Toasted Pita Wedges: Split 8 small pita bread
rounds; cut each half into 6 wedges. Place, cut sides
up, on an ungreased baking sheet. Bake in batches
in a 375° oven for 7 to 9 minutes or until lightly
browned. Store any leftovers in an airtight container.

Nutrition facts per serving dip and 6 pita wedges:
133 calories, 7 g total fat (4 g saturated fat), 22 mg
cholesterol, 246 mg sodium, 12 g carbohydrate, 0 g fiber,
5 g protein
Exchanges: ½ Starch, 2 Vegetable, 1 Fat

81 calories

Preparation time: 25 minutes ● **Chilling time:** 2 to 24 hours

layered bean dip

Ounce for ounce, our homemade Tortilla Crisps (recipe below) have one-third fewer calories than fried corn tortilla chips and much less fat, too.

**1 15-ounce can pinto or red kidney beans,
drained**
¼ cup salsa
**1 4½-ounce can diced green chili peppers,
drained**
**4 ounces bottled roasted red sweet peppers
or one 4-ounce jar pimientos, drained
and chopped (about ½ cup)**
1 cup low-fat cottage cheese
1 cup chopped tomato
¼ cup sliced green onions
¼ cup shredded reduced-fat cheddar cheese
**1 recipe Tortilla Crisps or assorted vegetable
dippers**

1 In a food processor bowl or blender container place beans and salsa. Cover and blend or process until smooth. Spread mixture evenly in a shallow bowl or a 9-inch pie plate. Top with chili peppers and roasted red peppers or pimientos.

2 Wash food processor bowl or blender container. Place cottage cheese in the food processor bowl or blender container. Cover and process or blend until smooth. Spread cottage cheese on top of peppers in bowl or pie plate. Cover; refrigerate for at least 2 or up to 24 hours.

3 To serve, sprinkle tomato, green onions, and cheddar cheese over dip. Serve with Tortilla Crisps or vegetables. Makes 18 (¼-cup) servings.

Tortilla Crisps: Cut twelve 6-inch flour or corn tortillas into 6 wedges each. Place wedges in a single layer on an ungreased baking sheet. Bake the tortillas in batches in a 350° oven for 8 to 10 minutes or until crisp.

Nutrition facts per ¼ cup dip and 4 Tortilla Crisps:
81 calories, 2 g total fat (1 g saturated fat),
2 mg cholesterol, 185 mg sodium, 12 g carbohydrate,
2 g fiber, 5 g protein
Exchanges: ½ Starch, 1 Vegetable

34 calories

Preparation time: 15 minutes

roasted red pepper dip

Cilantro, the leaves of the coriander plant, has a pungent almost musty aroma and a taste distinctive to Latin, Asian, and Eastern Mediterranean cooking. Taste it first and adjust the level according to your liking.

1	**7-ounce jar roasted red sweet peppers**
1	**teaspoon vinegar**
¼	**teaspoon lemon-pepper seasoning**
¼	**teaspoon garlic powder**
⅓	**cup fat-free dairy sour cream**
2	**teaspoons snipped fresh cilantro or parsley**
	Assorted vegetable dippers (such as carrot, jicama, and/or celery sticks)

1 Drain roasted peppers. Chop and set aside *2 tablespoons* of the roasted peppers. In a food processor bowl or blender container combine remaining roasted peppers, vinegar, lemon-pepper seasoning, and garlic powder. Cover and process or blend until mixture is smooth, scraping sides as necessary. Stir in sour cream, reserved roasted peppers, and *1 teaspoon* of the cilantro or parsley.

2 Transfer to a serving bowl. Sprinkle remaining cilantro on top. Serve immediately. (Or, cover and refrigerate for up to 24 hours.) Serve with vegetables dippers. Makes 5 (¼-cup) servings.

Nutrition facts per serving dip and 1 carrot:
34 calories, 0 g total fat, 0 mg cholesterol, 76 mg sodium, 7 g carbohydrate, 3 g fiber, 3 g protein
Exchanges: 1 Vegetable

81 calories

Preparation time: 10 minutes ● **Chilling time:** 4 to 24 hours

hummus

Traditional hummus is a Middle Eastern dip made of mashed garbanzo beans, garlic, lemon, and olive or sesame oil. Here we've skipped the oil and added fat-free yogurt, which gives it a creamier texture.

1 **15-ounce can garbanzo beans, rinsed and drained**
¼ **cup plain fat-free yogurt**
2 **tablespoons toasted sesame seeds**
2 **cloves garlic, halved**
2 **tablespoons lemon juice**
⅛ **teaspoon ground red pepper**
  Red, green, and/or yellow sweet pepper wedges, assorted vegetable dippers, or 1 recipe Toasted Pita Wedges (see recipe, page 51)

1 In a food processor bowl or blender container combine garbanzo beans, yogurt, sesame seeds, garlic, lemon juice, and ground red pepper. Cover and process or blend until almost smooth. Place in a serving bowl. Cover and refrigerate at least 4 hours or up to 24 hours to blend flavors.

2 Serve with sweet pepper wedges, other vegetable dippers, or Toasted Pita Wedges. Makes 6 (¼-cup) servings.

Nutrition facts per serving dip and ½ cup vegetable dippers: 81 calories, 3 g total fat (0 g saturated fat), 0 mg cholesterol, 234 mg sodium, 11 g carbohydrate, 3 g fiber, 4 g protein
Exchanges: ½ Starch, 1 Vegetable, ½ Fat

150 calories

Preparation time: 15 minutes ● **Chilling time:** 1 to 24 hours

guacamole

Unlike most other fruits and vegetables, avocados are high in fat. To lighten this guacamole, we added some fat-free yogurt and chopped tomatoes. The result is a great-tasting, extra-creamy dip.

1   **ripe medium avocado, halved, seeded, peeled, and cut up**
½   **cup plain fat-free yogurt**
½   **of a 4½-ounce can (¼ cup) diced green chili peppers, drained**
½   **of a small onion, cut up**
1   **tablespoon snipped fresh cilantro or parsley**
1   **tablespoon lemon or lime juice**
2   **cloves garlic, quartered**
2   **medium tomatoes, seeded and finely chopped**
    Chopped red sweet pepper (optional)
1   **recipe Tortilla Crisps (see recipe, page 52) or purchased baked tortilla chips**

1 In a food processor bowl or blender container combine the avocado, yogurt, chili peppers, onion, cilantro, lemon or lime juice, and garlic. Cover and process or blend until mixture is smooth, scraping sides of bowl as necessary. Stir in the tomatoes.

2 Spoon guacamole into a serving bowl. Cover the surface with plastic wrap and refrigerate for at least 1 hour or up to 24 hours. If desired, garnish with red sweet pepper. Serve with Tortilla Crisps or chips. Makes 8 (¼-cup) servings.

Nutrition facts per serving dip and 6 Tortilla Crisps: 150 calories, 6 g total fat (1 g saturated fat), 0 mg cholesterol, 155 mg sodium, 22 g carbohydrate, 2 g fiber, 4 g protein
Exchanges: 1 Starch, 1 Vegetable, 1 Fat

76 calories

Preparation time: 10 minutes ● **Baking time:** 20 minutes ● **Cooling time:** 30 minutes

curried snack mix

Do you crave salty, high-fat snacks, such as potato chips? Bake a batch of this snack mix and you'll save yourself about half the calories and more than half the fat of a similar serving of fat-laden chips.

3 plain rice cakes, broken into bite-size pieces
1 cup bite-size corn square cereal or oyster crackers
¾ cup pretzel sticks, halved (1 ounce)
1 tablespoon margarine or butter, melted
1 teaspoon Worcestershire sauce
½ to ¾ teaspoon curry powder

1 In a 13×9×2-inch baking pan stir together broken rice cakes, corn cereal or oyster crackers, and pretzels.

2 In a custard cup stir together melted margarine or butter, Worcestershire sauce, and curry powder. Drizzle margarine or butter mixture over cereal mixture. Toss cereal mixture until coated. Bake in a 300° oven for 20 minutes, stirring twice. Cool before serving. Store leftovers in a tightly covered container. Makes 6 to 8 (½-cup) servings.

Nutrition facts per serving: 76 calories, 2 g total fat (1 g saturated fat), 0 mg cholesterol, 175 mg sodium, 12 g carbohydrate, 0 g fiber, 1 g protein
Exchanges: ½ Starch, ½ Fat

32 calories

Preparation time: 15 minutes ● **Baking time:** 15 minutes ● **Cooling time:** 30 minutes

sugar and spice popcorn

Plain air-popped popcorn is the recommended choice for dieters. But why eat that flavorless stuff when you can enjoy this version spiced with cinnamon, nutmeg, and ginger?

Nonstick spray coating
6 **cups popped popcorn (using no oil)**
2 **tablespoons sugar**
2 **teaspoons water**
¼ **teaspoon ground cinnamon**
⅛ **teaspoon ground nutmeg**
⅛ **teaspoon ground ginger**

1 Spray a 13×9×2-inch baking pan with nonstick coating. Place popcorn in the pan.

2 In a small mixing bowl stir together sugar, water, cinnamon, nutmeg, and ginger. Drizzle spice mixture over popcorn in baking pan. Toss popcorn until coated. Bake in a 350° oven for 15 minutes, stirring once or twice.

3 Transfer the hot popcorn from baking pan to a large piece of foil. Cool popcorn completely. Store leftovers in a tightly covered container. Makes 8 (¾-cup) servings.

Nutrition facts per serving: 32 calories, 0 g total fat, 0 mg cholesterol, 0 mg sodium, 7 g carbohydrate, 0 g fiber, 1 g protein
Exchanges: ½ Starch

79 calories

Preparation time: 30 minutes ● **Baking time:** 20 minutes

pizza margherita

Roma tomatoes, sometimes called plum or Italian tomatoes, have rich tomato flavor.
They hold their shape well when baked on top of this pizza.

¾ **cup shredded part-skim mozzarella cheese**
    (3 ounces)
1 **recipe Whole Wheat Pizza Crust**
1 **tablespoon snipped fresh basil or**
    ½ **teaspoon dried basil, crushed**
4 **Roma tomatoes, thinly sliced**
½ **cup thin strips green and/or yellow sweet**
    pepper
2 **tablespoons finely shredded Parmesan**
    cheese

1 Sprinkle mozzarella cheese over the Whole
Wheat Pizza Crust. Sprinkle with dried basil (if
using). Arrange the tomato slices and pepper strips
over mozzarella cheese. Sprinkle with Parmesan
cheese. Bake in a 425° oven for 10 to 15 minutes
or until heated through. Sprinkle with fresh basil
(if using). Makes 12 servings.

Whole Wheat Pizza Crust: In a medium mixing
bowl combine ⅔ cup *all-purpose flour,* 1 package
active dry yeast, and ⅛ teaspoon *salt.* Add ½ cup

warm water (120° to 130°) and ½ teaspoon *olive*
or *cooking oil.* Beat with an electric mixer on low
speed for 30 seconds. Beat on high speed for
3 minutes. Using a wooden spoon, stir in ½ cup
whole wheat flour and 2 tablespoons *all-purpose*
flour. On a lightly floured surface, knead in 1 to
2 tablespoons additional *all-purpose flour* to make
a moderately stiff dough that is smooth and elastic
(3 to 4 minutes total). Cover and let rest 10 minutes.

    Spray a 12-inch pizza pan or large baking sheet
with *nonstick spray coating.* Pat or roll dough into
a 13-inch circle. Transfer to the prepared pan. Build
up the edge slightly. Prick crust with a fork. *Do not*
let rise. Bake in a 425° oven about 10 minutes or
until lightly browned.

Nutrition facts per serving: 79 calories, 2 g total fat
(1 g saturated fat), 5 mg cholesterol, 71 mg sodium,
12 g carbohydrate, 1 g fiber, 4 g protein
Exchanges: 1 Starch

31 calories

Preparation time: 20 minutes ● **Standing time:** 30 minutes ● **Baking time:** 5 minutes

tomato-topped garlic toasts

To quickly seed tomatoes, cut in half crosswise. Gently squeeze out the seeds or push them out with the tip of the knife or a small spoon.

2 cups chopped, seeded tomato
⅓ cup finely chopped green onions
1 clove garlic, minced
2 teaspoons Dijon-style mustard
¼ teaspoon coarsely ground black pepper
1 tablespoon capers (optional)
1 teaspoon snipped fresh thyme
½ of a 16-ounce loaf baguette-style French bread
Short, thin green sweet pepper strips (optional)

1 In a medium bowl combine tomato, green onions, garlic, mustard, and pepper. Gently stir in capers (if using) and thyme. Cover and let stand for 30 minutes at room temperature to blend flavors. (Or, cover and refrigerate for up to 24 hours.)

2 For toast, cut bread into ¼-inch-thick slices (about 24). Place slices on an ungreased baking sheet. Bake in a 425° oven about 5 minutes or until crisp and light brown, turning once.

3 To assemble, top each piece of toast with about 1 tablespoon tomato mixture. If desired, garnish each piece with sweet pepper strips. Makes about 24 servings.

Nutrition facts per serving: 31 calories, 0 g total fat, 0 mg cholesterol, 70 mg sodium, 6 g carbohydrate, 0 g fiber, 1 g protein
Exchanges: ½ Starch

78 calories

Preparation time: 15 minutes ● **Baking time:** 20 minutes

herbed potato wedges

*Balsamic vinegar adds a wonderful tang to these wedges. If you've never bought balsamic vinegar,
it's worth a try. Its slightly sweet flavor adds flair to salad dressings, sauces, and stir-fries.*

2 teaspoons olive oil
2 teaspoons balsamic vinegar
1 tablespoon grated Parmesan cheese
1 tablespoon fine dry bread crumbs
½ teaspoon dried Italian seasoning, crushed
⅛ teaspoon pepper
2 medium baking potatoes
  Nonstick spray coating
½ cup fat-free dairy sour cream
1 tablespoon snipped fresh chives
¼ teaspoon garlic powder

1 In a custard cup or small bowl combine olive oil and balsamic vinegar. In another small bowl combine Parmesan cheese, bread crumbs, Italian seasoning, and pepper.

2 Scrub potatoes with a soft vegetable brush under running water. Cut the potatoes in half lengthwise, then cut each half lengthwise into 4 wedges. Spray a foil-lined baking sheet with nonstick coating. Arrange wedges on sheet, skin sides down, so they don't touch. Brush with olive oil mixture and coat with Parmesan mixture.

3 Bake in a 425° oven 20 to 25 minutes or until potatoes are tender and edges are crisp.

4 Meanwhile, in a small bowl combine sour cream, chives, and garlic powder. Serve potatoes warm with sour cream mixture. Makes 8 servings.

Nutrition facts per serving: 78 calories, 2 g total fat (0 g saturated fat), 1 mg cholesterol, 34 mg sodium, 14 g carbohydrate, 0 g fiber, 2 g protein
Exchanges: 1 Starch

74 calories

Preparation time: 20 minutes ● **Baking time:** 25 minutes ● **Cooling time:** 1 hour

apricot-oatmeal bars

Sweet attacks are natural. So it's OK to enjoy something sweet as long as you choose wisely.
These bars satisfy your sweet tooth while keeping fat and calories in check.

 1 **cup all-purpose flour**
½ **cup whole wheat flour**
½ **teaspoon salt**
½ **teaspoon baking powder**
½ **teaspoon ground cinnamon**
¼ **teaspoon baking soda**
 1 **beaten egg**
¼ **cup packed brown sugar**
½ **cup plain low-fat yogurt**
¼ **cup water**
¼ **cup molasses**
¼ **cup cooking oil**
 1 **cup quick-cooking rolled oats**
¾ **cup snipped dried apricots**
½ **cup raisins**
¾ **cup sifted powdered sugar**
 1 **to 2 tablespoons orange juice or milk**

1 In a large mixing bowl combine the all-purpose flour, whole wheat flour, salt, baking powder, cinnamon, and baking soda.

2 In a medium mixing bowl combine egg, brown sugar, yogurt, water, molasses, and oil. Stir into flour mixture; mix well.

3 Stir in oats, apricots, and raisins. Spread in a 13×9×2-inch baking pan.

4 Bake in a 350° oven about 25 minutes or until lightly browned. Cool in pan on a wire rack. Cut into bars.

5 For glaze, stir together powdered sugar and enough of the orange juice or milk to make of drizzling consistency. Drizzle over bars. Store in an airtight container. Makes 36 bars.

Nutrition facts per bar: 74 calories, 2 g total fat (0 g saturated fat), 6 mg cholesterol, 49 mg sodium, 13 g carbohydrate, 1 g fiber, 1 g protein
Exchanges: 1 Starch

152 calories

Preparation time: 20 minutes ● **Baking time:** 20 minutes ● **Cooling time:** 1 hour

carrot snack cake

All you need is a small serving of this spiced cake. The decorative powdered sugar replaces the traditional high-fat, high-calorie cream cheese frosting, making it lighter and more healthful.

¼ **cup margarine or butter, softened**
½ **cup granulated sugar**
 1 **egg**
¾ **cup finely shredded carrot**
¼ **cup skim milk**
½ **teaspoon vanilla**
 1 **cup all-purpose flour**
1¼ **teaspoons baking powder**
½ **teaspoon ground cinnamon**
⅛ **teaspoon salt**
⅛ **teaspoon ground nutmeg**
  Nonstick spray coating
 1 **to 2 teaspoons sifted powdered sugar**

1 In a medium mixing bowl beat margarine or butter and granulated sugar until thoroughly combined. Beat in egg. Stir in carrot, milk, and vanilla.

2 In another bowl combine flour, baking powder, cinnamon, salt, and nutmeg. Add to carrot mixture and stir until thoroughly combined.

3 Spray an 8×8×2-inch baking pan with nonstick coating. Pour batter evenly into pan.

4 Bake in a 350° oven for 20 to 25 minutes or until a toothpick inserted near the center of the cake comes out clean. Cool completely in pan on wire rack. (Or, remove from pan after cooling 10 minutes. Then cool completely.)

5 Place a paper doily on top of the cake. Lightly sift the powdered sugar evenly over the doily. Carefully remove the doily. Makes 9 servings.

Nutrition facts per serving: 152 calories, 6 g total fat (1 g saturated fat), 24 mg cholesterol, 154 mg sodium, 23 g carbohydrate, 1 g fiber, 2 g protein
Exchanges: 1½ Starch, 1 Fat

104 calories

Preparation time: 12 minutes ● **Baking time:** 20 minutes ● **Cooling time:** 1 hour

brownie bites

A small pan of these sweet treasures will satisfy your longing for chocolate.
Little harm will be done to your waistline—especially if you share.

2 tablespoons margarine or butter
⅓ cup granulated sugar
¼ cup cold water
½ teaspoon vanilla
½ cup all-purpose flour
2 tablespoons unsweetened cocoa powder
½ teaspoon baking powder
2 tablespoons chopped walnuts or pecans
**   Nonstick spray coating**
1 teaspoon powdered sugar

1 In a small saucepan melt margarine or butter; remove from heat. Stir in granulated sugar, cold water, and vanilla. Stir in flour, cocoa powder, and baking powder until thoroughly combined. Stir in nuts.

2 Spray the bottom of an 8×4×2-inch loaf pan with nonstick coating. Pour batter into pan.

3 Bake in a 350° oven about 20 minutes or until a toothpick inserted near the center comes out clean. Cool completely in pan on wire rack. Remove from pan. Cut into 8 bars. Sprinkle with powdered sugar. Makes 8 servings.

Nutrition facts per serving: 104 calories, 4 g total fat (1 g saturated fat), 0 mg cholesterol, 57 mg sodium, 15 g carbohydrate, 0 g fiber, 1 g protein
Exchanges: 1 Starch, ½ Fat

186 calories

Preparation time: 8 minutes

mocha milk shakes

Even adults swoon for a milk shake. This variation takes a childhood-favorite drink and gives it grown-up appeal with a hint of coffee flavor.

2 cups chocolate low-fat frozen yogurt
½ cup skim milk
2 to 3 teaspoons instant coffee crystals

1 Place frozen yogurt, milk, and coffee crystals in a blender container. Cover and blend until smooth. Serve immediately. Makes 2 (8-ounce) servings.

Nutrition facts per serving: 186 calories, 3 g total fat (2 g saturated fat), 21 mg cholesterol, 163 mg sodium, 36 g carbohydrate, 0 g fiber, 8 g protein
Exchanges: 2 Starch, ½ Milk

Chocolate-Banana Milk Shakes: Prepare Mocha Milk Shakes as directed, except omit the coffee crystals and add 1 ripe *banana,* cut up.

Nutrition facts per serving: 234 calories, 3 g total fat (2 g saturated fat), 21 mg cholesterol, 162 mg sodium, 48 g carbohydrate, 1 g fiber, 9 g protein
Exchanges: 1½ Starch, 1 Fruit, ½ Milk

Chocolate-Mint Milk Shakes: Prepare Mocha Milk Shakes as directed, except omit the coffee crystals and add a few drops *peppermint* or *mint flavoring.*

Nutrition facts per serving: 182 calories, 3 g total fat (2 g saturated fat), 21 mg cholesterol, 162 mg sodium, 35 g carbohydrate, 0 g fiber, 8 g protein
Exchanges: 2 Starch, ½ Milk

95 calories

Preparation time: 10 minutes

tropical banana milk shakes

Choose a low-fat ice cream for this blended shake to keep the fat and calories under control. As a midafternoon snack, share it with your kids and feel good about it being good for them, too.

1 **small banana**
1 **cup orange juice**
1 **cup vanilla low-fat or light ice cream**
¼ **teaspoon vanilla**
  Ground nutmeg
  Orange slices, halved (optional)
  Orange peel strips (optional)

1 Peel and cut up banana. Place in freezer container or bag; freeze until firm.

2 In a blender container combine banana, orange juice, ice cream, and vanilla. Cover and blend until smooth. Sprinkle each serving with nutmeg. If desired, garnish with orange slice halves and orange peel strips. Makes 4 (6-ounce) servings.

Nutrition facts per serving: 95 calories, 2 g total fat (1 g saturated fat), 5 mg cholesterol, 29 mg sodium, 19 g carbohydrate, 1 g fiber, 2 g protein
Exchanges: ½ Fruit, ½ Milk

Banana Shakes: Prepare Tropical Banana Milk Shakes as directed, except substitute 1 cup *skim milk* for the orange juice.

Nutrition facts per serving: 88 calories, 2 g total fat (1 g saturated fat), 6 mg cholesterol, 60 mg sodium, 16 g carbohydrate, 0 g fiber, 4 g protein
Exchanges: ½ Fruit, ½ Milk

48 calories

Preparation time: 10 minutes

peppy tomato sipper

Having trouble eating enough vegetables? Drink up! This refreshing choice can be served over ice or blended into a frosty slush. Make it as peppy as you like by varying the amount of hot pepper sauce.

2 **cups tomato juice or vegetable juice**
2 **tablespoons lime or lemon juice**
1 **teaspoon Worcestershire sauce**
½ **teaspoon prepared horseradish (optional)**
   Few drops bottled hot pepper sauce
   Ice cubes
   Celery leaves (optional)

1 In a small pitcher stir together tomato juice or vegetable juice, lime or lemon juice, Worcestershire sauce, horseradish (if using), and hot pepper sauce.

2 Pour mixture over ice in glasses. If desired, garnish each serving with celery leaves. Makes 2 (8-ounce) servings.

Peppy Tomato Slush: Prepare Peppy Tomato Sipper as directed, except omit ice cubes. Pour tomato mixture into a 2-quart square dish. Cover and freeze for 1 to 2 hours or until slushy. Spoon into glasses.

Nutrition facts per serving: 48 calories, 0 g total fat, 0 mg cholesterol, 906 mg sodium, 12 g carbohydrate, 3 g fiber, 2 g protein
Exchanges: 2 Vegetable

39 calories

Preparation time: 15 minutes

orange and spice tea

Squelch any hunger pangs with a cup of this tea that gets a boost of citrus flavor from orange juice.
Satisfying and soothing, it has only 39 calories per serving.

2 cups water
3 inches stick cinnamon, broken
6 whole cloves
3 tea bags
1 cup orange juice
1 tablespoon brown sugar
   Orange slices, quartered (optional)

1 In a saucepan combine water, cinnamon, and cloves. Bring to boiling; remove from heat.

2 Add tea bags; let stand for 5 minutes. Remove tea bags.

3 Stir in orange juice and brown sugar; heat mixture through.

4 Pour mixture through a wire strainer into 4 mugs or cups. If desired, serve with orange slice quarters. Makes 4 (6-ounce) servings.

Nutrition facts per serving: 39 calories, 0 g total fat, 0 mg cholesterol, 5 mg sodium, 9 g carbohydrate, 1 g fiber, 0 g protein
Exchanges: ½ Fruit

Breakfast

& BRUNCHES

chapter index

120 calories

Preparation time: 10 minutes ● **Cooking time:** 12 minutes

breakfast rice cereal

Breakfast is especially important when you're dieting. Try this tasty hot cereal for a change. Added fruit, a little brown sugar, and nutmeg transform brown rice into a breakfast fit for any svelte-to-be queen or king.

1½ **cups water**
⅛ **teaspoon salt**
1 **cup quick-cooking brown rice**
⅓ **cup mixed dried fruit bits**
¾ **cup skim milk**
   Dash ground nutmeg
4 **teaspoons brown sugar**

1 In a 2-quart saucepan bring the water and salt to boiling. Add brown rice; reduce heat. Cover and simmer for 7 minutes. Stir in fruit bits. Cover and simmer for 5 to 7 minutes more or until rice is tender and liquid is absorbed. Stir in milk and nutmeg. Heat through. To serve, sprinkle each with *1 teaspoon* brown sugar. Makes 4 servings.

Nutrition facts per serving: 120 calories, 1 g total fat, (0 g saturated fat), 1 mg cholesterol, 104 mg sodium, 27 g carbohydrate, 1 g fiber, 3 g protein
Exchanges: 1 Starch, ½ Fruit

216 calories

Preparation time: 12 minutes ● **Baking time:** 45 minutes ● **Cooling time:** 30 minutes

granola

*Shredded apples add flavor and texture to this honey-sweetened granola. Sprinkle the granola
over low-fat yogurt for a quick snack or breakfast on the go.*

3 cups regular rolled oats
1 cup coarsely shredded unpeeled apple
½ cup toasted wheat germ
¼ cup honey
¼ cup water
1½ teaspoons ground cinnamon
**1 teaspoon vanilla or ½ teaspoon almond
   extract**
Nonstick spray coating
Skim milk

1 In a large bowl combine oats, apple, and wheat germ; mix well. In a small saucepan stir together honey, water, and cinnamon. Heat to boiling; remove from heat. Stir in vanilla or almond extract. Pour over oat mixture; mix well.

2 Spray a 15×10×1-inch baking pan with nonstick coating. Spread oat mixture evenly in pan. Bake in a 325° oven about 45 minutes or until golden brown, stirring occasionally. Spread onto foil to cool. (To store, place cooled granola in an airtight container in the refrigerator for up to 2 weeks.) Serve with milk. Makes 8 (½-cup) servings.

Nutrition facts per serving with ⅓ cup skim milk:
216 calories, 3 g total fat (1 g saturated fat),
1 mg cholesterol, 44 mg sodium, 39 g carbohydrate,
0 g fiber, 10 g protein
Exchanges: 2 Starch, ½ Milk

141 calories

Preparation time: 15 minutes

fruity oatmeal

In just 15 minutes you'll have a warm breakfast for a cold winter morning. If you have a penchant for pears or apricots, substitute them for the peaches or apple.

2 cups water
¼ teaspoon salt
1 cup regular rolled oats
1 cup coarsely chopped peeled peaches or chopped apple
¼ cup raisins or snipped pitted whole dates
⅛ teaspoon ground cinnamon
2 teaspoons brown sugar
½ cup skim milk

1 In a medium saucepan bring the water and salt to boiling. Stir in oats, peaches or apple, raisins or dates, and cinnamon. Reduce heat. Simmer, uncovered, for 5 minutes, stirring occasionally. Remove from heat. Cover; let stand for 2 minutes. Stir in brown sugar.

2 Divide the hot oat mixture among 4 bowls. Pour 2 tablespoons milk over each serving. Serve immediately. Makes 4 servings.

Nutrition facts per serving: 141 calories, 1 g total fat (0 g saturated fat), 1 mg cholesterol, 155 mg sodium, 29 g carbohydrate, 1 g fiber, 5 g protein
Exchanges: 2 Starch

227 calories

Preparation time: 5 minutes ● **Cooking time:** 10 minutes

grain and fruit hot cereal

*Cornmeal and bulgur pair up in this ready-to-cook, delicious breakfast.
It makes enough cereal mix for 8 servings.*

1 **cup cornmeal**
⅔ **cup bulgur**
1 **6-ounce package mixed dried fruit bits**
½ **cup slivered almonds, toasted**
½ **teaspoon ground cinnamon**
   Skim milk
   Brown sugar (optional)

1 In an airtight container stir together the cornmeal, bulgur, dried fruit bits, almonds, and ground cinnamon. Cover and store in the refrigerator up to 1 month.

2 To cook 1 serving, in a small saucepan bring 1 cup *water* and a dash *salt* to boiling. Slowly stir in ⅓ cup cereal mixture. Simmer, uncovered, about 10 minutes or to desired consistency, stirring occasionally. Stir in *3 tablespoons* milk and, if desired, *1 teaspoon* brown sugar. Serve immediately. Makes enough mix for 8 servings.

Nutrition facts per serving: 227 calories, 5 g total fat (1 g saturated fat), 1 mg cholesterol, 49 mg sodium, 42 g carbohydrate, 4 g fiber, 7 g protein
Exchanges: 3 Starch

140 calories

Preparation time: 20 minutes

saucy prunes and peaches

Wake up your morning with this spicy fruit combo. Eat it as is or spoon it over hot oatmeal. A half cup of cooked oatmeal adds 70 calories and 1 gram of fat (1 Starch exchange) to your nutrition total.

 1 **cup orange juice**
 2 **tablespoons sugar**
¼ **teaspoon ground cinnamon**
⅛ **teaspoon ground cloves**
½ **cup halved pitted prunes**
 4 **medium peaches or nectarines, peeled,
      pitted, and sliced, or 4 cups frozen sliced
      peaches, thawed**
      Hot cooked oatmeal (optional)

1 In a 2-quart saucepan stir together the orange juice, sugar, cinnamon, and cloves. Add the prunes. Bring to boiling; reduce heat. Cover and simmer for 5 minutes.

2 Add the peaches or nectarines. Heat through. Serve immediately. If desired, serve over hot oatmeal. Makes 5 servings.

Nutrition facts per serving: 140 calories, 0 g total fat, 0 mg cholesterol, 1 mg sodium, 36 g carbohydrate, 4 g fiber, 2 g protein
Exchanges: 2 Fruit

89 calories

Preparation time: 12 minutes ● **Broiling time:** 10 minutes

turkey and apple sausage

*To ensure your sausage is the lowest in fat and calories possible, grind your own turkey without the skin.
Or, have your butcher grind it for you without adding the skin.*

2 tablespoons soft bread crumbs
½ cup shredded peeled apple
1½ teaspoons snipped fresh sage or
½ teaspoon dried sage, crushed
¼ teaspoon black pepper
⅛ teaspoon salt
⅛ teaspoon paprika
⅛ teaspoon ground red pepper
Dash ground nutmeg
8 ounces ground raw turkey
Nonstick spray coating

1 In a large bowl combine bread crumbs, apple, sage, black pepper, salt, paprika, ground red pepper, and nutmeg; add turkey and mix well. Shape mixture into four ½-inch-thick patties.

2 Spray the unheated rack of a broiler pan with nonstick coating. Arrange patties on rack. Broil 4 to 5 inches from the heat about 10 minutes or until no longer pink; turn once. (Or, spray an unheated large skillet with nonstick coating. Preheat over medium heat. Add sausage and cook for 8 to 10 minutes or until no longer pink.) Makes 4 servings.

Nutrition facts per serving: 89 calories, 5 g total fat (1 g saturated fat), 21 mg cholesterol, 99 mg sodium, 4 g carbohydrate, 0 g fiber, 8 g protein
Exchanges: 1 Lean Meat, ½ Fruit

Mexican-Style Turkey Sausage: Prepare as directed, except substitute one 4½-ounce can *diced green chili peppers* for the apple and omit the sage, paprika, and nutmeg. Add 1 large clove *garlic,* finely chopped; ¼ teaspoon *ground cumin;* and ¼ teaspoon *dried oregano,* crushed, to the turkey mixture. Continue as directed.

Nutrition facts per serving: 83 calories, 5 g total fat (1 g saturated fat), 21 mg cholesterol, 179 mg sodium, 2 g carbohydrate, 0 g fiber, 8 g protein
Exchanges: 1 Lean Meat, ½ Fruit

268 calories

Preparation time: 25 minutes

pancakes with orange sauce

*Tempt your family with a breakfast of whole wheat pancakes. The bright mandarin orange
and walnut sauce is a tangy alternative to maple syrup.*

¾ **cup whole wheat flour**
¼ **cup all-purpose flour**
1½ **teaspoons baking powder**
⅛ **teaspoon salt**
¾ **cup skim milk**
1 **tablespoon honey**
1 **teaspoon cooking oil**
2 **stiffly beaten egg whites**
 Nonstick spray coating
1 **recipe Orange Sauce**

1 In a medium mixing bowl combine whole wheat flour, all-purpose flour, baking powder, and salt. In a small mixing bowl combine milk, honey, and oil; add to flour mixture. Stir just until moistened. Fold in egg whites.

2 Spray an unheated griddle with nonstick coating. Preheat griddle over medium heat. For each pancake, pour about ¼ cup batter onto hot griddle.

Cook until golden brown on both sides, turning when pancakes have bubbly surfaces and slightly dry edges. Serve with warm Orange Sauce. Makes 4 servings (8 pancakes).

Orange Sauce: In a small saucepan combine 2 tablespoons *sugar* and 1 tablespoon *cornstarch*. Stir in 1 cup *water* and 3 tablespoons *frozen orange juice concentrate*. Cook and stir until thickened and bubbly. Cook and stir 2 minutes more. Gently stir in one 11-ounce can *mandarin orange sections*, drained, and 2 tablespoons chopped *walnuts*. Keep warm. Makes about 1½ cups.

Nutrition facts per serving: 268 calories, 5 g total fat (0 g saturated fat), 1 mg cholesterol, 263 mg sodium, 52 g carbohydrate, 3 g fiber, 8 g protein
Exchanges: 2 Starch, 1 Fruit, ½ Fat

152 calories

Preparation time: 30 minutes

pancakes with strawberry sauce

*Strawberry sauce makes these pancakes a special treat. Use fresh or frozen berries in the sauce
and dust pancakes with powdered sugar before serving.*

½ **cup whole wheat flour**
½ **cup all-purpose flour**
 1 **tablespoon granulated sugar**
 2 **teaspoons baking powder**
¼ **teaspoon salt**
¾ **cup skim milk**
 1 **teaspoon cooking oil**
 2 **stiffly beaten egg whites**
    Nonstick spray coating
 1 **recipe Strawberry Sauce**
 1 **tablespoon powdered sugar (optional)**

1 In a mixing bowl combine whole wheat flour,
all-purpose flour, granulated sugar, baking powder,
and salt. Stir in milk and oil. Fold in egg whites.

2 Spray an unheated griddle with nonstick
coating. Preheat griddle over medium heat. For each
pancake, pour about ¼ cup batter onto the hot

griddle. Cook until golden brown on both sides,
turning when pancakes have bubbly surfaces and
slightly dry edges. Serve pancakes with Strawberry
Sauce. If desired, sift powdered sugar over
pancakes. Makes 5 servings (10 pancakes).

Strawberry Sauce: In a food processor bowl or
blender container combine 1½ cups fresh or thawed
frozen unsweetened *strawberries,* 1 to 2 tablespoons
granulated sugar, and 1 teaspoon *vanilla.* Cover
and process or blend until smooth. Stir in ½ cup
chopped *strawberries.* In a small saucepan heat
sauce through. Makes about 1 cup.

Nutrition facts per serving: 152 calories, 2 g total fat
(0 g saturated fat), 1 mg cholesterol, 294 mg sodium,
29 g carbohydrate, 3 g fiber, 6 g protein
Exchanges: 2 Starch

171 calories

Preparation time: 25 minutes

no - fry french toast

Once you try this oven-baked French toast, you'll never make it the old way again. On a griddle or in a skillet, French toast must be made in batches. Baking allows you to make eight at one time.

Nonstick spray coating
- 1 **slightly beaten egg**
- 1 **slightly beaten egg white**
- ¾ **cup skim milk**
- 1 **teaspoon vanilla**
- ⅛ **teaspoon ground cinnamon**
- 8 **½-inch-thick slices French bread**
- ¼ **teaspoon finely shredded orange peel**
- ½ **cup orange juice**
- 1 **tablespoon honey**
- 1 **teaspoon cornstarch**
- ⅛ **teaspoon ground cinnamon**
- 1 **tablespoon powdered sugar (optional)**

1 Spray a large baking sheet with nonstick coating. In a pie plate combine egg, egg white, milk, vanilla, and ⅛ teaspoon ground cinnamon. Soak bread slices in egg mixture for about 1 minute per side. Place on prepared baking sheet.

2 Bake in a 450° oven about 6 minutes or until bread is lightly browned. Turn bread over and bake 5 to 8 minutes more or until golden brown.

3 Meanwhile, for orange syrup, in a small saucepan stir together orange peel, orange juice, honey, cornstarch, and ⅛ teaspoon cinnamon. Cook and stir until thickened and bubbly. Cook and stir 2 minutes more.

4 If desired, sift powdered sugar over toast. Serve with warm orange syrup. Makes 4 servings.

Nutrition facts per serving: 171 calories, 3 g total fat (1 g saturated fat), 54 mg cholesterol, 263 mg sodium, 29 g carbohydrate, 0 g fiber, 7 g protein
Exchanges: 2 Starch

111 calories

Preparation time: 30 minutes ● **Baking time:** 15 minutes

breakfast blintzes

Plan a brunch around these ricotta-filled crepes. You can make the crepes up to two days in advance.
Layer the cooled crepes between waxed paper and store in an airtight container in the refrigerator.

　1　**egg**
　1½　**cups skim milk**
　1　**cup all-purpose flour**
　　　Nonstick spray coating
　½　**teaspoon shortening**
　1　**15-ounce carton low-fat or light ricotta**
　　　cheese
　2　**tablespoons orange marmalade**
　1　**tablespoon sugar**
　⅛　**teaspoon ground cinnamon**
　⅔　**cup light dairy sour cream**
　5　**tablespoons orange marmalade**
　½　**cup fresh raspberries or blueberries**

　1 For crepes, combine egg, milk, and flour. Beat with rotary beater until well mixed. Spray an unheated 6-inch skillet or crepe pan with nonstick coating. Preheat skillet over medium heat. Remove from heat and pour in about 2 tablespoons batter. Lift and tilt skillet to spread batter. Return skillet to heat; cook 30 to 60 seconds or until browned on 1 side only. Remove from pan. Repeat with remaining batter to make 15 crepes. Lightly brush skillet with shortening between cooking, as needed.

　2 For filling, in a mixing bowl combine ricotta cheese, the 2 tablespoons orange marmalade, the sugar, and cinnamon. Spoon about 2 tablespoons cheese mixture onto the unbrowned side of a crepe; spread out slightly. Fold in half. Fold in half again, forming a wedge. Repeat with remaining filling and remaining crepes.

　3 Spray a shallow baking pan with nonstick coating. Arrange blintzes in pan. Bake in a 350° oven for 15 to 20 minutes or until heated through. To serve, spoon about 2 teaspoons of the sour cream and a teaspoon of marmalade onto each blintz. Sprinkle with berries. Makes 15 blintzes.

Nutrition facts per blintz: 111 calories, 2 g total fat (1 g saturated fat), 21 mg cholesterol, 51 mg sodium, 17 g carbohydrate, 1 g fiber, 6 g protein
Exchanges: 1 Starch, ½ Lean Meat

152 calories

Preparation time: 40 minutes

puffy omelet squares

*Topped with a savory zucchini and tomato sauce, these fluffy, puffy squares are
a delicious, quick choice for any meal of the day.*

Nonstick spray coating
6 eggs, separated
½ teaspoon onion powder
¼ teaspoon salt
⅛ teaspoon pepper
**1 14½-ounce can pasta-style stewed tomatoes,
undrained and cut up if necessary**
**1 medium zucchini, quartered lengthwise
and sliced (about 1 cup)**
⅛ teaspoon pepper

1 Spray a 2-quart square baking dish with
nonstick coating; set aside. For omelet, beat egg
yolks, onion powder, salt, and ⅛ teaspoon pepper
with an electric mixer on medium speed about
4 minutes or until thick and lemon colored; set aside.
Wash beaters thoroughly. Beat egg whites until soft
peaks form (tips curl); fold into yolk mixture.

2 Spread egg mixture evenly into prepared dish.
Bake in a 350° oven for 22 to 25 minutes or until a
knife inserted near the center comes out clean.

3 Meanwhile, for sauce, in a medium saucepan
combine undrained tomatoes, zucchini, and
⅛ teaspoon pepper. Bring to boiling; reduce heat.
Simmer, covered, about 5 minutes or until zucchini
is tender. Simmer, uncovered, for 10 to 12 minutes
more or until of desired consistency. To serve,
cut omelet into quarters; top with sauce. Makes
4 servings.

Nutrition facts per serving: 152 calories, 8 g total fat
(2 g saturated fat), 320 mg cholesterol, 549 mg sodium,
10 g carbohydrate, 0 g fiber, 11 g protein
Exchanges: 1 Medium-Fat Meat, 2 Vegetable, ½ Fat

161 calories

Preparation time: 25 minutes ● **Broiling time:** 2 minutes

ham and cheese frittata

A frittata is an Italian egg dish that resembles an omelet. It is cooked on top of the stove until almost set, then placed under the broiler to finish cooking. A cast-iron skillet works well for both cooking phases.

Nonstick spray coating
- 1 **cup chopped cooked ham (about 5 ounces)**
- ½ **cup chopped onion**
- ½ **cup chopped green or red sweet pepper**
- 6 **slightly beaten eggs**
- ¾ **cup low-fat cottage cheese**
- ⅛ **teaspoon black pepper**
- 2 **Roma tomatoes, thinly sliced**
- ¼ **cup shredded reduced-fat cheddar cheese (1 ounce)**

1 Spray an unheated 10-inch broiler-proof skillet with nonstick coating. Preheat skillet over medium heat. Add ham, onion, and sweet pepper. Cook about 4 minutes or until vegetables are tender and ham is lightly browned.

2 Meanwhile, in a mixing bowl combine eggs, cottage cheese, and black pepper. Pour over ham mixture in skillet.

3 Cook over medium-low heat. As egg mixture sets, run a spatula around the edge of the skillet, lifting the egg mixture so uncooked portion flows underneath. Continue cooking and lifting edge until egg mixture is almost set (surface will be moist).

4 Place skillet under broiler 5 inches from heat. Broil for 1 to 2 minutes or until top is just set.

5 Arrange tomato slices on top of frittata. Sprinkle cheddar cheese over tomato. Broil 1 minute more. Makes 6 servings.

Nutrition facts per serving: 161 calories, 8 g total fat (3 g saturated fat), 231 mg cholesterol, 494 mg sodium, 5 g carbohydrate, 1 g fiber, 17 g protein
Exchanges: 2 Medium-Fat Meat, 1 Vegetable

254 calories

Preparation time: 25 minutes ● **Chilling time:** 2 hours ● **Baking:** 35 minutes ● **Standing:** 5 minutes

mexican strata

To lower the sodium in this make-ahead breakfast dish, use ground raw turkey instead of the breakfast sausage and add an herb such as thyme or oregano.

Nonstick spray coating
5 slices white or whole wheat bread, cubed (3¾ cups)
6 ounces ground turkey sausage
3 eggs
1 cup skim milk
½ cup light dairy sour cream
½ cup shredded Monterey Jack cheese with jalapeño peppers (2 ounces)
⅓ cup shredded reduced-fat sharp cheddar cheese
⅓ cup salsa

1 Spray a 9- or 10-inch quiche dish with nonstick coating. Spread bread cubes evenly in the quiche dish. Set aside.

2 Crumble turkey sausage into a medium skillet; cook until brown. Drain off fat. Pat with paper towels to remove excess fat. Sprinkle cooked sausage over bread cubes in quiche dish.

3 In medium mixing bowl beat together eggs, milk, and sour cream. Stir in Monterey Jack and cheddar cheeses. Pour egg mixture over sausage in quiche dish. Cover and refrigerate for at least 2 hours or up to 24 hours.

4 Uncover and bake in a 325° oven for 35 to 40 minutes or until center is set and top is golden brown. Let stand for 5 to 10 minutes before cutting.

5 To serve, cut strata into wedges. Spoon some salsa on top of each serving. Makes 6 servings.

Nutrition facts per serving: 254 calories, 13 g total fat (6 g saturated fat), 134 mg cholesterol, 556 mg sodium, 17 g carbohydrate, 0 g fiber, 18 g protein
Exchanges: 1 Starch, 2 Medium-Fat Meat, 1 Vegetable

163 calories

Preparation time: 30 minutes • **Standing time:** 3 to 4 minutes

spring vegetables and egg skillet

Using an egg substitute keeps the fat and cholesterol down in this egg dish. For heartier appetites, serve it with toasted bagels spread with fat-free cream cheese.

    8 ounces tiny new red potatoes (about 6), cut
          into ¼-inch-thick slices
    1 cup ½-inch pieces asparagus
          Nonstick spray coating
 1½ cups refrigerated or frozen egg product,
          thawed, or 6 eggs
    1 tablespoon snipped fresh parsley
    1 teaspoon snipped fresh rosemary or
          ½ teaspoon dried rosemary, crushed
   ¼ to ½ teaspoon onion powder
   ¼ teaspoon salt
   ¼ teaspoon pepper
    1 large tomato, seeded and coarsely chopped
    1 tablespoon finely shredded or grated
          Parmesan cheese

1 In a large covered nonstick skillet cook potatoes in a small amount of *boiling water* for 5 minutes. Add the asparagus; cover and cook for 5 to 7 minutes more or until the vegetables are tender. Drain. Dry and cool the skillet.

2 Spray the cooled skillet with nonstick coating. Return vegetables to skillet. In a medium bowl combine egg product, parsley, rosemary, onion powder, salt, and pepper. Pour into skillet over vegetables. Cook over medium heat. As mixture sets, run a spatula around the edge of the skillet, lifting egg mixture so uncooked portion flows underneath. Continue cooking and lifting edge until egg mixture is almost set (surface will be moist).

3 Remove skillet from heat. Cover and let stand for 3 to 4 minutes or until top is set. Spoon onto plates. Top with chopped tomato and sprinkle with Parmesan cheese. Makes 4 servings.

Nutrition facts per serving: 163 calories, 4 g total fat (1 g saturated fat), 2 mg cholesterol, 348 mg sodium, 17 g carbohydrate, 2 g fiber, 15 g protein
Exchanges: 1 Starch, 1 Lean Meat, 1 Vegetable

192 calories

Preparation time: 18 minutes ● **Baking time:** 4 minutes

oven omelet

*Reduced-fat cream cheese and smoked turkey fill this oven omelet. Another time, add ½ cup cooked
vegetables, such as chopped broccoli, sliced mushrooms, or cut asparagus in place of the meat.*

3 **egg whites**
 Dash salt
 Dash black pepper
3 **egg yolks**
1 **tablespoon snipped fresh parsley**
 Nonstick spray coating
2 **ounces smoked turkey, smoked salmon, or
 cooked ham, chopped**
¼ **cup chopped red or green sweet pepper**
1 **ounce reduced-fat cream cheese
 (Neufchâtel), cut up**
1 **to 2 teaspoons skim milk**
½ **teaspoon snipped fresh thyme or
 ⅛ teaspoon dried thyme, crushed
 Fresh thyme (optional)**

1 In a small mixing bowl beat egg whites, salt,
and black pepper with an electric mixer until stiff
peaks form (tips stand straight). In another bowl
lightly beat yolks with a fork. Stir in parsley. Fold
whites into yolks.

2 Spray an unheated 10-inch ovenproof skillet
with nonstick coating. Preheat the skillet over
medium-high heat. Spread the egg mixture in the
skillet. Cook 3 to 5 minutes or until the bottom of
the omelet is golden brown. Place skillet in a 350°
oven. Bake 3 minutes or until nearly dry.

3 Meanwhile in a small skillet cook and stir
turkey, salmon, or ham; sweet pepper; cream
cheese; milk; and thyme until cheese is melted.
Carefully spoon the turkey mixture over baked egg
mixture. Bake 1 minute more.

4 To serve, fold omelet in half. If desired,
garnish with fresh thyme. Makes 2 servings.

Nutrition facts per serving: 192 calories, 13 g total fat
(5 g saturated fat), 346 mg cholesterol, 509 mg sodium,
3 g carbohydrate, 0 g fiber, 17 g protein
Exchanges: 3 Medium-Fat Meat

238 calories

Preparation time: 25 minutes ● **Chilling time:** 2 hours ● **Baking:** 32 minutes ● **Standing:** 5 minutes

breakfast casserole

*Like a traditional strata, this cheesy sausage casserole is assembled the night before. The difference
is that this version is leaner in fat and calories.*

6 slices whole wheat bread
Nonstick spray coating
4 ounces ground turkey sausage
**1 medium red or green sweet pepper,
chopped**
½ cup chopped fresh mushrooms
**½ cup shredded reduced-fat sharp cheddar
cheese (2 ounces)**
**1 10¾-ounce can reduced-fat and -sodium
condensed cream of mushroom soup**
**1 cup refrigerated or frozen egg product,
thawed**
1 cup evaporated skim milk
¾ teaspoon dry mustard
¼ teaspoon black pepper

1 Cut bread into cubes; place in a large shallow
pan. Bake in a 350° oven for 8 to 10 minutes or
until toasted, stirring once. Spray a 2-quart
rectangular baking dish with nonstick coating. Place
half of toasted bread cubes in the dish. Set aside.

2 Meanwhile, in a large skillet cook sausage,
sweet pepper, and mushrooms over medium-high
heat until sausage is brown. Drain off fat. Pat
mixture with a paper towel to remove excess fat.
Spoon mixture over bread cubes in dish. Sprinkle
with *half* of the cheese. Top with remaining bread.

3 In a medium mixing bowl combine soup, egg
product, evaporated milk, dry mustard, and black
pepper. Pour over bread, pressing down cubes with
back of spoon to moisten. Cover and refrigerate for
at least 2 hours or up to 24 hours.

4 Uncover and bake in a 350° oven for
30 minutes or until a knife inserted near the center
comes out clean. Sprinkle with remaining cheese.
Bake 2 to 3 minutes more. Let stand for 5 to
10 minutes before serving. Makes 8 servings.

Nutrition facts per serving: 238 calories, 8 g total fat
(2 g saturated fat), 17 mg cholesterol, 719 mg sodium,
23 g carbohydrate, 3 g fiber, 18 g protein
Exchanges: 1 Starch, 2 Lean Meat, 1 Vegetable

317 calories

Preparation time: 30 minutes ● **Baking time:** 20 minutes

brunch turnovers

A sausage and mozzarella cheese filling makes these turnovers taste like a pizza.
For a weekend brunch, simply serve with fresh fruit.

8 ounces ground turkey sausage
1 8-ounce can low-sodium tomato sauce
½ of a 10-ounce package frozen chopped spinach or broccoli, thawed and well-drained
⅓ cup shredded part-skim mozzarella cheese
3 tablespoons sliced green onion
1 teaspoon dried Italian seasoning, crushed
⅛ teaspoon garlic salt
¾ cup reduced-fat packaged biscuit mix
½ cup whole wheat flour
⅓ cup skim milk
Skim milk
½ teaspoon sugar

1 Line a baking sheet with foil; set aside. For filling, cook sausage in a skillet until brown. Drain off fat. Stir in ¼ *cup* of the tomato sauce, the spinach or broccoli (cut up large pieces of broccoli), cheese, green onion, ½ *teaspoon* of the Italian seasoning, garlic salt, and dash *pepper*. Set aside.

2 In a mixing bowl stir together biscuit mix and whole wheat flour. Stir in the ⅓ cup milk just until moistened. Turn dough out onto a lightly floured surface and knead 10 to 12 strokes. Divide dough into 4 equal pieces. Roll each into a 7-inch circle.

3 Spoon one-fourth of the filling onto half of each circle of dough. Brush edges of circles with additional milk. Fold the other half of each circle over the filling and seal edges with the tines of a fork. Place turnovers on foil-lined baking sheet. Brush tops of turnovers with additional milk. Cut slits in tops for steam to escape. Bake in a 400° oven about 20 minutes or until golden brown.

4 Meanwhile, in a saucepan heat remaining tomato sauce, Italian seasoning, and the sugar until heated through. Serve with hot turnovers. Serves 4.

Nutrition facts per serving: 317 calories, 9 g total fat (4 g saturated fat), 28 mg cholesterol, 857 mg sodium, 35 g carbohydrate, 3 g fiber, 21 g protein
Exchanges: 2 Starch, 2 Medium-Fat Meat, 1 Vegetable

216 calories

Preparation time: 25 minutes ● **Baking time:** 18 minutes

canadian bacon brunch pizza

Why not pizza for brunch? This fresh, colorful midmorning treat will surely become a favorite.
Plus, it's a great way to get some fruit into your diet.

1 **Whole Wheat Pizza Crust (see recipe, page 58)**

3 **ounces pizza-style Canadian-style bacon, quartered**

1 **11-ounce can mandarin orange sections, drained**

1 **8-ounce can pineapple tidbits (juice-packed), drained**

½ **cup chopped green sweet pepper**

1 **tablespoon snipped fresh basil or ½ teaspoon dried basil, crushed**

¾ **cup shredded part-skim mozzarella cheese (3 ounces)**

2 **tablespoons grated Parmesan cheese**

1 Bake Whole Wheat Pizza Crust as directed. Arrange the Canadian-style bacon, drained fruits, and sweet pepper over crust. Sprinkle with the basil, then with the mozzarella and Parmesan cheeses. Bake in a 425° oven for 8 to 10 minutes more or until cheese is melted and crust is browned. Makes 6 servings.

Nutrition facts per serving: 216 calories, 4 g total fat (2 g saturated fat), 15 mg cholesterol, 293 mg sodium, 35 g carbohydrate, 3 g fiber, 11 g protein
Exchanges: 1 Starch, 1 Lean Meat, 1 Fruit

132 calories

Preparation time: 10 minutes

berry - banana smoothie

*Keep frozen bananas on hand by placing peeled, cut-up, ripe bananas in a freezer container or plastic bag.
Use the frozen banana pieces right from the freezer for this fruity shake.*

1 **small banana, peeled, cut up, and frozen**
¼ **cup fresh or frozen assorted berries**
   **(such as raspberries, blackberries, and/or
   strawberries)**
1 **cup orange juice**
3 **tablespoons vanilla low-fat yogurt**
   Fresh mint (optional)
   Fresh berries (optional)

1 In a blender container combine the frozen banana pieces, desired fresh or frozen berries, orange juice, and yogurt. Cover and blend until smooth. To serve, pour into glasses. If desired, garnish with fresh mint and additional berries. Makes 2 (8-ounce) servings.

Nutrition facts per serving: 132 calories, 0 g total fat, 1 mg cholesterol, 14 mg sodium, 29 g carbohydrate, 2 g fiber, 2 g protein
Exchanges: 2 Fruit

220 calories

Preparation time: 10 minutes

strawberry and papaya shake

*The pear-shaped papaya is famous for its mellow, buttery taste. For the ultimate flavor,
use a ripe fruit that is mostly yellow and feels somewhat soft when pressed.*

½ **cup skim milk**
½ **cup plain fat-free yogurt**
½ **cup fresh strawberries**
½ **of a medium papaya, seeded, peeled,
and chopped (about ¾ cup)**
1 **tablespoon honey**
3 **large ice cubes**

1 In a blender container combine milk, yogurt,
strawberries, papaya, and honey. Cover and blend
until smooth. With the blender running, add ice
cubes, 1 at a time, through the opening in lid. Blend
until smooth. Pour into glasses; serve immediately.
Makes 2 (10-ounce) servings.

Nutrition facts per serving: 220 calories, 1 g total fat
(0 g saturated fat), 2 mg cholesterol, 91 mg sodium,
48 g carbohydrate, 5 g fiber, 6 g protein
Exchanges: 2 Fruit, 1 Milk

Lunch

chapter index

163 calories

Preparation time: 15 minutes

fruited cottage cheese salad

Apples, dried fruit, and a dash of cinnamon transform cottage cheese into a satisfying single-serving lunch.
To make enough for the whole family, simply double, triple, or quadruple the recipe as needed.

½ **cup low-fat cottage cheese**
1 **small apple, chopped (½ cup)**
2 **tablespoons mixed dried fruit bits or raisins**
   Dash ground cinnamon, ground nutmeg, or apple pie spice
1 **lettuce leaf**

1 In a small mixing bowl stir together cottage cheese; apple; dried fruit bits or raisins; and cinnamon, nutmeg, or apple pie spice.

2 To serve, line a plate with lettuce leaf. Spoon cottage cheese mixture on lettuce leaf. (If desired, cover and refrigerate for up to 24 hours.) Makes 1 main-dish serving.

To tote for lunch: Pack 1 lettuce leaf in a small plastic bag. Place 1 serving of the salad in an airtight container. Place the bag of lettuce and the container of the salad in an insulated lunch box with a frozen ice pack.

Nutrition facts per serving: 163 calories, 2 g total fat (1 g saturated fat), 5 mg cholesterol, 380 mg sodium, 23 g carbohydrate, 1 g fiber, 15 g protein
Exchanges: 2 Lean Meat, 1 Fruit

75 calories

Preparation time: 15 minutes

garden-style cottage cheese

Serve this fat-free vegetable-filled salad solo or spoon it onto pita bread wedges, as we have done here.
Add about 40 calories (½ Starch) to your meal for half of a pita bread round.

½ **cup fat-free cottage cheese, drained**
⅓ **cup finely chopped red, green, or yellow**
    sweet pepper
⅓ **cup finely shredded carrot**
¼ **cup finely chopped green onions**
1½ **teaspoons Dijon-style mustard**

1 In a medium bowl combine cottage cheese, sweet pepper, carrot, green onions, and mustard. Serve immediately or cover and refrigerate for up to 24 hours. Makes 2 main-dish servings.

Nutrition facts per serving: 75 calories, 0 g total fat, 7 mg cholesterol, 208 mg sodium, 7 g carbohydrate, 1 g fiber, 11 g protein
Exchanges: 1 Lean Meat, 1 Vegetable

111 calories

Preparation time: 30 minutes ● **Chilling time:** 4 to 24 hours

thai-style potato salad

For variety, try another flavor of yogurt—such as orange or lemon—the next time you make this refreshing salad. The curly carrot garnish (in photo) was made with an kitchen tool called a spiral slicer or cutter.

1 **pound whole tiny new potatoes**
1 **cup fresh pea pods**
½ **of an 8-ounce carton pineapple low-fat yogurt**
1 **teaspoon reduced-sodium soy sauce**
¼ **teaspoon crushed red pepper**
⅛ **teaspoon ground ginger**
1 **small yellow summer squash, washed, halved lengthwise, and thinly sliced**
½ **cup bias-sliced carrots**
Curly carrot (optional)

1 Scrub potatoes with a vegetable brush, then cut into halves or quarters. In a large saucepan cook potatoes in a small amount of *boiling water* for 15 to 20 minutes or until tender.

2 Meanwhile, wash pea pods; remove tips and strings. Cut pea pods in half crosswise. Add to the hot *cooked* potatoes and hot cooking water in saucepan. Immediately drain potatoes and pea pods. Drain in a colander.

3 In a large mixing bowl combine yogurt, soy sauce, crushed red pepper, and ginger. Add potatoes and pea pods, yellow summer squash, and carrots; stir until all vegetables are coated.

4 Cover and refrigerate for at least 4 hours or up to 24 hours. Stir salad before serving. If desired, garnish with curly carrot. Makes 6 side-dish servings.

Nutrition facts per serving: 111 calories, 0 g total fat, 1 mg cholesterol, 53 mg sodium, 24 g carbohydrate, 2 g fiber, 4 g protein
Exchanges: 1 Starch, 1 Vegetable

297 calories

Preparation time: 1 hour ● **Chilling time:** 4 to 24 hours

toasted barley salad

Barley and nuts contribute the protein to this main-dish salad. Toasting the barley in a skillet brings out the rich, nutty flavor and improves the texture, too.

½ **cup regular barley**
1 **14½-ounce can reduced-sodium chicken broth**
1 **cup frozen Italian green beans or desired frozen vegetables**
2 **tablespoons white wine vinegar or vinegar**
2 **teaspoons salad oil**
1 **teaspoon snipped fresh rosemary or ¼ teaspoon dried rosemary, crushed**
1 **cup chopped seeded cucumber**
2 **tablespoons broken walnuts or pecans, toasted**

1 To toast the barley, heat in a large, heavy skillet over medium heat for 4 to 5 minutes or until lightly browned, stirring occasionally with a wooden spoon. (Do not overheat; barley continues to brown after skillet is removed from heat.) Set skillet aside to cool slightly. Carefully stir in chicken broth. Bring to boiling; reduce heat. Simmer, covered, about 45 minutes or until broth is absorbed, stirring occasionally.

2 Cook frozen beans or other desired vegetables according to package directions. Drain.

3 In a mixing bowl combine the vinegar, oil, and rosemary. Add cooked barley, beans, cucumber, and nuts, stirring to coat all ingredients.

4 Cover and refrigerate for at least 4 hours or up to 24 hours. Makes 2 main-dish servings.

To tote for lunch: Place 1 serving in an airtight container. Place in an insulated lunch box with a frozen ice pack.

Nutrition facts per serving: 297 calories, 11 g total fat (1 g saturated fat), 0 mg cholesterol, 595 mg sodium, 43 g carbohydrate, 8 g fiber, 10 g protein
Exchanges: 2 Starch, 1 Vegetable, 2 Fat

174 calories

Preparation time: 15 minutes ● **Chilling time:** 4 to 24 hours

minted pea – egg salad

Mint freshens up an otherwise ordinary pea salad, making it a welcome addition to your simple lunch-box sandwich.

2 tablespoons shredded reduced-fat cheddar cheese (optional)
1 tablespoon fat-free mayonnaise dressing or salad dressing
½ teaspoon snipped fresh mint or thyme or ⅛ teaspoon dried mint or thyme, crushed
⅔ cup frozen peas
1 hard-cooked egg, chopped
¼ cup chopped celery
   Salt (optional)
   Pepper (optional)

1 In a mixing bowl stir together the cheese (if using), mayonnaise dressing or salad dressing, and mint or thyme. Add frozen peas, egg, and celery. If desired, season to taste with salt and pepper. Cover and refrigerate for at least 4 hours or up to 24 hours. Makes 1 side-dish serving.

To tote for lunch: Place 1 serving in an airtight container. Place in an insulated lunch box with a frozen ice pack.

Nutrition facts per serving: 174 calories, 7 g total fat (2 g saturated fat), 220 mg cholesterol, 368 mg sodium, 17 g carbohydrate, 4 g fiber, 12 g protein
Exchanges: 1 Starch, 2 Lean Meat

297 calories

Preparation time: 25 minutes ● **Chilling time:** 4 to 24 hours

beet-spinach salad

Powdered fruit pectin and honey add body and thickness to the oil-free dressing. Look for the powdered fruit pectin with the jellymaking supplies in your grocery store.

¼ teaspoon finely shredded orange peel
⅓ cup orange juice
1 tablespoon wine vinegar
1 tablespoon powdered fruit pectin
1 tablespoon honey
¼ teaspoon poppy seed
2 cups torn fresh spinach
1 8¼-ounce can sliced beets, drained
1 cup cooked chicken strips
1 green onion, thinly sliced
2 tablespoons chopped walnuts or pecans,
   toasted
   Orange, thinly sliced and cut into wedges
   (optional)

1 For dressing, in a small bowl combine orange peel, orange juice, vinegar, pectin, honey, and poppy seed. Stir well. Cover and refrigerate for at least 4 hours or up to 24 hours.

2 To serve, line 2 plates with torn spinach. Arrange beets and chicken strips on spinach. Sprinkle with green onion and toasted walnuts or pecans. Drizzle with dressing. If desired, garnish with orange wedges. Makes 2 main-dish servings.

Nutrition facts per serving: 297 calories, 11 g total fat (2 g saturated fat), 68 mg cholesterol, 350 mg sodium, 26 g carbohydrate, 4 g fiber, 26 g protein
Exchanges: 3 Lean Meat, 2 Vegetable, 1 Fruit, ½ Fat

259 calories

Preparation time: 20 minutes ● **Chilling time:** 4 to 24 hours

tortellini - vegetable salad

Simple ingredients turn cheese-filled tortellini into a main-dish salad to look forward to. Try another variety of frozen vegetables—such as an Italian combination—to suit your taste.

1 9-ounce package refrigerated cheese-filled tortellini
1 10-ounce package frozen peas and carrots
½ cup fat-free mayonnaise dressing or salad dressing
2 tablespoons skim milk
1 to 2 tablespoons stone-ground mustard or Dijon-style mustard

1 In a saucepan cook tortellini according to package directions, except stir in frozen peas and carrots along with tortellini. Drain.

2 In a mixing bowl combine mayonnaise dressing or salad dressing, milk, and mustard. Add cooked tortellini and vegetables, stirring to coat.

3 Cover and refrigerate for at least 4 hours or up to 24 hours. Makes 4 main-dish servings.

To tote for lunch: Place 1 serving in an airtight container. Place in an insulated lunch box with a frozen ice pack.

Nutrition facts per serving: 259 calories, 5 g total fat (2 g saturated fat), 30 mg cholesterol, 714 mg sodium, 43 g carbohydrate, 2 g fiber, 12 g protein
Exchanges: 2½ Starch, 1 Vegetable, ½ Fat

161 calories

Preparation time: 25 minutes ● **Marinating time:** 2 hours

shrimp and fruit salad

Treat yourself to a spectacular luncheon salad. The flavorful lemon-mint dressing perfectly complements the shrimp, pineapple, and orange combination.

12 **ounces fresh or frozen peeled and deveined**
   shrimp
 1 **15¼-ounce can pineapple chunks**
   (juice-packed)
 1 **medium orange, peeled and sectioned**
 1 **tablespoon snipped fresh mint**
   or 1 teaspoon dried mint, crushed
   Dash salt
   Dash pepper
 ½ **cup sliced celery**
 ½ **cup lemon low-fat yogurt**
 4 **cantaloupe wedges (optional)**

1 In a large saucepan cook shrimp in a large amount of *boiling water* about 3 minutes or until shrimp turn pink. Drain. Rinse shrimp under cold water; drain well.

2 Drain pineapple chunks, reserving ¼ cup juice. Combine pineapple chunks and orange sections; cover and refrigerate.

3 For marinade, in a medium bowl combine the reserved pineapple juice, the mint, salt, and pepper.

4 Stir in cooked shrimp and the celery. Cover and marinate in the refrigerator for 2 hours. Drain, discarding marinade.

5 Stir pineapple and orange into shrimp mixture. Fold in the yogurt. If desired, serve with cantaloupe wedges. Store leftovers, covered, in the refrigerator for up to 2 days. Makes 4 main-dish servings.

To tote for lunch: Place 1 serving in an airtight container. If desired, place a cantaloupe wedge in a self-sealing plastic bag. Carry the salad and cantaloupe wedge in an insulated lunch box with a frozen ice pack. To serve, spoon the salad over the cantaloupe wedge.

Nutrition facts per serving: 161 calories, 1 g total fat (0 g saturated fat), 132 mg cholesterol, 281 mg sodium, 22 g carbohydrate, 1 g fiber, 16 g protein
Exchanges: 2 Lean Meat, 1½ Fruit

140 calories

Preparation time: 25 minutes ● **Chilling time:** 4 to 24 hours

cabbage – broccoli salad

If you're short on time, substitute 5 cups packaged coleslaw mix (shredded cabbage and carrot) for the red cabbage and carrot. The cabbage will be green instead of red, but the flavor will be the same.

- **1 small bunch broccoli (about 12 ounces)**
- **4 cups shredded red cabbage**
- **1 cup shredded carrot**
- **¼ cup thinly sliced green onions**
- **1 8-ounce carton lemon low-fat yogurt**
- **1 tablespoon snipped fresh basil or oregano or 1 teaspoon dried basil or oregano, crushed**
- **¼ teaspoon dry mustard**
- **1 clove garlic, minced**
- **1 tablespoon cider vinegar**
- **4 ounces lower-fat, lower-sodium cooked ham, cut into small cubes (about ¾ cup)**

1 Wash broccoli and trim off ends. Separate flowerets into small pieces. Thinly slice stalks (should have about 3 cups). In a large bowl combine broccoli, cabbage, carrot, and green onions. In a small bowl combine yogurt, basil or oregano, mustard, and garlic. Stir in vinegar. Pour over broccoli mixture, tossing to coat.

2 Cover and refrigerate salad for at least 4 hours or up to 24 hours. To serve, stir in the ham. Makes 4 main-dish servings.

To tote for lunch: Place one-fourth of the cabbage mixture in an airtight container. Top mixture with one-fourth of the ham. Place in an insulated lunch box with a frozen ice pack. If desired, take along ½ of a *whole wheat pita bread round* to serve with the salad.

Nutrition facts per serving: 140 calories, 2 g total fat (1 g saturated fat), 14 mg cholesterol, 387 mg sodium, 23 g carbohydrate, 5 g fiber, 11 g protein
Exchanges: 1 Lean Meat, 3 Vegetable

92 calories

Preparation time: 20 minutes ● **Chilling time:** 4 to 24 hours

fruited orzo

If you haven't tried orzo, this fresh-tasting salad will inspire you. Although orzo means barley in Italian, it's really just tiny, rice-shaped pasta. It's a nice change from ordinary rice.

1 8-ounce can crushed pineapple
  (juice-packed)
¼ cup snipped dried apricots
½ cup orange or lemon low-fat yogurt
½ teaspoon snipped fresh mint
1 cup cooked orzo
½ cup fresh blueberries or raspberries
½ cup sliced fresh strawberries

1 Drain pineapple, reserving ¼ cup juice. Combine reserved juice and apricots. Set aside.

2 In a mixing bowl combine pineapple, yogurt, and mint. Add orzo, blueberries or raspberries, and strawberries. Stir in apricots and juice. Cover and refrigerate for at least 4 hours or up to 24 hours. Makes 6 side-dish servings.

To tote for lunch: Place 1 serving in an airtight container. Place in an insulated lunch box with a frozen ice pack.

Nutrition facts per serving: 92 calories, 0 g total fat, 1 mg cholesterol, 13 mg sodium, 21 g carbohydrate, 2 g fiber, 2 g protein
Exchanges: ½ Starch, 1 Fruit

219 calories

Preparation time: 40 minutes ● **Chilling time:** 4 to 24 hours

herbed chicken and bean salad

Canned beans are high in sodium, so we call for cooked dried beans in this recipe to reduce the sodium. If you use canned beans for convenience, be sure and rinse them well before adding them to the salad.

⅔ **cup herb vinegar, such as tarragon, basil, or dill**
2 **tablespoons sugar**
2 **cups cooked red kidney beans and/or cannellini beans or other white beans***
1 **cup chopped cooked chicken or turkey**
½ **cup thinly sliced celery**
½ **cup chopped red sweet pepper**
2 **tablespoons snipped fresh parsley**
   Kale leaves (optional)

1 In a small saucepan combine the vinegar and sugar. Cook and stir over medium heat until the sugar is dissolved.

2 Meanwhile, in a mixing bowl combine beans, chicken or turkey, celery, sweet pepper, and parsley. Add vinegar mixture; stir to coat.

3 Cover and refrigerate for at least 4 hours or up to 24 hours. If desired, serve in kale leaf-lined salad bowls. Makes 4 main-dish servings.

To tote for lunch: Place 1 serving in an airtight container. Place in an insulated lunch box with a frozen ice pack.

*****Note:** To cook dried beans, first soak about ¾ cup of well-rinsed beans in *cold water* overnight. Drain and rinse. In a large pot cook the beans in *boiling water* for 1 to 1½ hours or until tender, stirring occasionally. (To keep cooked beans on hand, prepare double or triple the amount you need. Place cooked beans in an airtight, freezer-safe container. Freeze for up to 6 months.)

Nutrition facts per serving: 219 calories, 3 g total fat (1 g saturated fat), 34 mg cholesterol, 50 mg sodium, 31 g carbohydrate, 5 g fiber, 19 g protein
Exchanges: 1½ Starch, 2 Lean Meat, 1 Vegetable

185 calories

Preparation time: 20 minutes • **Chilling time:** 4 to 24 hours

garbanzo bean and vegetable salad

Garbanzo beans, also known as chickpeas, have a mild, nutty flavor. If you don't have any on hand, substitute any type of canned beans. Beans are filling and contain significant amounts of fiber and protein.

2 **tablespoons lemon juice**
1 **clove garlic, minced**
1 **tablespoon snipped fresh basil**
   or 1 teaspoon dried basil, crushed
⅛ **teaspoon pepper**
1 **15-ounce can garbanzo beans, rinsed and**
   drained
1½ **cups coarsely chopped broccoli**
1 **7½-ounce can tomatoes, undrained and**
   cut up
1 **cup cubed reduced-fat Monterey Jack**
   cheese or part-skim mozzarella cheese
   (4 ounces)
½ **cup sliced carrots**

1 In a large mixing bowl combine lemon juice, garlic, basil, and pepper.

2 Stir in the beans, broccoli, undrained tomatoes, cubed cheese, and carrots. Toss to mix well.

3 Cover and refrigerate for at least 4 hours or up to 24 hours. Makes 4 main-dish servings.

To tote for lunch: Place 1 serving in an airtight container. Place in an insulated lunch box with a frozen ice pack.

Nutrition facts per serving: 185 calories, 7 g total fat (3 g saturated fat), 20 mg cholesterol, 568 mg sodium, 19 g carbohydrate, 6 g fiber, 14 g protein
Exchanges: ½ Starch, 1 Medium-Fat Meat, 2 Vegetable

211 calories

Preparation time: 20 minutes

tortilla triangles

This lima bean and lentil spread is similar to hummus, a dip from the Middle East. Spread it on flour tortillas to make a sandwich that's far from ordinary.

¼ **cup dry red or brown lentils**
1 **cup cold water**
1 **8½-ounce can lima beans, rinsed and drained**
2 **to 3 cloves garlic, peeled**
2 **tablespoons lemon juice**
1 **tablespoon olive oil or cooking oil**
¼ **teaspoon ground cumin**
½ **cup shredded carrot**
4 **8-inch flour tortillas**
4 **small fresh spinach or lettuce leaves**

1 Rinse lentils. In a small saucepan combine the lentils and the water. Bring to boiling; reduce heat. Simmer, covered, until tender (allow about 5 minutes for red lentils and 20 minutes for brown lentils).

2 Drain lentils; transfer to a blender container or food processor bowl. Add the lima beans, garlic, lemon juice, oil, and cumin. Cover and blend or process until smooth, stopping and scraping sides of container as necessary. Stir in the carrot.

3 Spread about ¼ cup lentil mixture over half of 1 tortilla; fold plain half of the tortilla over lentil mixture. Spread another 2 tablespoons lentil mixture over half of the folded tortilla. Top lentil mixture with a spinach or lettuce leaf. Fold tortilla again to form a triangle. Repeat with remaining bean mixture, remaining tortillas, and remaining spinach or lettuce. Makes 4 main-dish servings.

Nutrition facts per serving: 211 calories, 6 g total fat (1 g saturated fat), 0 mg cholesterol, 130 mg sodium, 32 g carbohydrate, 4 g fiber, 8 g protein
Exchanges: 2 Starch, 1 Fat

312 calories

Preparation time: 45 minutes ● **Rising/rising time:** 1 hour 15 minutes ● **Baking time:** 20 minutes

ham and cheese focaccia

To make these ahead, cool completely, place in airtight containers, and refrigerate for up to two days.
To serve, wrap each focaccia in foil and heat in a 300° oven for 15 to 20 minutes.

2½ **to 3 cups bread flour or all-purpose flour**
 ¾ **cup rye flour**
 1 **package active dry yeast**
 1 **teaspoon sugar**
1¼ **cups warm water (120° to 130°)**
 1 **tablespoon olive oil or cooking oil**
 ½ **cup chopped onion**
 ⅔ **cup chopped lower-fat, lower-sodium cooked ham**
 6 **tablespoons shredded reduced-fat Swiss cheese**

1 In a large mixing bowl combine ½ *cup* of the bread flour, the rye flour, the yeast, sugar, and ½ teaspoon *salt*. Add the warm water and oil. Beat with an electric mixer on low to medium speed for 30 seconds, scraping sides of bowl constantly. Beat on high speed for 3 minutes. Using a spoon, stir in as much of the remaining flour as you can.

2 Turn dough out onto a lightly floured surface. Knead in enough of the remaining flour to make a stiff dough that is smooth and elastic (8 to 10 minutes total). Shape dough into a ball. Place in a lightly greased bowl; turn once. Cover; let rise in a warm place until double (45 minutes to 1 hour).

3 Lightly grease 2 large baking sheets. Punch dough down. Turn out onto a floured surface; divide into 6 portions. Cover; let rest 10 minutes. Roll each to a 6-inch circle. Place 2 inches apart on baking sheets. Cover; let rise for 20 to 30 minutes.

4 In a skillet cook onion in ¼ cup *water* until onion is tender and water has evaporated. Remove from heat; stir in ham. Spoon about 2 tablespoons ham mixture over each bread round, pressing lightly into bread. Sprinkle 1 tablespoon cheese over each. Bake in a 400° oven about 20 minutes or until lightly browned. Makes 6 main-dish servings.

Nutrition facts per serving: 312 calories, 5 g total fat (1 g saturated fat), 10 mg cholesterol, 427 mg sodium, 54 g carbohydrate, 4 g fiber, 13 g protein
Exchanges: 3½ Starch, ½ Fat

236 calories

Preparation time: 30 minutes ● **Baking time:** 12 minutes

zesty turkey turnovers

These tasty turnovers are a cinch to make with refrigerated biscuits. They're like a big chicken taco—without the taco shell—baked inside a flaky turnover.

1¼ **cups chopped cooked turkey or chicken**
1 **4½-ounce can diced green chili peppers, drained**
¾ **cup shredded reduced-fat Monterey Jack or cheddar cheese (3 ounces)**
½ **cup shredded carrot**
½ **teaspoon ground cumin**
1 **package (10) refrigerated reduced-fat biscuits**
 Nonstick spray coating
1 **tablespoon skim milk**
1 **teaspoon sesame seeds**

1 For filling, in a medium mixing bowl combine turkey or chicken, chili peppers, cheese, carrot, and cumin. Set aside.

2 On a floured surface, roll each biscuit into a 5-inch circle. Place about ½ cup of filling on each of 5 of the circles, spreading to within ½ inch of edge.

3 Spray a baking sheet with nonstick coating. Moisten edges of dough with water. Top with remaining circles of dough. Press edges of dough together to seal in filling. Cut slits in the top of each to allow steam to escape. Place turnovers on prepared baking sheet. Brush the tops with the milk and sprinkle with sesame seeds.

4 Bake the turnovers in a 400° oven for 12 to 14 minutes or until golden brown. Serve warm. Makes 5 main-dish servings.

Nutrition facts per serving: 236 calories, 9 g total fat (4 g saturated fat), 47 mg cholesterol, 762 mg sodium, 23 g carbohydrate, 1 g fiber, 20 g protein
Exchanges: 1½ Starch, 2 Lean Meat

257 calories

Preparation time: 30 minutes

clam - corn chowder

If you plan to tote the soup for lunch, make it the night before. Cover and refrigerate it. In the morning, heat soup on the stove. Carry it in a preheated insulated vacuum bottle (see below).

½ cup chopped celery
¼ cup chopped onion
 1 tablespoon margarine or butter
¼ cup all-purpose flour
1½ teaspoons snipped fresh marjoram
     or ½ teaspoon dried marjoram, crushed
1½ teaspoons snipped fresh thyme
     or ½ teaspoon dried thyme, crushed
½ teaspoon dry mustard
¼ teaspoon pepper
2⅔ cups skim milk
 1 8-ounce bottle clam juice
 1 teaspoon instant chicken bouillon granules
 1 15-ounce can cream-style corn
 1 6½-ounce can minced clams, drained

1 In a large saucepan cook celery and onion in margarine or butter until tender. Stir in flour, marjoram, thyme, mustard, and pepper. Add the milk, clam juice, and bouillon granules all at once.

Cook and stir until thickened and bubbly. Cook and stir for 1 minute more. Stir in corn and clams; heat through. (If desired, divide chowder among 4 airtight containers. Store up to 3 days in the refrigerator.) Makes 4 main-dish servings.

To tote for lunch: If using chilled soup, transfer to a small saucepan. Heat soup just to boiling, stirring often. Transfer hot soup to a preheated insulated vacuum bottle. (To preheat the bottle, fill with hot tap water. Cover with lid; let stand about 5 minutes. Pour out water and immediately fill with the hot soup.)

Nutrition facts per serving: 257 calories, 5 g total fat (1 g saturated fat), 34 mg cholesterol, 796 mg sodium, 35 g carbohydrate, 2 g fiber, 21 g protein
Exchanges: 1 Starch, 1 Lean Meat, 1 Vegetable, 1 Milk

203 calories

Preparation time: 30 minutes ● **Cooking time:** 20 minutes

hearty italian-style soup

Package this soup in single-serving containers and stockpile a supply in your freezer. You'll be ready for anything—a quick meal, on-the-go lunches, or those days when everyone eats in shifts.

2 **14½-ounce cans beef broth**
2 **cups shredded cabbage**
1 **14½-ounce can low-sodium tomatoes, undrained and cut up**
2 **medium potatoes (unpeeled, if desired), cubed**
½ **cup chopped carrot**
½ **cup sliced celery**
½ **cup chopped onion**
¼ **cup snipped fresh parsley**
1 **teaspoon dried Italian seasoning, crushed**
¼ **teaspoon garlic salt**
¼ **teaspoon pepper**
1 **15- or 19-ounce can white kidney beans, rinsed and drained**
1½ **cups chopped cooked beef or chicken (about 8 ounces)**

1 In a large saucepan or Dutch oven combine beef broth, cabbage, undrained tomatoes, potatoes, carrot, celery, onion, parsley, Italian seasoning,

garlic salt, and pepper. Bring to boiling; reduce heat. Simmer, covered, about 20 minutes or until vegetables are tender.

2 Stir in the beans and beef or chicken. Cook and stir for 2 to 3 minutes or until heated through. (If desired, divide hot soup among 6 airtight containers. Store up to 3 days in the refrigerator.) Makes 6 main-dish servings.

To tote for lunch: Transfer hot soup to a preheated insulated vacuum bottle. (To preheat the bottle, fill with hot tap water. Cover with lid; let stand about 5 minutes. Pour out water and immediately fill with the hot soup.) If using chilled soup, transfer to a small saucepan. Heat just to boiling, stirring often. Reduce heat. Simmer, covered, for 3 minutes. Transfer to preheated bottle.

Nutrition facts per serving: 203 calories, 4 g total fat (1 g saturated fat), 34 mg cholesterol, 711 mg sodium, 28 g carbohydrate, 6 g fiber, 19 g protein
Exchanges: 1½ Starch, 2 Lean Meat, 1 Vegetable

159 calories

Preparation time: 35 minutes ● **Cooking time:** 20 minutes

potato soup

This soup is pureed, so use whatever type of potato you happen to have on hand. Strain the soup, if you like, to remove any remaining strands of the celery.

3 medium potatoes (1 pound), peeled and quartered
2 cups water
½ cup chopped onion
½ cup sliced celery
½ cup sliced carrot
1 clove garlic, minced
1 tablespoon snipped fresh thyme
**   or ½ teaspoon dried thyme, crushed**
1 teaspoon instant chicken bouillon granules
⅛ teaspoon pepper
2 cups skim milk

1 In a large saucepan combine potatoes, water, onion, celery, carrot, garlic, thyme, bouillon granules, and pepper. Bring to boiling; reduce heat. Simmer, covered, for 20 to 25 minutes or until potatoes are tender. Remove from heat. Cool slightly. Place, a portion at a time, in blender container or food processor bowl. Cover and process until nearly smooth. If desired, strain. Return all to saucepan. Stir in milk; heat just to boiling. (If desired, divide hot soup among 4 airtight containers. Store for up to 3 days in refrigerator.) Makes 4 side-dish servings.

To tote for lunch: Transfer soup to a preheated insulated vacuum bottle. (To preheat the vacuum bottle, fill the bottle with hot tap water. Cover with lid and let stand about 5 minutes. Pour out the water and immediately fill with the hot soup.) If using chilled soup, transfer to a small saucepan. Heat just to boiling, stirring often. Transfer soup to preheated bottle.

Nutrition facts per serving: 159 calories, 0 g total fat, 2 mg cholesterol, 314 mg sodium, 33 g carbohydrate, 3 g fiber, 7 g protein
Exchanges: 1 Starch, 1 Vegetable, ½ Milk

57 calories

Preparation time: 10 minutes • **Chilling time:** 8 to 24 hours

gazpacho

For a light but refreshing lunch, pair this chilled vegetable soup with cheese and crackers.
For the best marriage of flavors, make the soup the night before.

1 6-ounce can vegetable juice or tomato juice
¼ cup chopped cucumber
¼ cup chopped green sweet pepper
1 tablespoon sliced green onion
1 teaspoon lemon juice
  Dash black pepper
  Dash bottled hot pepper sauce
  Dash Worcestershire sauce

1 In a small bowl combine the vegetable juice, cucumber, sweet pepper, green onion, lemon juice, black pepper, hot pepper sauce, and Worcestershire sauce. Cover and refrigerate for at least 8 hours or up to 24 hours. Makes 1 side-dish serving.

To tote for lunch: Place chilled soup in a prechilled insulated vacuum bottle. (To prechill the vacuum bottle, fill the bottle with cold water. Cover with the lid; let stand for 5 minutes. Pour out the water and immediately fill with the cold soup.)

Nutrition facts per serving: 57 calories, 0 g total fat, 0 mg cholesterol, 668 mg sodium, 13 g carbohydrate, 1 g fiber, 2 g protein
Exchanges: 2 Vegetable

319 calories

Preparation time: 20 minutes ● **Cooking time:** 13 minutes

chicken and salsa soup

Chunky bottled salsa provides the heat in this Mexican-inspired soup. It also makes the soup easy enough to whip together for a quick lunch.

1¾ **cups water**

1 **14½-ounce can reduced-sodium chicken broth**

8 **ounces skinless, boneless chicken, cut into bite-size pieces**

1 **to 2 teaspoons chili powder**

1 **11-ounce can whole kernel corn with sweet peppers, drained**

1 **cup chunky garden-style salsa**

3 **cups broken baked tortilla chips**

2 **ounces Monterey Jack cheese with jalapeño peppers, shredded (½ cup)**

1 In a 3-quart saucepan combine the water, chicken broth, chicken, and chili powder. Bring to boiling; reduce heat. Simmer, covered, for 8 minutes. Add corn. Simmer, uncovered, about 5 minutes more. Stir in salsa; heat through.

2 To serve, ladle into soup bowls. Top with tortilla chips and sprinkle with the cheese. Makes 4 main-dish servings.

Nutrition facts per serving: 319 calories, 9 g total fat (3 g saturated fat), 42 mg cholesterol, 989 mg sodium, 32 g carbohydrate, 3 g fiber, 20 g protein
Exchanges: 2 Starch, 2 Lean Meat

MAIN-DISH Salads

chapter index

313 calories

Preparation time: 20 minutes ● **Cooking time:** 45 minutes ● **Chilling time:** 2 to 6 hours

smoked turkey and wild rice salad

Wild rice is not really rice, but the nutty-flavored seed of a marsh grass. Here it's combined with brown rice, turkey, and fruit for a refreshing yet hearty salad.

1¾ cups water
⅛ teaspoon salt
⅛ teaspoon pepper
½ cup brown rice
⅓ cup wild rice, rinsed and drained
8 ounces smoked turkey breast, cut into
   bite-size pieces (about 1½ cups)
½ cup thinly sliced celery
¼ cup sliced green onions
¼ cup pitted whole dates, snipped
2 medium pears or apples, cored and
   chopped
⅓ cup frozen apple juice concentrate, thawed
2 tablespoons cider vinegar
2 teaspoons snipped fresh tarragon or
   ½ teaspoon dried tarragon, crushed
Lettuce leaves

1 In a medium saucepan bring the water, salt, and pepper to boiling. Stir in brown rice and wild rice. Return to boiling; reduce heat. Simmer, covered, about 45 minutes or until rices are tender and liquid is absorbed. Let stand, covered, for 5 minutes. Stir in smoked turkey, celery, green onions, and dates. Cover and refrigerate for at least 2 hours or up to 6 hours.

2 Before serving, gently stir pears or apples into rice mixture. For dressing, in a small bowl stir together the apple juice concentrate, vinegar, and tarragon. Drizzle dressing over rice mixture. Toss to coat. Serve in 4 lettuce-lined bowls. Makes 4 servings.

Nutrition facts per serving: 313 calories, 2 g total fat (0 g saturated fat), 24 mg cholesterol, 659 mg sodium, 60 g carbohydrate, 5 g fiber, 17 g protein
Exchanges: 2 Starch, 1 Lean Meat, 2 Fruit

204 calories

Preparation time: 25 minutes

sweet-sour turkey salad

*For this no-fat peach and ginger dressing, start with fruit spread. It's easy to make and versatile, too.
Try another fruit spread flavor to fit your personal preference for other salads.*

½ **cup peach or apricot spreadable fruit**
2 **tablespoons cider vinegar**
1 **tablespoon reduced-sodium soy sauce**
⅛ **teaspoon ground ginger**
6 **cups torn mixed greens**
6 **ounces boneless cooked turkey breast, cut
into thin bite-size strips (about 1¼ cups)**
1 **11-ounce can mandarin orange sections,
drained, or 2 medium oranges, sectioned**
1 **cup broccoli flowerets**
1 **cup cauliflower flowerets**

1 For dressing, in a small saucepan stir together spreadable fruit, vinegar, soy sauce, and ginger. Cook and stir over low heat until bubbly. Remove from heat. Set aside to cool slightly.

2 In a large mixing bowl toss together greens, turkey breast, orange sections, broccoli, and cauliflower. Divide salad among 4 plates. Drizzle with dressing. Makes 4 servings.

Nutrition facts per serving: 204 calories, 1 g total fat (0 g saturated fat), 35 mg cholesterol, 180 mg sodium, 39 g carbohydrate, 2 g fiber, 16 g protein
Exchanges: 1 Lean Meat, 2 Vegetable, 2 Fruit

180 calories

Preparation time: 25 minutes

turkey and nectarine salad

Buttermilk adds a tang to this creamy dill dressing. Although you may think buttermilk is high in fat due to its name, it has only slightly more fat and calories than skim milk.

⅔ **cup buttermilk**
2 **tablespoons light mayonnaise dressing or salad dressing**
2 **to 3 teaspoons snipped fresh dill or ¼ to ½ teaspoon dried dillweed**
⅛ **teaspoon salt**
⅛ **teaspoon onion powder**
⅛ **teaspoon garlic powder**
6 **cups torn mixed greens**
8 **ounces boneless cooked turkey breast, thinly sliced**
2 **medium nectarines, pitted and sliced, or 2 medium peaches, peeled, pitted, and sliced**
¼ **cup chopped red sweet pepper**
Coarsely ground black pepper (optional)
Snipped fresh dill (optional)

1 For dressing, in a small bowl gradually stir buttermilk into mayonnaise dressing or salad dressing until smooth. Stir in dill, salt, onion powder, and garlic powder.

2 Arrange greens on 4 plates. Top with turkey, nectarines or peaches, and sweet pepper. Pour dressing over salads. If desired, sprinkle with black pepper and additional dill. Makes 4 servings.

Nutrition facts per serving: 180 calories, 5 g total fat (1 g saturated fat), 41 mg cholesterol, 228 mg sodium, 13 g carbohydrate, 2 g fiber, 21 g protein
Exchanges: 2 Lean Meat, 1 Vegetable, ½ Fruit

153 calories

Preparation time: 25 minutes ● **Chilling time:** 2 to 6 hours

chicken and basil pasta salad

A simple pasta salad becomes a real treat when you play up fresh ingredients, such as basil, zucchini, and in-season tomatoes. Chicken makes it into a satisfying main dish.

4 ounces packaged dried corkscrew macaroni (about 1 cup)
8 ounces skinless, boneless chicken breasts
Nonstick spray coating
⅛ teaspoon salt
⅛ teaspoon pepper
4 plum tomatoes, halved lengthwise and sliced
1 small zucchini and/or yellow summer squash, halved lengthwise and sliced
¼ cup sliced green onions
⅔ cup reduced-calorie or fat-free clear Italian salad dressing
¼ cup snipped fresh basil

1 Cook macaroni according to package directions, except omit any oil and use ¼ teaspoon *salt*. Drain pasta. Rinse with cold water. Drain.

2 Meanwhile, rinse chicken; pat dry with paper towels. Cut chicken into 1-inch pieces. Spray an unheated large skillet with nonstick coating. Preheat over medium-high heat. Add the chicken and stir-fry for 3 to 4 minutes or until chicken is no longer pink. Sprinkle with the salt and pepper. Remove chicken from heat.

3 In a large mixing bowl toss together cooked macaroni, chicken, tomatoes, zucchini or summer squash, and green onions. Drizzle with salad dressing. Sprinkle with basil. Toss to coat. Cover and refrigerate at least 2 hours or up to 6 hours. Toss salad before serving. Makes 6 servings.

Nutrition facts per serving: 153 calories, 4 g total fat (1 g saturated fat), 22 mg cholesterol, 277 mg sodium, 18 g carbohydrate, 1 g fiber, 10 g protein
Exchanges: 1 Starch, 1 Lean Meat, 1 Vegetable

170 calories

Preparation time: 25 minutes

chicken and vegetable salad

Pureed cottage cheese makes a creamy dressing for this refreshing salad. For a quick-fix summer supper, serve it with bread sticks and iced tea, and add fresh fruit for dessert.

½ **cup low-fat cottage cheese or fat-free cottage cheese**
1 **tablespoon catsup**
1 **hard-cooked egg, chopped (optional)**
1 **tablespoon thinly sliced green onion**
1 **tablespoon sweet pickle relish**
⅛ **teaspoon salt**
1½ **cups chopped cooked chicken (about 8 ounces)**
½ **cup sliced celery**
½ **cup chopped red or green sweet pepper**
 Lettuce leaves
2 **tablespoons toasted sliced almonds**

1 For dressing, in a food processor bowl combine cottage cheese and catsup. Cover and process until smooth; transfer to a small mixing bowl. Stir in egg (if using), green onion, pickle relish, and salt. Set aside.

2 In a medium mixing bowl combine chicken, celery, and sweet pepper. Add dressing and toss gently to mix.

3 To serve, divide salad among 4 lettuce-lined plates. Sprinkle with the toasted almonds. Makes 4 servings.

Nutrition facts per serving: 170 calories, 6 g total fat (2 g saturated fat), 53 mg cholesterol, 326 mg sodium, 6 g carbohydrate, 1 g fiber, 22 g protein
Exchanges: 3 Lean Meat, 1 Vegetable

202 calories

Preparation time: 30 minutes ● **Marinating time:** 6 to 24 hours ● **Grilling time:** 12 minutes

grilled chicken salad

To streamline this hearty salad, begin the night before you plan to serve it. Start the chicken marinating and prepare the dressing (cover and refrigerate both). Opt for packaged prewashed salad greens to save even more time.

4 small skinless, boneless chicken breast halves (about 12 ounces total)
¼ cup frozen orange juice concentrate, thawed
2 teaspoons finely shredded lemon peel
2 tablespoons lemon juice
2 teaspoons olive oil
2 cloves garlic, minced
½ cup fat-free mayonnaise dressing or salad dressing
2 tablespoons milk
1 tablespoon frozen orange juice concentrate, thawed
1 tablespoon coarse-grain brown mustard
6 cups torn mixed greens
2 medium apples, cored and thinly sliced
1 tablespoon broken walnuts, toasted (optional)

1 Rinse chicken; pat dry with paper towels. Place in a plastic bag set in a shallow dish. For marinade, stir together the ¼ cup orange juice concentrate, the lemon peel, lemon juice, oil, and garlic. Pour over chicken. Close bag. Marinate in the refrigerator for 6 to 24 hours; turn bag occasionally.

2 For dressing, in a bowl stir together mayonnaise dressing, milk, the 1 tablespoon orange juice concentrate, the mustard, and ¼ teaspoon *pepper.* Cover; refrigerate until serving time.

3 Drain chicken, discarding marinade. Grill chicken on the rack of an uncovered grill directly over medium coals for 12 to 15 minutes or until chicken is tender and no longer pink, turning once. Arrange mixed greens and apple slices on 4 plates.

4 To serve, cut chicken breast halves into slices. Arrange slices on top of greens; drizzle with dressing. If desired, sprinkle with walnuts. Serves 4.

Nutrition facts per serving: 202 calories, 4 g total fat (1 g saturated fat), 45 mg cholesterol, 502 mg sodium, 23 g carbohydrate, 3 g fiber, 19 g protein
Exchanges: 2 Lean Meat, 1 Vegetable, 1 Fruit

195 calories

Preparation time: 20 minutes ● **Chilling time:** 2 to 4 hours

chicken and fruit salad

If you want to make this salad ahead, prepare the dressing; cover and chill. Cut up and combine the melon, grapes, and celery; cover and chill separately. Just before serving, toss dressing with melon mixture and chicken.

1 **8-ounce carton lemon, peach, or pineapple low-fat yogurt**
¼ **cup fat-free mayonnaise dressing or salad dressing**
½ **teaspoon ground ginger**
½ **teaspoon finely shredded lemon peel**
3 **cups cubed cantaloupe, watermelon and/or honeydew melon**
2 **cups cubed cooked chicken breast or turkey breast**
1 **cup halved seedless red grapes**
¾ **cup sliced celery**
  Lettuce and/or purple kale leaves

1 In a mixing bowl stir together yogurt, mayonnaise dressing or salad dressing, ginger, and lemon peel. Add melon, chicken, grapes, and celery. Toss until mixed.

2 Cover and refrigerate for at least 2 hours or up to 4 hours. Serve on 6 lettuce- and/or kale-lined plates. Makes 6 servings.

Nutrition facts per serving: 195 calories, 5 g total fat (1 g saturated fat), 47 mg cholesterol, 215 mg sodium, 22 g carbohydrate, 1 g fiber, 17 g protein
Exchanges: 2 Lean Meat, 1½ Fruit

251 calories

Preparation time: 20 minutes ● **Chilling time:** 4 to 6 hours

curried chicken and apple salad

Chutney—a blend of fruit, vinegar, sugar, and spices—originated in East India. Look for mango chutney in grocery stores. Shop specialty food stores for other flavors, such as pear or cranberry.

1 **8-ounce carton plain fat-free yogurt**
¼ **cup chutney**
1 **teaspoon curry powder**
2 **cups chopped cooked chicken or turkey**
1½ **cups sliced celery**
1 **medium apple, cored and cut into chunks**
¼ **cup sliced green onions**
    Purple kale and/or red-tipped leaf lettuce

1 In a medium mixing bowl stir together yogurt, chutney, and curry powder. Stir in chicken or turkey, celery, apple, and green onions. Cover and refrigerate for at least 4 hours or up to 6 hours.

2 Before serving, stir chicken mixture. Serve on 4 kale- and/or lettuce-lined plates. Makes 4 servings.

Nutrition facts per serving: 251 calories, 6 g total fat (2 g saturated fat), 69 mg cholesterol, 157 mg sodium, 23 g carbohydrate, 3 g fiber, 26 g protein
Exchanges: 3 Lean Meat, 1 Vegetable, 1 Fruit

203 calories

Preparation time: 35 minutes

three - citrus chicken salad

Using a strong-flavored oil, such as olive oil, in the dressing allows you to boost the flavor without using very much.
Also try orange or lemon juice instead of lime and add a fresh herb, such as basil, for variety.

9 cups torn mixed greens (such as romaine,
    Boston or bibb lettuce, arugula, curly leaf
    lettuce, or red leaf lettuce)
2 cups cooked chicken cut into strips
1½ cups grapefruit sections (about
    2 grapefruit)
1½ cups orange sections (about 3 oranges)
1 cup thinly sliced red onion
2 tablespoons olive oil or salad oil
2 tablespoons lime juice
2 tablespoons water
1 teaspoon Dijon-style mustard
⅛ teaspoon salt
⅛ teaspoon pepper

1 Divide greens among 6 plates. Arrange chicken, grapefruit sections, orange sections, and red onion slices on top of greens.

2 For the dressing, in a screw-top jar combine oil, lime juice, water, mustard, salt, and pepper. Cover; shake well. Drizzle dressing over salads. Makes 6 servings.

Nutrition facts per serving: 203 calories, 9 g total fat (2 g saturated fat), 45 mg cholesterol, 116 mg sodium, 16 g carbohydrate, 3 g fiber, 17 g protein
Exchanges: 2 Lean Meat, 1 Vegetable, 1 Fruit, ½ Fat

225 calories

Preparation time: 25 minutes ● **Roasting time:** 25 minutes

honey - mustard pork salad

This salad rates special enough for a casual summer get-together. Substitute leftover sliced roast pork or beef if you don't have the time to roast the pork tenderloin.

1 **tablespoon honey**
2 **teaspoons Dijon-style mustard**
⅛ **teaspoon ground ginger**
1 **12-ounce pork tenderloin**
⅓ **cup fat-free mayonnaise dressing or salad dressing**
⅓ **cup pineapple juice or orange juice**
1 **tablespoon honey**
1 **tablespoon Dijon-style mustard**
⅛ **teaspoon ground ginger**
6 **cups torn mixed greens**
2 **cups fresh strawberries, halved**
1 **papaya, seeded, peeled, sliced lengthwise, and halved**
   Freshly ground black pepper (optional)

1 In a small bowl or custard cup stir together the 1 tablespoon honey, the 2 teaspoons Dijon-style mustard, and ⅛ teaspoon ginger. Trim fat from pork tenderloin. Place on a rack in a shallow, foil lined,

roasting pan. Brush mustard mixture over outside of tenderloin. Insert a meat thermometer in center of tenderloin. Roast, uncovered, in a 425° oven for 25 to 35 minutes or until thermometer registers 160°.

2 Meanwhile, for dressing, in a mixing bowl whisk together mayonnaise dressing or salad dressing, pineapple or orange juice, the remaining 1 tablespoon honey, the 1 tablespoon Dijon-style mustard, and ⅛ teaspoon ginger. Cover and refrigerate until serving time.

3 To serve, arrange the torn greens, strawberries, and papaya on 4 salad plates. Thinly slice warm tenderloin and arrange on salads. Drizzle with the dressing. If desired, sprinkle with black pepper. Makes 4 servings.

Nutrition facts per serving: 225 calories, 4 g total fat (1 g saturated fat), 60 mg cholesterol, 464 mg sodium, 26 g carbohydrate, 3 g fiber, 21 g protein
Exchanges: 3 Lean Meat, 2 Vegetable, 1 Fruit

227 calories

Preparation time: 30 minutes

balsamic pork and berry salad

Balsamic vinegar is made from white Trebbiano grape juice that's been aged in wooden barrels. Look for it at your grocery store or in specialty food stores. In this dressing, balsamic vinegar adds a delicate sweetness.

6 cups torn romaine
2 cups sliced fresh strawberries
½ cup thinly sliced celery
1 teaspoon snipped fresh chives
8 ounces pork tenderloin
** Nonstick spray coating**
1 teaspoon olive oil or salad oil
2 cloves garlic, minced
¼ cup honey
¼ cup balsamic vinegar
¼ teaspoon pepper
2 tablespoons chopped pecans or walnuts,
** toasted**

1 In a large mixing bowl toss together romaine, strawberries, celery, and chives. Set aside.

2 Trim any fat from pork. Cut into ¼-inch-thick slices. Spray an unheated large skillet with nonstick coating. Preheat over medium-high heat. Add half of the pork; cook for 3 to 4 minutes or until no longer pink, turning once. Repeat with remaining pork. Remove all pork from skillet. Cover to keep warm.

3 For dressing, add oil to skillet. Add garlic; cook and stir for 15 seconds. Stir in honey, vinegar, and pepper. Cook and stir until heated through.

4 Place romaine mixture on 4 plates. Top with the pork. Drizzle dressing over. Sprinkle with pecans or walnuts. Serve immediately. Makes 4 servings.

Nutrition facts per serving: 227 calories, 6 g total fat (1 g saturated fat), 40 mg cholesterol, 54 mg sodium, 30 g carbohydrate, 3 g fiber, 15 g protein
Exchanges: 2 Lean Meat, 2 Vegetable, 1 Fruit

224 calories

Preparation time: 35 minutes ● **Chilling time:** 4 to 8 hours

ham and orzo salad

*Use any tiny pasta you have on hand. Orzo, shown in the photograph, is shaped like
grains of rice; tripolini is shaped like tiny bow ties.*

½ **cup packaged dried orzo, tripolini, tiny
  tube macaroni, or tiny star macaroni**
1 **cup frozen peas and carrots or frozen
  mixed vegetables**
6 **ounces lower-fat, lower-sodium cooked
  ham, cut into ½-inch cubes (about 1 cup)**
4 **green onions, sliced**
½ **cup light dairy sour cream**
2 **tablespoons reduced-calorie ranch salad
  dressing**
1 **teaspoon snipped fresh dill or ¼ teaspoon
  dried dillweed**
2 **medium tomatoes, sliced**
1 **green sweet pepper, cut into half rings
  Lettuce leaves**

1 In a medium saucepan bring a large amount
of *water* to boiling. Add the pasta and the frozen
vegetables. Return to boiling. Boil, uncovered, for
5 to 8 minutes or until pasta and vegetables are
tender. Immediately drain mixture in a colander.
Rinse with cold water. Drain.

2 In a medium mixing bowl stir together pasta
mixture, ham, and green onions. In a small mixing
bowl stir together sour cream, salad dressing, and
dill. Pour sour cream mixture over pasta mixture.
Toss until well coated. Cover and refrigerate for at
least 4 hours or up to 8 hours.

3 To serve, arrange the tomato slices and sweet
pepper on 4 lettuce-lined plates. Stir the pasta
mixture; spoon onto the plates. Makes 4 servings.

Nutrition facts per serving: 224 calories, 6 g total fat
(1 g saturated fat), 22 mg cholesterol, 597 mg sodium,
31 g carbohydrate, 3 g fiber, 15 g protein
Exchanges: 1 Starch, 2 Lean Meat, 2 Vegetable

120 calories

Preparation time: 30 minutes

hot ham and apple slaw

*A tangy sweet-and-sour dressing coats the stir-fried ham and cabbage. If you're in a hurry, use
3½ cups of packaged coleslaw mix instead of shredding your own cabbage and carrot.*

⅓ **cup apple juice**
1 **tablespoon vinegar**
2 **teaspoons cornstarch**
¼ **teaspoon celery seed**
⅛ **teaspoon pepper**
   Nonstick spray coating
½ **cup chopped onion**
2½ **cups coarsely shredded cabbage**
1 **cup shredded carrot**
1 **teaspoon cooking oil (optional)**
8 **ounces lower-fat, lower-sodium cooked
   ham, cubed (about 1½ cups)**
1 **medium apple, coarsely chopped**
   Apple slices (optional)

1 For sauce, stir together apple juice, vinegar, cornstarch, celery seed, and pepper. Set aside.

2 Spray an unheated wok or large skillet with nonstick coating. Preheat over medium-high heat. Add onion and stir-fry for 2 minutes. Add cabbage and carrot; stir-fry about 2 minutes or until vegetables are crisp-tender. Remove from wok.

3 If necessary, add oil to hot wok. Add ham and stir-fry for 2 to 3 minutes or until heated through. Push ham from center of wok.

4 Stir sauce; add to center of wok. Cook and stir until thickened and bubbly. Cook and stir for 1 minute more. Return vegetables to wok. Add chopped apple. Stir to coat all with sauce. Cook and stir for 1 minute. If desired, garnish with apple slices. Makes 4 servings.

Nutrition facts per serving: 120 calories, 3 g total fat (1 g saturated fat), 24 mg cholesterol, 641 mg sodium, 16 g carbohydrate, 3 g fiber, 11 g protein
Exchanges: 1 Lean Meat, 1 Vegetable, ½ Fruit

209 calories

Preparation time: 35 minutes ● **Marinating time:** 2 to 8 hours

asian-style beef salad

Speed preparation by substituting 8 ounces cooked lean deli roast beef for the broiled steak. Just cut the sliced beef into bite-size strips and let it marinate in the lime-flavored dressing.

12 **ounces boneless beef sirloin steak, cut 1 inch thick**
1 **fresh jalapeño pepper, seeded and finely chopped***
½ **teaspoon finely shredded lime peel**
3 **tablespoons lime juice**
2 **tablespoons reduced-sodium soy sauce**
1 **tablespoon snipped fresh cilantro**
2 **teaspoons toasted sesame oil**
1 **teaspoon sugar**
2 **cloves garlic, minced**
6 **cups torn napa cabbage and/or bok choy**
½ **cup red sweet pepper strips or fresh pea pods**
¼ **cup sliced green onions**

1 Trim fat from steak. Place on the unheated rack of a broiler pan. Broil 3 to 4 inches from the heat for 12 to 15 minutes or to desired doneness. Let steak stand for 5 minutes. Cut across the grain into thin bite-size strips.

2 Meanwhile, in a medium mixing bowl stir together jalapeño pepper, lime peel, lime juice, soy sauce, cilantro, sesame oil, sugar, and garlic. Stir in beef. Marinate in the refrigerator for 2 to 8 hours.

3 To serve, in a salad bowl toss together napa cabbage and/or bok choy, sweet pepper or pea pods, and green onions. Stir beef mixture; arrange in center of cabbage mixture. Makes 4 servings.

***Note:** Because chili peppers, such as jalapeños, contain volatile oils that can burn your skin and eyes, avoid direct contact with them as much as possible. When working with chili peppers, wear plastic gloves. If your bare hands touch the chili peppers, wash your hands well with soap and water.

Nutrition facts per serving: 209 calories, 10 g total fat (3 g saturated fat), 57 mg cholesterol, 317 mg sodium, 8 g carbohydrate, 1 g fiber, 22 g protein
Exchanges: 3 Lean Meat, 2 Vegetable

197 calories

Preparation time: 30 minutes

beef and new potato salad

No need to peel the potatoes. Leaving the skin on the potatoes hastens preparation and adds a little extra fiber to these salads.

6 to 8 whole tiny new potatoes
4 cups torn mixed greens
1 medium cucumber, halved lengthwise and sliced
4 radishes, sliced
4 ounces very thinly sliced cooked roast beef or turkey
2 small tomatoes, cut into wedges
½ cup low-calorie creamy cucumber or ranch salad dressing
1 teaspoon snipped fresh dill or ¼ teaspoon dried dillweed

1 Scrub new potatoes; cut into quarters.

2 In a medium saucepan cook potatoes in a small amount of lightly salted *boiling water* for 10 to 15 minutes or until tender. Drain. Rinse with cold water. Drain.

3 In a mixing bowl gently toss together greens, cucumber, and radishes. Add potatoes. Gently toss. Arrange on 4 plates. Roll up the roast beef slices and arrange on top of greens mixture. Place a few tomato wedges to the side of each salad.

4 In a small mixing bowl stir together salad dressing and dill. Drizzle over salads. Makes 4 servings.

Nutrition facts per serving: 197 calories, 7 g total fat (1 g saturated fat), 25 mg cholesterol, 494 mg sodium, 20 g carbohydrate, 3 g fiber, 12 g protein
Exchanges: 1 Starch, 1 Lean Meat, 1 Vegetable, ½ Fat

279 calories

Total preparation time: 1 hour

taco salad

By replacing ground beef with strips of lean beef steak and the fried tortilla shells with baked flour tortilla wedges, we were able to lower both calories and fat in this Mexican favorite.

6 **ounces boneless beef top round steak**
4 **7- or 8-inch flour tortillas**
  Nonstick spray coating
1 **cup frozen corn**
1 **clove garlic, minced**
1 **cup salsa**
1 **8-ounce can kidney beans, rinsed and drained**
6 **cups shredded lettuce**
¼ **cup light dairy sour cream**
  Thinly sliced green onion (optional)

1 Trim fat from beef. Partially freeze beef (about 30 minutes). Cut into thin bite-size strips.

2 Meanwhile, cut each tortilla into 8 wedges. Place in a single layer on an ungreased baking sheet. Bake in a 350° oven for 10 to 12 minutes or until golden brown; set aside to cool.

3 Spray an unheated large skillet with nonstick coating. Preheat over medium heat. Add corn and garlic. Cook and stir for 2 minutes. Push to side. Add beef. Cook and stir for 2 to 3 minutes or until beef is of desired doneness. Stir in salsa and kidney beans. Heat through. Divide lettuce among 4 plates or large bowls. Spoon meat mixture atop lettuce. Place several tortilla wedges to side of each salad. Top salads with sour cream and, if desired, sprinkle with green onion. Makes 4 servings.

Nutrition facts per serving: 279 calories, 8 g total fat (2 g saturated fat), 29 mg cholesterol, 495 mg sodium, 39 g carbohydrate, 5 g fiber, 20 g protein
Exchanges: 2 Starch, 2 Lean Meat, 1 Vegetable

238 calories

Preparation time: 30 minutes

beef, beet, and basil salad

Ruby red beets as well as an assortment of fresh vegetables add vibrant color to this robust salad.
Serve it with rye rolls or Italian bread for a satisfying lunch or dinner.

6 cups torn mixed greens
8 ounces lean cooked beef or turkey breast,
   cut into thin strips
1 small parsnip or carrot, thinly sliced
1 medium carrot, thinly sliced
½ of a small zucchini, sliced
½ cup broccoli flowerets
1 recipe Fresh Basil Dressing
½ of a 16-ounce can julienned beets, well
   drained

1 For salad, toss together the mixed greens, beef or turkey, parsnip, carrot, zucchini, and broccoli. Add the Fresh Basil Dressing and toss to coat. Divide among 4 plates. Top with drained beets. Makes 4 servings.

Fresh Basil Dressing: In a small mixing bowl stir together ⅓ cup *buttermilk;* 3 tablespoons *light mayonnaise dressing* or *salad dressing;* 1 tablespoon snipped *fresh basil* or 1 teaspoon *dried basil,* crushed; 1 tablespoon *lemon juice;* 1 teaspoon *sugar;* and dash *pepper.* Cover and refrigerate until serving time.

Nutrition facts per serving: 238 calories, 10 g total fat (3 g saturated fat), 51 mg cholesterol, 268 mg sodium, 16 g carbohydrate, 4 g fiber, 21 g protein
Exchanges: 2 Lean Meat, 3 Vegetable, ½ Fat

185 calories

Preparation time: 20 minutes ● **Chilling time:** 2 to 24 hours ● **Baking time:** 45 minutes ● **Standing time:** 20 minutes

beef and asparagus salad

Oven-roasted tomatoes yield a rich tasting dressing that's fat-free. Be sure to use plum tomatoes; they are meatier and less juicy than other tomatoes, so they give the dressing a thicker consistency and better flavor.

 1 **pound fresh asparagus**
 6 **cups torn mixed greens**
 8 **ounces cooked lean roast beef, thinly sliced**
 ¼ **cup sliced radishes**
 1 **recipe Roasted Tomato Dressing**

1 Wash asparagus. Break off woody bases where spears snap easily. Scrape off scales. In a medium covered saucepan cook asparagus in a small amount of *boiling water* for 4 to 6 minutes or until crisp-tender. Drain. Rinse with cold water. Drain. Cover and refrigerate at least 2 hours or up to 24 hours.

2 To serve, divide greens among 4 plates. Arrange chilled asparagus, roast beef, and radish slices on top of greens. Drizzle Roasted Tomato Dressing over salads. Makes 4 servings.

Roasted Tomato Dressing: Spray a shallow baking pan with nonstick coating. Arrange 4 *plum tomatoes,* halved lengthwise, cut sides up, in pan. Bake, uncovered, in a 425° oven about 45 minutes or until very soft and skins are slightly dark. Let stand for 20 minutes.

In a blender container combine tomatoes, ¼ cup *water,* 2 tablespoons *red wine vinegar,* 1 tablespoon *sugar,* ¼ teaspoon *salt,* ¼ teaspoon *pepper,* and dash *bottled hot pepper sauce* (if desired). Cover and blend until smooth.

Nutrition facts per serving: 185 calories, 7 g total fat (2 g saturated fat), 51 mg cholesterol, 207 mg sodium, 12 g carbohydrate, 4 g fiber, 21 g protein
Exchanges: 2 Lean Meat, 3 Vegetable

269 calories

Preparation time: 18 minutes

greek-style salad

*Preparation is easy—make the dressing and arrange the salad ingredients
on serving plates while the meat broils.*

12 **ounces boneless lamb leg center slice or
  beef top round steak, cut 1 inch thick**
1 **teaspoon finely shredded lemon peel**
¼ **cup lemon juice**
1 **tablespoon olive oil or salad oil**
1 **tablespoon water**
1 **tablespoon snipped fresh oregano
  or 1 teaspoon dried oregano, crushed**
1 **clove garlic, minced**
¼ **teaspoon salt**
¼ **teaspoon pepper**
6 **cups torn fresh spinach and/or romaine
  leaves**
1 **medium cucumber, thinly sliced**
¼ **cup chopped red onion**
4 **ripe olives, halved**
2 **tablespoons crumbled feta cheese**
2 **small pita bread rounds, cut in wedges
  and toasted**

1 Trim fat from meat. Place on the unheated
rack of a broiler pan. Broil 3 to 4 inches from heat
for 12 to 15 minutes or to desired doneness, turning
meat once.

2 Meanwhile, for the dressing, in a screw-top
jar combine the lemon peel, lemon juice, oil, water,
oregano, garlic, salt, and pepper. Cover and shake
well. Set aside.

3 Divide spinach and/or romaine leaves among
4 plates. Cut the broiled meat across the grain into
thin, bite-size strips. Arrange warm sliced meat,
cucumber, red onion, olives, and feta cheese on top
of greens. Drizzle dressing over salads. Serve with
toasted pita bread wedges. Makes 4 servings.

Nutrition facts per serving: 269 calories, 11 g total fat
(4 g saturated fat), 50 mg cholesterol, 504 mg sodium,
25 g carbohydrate, 3 g fiber, 21 g protein
Exchanges: 1 Starch, 2 Lean Meat, 2 Vegetable, ½ Fat

207 calories

Preparation time: 20 minutes ● **Chilling time:** 2 to 8 hours

easy corn and bean salad

Serve this refreshing salad and a lettuce leaf wrapped inside flour tortillas for an tasty out-of-hand lunch.

1 16-ounce package frozen whole kernel corn
1 15-ounce can dark red kidney beans, drained and rinsed
½ cup chopped green sweet pepper
½ cup salsa
2 tablespoons snipped fresh cilantro
¼ teaspoon ground cumin
1 clove garlic, minced
   Lettuce and/or purple kale leaves

1 Cook frozen corn according to package directions, except omit any salt and margarine or butter. Drain. Rinse with cold water. Drain.

2 In a mixing bowl stir together corn, kidney beans, sweet pepper, salsa, cilantro, cumin, and garlic. Cover and refrigerate for at least 2 hours or up to 8 hours.

3 To serve, mound corn mixture on 4 lettuce-lined plates. Makes 4 servings.

Nutrition facts per serving: 207 calories, 2 g total fat (0 g saturated fat), 0 mg cholesterol, 293 mg sodium, 46 g carbohydrate, 6 g fiber, 12 g protein
Exchanges: 3 Starch

256 calories

Preparation time: 25 minutes ● **Chilling time:** 2 to 8 hours

black bean and rice salad

Black beans are a good source of soluble fiber, which has been linked with reducing blood cholesterol levels. They're also a good source of protein, so you can serve this salad as a main dish.

1⅓ cups water
⅔ cup long grain rice
1 15-ounce can black beans, drained and rinsed
½ cup chopped red sweet pepper
¼ cup sliced green onions
3 tablespoons rice wine vinegar
2 tablespoons olive oil or salad oil
1 tablespoon snipped fresh oregano
    or 1 teaspoon dried oregano, crushed
¼ teaspoon salt
¼ teaspoon black pepper
¼ teaspoon paprika
2 cloves garlic, minced
4 flour tortillas, softened (optional)*
Lettuce leaves

1 In a medium saucepan stir together the water and rice. Bring to boiling; reduce heat. Simmer, covered, about 15 minutes or until rice is tender and water is absorbed.

2 In a mixing bowl stir together cooked rice and black beans. Stir in sweet pepper and green onions.

3 For dressing, in a screw-top jar combine vinegar, oil, oregano, salt, black pepper, paprika, and garlic. Cover and shake well. Drizzle over rice mixture. Toss to coat. Cover and refrigerate for at least 2 hours or up to 8 hours.

4 To serve, if desired, place a folded tortilla on each serving plate; top with a lettuce leaf. Spoon rice mixture onto lettuce leaves. Makes 4 servings.

*Note: To soften tortillas, wrap tortillas in foil. Heat in a 350° oven about 10 minutes. Fold tortillas into fourths. Allow to cool slightly before serving.

Nutrition facts per serving: 256 calories, 7 g total fat (1 g saturated fat), 0 mg cholesterol, 405 mg sodium, 43 g carbohydrate, 6 g fiber, 10 g protein
Exchanges: 3 Starch, ½ Fat

248 calories

Preparation time: 30 minutes ● **Chilling time:** 2 to 6 hours

lentil - vegetable salad

Cook lentils just as you would pasta—until al dente, or slightly firm to the bite.

½ **cup dry lentils**
1¼ **cups water**
½ **teaspoon instant chicken bouillon granules**
¼ **teaspoon black pepper**
2 **cups small broccoli flowerets**
1 **cup cubed cooked chicken or turkey**
1 **cup thinly sliced carrot**
1 **red sweet pepper, cut into strips**
¼ **cup sliced green onions**
¼ **cup rice vinegar or white wine vinegar**
2 **tablespoons salad oil**
2 **teaspoons snipped fresh thyme or basil or**
  ½ **teaspoon dried thyme or basil, crushed**
1 **teaspoon Dijon-style mustard**
1 **clove garlic, minced**
  Napa cabbage or lettuce leaves

1 Rinse lentils. Drain. In a small saucepan combine lentils, water, bouillon granules, and black pepper. Bring to boiling; reduce heat. Simmer, covered, about 20 minutes or until lentils are tender; drain off excess liquid. Combine drained lentils with broccoli, chicken or turkey, carrot, sweet pepper, and green onions.

2 Meanwhile, for dressing, in a screw-top jar combine vinegar, oil, thyme or basil, mustard, and garlic. Cover and shake well. Drizzle over lentil mixture. Toss to mix. Cover and refrigerate for at least 2 hours or up to 6 hours.

3 Serve on 4 cabbage- or lettuce-lined plates. Makes 4 servings.

Nutrition facts per serving: 248 calories, 10 g total fat (2 g saturated fat), 34 mg cholesterol, 201 mg sodium, 22 g carbohydrate, 4 g fiber, 19 g protein
Exchanges: 1 Starch, 2 Lean Meat, 1 Vegetable, ½ Fat

155 calories

Preparation time: 20 minutes ● **Cooking time:** 6 minutes ● **Chilling time:** 2 to 24 hours

chilled lobster with curry dressing

Reserve this salad for a special celebration—perhaps the loss of your first 10 pounds? Lobster, a true treat, is readily found at most supermarkets and not that difficult to prepare.

2 fresh or frozen medium rock lobster tails (about 5 ounces each)
2 tablespoons light mayonnaise dressing or salad dressing
2 tablespoons light dairy sour cream
1 tablespoon snipped fresh parsley
1 teaspoon lime juice or lemon juice
¼ to ½ teaspoon curry powder
1 to 2 drops bottled hot pepper sauce
Leaf lettuce (optional)
Tomato wedges (optional)
Cucumber strips (optional)

1 Thaw lobster, if frozen. In a large saucepan bring 6 cups *water* to boiling. Add lobster tails. Return to boiling; reduce heat. Simmer, uncovered, for 6 to 10 minutes or until lobster shells turn bright red and meat is tender. Drain. Cover and refrigerate for at least 2 hours or up to 24 hours.

2 For dressing, in a small mixing bowl stir together mayonnaise dressing or salad dressing, sour cream, parsley, lime or lemon juice, curry powder, and hot pepper sauce. Cover and refrigerate until serving time.

3 To serve, if desired, line 2 plates with leaf lettuce; arrange tomato wedges and cucumber strips on plates. Place lobster on cutting surface with underside facing up. With kitchen shears, cut along both sides of the tail and remove the membrane to expose the meat. Cut the meat lengthwise. Place 1 lobster tail, shell side down, on each plate. Serve with the dressing. Makes 2 servings.

Nutrition facts per serving: 155 calories, 7 g total fat (2 g saturated fat), 63 mg cholesterol, 453 mg sodium, 4 g carbohydrate, 0 g fiber, 18 g protein
Exchanges: 3 Lean Meat

216 calories

Preparation time: 30 minutes ● **Chilling time:** 4 to 24 hours

salmon-and-pasta-stuffed tomatoes

If you want to skip the tomato stars, slice the tomatoes and serve them with this colorful macaroni salad on lettuce-lined plates. A few whole wheat crackers and a glass of skim milk make this a satisfying lunch.

1 cup four-color corkscrew macaroni
½ cup plain low-fat yogurt
½ cup shredded cucumber or zucchini
¼ cup shredded carrot
2 tablespoons light mayonnaise dressing or salad dressing
½ teaspoon snipped fresh dill or ¼ teaspoon dried dillweed
¼ teaspoon salt
⅛ teaspoon pepper
1 7½-ounce can salmon, drained, flaked, and skin and bones removed
4 medium tomatoes

1 Cook macaroni according to package directions, except omit any oil and salt. Drain; set aside. In a large mixing bowl combine yogurt, cucumber or zucchini, carrot, mayonnaise dressing or salad dressing, dill, salt, and pepper. Add cooked pasta and salmon; toss gently to coat. Cover and refrigerate for at least 4 hours or up to 24 hours.

2 Meanwhile, for tomato stars, cut out ½ inch of the core from each tomato. Invert tomatoes. For each tomato, cut from the top to, but not quite through, the stem end to make 6 wedges.

3 To serve, place tomatoes on plates. Spread wedges apart slightly; fill with salmon-pasta mixture. Makes 4 servings.

Nutrition facts per serving: 216 calories, 7 g total fat (2 g saturated fat), 31 mg cholesterol, 517 mg sodium, 23 g carbohydrate, 2 g fiber, 16 g protein
Exchanges: 1 Starch, 2 Lean Meat, 1 Vegetable

112 calories

Preparation time: 35 minutes ● **Cooking time:** 8 minutes ● **Chilling time:** 1 to 2 hours

orange tarragon halibut salad

Choose your favorite greens for this salad. Romaine, spinach, and Boston or bibb lettuce all work well.

8 **ounces fresh or frozen halibut, swordfish,**
 haddock, or orange roughy steaks, cut
 1 inch thick
3 **oranges**
 Orange juice
2 **tablespoons salad oil**
1 **tablespoon tarragon vinegar or white wine**
 vinegar
1 **teaspoon snipped fresh tarragon or**
 ¼ teaspoon dried tarragon, crushed
¼ **teaspoon pepper**
1 **clove garlic, minced**
6 **cups torn mixed greens**
¼ **cup sliced green onions**
4 **radishes, thinly sliced**
 Fresh tarragon sprigs (optional)

 1 In a medium skillet place enough *water* to reach ½ inch up the sides of the fish steaks. Bring to boiling. Carefully add fish. Return to boiling; reduce heat. Simmer, covered, for 8 to 12 minutes or until fish just flakes when tested with a fork. Remove fish

from water. Cool slightly. When fish steaks are cool enough to handle, remove and discard skin and bones. Break fish into chunks. Place in a bowl.

 2 Peel oranges. Using a knife, prepare oranges by cutting away the peel and white rind. Working over a bowl, cut fruit between the flesh and the membrane into sections. Reserve ⅓ cup of the juice. (If necessary, add additional orange juice to equal ⅓ cup.) Cover and refrigerate orange sections.

 3 In a screw-top jar combine reserved orange juice, oil, vinegar, tarragon, pepper, and garlic. Cover; shake well. Pour over fish in bowl. Cover and refrigerate for at least 1 hour or up to 2 hours.

 4 In a large salad bowl toss together orange sections, greens, green onions, and radishes. Arrange fish mixture in center of greens mixture. If desired, garnish with tarragon sprigs. Toss before serving. Makes 6 servings.

Nutrition facts per serving: 112 calories, 6 g total fat (1 g saturated fat), 12 mg cholesterol, 26 mg sodium, 7 g carbohydrate, 2 g fiber, 9 g protein
Exchanges: 1 Lean Meat, 1 Vegetable, ½ Fruit, ½ Fat

109 calories

Preparation time: 15 minutes ● **Chilling time:** 1 to 4 hours

tuna – vegetable salad

For a great chilled sandwich, spread the tuna mixture between slices of whole wheat bread and top with tomato slices and lettuce leaves.

1 **cup chopped celery and/or chopped seeded cucumber**
½ **cup shredded carrot**
2 **tablespoons sliced green onion**
⅓ **cup fat-free mayonnaise dressing or salad dressing**
1½ **teaspoons snipped fresh dill or ½ teaspoon dried dillweed**
½ **teaspoon finely shredded lemon peel**
⅛ **teaspoon garlic powder**
⅛ **teaspoon pepper**
1 **6½-ounce can low-sodium chunk light or white tuna (water pack), drained and broken into chunks**
4 **medium tomatoes, sliced**
   Fresh dill (optional)

1 In a medium mixing bowl combine celery or cucumber, carrot, and green onion. Add mayonnaise dressing or salad dressing, dill, lemon peel, garlic powder, and pepper. Gently fold in tuna. Cover and refrigerate for at least 1 hour or up to 4 hours.

2 To serve, place the sliced tomatoes on each of 4 salad plates. Spoon the tuna mixture into tomato slices. If desired, garnish with fresh dill. Makes 4 servings.

Nutrition facts per serving: 109 calories, 1 g total fat (0 g saturated fat), 15 mg cholesterol, 314 mg sodium, 13 g carbohydrate, 3 g fiber, 13 g protein
Exchanges: 1½ Lean Meat, 2 Vegetable

292 calories

Preparation time: 20 minutes ● **Marinating time:** 30 minutes

antipasto salad

Antipasto is an Italian term that literally means "before the pasta"; it refers to a variety of hors d'oeuvres. In this recipe, several items traditionally served as cold appetizers are arranged on a plate of greens.

1 **9-ounce package frozen artichoke hearts**
½ **cup white wine vinegar**
2 **tablespoons olive oil or salad oil**
1 **tablespoon water**
1 **tablespoon snipped fresh basil or**
    1 **teaspoon dried basil, crushed**
    Dash salt
    Dash pepper
2 **cups small fresh mushrooms**
2 **medium tomatoes, cut into wedges**
1 **6½-ounce can white tuna (water pack),**
    drained and broken into chunks
4 **ounces part-skim mozzarella cheese, cut**
    into strips
    Lettuce leaves

1 Cook artichoke hearts according to package directions; drain well.

2 Meanwhile, for the dressing, in a medium bowl combine vinegar, oil, water, basil, salt, and pepper. Add the cooked artichoke hearts and mushrooms; toss to coat. Marinate at room temperature for 30 minutes, tossing occasionally. Drain vegetables, reserving dressing.

3 Arrange artichoke hearts, mushrooms, tomatoes, tuna, and cheese on 4 lettuce-lined plates. Drizzle with reserved dressing. Makes 4 servings.

Nutrition facts per serving: 292 calories, 13 g total fat (4 g saturated fat), 28 mg cholesterol, 419 mg sodium, 25 g carbohydrate, 1 g fiber, 25 g protein
Exchanges: 3 Lean Meat, 3 Vegetable, 1 Fat

237 calories

Preparation time: 40 minutes

shrimp with tarragon dressing

To make ahead, arrange the potatoes and shrimp on lettuce-lined plates; cover and refrigerate.
Cover and chill the dressing. To serve, drizzle the dressing over the shrimp and potatoes.

1 pound fresh or frozen shrimp in shells
3 medium potatoes, sliced ¼ inch thick
¼ cup light mayonnaise dressing or salad
    dressing
¼ cup buttermilk or plain low-fat yogurt
2 green onions, sliced
2 tablespoons snipped fresh parsley
1 teaspoon snipped fresh tarragon
    or ¼ teaspoon dried tarragon, crushed
1 clove garlic, minced
4 cups water
2 tablespoons vinegar
½ teaspoon salt
    Lettuce leaves
8 cherry tomatoes (optional)

1 Thaw shrimp, if frozen. Peel and devein shrimp, leaving tails on if desired. Cover and refrigerate until needed.

2 In a saucepan cook potatoes in a small amount of lightly salted *boiling water* for 8 to 12 minutes or until tender. Drain. Set aside.

3 Meanwhile, for dressing, in a blender container combine mayonnaise dressing or salad dressing, buttermilk or yogurt, green onions, parsley, tarragon, and garlic. Cover and blend until smooth. Set aside.

4 In a saucepan combine the water, vinegar, and salt. Bring to boiling. Add shrimp. Simmer, uncovered, for 1 to 3 minutes or until shrimp turn pink. Drain. Rinse with cold water. Drain.

5 Arrange potato slices and shrimp on 4 lettuce-lined plates. If necessary, stir some water into the dressing to make of drizzling consistency. Drizzle dressing over potatoes and shrimp. If desired, garnish with cherry tomatoes. Makes 4 servings.

Nutrition facts per serving: 237 calories, 6 g total fat (1 g saturated fat), 131 mg cholesterol, 553 mg sodium, 28 g carbohydrate, 1 g fiber, 17 g protein
Exchanges: 1½ Starch, 2 Lean Meat

163 calories

Preparation time: 30 minutes ● **Marinating time:** 2 to 3 hours

marinated shrimp salad

Marinades perk up the flavor of seafood, poultry, or meat. Be stingy, though, with the amount of oil you use to keep fat and calories down. Just a little olive oil adds flavor to this marinade, which doubles as dressing.

1 **pound fresh or frozen large shrimp in shells**
4 **cups water**
¼ **teaspoon finely shredded lemon peel**
⅓ **cup lemon juice**
2 **tablespoons olive oil**
2 **tablespoons thinly sliced green onion**
1 **tablespoon snipped fresh oregano or 1 teaspoon dried oregano, crushed**
½ **teaspoon sugar**
¼ **teaspoon crushed red pepper**
¼ **teaspoon salt**
⅛ **teaspoon black pepper**
1 **clove garlic, minced**
6 **cups torn mixed greens**
2 **cups sliced papaya or mango and/or 2 cups strawberries, halved lengthwise**

1 Thaw shrimp, if frozen. Peel and devein shrimp. In a medium saucepan bring the water to boiling. Add shrimp. Return to boiling; reduce heat.

Simmer, uncovered, for 1 to 3 minutes or until shrimp turn pink. Drain. Rinse with cold water. Drain. Set aside.

2 For marinade, in a small mixing bowl stir together lemon peel, lemon juice, oil, green onion, oregano, sugar, crushed red pepper, salt, black pepper, and garlic. Place shrimp in a plastic bag set in a deep bowl. Pour marinade over shrimp. Close bag. Marinate in the refrigerator for 2 to 3 hours, turning occasionally.

3 To serve, divide greens among 4 individual salad plates. Drain shrimp, reserving marinade. Arrange shrimp and fruit on greens mixture. Drizzle reserved marinade over salads. Makes 4 servings.

Nutrition facts per serving: 163 calories, 8 g total fat (1 g saturated fat), 131 mg cholesterol, 312 mg sodium, 8 g carbohydrate, 2 g fiber, 16 g protein
Exchanges: 2 Lean Meat, 1 Vegetable, ½ Fruit

334 calories

Preparation time: 25 minutes ● **Chilling time:** 2 to 24 hours

couscous and shrimp salad

Check out the many varieties of fresh mushrooms available at your grocery store. Use an assortment of chanterelle, white or brown button, and shiitake to add a mixture of shapes and flavors to this delicious salad.

 3 **cups sliced fresh assorted mushrooms**
 1 **14½-ounce can reduced-sodium chicken broth**
 2 **tablespoons water**
 ½ **teaspoon dried Italian seasoning, crushed**
 1 **cup quick-cooking couscous**
 1 **cup chopped red, yellow, or green sweet pepper**
 ⅓ **cup sliced green onions**
 ¼ **cup balsamic vinegar**
 1 **tablespoon olive oil**
 1 **cup frozen peas, thawed**
 8 **ounces peeled, deveined, and cooked shrimp**
   Romaine or lettuce leaves
 1 **small red sweet pepper, thinly sliced into rings (optional)**

1 In a large saucepan combine mushrooms, broth, water, and Italian seasoning. Bring to boiling; reduce heat. Simmer, covered, for 2 to 4 minutes or until mushrooms are tender. Remove from heat. Stir in couscous. Let stand, covered, for 5 minutes.

2 Stir sweet pepper and green onions into couscous mixture. Drizzle vinegar and oil over mixture. Toss to coat. Cover and refrigerate for at least 2 hours or up to 24 hours. Before serving, stir in peas and shrimp. Serve in 4 romaine- or lettuce-lined bowls. If desired, garnish with the sweet pepper rings. Makes 4 servings.

Nutrition facts per serving: 334 calories, 5 g total fat (1 g saturated fat), 111 mg cholesterol, 454 mg sodium, 49 g carbohydrate, 9 g fiber, 22 g protein
Exchanges: 2 Starch, 2 Lean Meat, 2 Vegetable

Beef
& VEAL

chapter index

318 calories

Preparation time: 25 minutes

beef and bean burritos

To keep the spicy beef filling lean, we replaced the traditional refried beans, which have added fat, with black beans. If you like, substitute pinto or other small red beans.

4 **10-inch flour tortillas**
8 **ounces lean ground beef**
1 **cup chopped onion**
1 **15-ounce can black beans, rinsed and drained**
1 **10-ounce can chopped tomatoes and green chili peppers, undrained**
1 **to 2 teaspoons chili powder**
2 **tablespoons chopped green onion**
1 **recipe Quick-to-Fix Spanish Rice (optional)**

1 Wrap tortillas in foil. Heat in a 350° oven for 10 minutes to soften. Meanwhile, for filling, in a large skillet cook ground beef and onion until meat is brown and onion is tender. Drain off fat. Stir in beans, undrained tomatoes and chili peppers, and chili powder. Bring to boiling; reduce heat. Simmer, uncovered, for 5 minutes or to desired consistency.

2 Set aside ¼ cup filling. For each burrito, spoon one-fourth of the remaining filling onto each tortilla just below center. Fold plain side of tortilla over filling. Fold in the opposite sides of tortilla, just until they meet; roll up. Top with the reserved filling. Sprinkle with green onion. If desired, serve with Quick-to-Fix Spanish Rice. Makes 4 servings.

Nutrition facts per serving: 318 calories, 9 g total fat (3 g saturated fat), 36 mg cholesterol, 755 mg sodium, 42 g carbohydrate, 7 g fiber, 21 g protein
Exchanges: 2½ Starch, 2 Lean Meat, 1 Vegetable

Quick-to-Fix Spanish Rice: Prepare 2 cups *hot cooked rice.* Stir in 1 cup *chopped tomato* and one 4½-ounce can *diced green chili peppers;* heat the mixture through. Makes 4 servings.

Nutrition facts per serving: 120 calories, 1 g total fat (0 g saturated fat), 0 mg cholesterol, 84 mg sodium, 26 g carbohydrate, 1 g fiber, 3 g protein
Exchanges: 1½ Starch

335 calories

Preparation time: 25 minutes ● **Baking time:** 20 minutes ● **Standing time:** 5 minutes

beefy corn bread

This meat pie with a Mexican flair boasts a ground beef and corn filling topped with corn bread, cheese, and salsa. Serve with a mixed greens salad.

10 **ounces lean ground beef**
 1 **teaspoon chili powder**
¼ **teaspoon ground cumin**
½ **cup loose-pack frozen whole kernel corn, thawed**
¼ **cup salsa**
¾ **cup cornmeal**
¾ **cup all-purpose flour**
 2 **tablespoons sugar**
 2 **teaspoons baking powder**
 2 **beaten eggs**
¾ **cup skim milk**
 2 **tablespoons cooking oil**
½ **cup shredded reduced-fat cheddar cheese**
⅓ **cup salsa, heated**
 Fresh cilantro (optional)
 Jalapeño pepper slices (optional)

1 In a large skillet cook ground beef, chili powder, and cumin until meat is brown. Drain off fat. Stir corn and the ¼ cup salsa into meat.

2 Meanwhile, in a medium bowl stir together the cornmeal, flour, sugar, baking powder, and ½ teaspoon *salt*. In a small bowl combine the eggs, milk, and oil; add to the flour mixture, stirring just until moistened.

3 Spray a 2-quart rectangular baking dish with *nonstick coating*. Spread half of the cornmeal mixture in dish. Spoon meat mixture over batter and sprinkle half of cheese over meat. Spoon remaining cornmeal mixture over cheese; spread to cover the meat layer. Bake, uncovered, in a 375° oven about 20 minutes or until wooden toothpick inserted near the center comes out clean. Sprinkle with remaining cheese. Let stand 5 minutes. Serve with the ⅓ cup heated salsa. If desired, garnish with fresh cilantro and jalapeño pepper slices. Makes 6 servings.

Nutrition facts per serving: 335 calories, 14 g total fat (4 g saturated fat), 108 mg cholesterol, 512 mg sodium, 35 g carbohydrate, 1 g fiber, 18 g protein
Exchanges: 2 Starch, 2 Lean Meat, 1 Fat

238 calories

Preparation time: 40 minutes ● **Baking time:** 22 minutes

southwest-style stuffed peppers

Chili peppers and cumin spice up these stuffed peppers. For a real southwestern kick, use 1 or 2 chopped fresh jalapeño peppers in place of the mild green chili peppers.

2 **large green sweet peppers**
8 **ounces lean ground beef**
¼ **cup chopped onion**
1 **14½-ounce can low-sodium tomatoes, undrained and cut up**
½ **cup water**
⅓ **cup long grain rice**
1 **4½-ounce can diced green chili peppers, drained**
1 **teaspoon chili powder**
½ **teaspoon garlic salt**
¼ **teaspoon ground cumin**
1 **cup loose-pack frozen whole kernel corn**
2 **tablespoons shredded reduced-fat cheddar cheese**

1 Halve sweet peppers lengthwise, removing stem ends, seeds, and membranes. Immerse sweet peppers into *boiling water* for 3 minutes. Invert on paper towels to drain well.

2 In a large skillet cook ground beef and onion until meat is brown and onion is tender. Drain off fat. Stir in undrained tomatoes, water, uncooked rice, chili peppers, chili powder, garlic salt, and cumin. Bring to boiling. Stir in corn. Return to boiling; reduce heat. Simmer, covered, for 15 to 18 minutes or until rice and corn are tender.

3 Place pepper halves in a 2-quart square baking dish. Spoon meat mixture into peppers. Spoon any remaining meat mixture into the dish around the peppers. Bake peppers, covered, in a 375° oven for 20 minutes or until heated through. Uncover; sprinkle with the cheddar cheese. Bake 2 minutes more. Makes 4 servings.

Nutrition facts per serving: 238 calories, 7 g total fat (3 g saturated fat), 38 mg cholesterol, 406 mg sodium, 30 g carbohydrate, 2 g fiber, 15 g protein
Exchanges: 1½ Starch, 1 Medium-Fat Meat, 2 Vegetable

291 calories

Preparation time: 20 minutes ● **Baking time:** 45 minutes

spaghetti squash with chili

You can afford a generous serving of this delicious chili-flavored meat sauce ladled over low-calorie spaghetti squash. If you don't have time to make the squash, serve the chili over spaghetti.

1   2½- to 3-pound spaghetti squash
12 ounces lean ground beef
½   cup chopped onion
1   clove garlic, minced
½   teaspoon cornstarch
1   8-ounce can low-sodium tomato sauce
⅔   cup tomato juice
1   11-ounce can whole kernel corn with sweet
    peppers, drained
2   teaspoons chili powder
1   teaspoon snipped fresh oregano
    or ½ teaspoon dried oregano, crushed
½   cup shredded Monterey Jack cheese
    (2 ounces) (optional)

1 Halve the spaghetti squash lengthwise and remove seeds. Place, cut sides down, on a baking sheet. Bake in a 350° oven for 45 to 50 minutes or until tender. Using a fork, shred and separate the spaghetti squash into strands.

2 Meanwhile, for sauce, in a large skillet cook beef, onion, and garlic until meat is brown and onion is tender. Drain off fat.

3 Stir in cornstarch. Add tomato sauce and tomato juice. Stir in corn, chili powder, and oregano. Cook and stir until slightly thickened and bubbly. Cook and stir 2 minutes more.

4 To serve, spoon the meat mixture over spaghetti squash. If desired, top with Monterey Jack cheese. Makes 4 servings.

Microwave Directions: Place squash halves, cut sides down, in a microwave-safe baking dish with ¼ cup *water.* Cover and microwave on 100% power (high) for 15 to 20 minutes or until tender, rearranging once. Continue as above.

Nutrition facts per serving: 291 calories, 9 g total fat (3 g saturated fat), 54 mg cholesterol, 529 mg sodium, 35 g carbohydrate, 7 g fiber, 20 g protein
Exchanges: 1½ Starch, 2 Medium-Fat Meat, 2 Vegetable

270 calories

Preparation time: 30 minutes ● **Broiling time:** 12 minutes ● **Chilling time:** 4 to 24 hours

feta-stuffed burgers

Just a little bit of feta cheese adds a rich, tangy flavor to these stuffed burgers. Feta is sometimes referred to as pickled cheese because it is stored in a salty brine similar to pickles.

¼ **cup refrigerated or frozen egg product, thawed**
2 **tablespoons water**
⅓ **cup rolled oats**
¼ **teaspoon pepper**
⅛ **teaspoon salt**
1 **pound lean ground beef**
2 **teaspoons Dijon-style mustard**
⅓ **cup crumbled feta cheese**
3 **English muffins, split and toasted**
1 **recipe Tomato-Basil Relish**
   Fresh basil (optional)

1 In a mixing bowl stir together egg product and water. Stir in oats, pepper, and salt. Add beef; mix well. Shape mixture into twelve ¼-inch-thick patties. Spread mustard on 1 side of 6 patties. Top with crumbled cheese. Place remaining patties on top of cheese, pressing edges to seal.

2 Place patties on the unheated rack of a broiler pan. Broil 4 to 5 inches from the heat for 12 to 14 minutes or until juices run clear. Serve patties on toasted English muffin halves. Top with Tomato-Basil Relish. If desired, garnish with fresh basil. Makes 6 servings.

Tomato-Basil Relish: In a small bowl stir together 2 chopped *plum tomatoes;* ½ cup chopped seeded *cucumber;* 2 tablespoons thinly sliced *green onion;* 1 tablespoon *red wine vinegar;* 1 tablespoon snipped *fresh basil* or 1 teaspoon *dried basil,* crushed; and ⅛ teaspoon *pepper.* Cover and refrigerate for at least 4 hours or up to 24 hours.

Nutrition facts per serving: 270 calories, 12 g total fat (5 g saturated fat), 60 mg cholesterol, 500 mg sodium, 20 g carbohydrate, 2 g fiber, 20 g protein
Exchanges: 1 Starch, 2 Medium-Fat Meat, 1 Vegetable

359 calories

Preparation time: 35 minutes

saucy beef and onions

With the vast variety of fat-free and reduced-fat products in your grocery store, low-fat cooking is easier than ever. Here, a jar of fat-free gravy and light sour cream create a saucy hamburger stroganoff.

12 ounces lean ground beef or veal
 2 cups sliced fresh mushrooms
 2 medium onions, cut into thin wedges
 1 clove garlic, minced
 1 12-ounce jar fat-free beef gravy
⅔ cup light dairy sour cream
 1 tablespoon Worcestershire sauce
¾ teaspoon snipped fresh thyme or sage or
    ¼ teaspoon dried thyme or sage, crushed
⅛ teaspoon pepper
 2 cups hot cooked rice or noodles
 2 tablespoons snipped fresh parsley

1 In a large skillet cook meat, mushrooms, onions, and garlic until meat is brown and onions are tender. Drain off fat.

2 In a mixing bowl stir together beef gravy, sour cream, Worcestershire sauce, thyme or sage, and pepper. Stir into meat mixture. Heat through.

3 Serve meat mixture over rice or noodles. Sprinkle with parsley. Makes 4 servings.

Nutrition facts per serving: 359 calories, 13 g total fat (5 g saturated fat), 59 mg cholesterol, 643 mg sodium, 38 g carbohydrate, 1 g fiber, 24 g protein
Exchanges: 2 Starch, 2 Medium-Fat Meat, 2 Vegetable

345 calories

Preparation time: 40 minutes ● **Cooking time:** 1 hour 20 minutes

harvest ragout

Dried fruit lightly sweeten this hearty stew. Add a small mixed salad drizzled with a low-calorie dressing, and you have a meal perfect for a wintry evening.

1 **pound lean beef stew meat, trimmed of separable fat and cut into 1-inch pieces**
2 **teaspoons cooking oil**
1 **cup chopped onion**
3 **cloves garlic, minced**
2 **14½-ounce cans low-sodium tomatoes, undrained and cut up**
2 **cups water**
1⅓ **cups low-sodium vegetable juice**
2 **teaspoons instant beef bouillon granules**
1 **teaspoon sugar**
1 **teaspoon dried thyme, crushed**
½ **teaspoon dried marjoram, crushed**
¼ **teaspoon pepper**
3 **cups cubed potatoes**
2 **cups sliced carrots**
¼ **cup cold water**
2 **teaspoons cornstarch**
¾ **cup mixed dried fruit bits or snipped dried apricots**
 Fresh marjoram (optional)

1 Spray an unheated Dutch oven with *nonstick spray coating*. Brown meat, half at a time, in pan. Remove meat from pan. Add the oil. Cook onion and garlic in hot oil until tender.

2 Stir in undrained tomatoes, the 2 cups water, vegetable juice, bouillon granules, sugar, thyme, marjoram, and pepper. Return meat to pan. Bring to boiling; reduce heat. Simmer, covered, for 50 to 60 minutes or until meat is nearly tender.

3 Stir in potatoes and carrots. Return to boiling; reduce heat. Simmer, covered, for 30 to 40 minutes or until vegetables are tender. Stir together the ¼ cup cold water and cornstarch. Stir into meat mixture. Stir in fruit bits. Cook and stir until thickened. Cook and stir for 2 minutes more. If desired, garnish with marjoram. Makes 6 servings.

Nutrition facts per serving: 345 calories, 9 g total fat (3 g saturated fat), 50 mg cholesterol, 409 mg sodium, 46 g carbohydrate, 4 g fiber, 22 g protein
Exchanges: 1 Starch, 2 Lean Meat, 3 Vegetable, 1 Fruit

312 calories

Preparation time: 20 minutes ● **Cooking time:** 42 minutes

curried beef with rice

Brown rice is the least processed type of rice. It takes longer to cook than white rice, but the nutty flavor and chewy texture are worth the wait.

1½ **cups water**
 1 **cup chopped onion**
 ½ **cup chopped carrot**
 2 **to 3 teaspoons curry powder**
1½ **teaspoons instant beef bouillon granules**
 1 **clove garlic, minced**
 ¾ **cup regular brown rice**
1½ **cups cubed cooked beef (about 8 ounces)**
 1 **cup frozen peas**
 1 **medium tomato, chopped**
 Tomato wedges (optional)

1 In a 2-quart saucepan stir together the water, onion, carrot, curry powder, bouillon granules, and garlic. Bring to boiling; stir in rice. Simmer, covered, for 40 to 45 minutes or until rice is tender and liquid is absorbed.

2 Stir beef, peas, and chopped tomato into rice mixture. Cook and stir for 2 to 3 minutes more or until heated through. If desired, garnish with tomato wedges. Makes 4 servings.

Nutrition facts per serving: 312 calories, 7 g total fat (3 g saturated fat), 51 mg cholesterol, 408 mg sodium, 38 g carbohydrate, 5 g fiber, 23 g protein
Exchanges: 2 Starch, 2 Lean Meat, 1 Vegetable

302 calories

Preparation time: 1 hour

peppery beef and vegetables

Nonstick spray coating helps reduce the amount of oil needed in stir-frying. Spray the unheated wok before cooking the first few ingredients; you may need a small amount of oil later in the process.

12 **ounces lean boneless beef, trimmed of separable fat**
4 **ounces packaged dried linguini, broken into 3-inch pieces**
¼ **cup low-sodium soy sauce**
2 **teaspoons cornstarch**
½ **teaspoon coarsely ground black pepper**
⅛ **teaspoon ground red pepper**
Nonstick spray coating
1 **clove garlic, minced**
1 **cup fresh or frozen pea pods, halved crosswise**
½ **cup coarsely chopped green or red sweet pepper**
1 **cup sliced fresh mushrooms**
1 **tablespoon cooking oil**

1 Partially freeze meat about 30 minutes. Thinly slice meat across grain into bite-size strips. Set aside.

2 Cook linguini according to package directions, except omit any oil and salt. Drain well; keep warm.

3 Meanwhile, for sauce, in a bowl stir together soy sauce, cornstarch, coarsely ground pepper, ground red pepper, and ½ cup *water*. Set aside.

4 Spray an unheated wok or large skillet with nonstick coating. Preheat over medium-high heat. Add garlic; stir-fry for 30 seconds. Add pea pods and sweet pepper; stir-fry for 1 minute. Add mushrooms; stir-fry 1 to 2 minutes more or until vegetables are crisp-tender. Remove vegetables from wok.

5 Add oil to wok. Stir-fry beef in hot oil for 2 to 3 minutes or to desired doneness. Push beef to side of wok. Stir sauce and pour into the center of wok. Cook and stir until thickened and bubbly. Return vegetables to wok; cook and stir for 2 minutes more. Toss with linguini. Makes 4 servings.

Nutrition facts per serving: 302 calories, 8 g total fat (2 g saturated fat), 54 mg cholesterol, 571 mg sodium, 29 g carbohydrate, 1 g fiber, 27 g protein
Exchanges: 1½ Starch, 3 Lean Meat, 1 Vegetable

340 calories

Preparation time: 25 minutes ● **Cooking time:** 1 hour

beef and brew with noodles

Beer subtly flavors and tenderizes the beef as it slowly simmers. Hearty Italian bread or a small fresh salad is all you need as an accompaniment.

1 12-ounce can light beer
½ cup reduced-sodium chicken broth
1 bay leaf
1 tablespoon snipped fresh thyme
   or 1 teaspoon dried thyme, crushed
¼ teaspoon salt
⅛ teaspoon black pepper
12 ounces boneless beef round steak, trimmed
   of separable fat and cut into 1-inch pieces
2 small onions, cut into wedges
2 medium green and/or red sweet peppers,
   cut into thin strips
2 tablespoons cold water
4 teaspoons cornstarch
3 cups hot cooked noodles

1 In large saucepan stir together beer, chicken broth, bay leaf, thyme, salt, and black pepper. Stir in beef. Bring to boiling; reduce heat. Simmer, covered, for 50 minutes. Add onions and sweet peppers; simmer about 10 minutes more or until beef and vegetables are tender. Discard bay leaf.

2 Stir together the cold water and cornstarch; stir into meat mixture. Cook and stir until thickened and bubbly. Cook and stir for 2 minutes more. Serve over noodles. Makes 4 servings.

Nutrition facts per serving: 340 calories, 6 g total fat (2 g saturated fat), 94 mg cholesterol, 265 mg sodium, 38 g carbohydrate, 3 g fiber, 27 g protein
Exchanges: 2 Starch, 3 Lean Meat, 1 Vegetable

319 calories

Preparation time: 40 minutes ● **Cooking time:** 2 hours

barbecue-sauced beef sandwiches

Serve half of these saucy sandwiches now and freeze the rest for later. When you're short on time or the shelves are bare, you'll have a ready-to-heat meal in the freezer.

1   **2-pound boneless beef round steak, cut ¾ to 1 inch thick and trimmed of separable fat**
1   **14½-ounce can tomatoes, undrained and cut up**
1   **cup chopped onion**
1   **cup chopped carrot**
2   **tablespoons Worcestershire sauce**
2   **tablespoons vinegar**
1   **tablespoon brown sugar**
2   **teaspoons chili powder**
1   **teaspoon dried oregano, crushed**
1   **clove garlic, minced**
1   **bay leaf**
8   **hamburger buns, split and toasted**

1 Cut meat into 4 to 6 pieces. Spray an unheated Dutch oven with *nonstick spray coating*. Add half of the steak pieces; brown each piece on both sides. Remove meat. Repeat to brown remaining meat. Drain off fat. Return all meat to Dutch oven.

2 Add undrained tomatoes, onion, carrot, Worcestershire sauce, vinegar, brown sugar, chili powder, oregano, ⅛ teaspoon *pepper,* garlic, and bay leaf. Bring to boiling; reduce heat. Simmer, covered, 2 to 2½ hours or until meat is tender.

3 Remove meat from sauce; shred meat. Return meat to sauce. If necessary, simmer, uncovered, for 5 to 10 minutes or until slightly thickened. Discard bay leaf. Serve in buns. Makes 8 servings.

Freezer Directions: If desired, transfer mixture to freezer containers. Cover, label, and freeze for up to 6 months. To reheat, transfer mixture to a saucepan; add 1 tablespoon *water.* Cook, covered, over medium-low heat until heated through, stirring occasionally to break up. (Allow 8 to 10 minutes for 1 or 2 servings; 25 to 30 minutes for 4 servings.)

Nutrition facts per serving: 319 calories, 8 g total fat (2 g saturated fat), 72 mg cholesterol, 393 mg sodium, 30 g carbohydrate, 2 g fiber, 31 g protein
Exchanges: 2 Starch, 3 Lean Meat, 1 Vegetable

HOW MUCH CAN I SAVE?

Choosing the Best Reduced-Fat Products

When you choose low-fat products over regular fat products, the savings in fat and calories can be quite substantial. Check this table to figure how much you can save when you choose low-fat products.

Food	Amount	Cal.	Fat (g)	Sat. Fat (g)
Regular cheddar cheese	1 ounce	114	9	6
Reduced-fat cheddar cheese*	1 ounce	90	5	3
Fat-free cheddar cheese*	1 ounce	41	0	0
Regular cream cheese	1 ounce	100	10	6
Reduced-fat cream cheese	1 ounce	74	7	7
Fat-free cream cheese	1 ounce	25	0	0
Regular dairy sour cream	¼ cup	123	23	8
Light dairy sour cream	¼ cup	80	4	2
Fat-free dairy sour cream	¼ cup	60	0	0
2-percent milk	1 cup	120	5	3
Skim milk	1 cup	86	0	0
Egg	1	75	5	2
Egg substitute	¼ cup	53	2	0
Egg substitute (no cholesterol)	¼ cup	30	1	0
Regular mayonnaise	1 tablespoon	100	11	2
Reduced-fat mayonnaise	1 tablespoon	50	5	1
Fat-free mayonnaise	1 tablespoon	12	0	0
Regular salad dressing	1 tablespoon	70	7	1
Reduced-fat salad dressing	1 tablespoon	45	4	1
Fat-free salad dressing	1 tablespoon	20	0	0

*__Note:__ Reduced-fat and fat-free cheeses need a little more care when melted. If heated or broiled at high temperatures, they can become tough and stringy. For best results, use only what is specified in the recipes and follow directions carefully.

332 calories

Preparation time: 55 minutes

oriental beef and broccoli

A spicy-sweet sauce richly coats this colorful family-style stir-fry. Make up the majority of the mixture with your favorite fresh vegetables, a great way to fill up without adding a lot of calories.

**12 ounces beef top round steak, trimmed of
     separable fat**
3 tablespoons vinegar
2 tablespoons reduced-sodium soy sauce
2 tablespoons molasses
1 clove garlic, minced
**¼ teaspoon crushed red pepper
     Nonstick spray coating**
2 teaspoons cooking oil
1 cup thinly bias-sliced carrot
6 cups fresh broccoli flowerets
¼ cup cold water
1 tablespoon cornstarch
2 cups hot cooked rice

1 Partially freeze meat about 30 minutes. Thinly slice meat across grain into bite-size strips. Set aside.

2 In a medium bowl stir together vinegar, soy sauce, molasses, garlic, and crushed red pepper. Stir in meat. Cover and let marinate at room temperature for 10 minutes.

3 Drain meat, reserving marinade. Spray an unheated large skillet or wok with nonstick coating. Preheat over medium-high heat. Add meat; cook and stir for 2 to 3 minutes or to desired doneness. Remove meat from skillet or wok. Add oil to skillet or wok.

4 Add carrot to skillet or wok. Cook and stir for 2 minutes. Add broccoli; cook and stir for 3 to 4 minutes or until crisp-tender. Push vegetables from center of skillet or wok.

5 Stir together cold water, cornstarch, and reserved marinade; add to center of skillet or wok. Cook and stir until thickened and bubbly. Add meat. Cook and stir 2 minutes more or until heated through. Serve with hot rice. Makes 4 servings.

Nutrition facts per serving: 332 calories, 7 g total fat (2 g saturated fat), 54 mg cholesterol, 359 mg sodium, 41 g carbohydrate, 5 g fiber, 27 g protein
Exchanges: 2 Starch, 2 Lean Meat, 2 Vegetable

268 calories

Preparation time: 55 minutes

beef curry and potatoes

This stir-fry pleases the family that loves meat and potatoes. Add as much or as little curry powder as you like, depending on your tastes.

12 **ounces beef top round steak, trimmed of separable fat**
2 **medium potatoes, halved and thinly sliced (about 12 ounces total)**
½ **cup beef broth**
2 **teaspoons cornstarch**
¼ **teaspoon salt**
  Nonstick spray coating
¾ **cup chopped onion**
¾ **cup chopped green or red sweet pepper**
1 **tablespoon cooking oil**
1 **to 3 teaspoons curry powder**
1 **medium tomato, chopped**

1 Partially freeze meat about 30 minutes. Thinly slice across the grain into bite-size strips. Set aside.

2 Cook potatoes in lightly *salted boiling water* about 5 minutes or until tender. Drain; set aside.

3 Meanwhile, for sauce, stir together beef broth, cornstarch, and salt.

4 Spray an unheated wok or large skillet with nonstick coating. Preheat over medium-high heat. Add onion and stir-fry for 2 minutes. Add sweet pepper and stir-fry about 2 minutes more or until vegetables are crisp-tender. Remove from wok.

5 Add oil to hot wok. Add meat and curry powder. Stir-fry for 2 to 3 minutes or to desired doneness. Push meat from center of wok.

6 Stir sauce and add to center of wok. Cook and stir until thickened and bubbly. Stir in onion mixture, potatoes, and tomato. Cook and stir for 2 minutes more. Makes 4 servings.

Nutrition facts per serving: 268 calories, 8 g total fat (2 g saturated fat), 54 mg cholesterol, 282 mg sodium, 26 g carbohydrate, 2 g fiber, 24 g protein
Exchanges: 1 Starch, 2 Lean Meat, 2 Vegetable

215 calories

Preparation time: 15 minutes ● **Marinating time:** 4 to 24 hours ● **Grilling time:** 18 minutes

herbed steak and onions

When testing the temperature of the coals, hold your hand over the coals at the height and place the meat will cook. For medium heat, you should be able to keep your hand there for four seconds. Any more and it's not hot enough.

1 **cup tomato juice**
1½ **teaspoons snipped fresh basil**
    or ½ teaspoon dried basil, crushed
1½ **teaspoons snipped fresh oregano**
    or ½ teaspoon dried oregano, crushed
1 **teaspoon olive oil or cooking oil**
⅛ **teaspoon pepper**
1 **clove garlic, minced**
1 **pound beef top round steak, cut 1 inch**
    thick and trimmed of separable fat
2 **large onions, thinly sliced and separated**
    into rings

1 For marinade, combine tomato juice, basil, oregano, oil, pepper, and garlic. Set aside.

2 Cut meat into 4 serving-size pieces. Place meat in a plastic bag set in a deep bowl. Pour marinade over meat. Seal bag; turn to coat meat well. Marinate in the refrigerator for 4 to 24 hours. Drain steak, reserving marinade.

3 Place onions on an 18-inch square of heavy foil. Turn edges of foil up slightly. Drizzle ½ cup of the reserved marinade over onions. Fold foil tightly to seal. Grill onion packet and meat on uncovered grill directly over medium coals for 10 minutes. Turn onion packet and meat; brush meat with reserved marinade. Grill meat to desired doneness. (For medium doneness, grill meat 8 to 10 minutes more.) Grill onions 8 minutes more or until tender.

4 Unwrap onions and serve with the meat. Makes 4 servings.

Nutrition facts per serving: 215 calories, 7 g total fat (2 g saturated fat), 72 mg cholesterol, 234 mg sodium, 9 g carbohydrate, 2 g fiber, 28 g protein
Exchanges: 3 Lean Meat, 2 Vegetable

282 calories

Preparation time: 50 minutes

orange and beef stir-fry

Partially freeze the steak until it's firm but not hard (30 to 45 minutes). The frozen meat will then be easier to cut into thin, bite-size strips.

12 **ounces beef top round steak, trimmed of separable fat**
1 **tablespoon cornstarch**
1 **teaspoon sugar**
1 **teaspoon instant beef bouillon granules**
1 **teaspoon finely shredded orange peel**
½ **cup orange juice**
1 **tablespoon reduced-sodium soy sauce**
4 **green onions, bias-sliced into 1-inch pieces**
1 **clove garlic, minced**
1 **tablespoon cooking oil (optional)***
6 **cups torn fresh spinach**
⅓ **cup sliced water chestnuts, drained**
2 **cups hot cooked rice**
  Orange slices, halved (optional)

1 Partially freeze meat about 30 minutes. Thinly slice meat across grain into bite-size strips. Set aside.

2 In a small bowl stir together cornstarch, sugar, and beef bouillon granules. Stir in orange peel, orange juice, and soy sauce. Set aside.

3 Spray an unheated wok or 12-inch skillet with *nonstick spray coating*. Preheat over medium-high heat. Add onions and garlic; stir-fry for 1 minute. Remove from wok. If necessary, add the oil. Add meat; stir-fry for 2 to 3 minutes or to desired doneness. Push meat away from center of wok.

4 Stir orange juice mixture and pour into the center of wok. Cook and stir until thickened and bubbly. Stir in spinach, water chestnuts, and onion mixture. Cover and cook for 2 minutes more. Serve over rice. If desired, garnish with halved orange slices. Makes 4 servings.

*****Note:** To keep the beef from sticking to the wok or skillet, you may need to add the 1 tablespoon oil, which adds 30 calories and 4 grams fat per serving.

Nutrition facts per serving: 282 calories, 5 g total fat (2 g saturated fat), 54 mg cholesterol, 456 mg sodium, 34 g carbohydrate, 3 g fiber, 26 g protein
Exchanges: 2 Starch, 2 Lean Meat, 1 Vegetable

296 calories

Preparation time: 50 minutes ● **Cooking time:** 30 minutes

chunky chili

To give the baked tortilla strips a decorative edge, cut the tortillas before baking with a pasta or pastry wheel.

12　ounces beef top round steak, trimmed of
　　　separable fat
2　corn tortillas
　　　Nonstick spray coating
½　cup chopped onion
1　clove garlic, minced
1　15-ounce can kidney beans, drained and
　　　rinsed
1　14½-ounce can low-sodium tomatoes,
　　　undrained
1　cup water
1　4½-ounce can diced green chili peppers
1½　teaspoons snipped fresh basil
　　　or ½ teaspoon dried basil, crushed
1　teaspoon chili powder
1　teaspoon instant beef bouillon granules
¼　teaspoon ground cumin
¼　teaspoon black pepper
¼　cup shredded reduced-fat cheddar cheese
　　　(1 ounce)

1 Partially freeze meat about 30 minutes. Thinly slice across the grain into bite-size strips.

2 Cut or tear tortillas into bite-size strips. Spread on an ungreased baking sheet. Bake in a 350° oven about 10 minutes or until crisp and dry. Set aside.

3 Spray an unheated large skillet with nonstick coating. Preheat over medium-high heat. Add meat, onion, and garlic. Cook and stir until meat is brown and onion is tender. Stir in the kidney beans, undrained tomatoes, water, chili peppers, basil, chili powder, bouillon granules, cumin, and black pepper. Bring to boiling; reduce heat. Simmer, covered, for 30 minutes or until meat is tender.

4 Ladle into individual serving bowls. Sprinkle each serving with some of the tortilla strips and 1 tablespoon shredded cheese. Makes 4 servings.

Nutrition facts per serving: 296 calories, 7 g total fat (2 g saturated fat), 59 mg cholesterol, 601 mg sodium, 31 g carbohydrate, 7 g fiber, 33 g protein
Exchanges: 1½ Starch, 3 Lean Meat, 2 Vegetable

354 calories

Preparation time: 35 minutes ● **Cooking time:** 1¼ hours

italian beef skillet

For another alternative, serve the beef mixture over Cheesy Polenta Squares (see recipe, page 373) instead of pasta.

1 **pound boneless beef round steak, trimmed**
  of separable fat
  Nonstick spray coating
2 **cups sliced fresh mushrooms**
1 **cup chopped onion**
1 **cup coarsely chopped green sweet pepper**
½ **cup chopped celery**
2 **cloves garlic, minced**
1 **14½-ounce can tomatoes, undrained and**
  cut up
½ **teaspoon dried basil, crushed**
¼ **teaspoon dried oregano, crushed**
¼ **teaspoon crushed red pepper**
8 **ounces packaged dried spaghetti**
2 **tablespoons grated Parmesan cheese**

1 Cut meat into 5 serving-size pieces. Spray an unheated large skillet with nonstick coating. Preheat over medium heat. Add meat pieces to skillet; brown on both sides of each piece. Remove meat from skillet.

2 Add mushrooms, onion, sweet pepper, celery, and garlic to the skillet. Cook until vegetables are nearly tender. Stir in undrained tomatoes, basil, oregano, and crushed red pepper. Add meat to skillet, spooning vegetable mixture over the meat. Simmer, covered, about 1¼ hours or until meat is tender, stirring occasionally. Meanwhile, cook spaghetti according to package directions, except omit any oil and salt.

3 Transfer meat to a serving platter. Spoon vegetable mixture over meat. Serve with hot cooked pasta. Sprinkle some of the Parmesan cheese over each serving. Makes 5 servings.

Nutrition facts per serving: 354 calories, 6 g total fat (2 g saturated fat), 60 mg cholesterol, 255 mg sodium, 43 g carbohydrate, 2 g fiber, 31 g protein
Exchanges: 2 Starch, 3 Lean Meat, 2 Vegetable

205 calories

Preparation time: 20 minutes ● **Roasting time:** 2 hours

cranberry pot roast

Although poultry most often comes to mind when you think of cranberries, the tart berry flavor also blends well with beef. Here, both cranberry juice and fresh berries flavor the gravy.

1 **2- to 2½-pound beef bottom round roast, trimmed of separable fat**
2 **teaspoons cooking oil**
1 **cup cranberry juice cocktail**
½ **cup beef broth**
½ **teaspoon dried thyme, crushed**
1 **16-ounce package frozen small whole onions**
¼ **cup packed brown sugar**
2 **cups cranberries**
3 **tablespoons cold water**
2 **tablespoons cornstarch**

1 In a Dutch oven quickly brown meat in hot oil over medium-high heat, turning to brown on all sides. Remove from heat.

2 Pour cranberry juice cocktail and beef broth over the meat. Add the thyme. Roast, covered, in a 325° oven for 1 hour. Stir onions and brown sugar into the pan juices. Roast meat, covered, for 1 to 1¼ hours more or until meat and onions are tender. Transfer meat to a serving platter, reserving juices. Cover meat to keep warm.

3 Strain pan juices, reserving onions. Measure pan juices. If necessary, add enough water to measure 2 cups liquid. Return to Dutch oven. Stir in cranberries and the onions. Bring to boiling. Stir together cold water and cornstarch. Stir into mixture in Dutch oven. Cook and stir until thickened and bubbly. Cook and stir for 2 minutes more. Serve over meat. Makes 10 servings.

Nutrition facts per serving: 205 calories, 5 g total fat (2 g saturated fat), 58 mg cholesterol, 85 mg sodium, 16 g carbohydrate, 2 g fiber, 22 g protein
Exchanges: 3 Lean Meat, 1 Fruit

272 calories

Preparation time: 25 minutes ● **Cooking time:** 2 hours and 5 minutes

wine-sauced pot roast

Subtly flavored with red wine and garlic, this pot roast is perfect for casual entertaining. To save time on scraping and cutting carrots, buy prepackaged cleaned baby carrots from the grocery store produce section.

Nonstick spray coating
1 **3-pound beef round rump roast, trimmed of separable fat**
1 **large onion, sliced**
¾ **cup dry red wine**
½ **cup water**
4 **cloves garlic, minced**
2 **teaspoons instant beef bouillon granules**
½ **teaspoon dried thyme, crushed**
¼ **teaspoon pepper**
1 **pound tiny whole carrots**
1 **16-ounce package frozen cut green beans**
2 **tablespoons cornstarch**
2 **tablespoons cold water**

1 Spray an unheated Dutch oven with nonstick coating. Preheat over medium heat. Add roast and brown on all sides. Drain off fat. Add the onion, wine, the ½ cup water, garlic, bouillon granules,

thyme, and pepper. Bring to boiling; reduce heat. Simmer, covered, for 1 hour. Turn roast over; cook, covered, 45 minutes more.

2 Add the carrots to the Dutch oven; simmer for 20 minutes. Add beans; simmer about 10 minutes more or until beans and meat are tender. Transfer to a serving platter. Keep warm.

3 For gravy, skim fat from pan juices. Stir together cornstarch and the 2 tablespoons cold water. Stir mixture into pan juices. Cook and stir until thickened and bubbly. Cook and stir for 2 minutes more. To serve, spoon gravy over meat and vegetables. Makes 10 servings.

Nutrition facts per serving: 272 calories, 10 g total fat (3 g saturated fat), 93 mg cholesterol, 268 mg sodium, 11 g carbohydrate, 2 g fiber, 32 g protein
Exchanges: 4 Lean Meat, 2 Vegetable

149 calories

Preparation time: 30 minutes ● **Roasting time:** 1½ to 2 hours ● **Standing time:** 15 minutes

beef roast with vegetable stuffing

Serve this impressive vegetable-filled roast with Brown Rice Pilaf (see recipe, page 389) for a dinner party.

1 **cup chopped red or green sweet pepper**
1 **cup shredded carrot**
½ **cup chopped onion**
2 **cloves garlic, minced**
2 **teaspoons margarine or butter**
2 **teaspoons snipped fresh basil, marjoram,**
   or thyme or ½ teaspoon dried basil,
   marjoram, or thyme, crushed
¼ **teaspoon black pepper**
1 **2- to 2½-pound beef eye of round roast,**
   trimmed of separable fat

1 For stuffing, in a medium covered saucepan cook sweet pepper, carrot, onion, and garlic in hot margarine or butter until tender, stirring once or twice. Stir in desired herb and black pepper.

2 To butterfly roast, make a lengthwise cut down the center, cutting to within ½ inch of the opposite side. Spread open. At the center of each half, make 1 parallel slit to the right of the V and 1 to the left.

Cover with plastic wrap. Working from center to edges, pound with flat side of meat mallet to ½- to ¾-inch thickness. Remove plastic wrap.

3 Spread vegetable mixture on roast. Roll up from a short side. Tie with string. Place on a rack in a shallow roasting pan. Cover loosely with foil. Insert meat thermometer into center of roast. Roast in a 325° oven until thermometer registers 145° for medium rare (1½ to 1¾ hours) or 160° for medium (1¾ to 2 hours), uncovering the last 15 to 20 minutes to allow meat to brown. Remove from oven. Cover again with the foil; let stand 15 minutes before carving. Makes 10 to 12 servings.

Nutrition facts per serving: 149 calories, 5 g total fat (2 g saturated fat), 58 mg cholesterol, 55 mg sodium, 3 g carbohydrate, 1 g fiber, 22 g protein
Exchanges: 3 Lean Meat, 1 Vegetable

166 calories

Preparation time: 35 minutes ● **Marinating time:** 6 to 24 hours ● **Roasting time:** 1¼ hours ● **Standing time:** 15 minutes

mushroom-stuffed beef roast

Serve these juicy, fork-tender meat slices with steamed asparagus and roasted new potatoes sprinkled with lemon-pepper seasoning.

1   **2-pound beef eye of round roast, trimmed of separable fat**
¼   **cup dry white wine**
8   **ounces fresh mushrooms, finely chopped**
¼   **cup water**
¼   **teaspoon fennel seed or dried dillweed, crushed**
⅛   **teaspoon salt**
⅓   **cup thinly sliced green onions**
1   **tablespoon light mayonnaise dressing or salad dressing**
½   **cup light dairy sour cream**
4   **teaspoons all-purpose flour**
⅛   **teaspoon pepper**
½   **cup beef broth**

1 Cut 8 evenly spaced crosswise pockets or slits in roast, making each 2½ to 3 inches deep. Place roast in a plastic bag set in a deep bowl. Pour wine over roast. Seal bag. Marinate in the refrigerator for 6 to 24 hours, turning bag occasionally.

2 For filling, in medium saucepan combine mushrooms, water, fennel seed or dillweed, and salt. Cook, uncovered, over medium heat for 15 minutes or until liquid is evaporated. Cool. Stir in green onions and mayonnaise dressing or salad dressing.

3 Remove roast from bag; discard marinade. Place roast in a shallow roasting pan. Spoon filling into pockets of roast. Insert meat thermometer in center of roast. Bake, uncovered, in a 325° oven for 1¼ to 1½ hours or until thermometer registers 145°. Cover; let roast stand 15 minutes (temperature will rise 5°).

4 For sauce, in a small saucepan stir together the sour cream, flour, and pepper. Stir in broth. Cook and stir over medium heat until thickened and bubbly. Cook and stir for 1 minute more. Slice meat between filled pockets. Serve with sauce. Serves 8.

Nutrition facts per serving: 166 calories, 6 g total fat (2 g saturated fat), 56 mg cholesterol, 154 mg sodium, 5 g carbohydrate, 0 g fiber, 22 g protein
Exchanges: 3 Lean Meat, 1 Vegetable

259 calories

Preparation time: 30 minutes ● **Cooking time:** 1¾ hours

herbed sweet pepper pot roast

Fresh herbs make any dish more special. If you prefer to use fresh rather than dried herbs, always add them during the final stages of cooking to retain their optimal flavor.

Nonstick spray coating
1 **2½-pound boneless beef chuck roast, cut 2 inches thick and trimmed of separable fat**
2 **medium onions, sliced**
⅓ **cup water**
¼ **cup dry white wine**
1 **tablespoon Worcestershire sauce**
½ **teaspoon salt**
½ **teaspoon dried rosemary or oregano, crushed**
¼ **teaspoon black pepper**
1 **clove garlic, minced**
2 **medium green and/or red sweet peppers, cut into bite-size strips**
1 **tablespoon cornstarch**
1 **tablespoon cold water**

1 Spray a 4-quart Dutch oven with nonstick coating. Preheat over medium-high heat. Add meat; brown on all sides. Add onions, the ⅓ cup water, the wine, Worcestershire sauce, salt, rosemary or oregano, black pepper, and garlic. Heat to boiling; reduce heat.

2 Simmer, covered, for 1¾ to 2 hours or until meat is tender, adding the sweet peppers for the last 15 minutes of cooking. Transfer the meat and vegetables to a serving platter, reserving the juices in pan. Keep warm.

3 For sauce, skim fat from pan juices. Measure juices. If necessary, add enough water to measure 1 cup liquid. Return mixture to Dutch oven.

4 Stir together cornstarch and the 1 tablespoon cold water; stir into pan juices. Cook and stir until thickened and bubbly. Cook and stir for 2 minutes more. Serve with meat and vegetables. Makes 8 servings.

Nutrition facts per serving: 259 calories, 10 g total fat (4 g saturated fat), 103 mg cholesterol, 221 mg sodium, 4 g carbohydrate, 0 g fiber, 34 g protein
Exchanges: 4 Lean Meat, 1 Vegetable

230 calories

Preparation time: 25 minutes ● **Cooking time:** 1 hour and 10 minutes

beef–barley soup

*Barley is readily available in two forms—regular and quick-cooking. In this vegetable soup,
quick-cooking barley is added for the last 10 minutes of cooking time.*

1½ **pounds boneless beef chuck, trimmed of
    separable fat**
6 **cups water**
2 **cups sliced celery**
2 **cups sliced fresh mushrooms**
1 **cup sliced carrot**
1 **cup chopped onion**
½ **teaspoon salt**
1 **teaspoon dried rosemary, crushed**
½ **teaspoon pepper**
1 **clove garlic, minced**
1 **6-ounce can tomato paste**
½ **cup quick-cooking barley**

1 Cut meat into ¾-inch cubes. In a Dutch oven combine the meat, water, celery, mushrooms, carrot, onion, salt, rosemary, pepper, and garlic. Bring to boiling; reduce heat. Simmer, covered, for 1 to 1¼ hours or until meat is tender. If necessary, skim off fat.

2 Stir in tomato paste and barley. Return to boiling; reduce heat. Simmer, covered, about 10 minutes or until barley is tender. Makes 8 servings.

Nutrition facts per serving: 230 calories, 7 g total fat (2 g saturated fat), 62 mg cholesterol, 122 mg sodium, 19 g carbohydrate, 4 g fiber, 23 g protein
Exchanges: ½ Starch, 2 Lean Meat, 2 Vegetable

304 calories

Preparation time: 45 minutes ● **Marinating time:** 15 minutes ● **Cooking time:** 5 minutes

pineapple beef

Fresh gingerroot gives a pleasant pungency to this stir-fry. For longer storage, place the fresh unpeeled root in a freezer bag and freeze it. Grate or cut off what you need from the frozen root.

12 ounces beef top round steak, cut ½ inch thick and trimmed of separable fat
1 8-ounce can pineapple slices (juice-packed)
2 tablespoons reduced-sodium soy sauce
½ teaspoon grated fresh gingerroot or ⅛ teaspoon ground ginger
¼ teaspoon crushed red pepper Nonstick spray coating
4 green onions, cut into ½-inch pieces
1 tablespoon cornstarch
1 6-ounce package frozen pea pods
1 medium tomato, cut into wedges
2 cups hot cooked rice

1 Partially freeze meat about 30 minutes. Thinly slice meat across the grain into bite-size strips. Drain pineapple, reserving juice. Cut pineapple slices into quarters; set aside.

2 In a bowl stir together reserved pineapple juice, soy sauce, gingerroot, and crushed red pepper. Add the meat; stir until coated. Cover and marinate meat at room temperature for 15 minutes. Drain, reserving marinade.

3 Spray an unheated large nonstick skillet or wok with nonstick coating. Preheat over medium heat. Add meat and green onions. Stir-fry for 2 to 3 minutes or until meat is desired doneness. Push from center of skillet.

4 For sauce, stir cornstarch into reserved marinade. Add sauce to center of skillet. Cook and stir until thickened and bubbly. Add pineapple, pea pods, and tomato. Cook and stir 2 minutes more. Serve over hot cooked rice. Makes 4 servings.

Nutrition facts per serving: 304 calories, 5 g total fat (1 g saturated fat), 54 mg cholesterol, 311 mg sodium, 40 g carbohydrate, 2 g fiber, 25 g protein
Exchanges: 2 Starch, 2 Lean Meat, 2 Vegetable

274 calories

Preparation time: 20 minutes ● **Marinating time:** 4 hours ● **Broiling time:** 7 minutes

beef saté with peanut sauce

Saté (sah-TAY), an Indonesian dish, typically is skewered meat, poultry, or seafood served with a peanut sauce. It can be served as an appetizer. As a main dish, serve with pasta and grilled vegetables.

1 **pound lean boneless beef sirloin steak, cut
    1 inch thick and trimmed of separable fat**
1 **small onion, cut up**
2 **tablespoons reduced-sodium soy sauce**
2 **tablespoons lime juice**
1 **teaspoon sugar**
1 **teaspoon ground cumin**
1 **clove garlic, minced**
¼ **cup reduced-sodium chicken broth**
2 **tablespoons peanut butter**
1 **tablespoon molasses or honey**
1 **teaspoon reduced-sodium soy sauce**
¼ **to ½ teaspoon crushed red pepper**
1 **clove garlic, minced**

1 Cut beef into 1¼-inch pieces. Place in a plastic bag set in a deep bowl.

2 For marinade, in a food processor bowl or blender container place onion, the 2 tablespoons soy sauce, the lime juice, sugar, cumin, and 1 clove garlic. Cover; process or blend until smooth. Pour over meat in bag; close bag. Marinate meat in the refrigerator about 4 hours, turning bag occasionally.

3 For sauce, in a saucepan gradually stir broth into peanut butter. Stir in molasses, the 1 teaspoon soy sauce, crushed red pepper, and 1 clove garlic. Cook and stir until heated through. Keep warm.

4 Drain meat, discarding marinade. Thread meat onto 4 skewers, leaving ¼-inch space between pieces. Arrange skewers on the unheated rack of a broiler pan. Broil 3 to 4 inches from the heat for 7 to 9 minutes or to desired doneness, turning occasionally to brown evenly. Serve sauce with meat for dipping. Makes 4 servings.

Nutrition facts per serving: 274 calories, 14 g total fat (5 g saturated fat), 76 mg cholesterol, 313 mg sodium, 7 g carbohydrate, 1 g fiber, 29 g protein
Exchanges: 4 Medium-Fat Meat, 1 Vegetable, ½ Fat

366 calories

Preparation time: 25 minutes ● **Marinating time:** 2 to 8 hours ● **Grilling time:** 8 to 12 minutes

chutney beef kabobs

Experience the flavors of India—chutney, curry powder, ginger, and cumin—in these delicious kabobs. Papaya and chutney stirred into rice make an ordinary side dish a worthy accompaniment.

12 ounces boneless beef sirloin steak, cut
    1 inch thick and trimmed of separable fat
1 8-ounce can pineapple chunks
    (juice-packed)
⅓ cup mango chutney
1 teaspoon curry powder
½ teaspoon ground ginger
½ teaspoon ground cumin
¼ teaspoon black pepper
1 clove garlic, quartered
1 medium green sweet pepper, cut into
    1-inch pieces
2 cups hot cooked rice
½ cup chopped, seeded, and peeled papaya
2 tablespoons mango chutney, snipped

1 Cut meat into 1-inch pieces. Place in a plastic bag set in a deep bowl. For marinade, drain pineapple chunks; reserve juice. Cover; refrigerate pineapple. In a food processor bowl or blender container combine reserved juice, the ⅓ cup chutney, curry powder, ginger, cumin, black pepper, and garlic. Cover; process or blend until smooth. Pour over meat in bag; close bag. Marinate in refrigerator 2 to 8 hours, turning bag occasionally.

2 Drain beef, reserving marinade. On 4 long or 8 short metal skewers, alternately thread beef, pineapple chunks, and sweet pepper pieces, leaving about ¼-inch space between pieces.

3 Grill kabobs on the rack of an uncovered grill directly over medium coals to desired doneness, turning once and brushing frequently with reserved marinade during the first 4 minutes of grilling. (Allow 8 to 12 minutes for medium-rare and 12 to 15 minutes for medium.) Meanwhile, stir together the rice, papaya, and the 2 tablespoons snipped chutney. Heat through. Serve with kabobs. Serves 4.

Nutrition facts per serving: 366 calories, 8 g total fat (3 g saturated fat), 57 mg cholesterol, 51 mg sodium, 50 g carbohydrate, 2 g fiber, 22 g protein
Exchanges: 1½ Starch, 2 Lean Meat, 1 Vegetable, 1½ Fruit

269 calories

Preparation time: 50 minutes

beef stir-fry with noodles

*Be sure to buy the Japanese chuka soba noodles. Unlike many other Oriental noodles,
they're not fried. Look for them in Asian grocery stores.*

12 ounces boneless beef sirloin steak, trimmed
   of separable fat
 2 cups fresh pea pods
 3 tablespoons reduced-sodium soy sauce
 2 tablespoons rice vinegar
 1 teaspoon grated fresh gingerroot
 ½ teaspoon crushed red pepper
 4 ounces Oriental-style noodles (chuka soba)
   or dried linguine
   Nonstick spray coating
 2 cloves garlic, minced
 2 cups thinly sliced carrot
 6 green onions, bias-sliced into ½-inch pieces
 2 teaspoons cooking oil

1 Partially freeze meat about 30 minutes. Thinly slice across the grain into bite-size strips. Set aside. Remove ends from pea pods; halve pea pods diagonally. For sauce, in a small mixing bowl stir together soy sauce, rice vinegar, gingerroot, and crushed red pepper. Set aside.

2 Cook noodles according to package directions, except omit any oil and salt. Drain. Rinse with cold water. Drain. Set aside.

3 Spray an unheated large skillet or wok with nonstick coating. Preheat over medium-high heat. Stir-fry garlic in skillet or wok for 15 seconds. Add pea pods, carrot, and green onions. Stir-fry for 2 to 3 minutes more or until crisp-tender. Remove vegetables from wok or skillet.

4 Pour oil into hot wok or skillet. (If necessary, add more oil during cooking.) Add beef to wok or skillet. Stir-fry for 2 to 3 minutes or to desired doneness. Push beef from center of wok. Add sauce to center of wok. Add vegetables and cooked noodles. Cook and stir until heated through and coated with sauce. Serve immediately. Serves 5.

Nutrition facts per serving: 269 calories, 9 g total fat (3 g saturated fat), 65 mg cholesterol, 396 mg sodium, 25 g carbohydrate, 4 g fiber, 21 g protein
Exchanges: 1 Starch, 2 Lean Meat, 2 Vegetable, ½ Fat

279 calories

Preparation time: 25 minutes

steak with caramelized onions

Caramelized onions splashed with balsamic vinegar makes a full-flavored, lower-calorie alternative to a high-fat sauce. Another time serve the onions with grilled pork chops.

- **4 teaspoons margarine or butter**
- **2 medium onions, sliced**
- **2 cloves garlic, minced**
- **1 tablespoon brown sugar**
- **⅛ teaspoon salt**
- **1 pound boneless beef sirloin steak or top loin steak, cut 1 inch thick and trimmed of separable fat**
- **¼ teaspoon pepper**
- **1 tablespoon balsamic vinegar**
- **1 tablespoon snipped fresh parsley**

1 In a medium skillet melt margarine or butter over medium-low heat. Add onions and garlic. Cook, covered, for 13 to 15 minutes or until onions are tender. Add brown sugar and salt. Cook, uncovered, over medium-high heat 4 to 5 minutes or until onions are golden brown, stirring constantly.

2 Meanwhile, cut meat into 4 serving-size pieces. Sprinkle pepper on both sides of each meat piece. Place on the unheated rack of a broiler pan. Broil 3 inches from the heat to desired doneness, turning once. (Allow 10 to 12 minutes for medium rare or 12 to 15 minutes for medium.) Stir vinegar into onions. Spoon onion mixture over steak. Sprinkle with parsley. Makes 4 servings.

Nutrition facts per serving: 279 calories, 14 g total fat (5 g saturated fat), 76 mg cholesterol, 171 mg sodium, 10 g carbohydrate, 1 g fiber, 27 g protein
Exchanges: 3 Lean Meat, 2 Vegetable, 1 Fat

241 calories

Preparation time: 30 minutes

southwest skillet steaks

Cubed steaks are already tenderized before you buy them. They cook quickly, which makes them a great choice for meals you need to make in a hurry.

¼ **cup all-purpose flour**
¼ **teaspoon garlic salt**
¼ **teaspoon ground cumin**
⅛ **teaspoon ground red pepper**
4 **4-ounce lean beef cubed steaks**
 Nonstick spray coating
1 **14½-ounce can low-sodium tomatoes, cut up**
1 **4½-ounce can diced green chili peppers, drained**
⅓ **cup low-sodium tomato paste (½ of a 6-ounce can)**
1 **tablespoon snipped fresh oregano or 1 teaspoon dried oregano, crushed**
1 **teaspoon sugar**
¼ **teaspoon salt**
 Hot cooked noodles (optional)
 Yellow or green sweet pepper strips (optional)

1 In a shallow dish stir together the flour, garlic salt, cumin, and ground red pepper. Coat steaks with flour mixture, shaking off any excess. Spray an unheated 12-inch skillet with nonstick coating. Preheat over medium-high heat. Add steaks and cook for 8 to 12 minutes or until no pink remains. (Reduce heat as necessary to prevent burning while steaks cook.)

2 Meanwhile, in a medium saucepan combine tomatoes, chili peppers, tomato paste, oregano, sugar, and salt. Bring to boiling; reduce heat. Simmer, uncovered, about 5 minutes or until of desired consistency. Serve tomato mixture over meat. If desired, serve with hot cooked noodles and top with sweet pepper strips. Makes 4 servings.

Nutrition facts per serving: 241 calories, 7 g total fat (2 g saturated fat), 72 mg cholesterol, 421 mg sodium, 16 g carbohydrate, 2 g fiber, 30 g protein
Exchanges: 3 Lean Meat, 3 Vegetable

195 calories

Preparation time: 15 minutes ● **Marinating time:** 4 to 24 hours ● **Grilling time:** 12 minutes

steaks with piquant sauce

*Each steak is enough to serve two people. For a quick and filling side dish, stir chunky purchased salsa
into hot cooked rice or prepare Quick-to-Fix Spanish Rice, page 146.*

2 **beef top loin steaks, cut 1 inch thick and
trimmed of separable fat (about 1 pound
total)**
⅓ **cup red wine vinegar**
2 **tablespoons reduced-sodium soy sauce**
2 **cloves garlic, minced**
Nonstick spray coating
3 **tablespoons bottled chili sauce**
2 **tablespoons seedless raspberry spreadable
fruit**
1 **tablespoon orange juice or apple juice**
1½ **teaspoons brown mustard or spicy brown
mustard**

1 Cut meat into 4 serving-size portions. Place in
a plastic bag set in a shallow bowl. For marinade,
stir together the vinegar, soy sauce, and garlic. Pour
over meat. Close bag and marinate in the refrigerator
for 4 to 24 hours, turning bag occasionally.

2 Drain meat, discarding marinade. Spray
unheated grill rack with nonstick coating. Grill
steaks on prepared rack directly over medium coals
for 12 to 15 minutes or to desired doneness,
turning once. Keep warm while preparing sauce.

3 For sauce, in a small saucepan stir together
chili sauce, raspberry spreadable fruit, orange or
apple juice, and mustard. Cook and stir over low
heat until heated through and spreadable fruit is
melted. Serve over meat. Makes 4 servings.

Nutrition facts per serving: 195 calories, 7 g total fat
(3 g saturated fat), 64 mg cholesterol, 312 mg sodium,
10 g carbohydrate, 0 g fiber, 22 g protein
Exchanges: 3 Lean Meat, ½ Fruit

264 calories

Preparation time: 20 minutes ● **Marinating time:** 2 to 4 hours ● **Grilling time:** 12 minutes

summer vegetables and beef kabobs

A light lemon-basil marinade flavors the grilled steak and complements the summer vegetables.

12 **ounces boneless beef sirloin, cut 1 inch**
   thick and trimmed of separable fat
 2 **teaspoons finely shredded lemon peel**
 ⅓ **cup lemon juice**
 3 **tablespoons olive oil or cooking oil**
 1 **tablespoon honey**
1½ **teaspoons snipped fresh basil**
   or ½ teaspoon dried basil, crushed
 1 **teaspoon coarsely cracked black pepper**
 ¼ **teaspoon garlic salt**
 8 **ounces packaged, peeled baby carrots**
 1 **medium zucchini**
   Hot cooked couscous or rice (optional)

1 Cut meat into 1-inch cubes. Place in a plastic bag set in a shallow bowl.

2 For marinade, stir together lemon peel, lemon juice, oil, honey, basil, pepper, and garlic salt. Pour half of marinade over meat in bag. Close bag.

Marinate in refrigerator for 2 to 4 hours, turning bag occasionally. Cover remaining marinade; refrigerate.

3 Meanwhile, in a medium covered saucepan cook carrots in a small amount of *boiling water* for 3 minutes. Drain. Cut zucchini in half lengthwise; cut into ½-inch-thick slices.

4 Drain meat, discarding marinade. On 8 long metal skewers, alternately thread beef, carrots, and zucchini slices, leaving about ¼-inch space between pieces.

5 Grill on rack of uncovered grill directly over medium coals for 12 to 14 minutes or until meat is of desired doneness, turning once, brushing often with refrigerated marinade. If desired, serve with hot couscous or rice. Makes 4 servings.

Nutrition facts per serving: 264 calories, 15 g total fat (4 g saturated fat), 57 mg cholesterol, 170 mg sodium, 12 g carbohydrate, 2 g fiber, 20 g protein
Exchanges: 2 Lean Meat, 2 Vegetable, 2 Fat

368 calories

Preparation time: 30 minutes ● **Cooking time:** 35 minutes

beef pot pie

Pot pies don't have to be loaded with fat. This lean version uses a modest amount of meat but lots of vegetables to make up for it. A made-from-scratch biscuit topper makes up the crust.

12 ounces boneless beef sirloin steak, trimmed of separable fat
½ cup chopped onion
1 clove garlic, minced
1½ cups low-sodium vegetable juice
1 10-ounce package frozen mixed vegetables
¾ cup beef broth
1 teaspoon dried basil, crushed
½ teaspoon dried marjoram, crushed
¼ teaspoon pepper
1 cup all-purpose flour
3 tablespoons cornmeal
2 teaspoons sugar
1½ teaspoons baking powder
3 tablespoons shortening
⅓ cup skim milk
¼ cup plain fat-free yogurt

1 Cut meat into ¾-inch cubes. Spray an unheated large Dutch oven with *nonstick spray coating*. Preheat over medium-high heat. Add meat

and cook until brown. Remove meat from pan. Add onion and garlic to pan. Cook and stir until onion is tender. Stir in vegetable juice, frozen vegetables, beef broth, basil, marjoram, and pepper. Stir in meat. Bring to boiling; reduce heat. Simmer, covered, for 20 to 25 minutes or until vegetables are tender.

2 For topper, in a mixing bowl stir together flour, cornmeal, sugar, baking powder, and ⅛ teaspoon *salt*. Cut in shortening until mixture resembles coarse crumbs. Stir together milk and yogurt. Add to flour mixture. Stir just until combined.

3 Spoon hot meat mixture into a 2-quart casserole. Immediately drop the topper in small mounds onto hot mixture. Bake in a 450° oven for 15 to 20 minutes or until topper is golden brown. Makes 5 servings.

Nutrition facts per serving: 368 calories, 14 g total fat (5 g saturated fat), 46 mg cholesterol, 368 mg sodium, 38 g carbohydrate, 2 g fiber, 22 g protein
Exchanges: 1½ Starch, 2 Lean Meat, 3 Vegetable, 1 Fat

287 calories

Preparation time: 50 minutes ● **Cooking time:** 15 minutes

beef paprika with noodles

Using fat-free yogurt or sour cream in this dish creates a creamy, rich-flavored sauce that won't sabotage your diet.

1 **pound boneless beef sirloin, trimmed of separable fat**
  Nonstick spray coating
2 **teaspoons cooking oil**
3 **cups sliced fresh mushrooms**
1 **medium onion, sliced and separated into rings**
1 **clove garlic, minced**
1⅓ **cups water**
1 **tablespoon paprika**
1½ **teaspoons instant beef bouillon granules**
¼ **teaspoon pepper**
½ **cup plain fat-free yogurt or fat-free dairy sour cream**
2 **tablespoons all-purpose flour**
3 **cups hot cooked curly noodles or brown rice**
2 **tablespoons snipped fresh parsley**

1 Partially freeze meat about 30 minutes. Thinly slice across the grain into bite-size strips. Spray an unheated large skillet with nonstick coating. Preheat over medium-high heat. Quickly brown beef, half at a time, in skillet. Remove all meat from skillet. Add oil to skillet. Cook mushrooms, onion, and garlic in hot oil. Cook and stir until mushrooms are tender.

2 Add the water, paprika, bouillon granules, and pepper to the skillet. Return meat to the skillet. Bring to boiling; reduce heat. Simmer, covered, about 15 minutes or until meat is tender. Stir together yogurt or sour cream and flour. Add to mixture in skillet. Cook and stir until thickened and bubbly. Cook and stir for 1 minute more.

3 Toss together hot noodles or rice and parsley. Serve meat mixture on the noodle or rice mixture. Makes 6 servings.

Nutrition facts per serving: 287 calories, 10 g total fat (3 g saturated fat), 76 mg cholesterol, 273 mg sodium, 26 g carbohydrate, 3 g fiber, 23 g protein
Exchanges: 1 Starch, 2 Lean Meat, 2 Vegetable, ½ Fat

173 calories

Preparation time: 20 minutes ● **Grilling time:** 8 minutes

beef with mushroom - tomato sauce

For a more elegant dinner, make the Beef With Red Wine Sauce but grill 12 ounces of beef tenderloin instead of eye of round steaks. The grilling time remains the same.

⅛ teaspoon pepper
4 3-ounce beef eye of round steaks, trimmed of separable fat
1 cup sliced fresh mushrooms
½ cup sliced green onions
2 cloves garlic, minced
2 teaspoons margarine or butter
2 teaspoons cornstarch
⅔ cup low-sodium vegetable juice
½ teaspoon instant beef bouillon granules

1 Rub pepper over meat. Grill steaks on the rack of an uncovered grill directly over medium coals to desired doneness; turn once. (Allow 8 to 12 minutes for medium rare or 12 to 15 minutes for medium.)

2 Meanwhile, in a saucepan cook mushrooms, onions, and garlic in hot margarine or butter until vegetables are tender. Stir in cornstarch. Add vegetable juice and bouillon granules. Cook and stir

until thickened. Cook and stir for 2 minutes more. Keep warm while cooking meat. Serve sauce over meat. Makes 4 servings.

Broiling Directions: Place the meat on the unheated rack of a broiler pan. Broil 4 to 5 inches from the heat to desired doneness, turning once. (Allow 10 to 12 minutes for medium rare or 12 to 15 minutes for medium.)

Nutrition facts per serving: 173 calories, 8 g total fat (2 g saturated fat), 58 mg cholesterol, 172 mg sodium, 5 g carbohydrate, 0 g fiber, 20 g protein
Exchanges: 3 Lean Meat, 1 Vegetable

Beef With Red Wine Sauce: Prepare as directed above, except substitute ⅓ cup *dry red wine* plus ⅓ cup *water* for the vegetable juice.

Nutrition facts per serving: 179 calories, 8 g total fat (2 g saturated fat), 58 mg cholesterol, 175 mg sodium, 3 g carbohydrate, 0 g fiber, 20 g protein
Exchanges: 3 Lean Meat, 1 Vegetable

189 calories

Preparation time: 15 minutes ● **Grilling time:** 45 minutes ● **Standing time:** 15 minutes

herbed beef tenderloin

Indirect grilling allows roasts to cook slowly so they will be tender and juicy when done. Buy an inexpensive foil pan at the grocery store to use as a drip pan. The size will depend on your grill.

¼ **cup finely snipped fresh parsley**
2 **tablespoons Dijon-style mustard**
1 **tablespoon snipped fresh rosemary**
2 **teaspoons snipped fresh thyme**
2 **cloves garlic, minced**
1 **teaspoon olive oil or cooking oil**
½ **teaspoon coarsely ground black pepper**
1 **2-pound beef tenderloin roast, trimmed of
    separable fat**
½ **cup light dairy sour cream**
2 **teaspoons Dijon-style mustard**

1 In small mixing bowl stir together parsley, the 2 tablespoons mustard, the rosemary, thyme, garlic, oil, and pepper. Rub over top and sides of meat.

2 In a covered grill arrange hot coals around a drip pan. Test for medium-hot heat above the drip pan.* Place roast on grill rack over drip pan, but not over coals. Insert a meat thermometer in center of roast. Lower the grill hood. Grill about 45 minutes or until thermometer registers 140°. (Or, place meat on

a rack in a shallow roasting pan. Insert a meat thermometer into center of meat. Roast, uncovered, in a 325° oven for 30 to 45 minutes or until thermometer registers 140°.)

3 Cover meat with foil and let stand for 15 minutes (the temperature of the meat will rise 5° during standing).

4 Meanwhile, stir together sour cream and the 2 teaspoons mustard. Thinly slice meat. Serve with sour cream mixture. If desired, sprinkle with additional *black pepper*. Makes 8 servings.

*Note: To check for medium heat, hold your hand, palm side down, over where the meat will cook and at about the same height of the meat. The heat is right when you can hold your hand there for only 3 seconds.

Nutrition facts per serving: 189 calories, 9 g total fat (3 g saturated fat), 66 mg cholesterol, 193 mg sodium, 3 g carbohydrate, 0 g fiber, 23 g protein
Exchanges: 3 Lean Meat

226 calories

Preparation time: 35 minutes

asparagus and beef dijon

Elegant, simple, delicious, and low in calories—what more can you ask for?

2 **teaspoons whole black pepper**
1 **pound beef flank steak, trimmed of**
    separable fat
1 **pound fresh asparagus or one 10-ounce**
    package frozen asparagus spears
1 **cup sliced fresh mushrooms**
¼ **cup thinly sliced green onions**
¼ **cup water**
½ **teaspoon instant beef bouillon granules**
⅓ **cup light dairy sour cream**
1 **tablespoon all-purpose flour**
2 **teaspoons Dijon-style mustard**

1 Coarsely crack the black pepper. Rub pepper into both sides of the steak. Place steak on the unheated rack of a broiler pan. Broil 3 inches from heat for 6 minutes. Turn steak over and broil for 6 to 8 minutes more or to desired doneness.

2 Meanwhile, snap off and discard woody bases from fresh asparagus. In a covered saucepan cook fresh asparagus in a small amount of *boiling water* for 4 to 6 minutes or until crisp-tender. (Or, cook frozen asparagus according to the package directions.) Drain. Keep warm.

3 For sauce, in a medium saucepan combine mushrooms, green onions, water, and bouillon granules. Cook, covered, over medium heat about 5 minutes or until mushrooms are tender. Stir together sour cream, flour, and mustard. Stir sour cream mixture into mushroom mixture. Cook and stir until thickened and bubbly. Cook and stir for 1 minute more.

4 To serve, thinly slice meat diagonally across the grain. Arrange meat slices and asparagus on dinner plates. Serve with sauce. Makes 4 servings.

Nutrition facts per serving: 226 calories, 10 g total fat (4 g saturated fat), 56 mg cholesterol, 264 mg sodium, 9 g carbohydrate, 2 g fiber, 26 g protein
Exchanges: 3 Lean Meat, 2 Vegetable

189 calories

Preparation time: 20 minutes ● **Grilling time:** 12 minutes

grilled flank steak with chili sauce

Score the flank steak on both sides by making shallow diagonal cuts about 1 inch apart in a diamond pattern. This tenderizes the steak and allows the sauce to penetrate the meat.

1 cup chopped onion
4 cloves garlic, minced
2 teaspoons chili powder
1 8-ounce can low-sodium tomato sauce
⅓ cup vinegar
2 tablespoons honey
½ teaspoon salt
¼ teaspoon pepper
1¼ pounds beef flank steak, trimmed of separable fat

1 For sauce, in a medium saucepan cook onion, garlic, and chili powder in ½ cup *water* until tender. Stir in tomato sauce, vinegar, honey, salt, and pepper. Bring to boiling, stirring constantly. Boil for 5 minutes or until sauce is slightly thickened.

2 Meanwhile, score meat by making shallow diagonal cuts on both sides. Brush lightly with sauce. Grill steak on the rack of an uncovered grill directly over medium coals* for 7 minutes. Turn;

brush lightly with sauce. Grill to desired doneness, allowing 5 to 7 minutes more for medium. In a small saucepan bring remaining sauce to boiling. To serve, thinly slice the flank steak across the grain. Pass remaining sauce. Makes 6 servings.

Broiling Directions: Place meat on unheated rack of a broiler pan. Brush lightly with sauce. Broil 3 inches from the heat for 6 minutes. Turn; brush lightly with sauce. Broil to desired doneness, allowing 6 to 8 minutes more for medium.

*****Note:** To check for medium heat, hold your hand, palm side down, over where the meat will cook and at about the same height of the meat. The heat is right when you can hold your hand there for only 3 seconds.

Nutrition facts per serving: 189 calories, 7 g total fat (3 g saturated fat), 44 mg cholesterol, 254 mg sodium, 13 g carbohydrate, 1 g fiber, 19 g protein
Exchanges: ½ Starch, 2 Lean Meat, 1 Vegetable

320 calories

Preparation time: 10 minutes ● **Broiling time:** 12 minutes

mustard-pepper steak sandwiches

Save calories by serving this sandwich open-face. Use a knife and fork for easier eating.

2 tablespoons Dijon-style mustard
1 teaspoon brown sugar
½ teaspoon coarsely cracked black pepper
1 clove garlic, minced
1 pound beef flank steak, trimmed of
　　separable fat
3 hoagie rolls, split and toasted
1 cup shredded lettuce
　 Thinly sliced tomato
　 Dijon-style mustard (optional)

1 In a small mixing bowl stir together mustard, brown sugar, pepper, and garlic. Set aside.

2 Place meat on the unheated rack of a broiler pan. Brush with some of the mustard mixture. Broil 4 to 5 inches from the heat for 6 minutes. Turn and brush the steak with the remaining mustard mixture. Broil to desired doneness, allowing 6 to 8 minutes more for medium.

3 To serve, thinly slice meat diagonally across the grain. Top each hoagie half with some of the lettuce and sliced tomato. Layer meat slices on each sandwich. If desired, serve with additional mustard. Makes 6 servings.

Nutrition facts per serving: 320 calories, 8 g total fat (3 g saturated fat), 35 mg cholesterol, 554 mg sodium, 40 g carbohydrate, 2 g fiber, 21 g protein
Exchanges: 2 Starch, 2 Lean Meat, 1 Vegetable

202 calories

Preparation time: 20 minutes ● **Broiling time:** 10 minutes

spinach-stuffed flank steak

Dried tomatoes pack a flavorful punch. To save on calories and fat, choose those that are not packed in oil. Just soften the tomatoes in hot water for 10 minutes before using.

¼ **cup dried tomatoes (not oil packed)**
1 **1-pound beef flank steak or top round steak, trimmed of separable fat**
⅛ **teaspoon salt**
⅛ **teaspoon pepper**
1 **10-ounce package frozen chopped spinach, thawed and well drained**
2 **tablespoons grated Parmesan cheese**
2 **tablespoons snipped fresh basil**

1 In a small bowl soak dried tomatoes in enough *hot water* to cover for 10 minutes. Drain. Snip into small pieces.

2 Meanwhile, score meat by making shallow diagonal cuts at 1-inch intervals in a diamond pattern on both sides. Place meat between 2 pieces of plastic wrap. Working from center to edges, pound with flat side of a meat mallet into 12×8-inch rectangle. Remove plastic wrap. Sprinkle with the salt and pepper.

3 Spread the spinach over the steak. Sprinkle with the softened tomatoes, Parmesan cheese, and basil. Roll the steak up from a short side. Secure with wooden toothpicks at 1-inch intervals, starting ½ inch from 1 end. Cut between the toothpicks into eight 1-inch-thick slices.

4 Place slices, cut sides down, on the unheated rack of a broiler pan. Broil 3 to 4 inches from the heat to desired doneness, turning once. (Allow 10 to 12 minutes for medium-rare or 12 to 16 minutes for medium.) Before serving, remove the toothpicks. Makes 4 servings.

Nutrition facts per serving: 202 calories, 9 g total fat (4 g saturated fat), 56 mg cholesterol, 303 mg sodium, 5 g carbohydrate, 0 g fiber, 25 g protein
Exchanges: 3 Lean Meat, 1 Vegetable

167 calories

Preparation time: 10 minutes ● **Cooking time:** 13 minutes

veal with apple - marsala sauce

Veal may be labeled "scaloppine" in your supermarket meat section. Scaloppine technically describes a thin scallop of meat that is quickly sautéed. It is generally cut ⅛ inch thick and does not need to be pounded.

Nonstick spray coating
12 ounces veal scaloppine or boneless veal leg round steak or beef top round steak,* cut ¼ inch thick and trimmed of separable fat
1 apple, thinly sliced
1 clove garlic, minced
½ cup dry Marsala
⅓ cup reduced-sodium chicken broth
1 tablespoon snipped fresh parsley

1 Spray an unheated large skillet with nonstick coating. Preheat over medium-high heat. Cook meat, half at a time, for 4 to 5 minutes or until no pink remains, turning once. Transfer to a serving platter. Keep warm.

2 Add sliced apple and garlic to skillet. Stir in Marsala and chicken broth. Bring to boiling; reduce heat. Boil gently, uncovered, for 4 to 5 minutes or until mixture is reduced by half. Spoon over meat. Sprinkle with parsley. Makes 4 servings.

*Note: If using round or beef steak, cut steak into 8 pieces. Place 1 piece of the cut steak between 2 pieces of plastic wrap. Working from center to edges, pound with flat side of meat mallet to ⅛-inch thickness. Remove plastic wrap. Repeat with remaining meat.

Nutrition facts per serving: 167 calories, 4 g total fat (1 g saturated fat), 69 mg cholesterol, 100 mg sodium, 7 g carbohydrate, 1 g fiber, 19 g protein
Exchanges: 2 Lean Meat, ½ Fruit

246 calories

Preparation time: 30 minutes

veal scaloppine

When pounding veal with a meat mallet, be sure to use the flat side. The ridged sides are for tenderizing tougher cuts of meat and would tear apart the delicate veal.

12 ounces boneless veal leg round steak or veal leg sirloin steak or beef top round steak, cut ¼ inch thick and trimmed of separable fat

½ cup chopped onion

2 cloves garlic, minced

¼ cup water

1 14½-ounce can tomatoes, undrained and cut up

3 tablespoons dry white wine

1 tablespoon snipped fresh oregano or 1 teaspoon dried oregano, crushed

1 tablespoon capers, drained (optional)

⅛ teaspoon pepper

Nonstick spray coating

2 cups hot cooked noodles

1 Cut meat into 8 pieces. Place 1 piece of meat between 2 pieces of plastic wrap. Working from center to edges, pound with flat side of meat mallet to about ⅛-inch thickness. Remove plastic wrap. Sprinkle meat lightly with *salt* and *pepper*. Repeat with remaining meat. Set aside.

2 For sauce, in a medium covered saucepan cook onion and garlic in the water until onion is tender. Stir in undrained tomatoes, wine, oregano, capers (if desired), and pepper. Bring to boiling; reduce heat. Simmer, uncovered, about 15 minutes or to desired consistency. Keep warm.

3 Meanwhile, spray an unheated large skillet with nonstick coating. Preheat over medium-high heat. Cook meat, half at a time, for 2 to 4 minutes or to desired doneness, turning once. Transfer meat to a serving platter. Keep warm.

4 To serve, spoon sauce over meat. Serve with hot cooked noodles. Makes 4 servings.

Nutrition facts per serving: 246 calories, 5 g total fat (1 g saturated fat), 94 mg cholesterol, 216 mg sodium, 25 g carbohydrate, 3 g fiber, 23 g protein
Exchanges: 1 Starch, 2 Lean Meat, 2 Vegetable

Pork
& HAM

chapter index

201 calories

Preparation time: 30 minutes

pork chops with italian vegetables

Cook the vegetables in a skillet while the chops are broiling. Fresh basil and oregano add the Italian touch.

1 **tablespoon frozen orange juice
concentrate, thawed**
1 **clove garlic, minced**
⅛ **teaspoon pepper**
4 **boneless pork loin chops, cut ½ inch thick
and trimmed of separable fat (about
1¼ pounds total)**
Nonstick spray coating
2 **medium zucchini and/or yellow summer
squash, cut into thin strips**
1 **small green and/or red sweet pepper, cut
into strips**
1 **small onion, sliced**
2 **teaspoons snipped fresh basil
or ¾ teaspoon dried basil, crushed**
1 **teaspoon snipped fresh oregano
or ½ teaspoon dried oregano, crushed**
⅛ **teaspoon salt**
8 **cherry tomatoes, halved**

1 Combine orange juice concentrate, garlic, and pepper. Set aside.

2 Place chops on the unheated rack of a broiler pan. Broil 3 to 4 inches from the heat for 5 minutes. Brush with orange juice mixture. Turn and broil about 5 minutes more or until chops are just slightly pink in center and juices run clear. Brush with remaining orange juice mixture.

3 Meanwhile, spray an unheated large skillet with nonstick coating. Add zucchini, sweet pepper, onion, dried basil (if using), dried oregano (if using), and salt. Cook and stir over medium-high heat for 4 minutes or until vegetables are crisp-tender. Stir in tomato halves and fresh basil and oregano (if using). Reduce heat; cover and cook for 1 minute more. Serve vegetables with pork chops. Makes 4 servings.

Nutrition facts per serving: 201 calories, 8 g total fat (3 g saturated fat), 71 mg cholesterol, 138 mg sodium, 8 g carbohydrate, 2 g fiber, 24 g protein
Exchanges: 3 Lean Meat, 2 Vegetable

223 calories

Preparation time: 20 minutes ● **Broiling time:** 8 minutes

spiced pear and pork chops

If you don't have pumpkin pie spice on hand, substitute a combination of ⅛ teaspoon each of ground ginger, cinnamon, nutmeg, and cloves.

1 cup pear nectar or white grape juice
½ cup coarsely chopped onion
1 teaspoon instant chicken bouillon granules
½ teaspoon pumpkin pie spice
2 medium pears, cored and sliced
4 pork loin chops, cut ½ inch thick and trimmed of separable fat (about 1¼ pounds total)

1 In a medium saucepan combine pear nectar or white grape juice, onion, bouillon granules, and pumpkin pie spice. Bring to boiling. Add pear slices. Return to boiling; reduce heat. Simmer, covered, for 3 to 4 minutes or until crisp-tender.

2 Using a slotted spoon, remove pear slices and onion from the saucepan. Keep warm.

3 Gently boil juice mixture in saucepan, uncovered, for 3 to 5 minutes or until reduced to ½ cup.

4 Meanwhile, place chops on the unheated rack of a broiler pan. Broil 3 to 4 inches from the heat for 4 minutes. Brush with some of the juice mixture. Turn and broil 4 to 6 minutes more or until pork is slightly pink in center and juices run clear. Brush again with some of the juice mixture.

5 To serve, place chops on a serving platter. Top with pear and onion mixture. Drizzle with any remaining juice mixture. Makes 4 servings.

Nutrition facts per serving: 223 calories, 8 g total fat (3 g saturated fat), 48 mg cholesterol, 256 mg sodium, 24 g carbohydrate, 3 g fiber, 15 g protein
Exchanges: 2 Lean Meat, 1½ Fruit

Spiced Apple and Pork Chops: Prepare as above, except substitute *apple juice* or *apple cider* for the pear nectar and 2 medium *apples* for the pears.

Nutrition facts per serving: 198 calories, 8 g total fat (3 g saturated fat), 48 mg cholesterol, 255 mg sodium, 17 g carbohydrate, 2 g fiber, 14 g protein
Exchanges: 2 Lean Meat, 1½ Fruit

193 calories

Preparation time: 25 minutes

pork chops in creamy vegetable sauce

This cream sauce combines reduced-fat soup and fat-free sour cream, which provides a seemingly high-fat richness that won't give its real secret away.

Nonstick spray coating
6 **pork rib chops, cut ½ inch thick and trimmed of separable fat (about 1¾ pounds total)**
1½ **cups sliced fresh mushrooms**
1 **medium green or red sweet pepper, cut into thin strips**
1 **10¾-ounce can condensed reduced-fat and reduced-sodium cream of mushroom soup**
½ **cup fat-free dairy sour cream**
¼ **cup skim milk**
1 **teaspoon paprika**
1 **medium tomato, seeded and chopped**
3 **cups hot cooked noodles or rice (optional)**

1 Spray an unheated 12-inch skillet with nonstick coating. Preheat over medium heat. Add pork chops; cook for 6 minutes. Turn chops; add mushrooms and sweet pepper. Cook about 6 minutes more or until pork is slightly pink in center and juices run clear. Remove chops and vegetables.

2 Meanwhile, for sauce, in a small mixing bowl stir together soup, sour cream, milk, and paprika. Stir mixture into skillet; heat to boiling.

3 Return chops and vegetables to skillet. Cook, covered, for 5 minutes. Add tomato. Cook for 1 to 2 minutes more or until heated through. If desired, serve with hot cooked noodles. Makes 6 servings.

Nutrition facts per serving: 193 calories, 9 g total fat (3 g saturated fat), 50 mg cholesterol, 264 mg sodium, 11 g carbohydrate, 1 g fiber, 17 g protein
Exchanges: ½ Starch, 2 Medium-Fat Meat, 1 Vegetable

152 calories

Preparation time: 20 minutes • **Cooking time:** 30 minutes

curried pork chops with oranges

A touch of honey mellows the tanginess of the orange and the spiciness of the curry.

2 **pork sirloin chops, cut ½ inch thick
   and trimmed of separable fat
   (about 1¼ pounds total)**
   Nonstick spray coating
½ **cup orange juice**
1 **tablespoon honey**
1 **to 1½ teaspoons curry powder**
⅛ **teaspoon salt**
2 **oranges**
1 **tablespoon cold water**
2 **teaspoons cornstarch**
1 **tablespoon snipped fresh chives or parsley**

1 Cut each chop in half. Spray an unheated large skillet with nonstick coating. Preheat over medium-high heat. Add pork chops and brown on both sides. Drain off fat.

2 Add orange juice, honey, curry powder, and salt to skillet. Bring to boiling; reduce heat. Simmer, covered, for 30 to 40 minutes or until pork is slightly pink in center and juices run clear.

3 Meanwhile, peel oranges. Slice crosswise, then halve circular slices. Set aside. Remove chops, reserving pan juices in skillet. Keep chops warm.

4 Combine cold water and cornstarch; add to pan juices. Cook and stir until thickened and bubbly. Cook and stir for 2 minutes more. Add orange slices and chives; heat through. Spoon over pork chops. Makes 4 servings.

Nutrition facts per serving: 152 calories, 5 g total fat
(1 g saturated fat), 36 mg cholesterol, 87 mg sodium,
17 g carbohydrate, 2 g fiber, 12 g protein
Exchanges: 2 Lean Meat, 1 Fruit

203 calories

Preparation time: 35 minutes ● **Grilling time:** 12 minutes

sweet-and-sour pork kabobs

Try pork tenderloin or loin chops for these kabobs. They're both boneless and lean cuts.
Serve the kabobs with couscous, which adds 57 calories (1 Starch) per ½ cup serving.

2 **medium carrots, bias-sliced into 1-inch**
    pieces
1 **8-ounce can pineapple slices (juice-packed)**
⅓ **cup wine vinegar**
2 **tablespoons reduced-sodium soy sauce**
1 **tablespoon cooking oil**
2 **teaspoons cornstarch**
1 **teaspoon sugar**
1 **clove garlic, minced**
2 **small green and/or red sweet peppers, cut**
    into 1-inch squares
12 **ounces lean boneless pork, cut into**
    1-inch pieces
    Hot cooked couscous (optional)

1 In a covered saucepan cook carrots in a small amount of *boiling water* for 8 minutes; drain well. Drain pineapple, reserving juice. Cut pineapple slices into quarters; set aside.

2 For sauce, in a saucepan combine reserved pineapple juice, vinegar, soy sauce, oil, cornstarch, sugar, and garlic. Cook and stir until thickened and bubbly. Cook and stir for 2 minutes more.

3 Thread carrots, pineapple, sweet peppers, and pork on 8 short or 4 long skewers, leaving about ¼ inch between pieces. Brush with sauce.

4 Grill kabobs on an uncovered grill directly over medium coals for 12 to 14 minutes or until pork is slightly pink in center and juices run clear. (Or, broil 4 to 5 inches from the heat for 15 to 18 minutes.) Turn the kabobs once and brush frequently with sauce during the first half of cooking time. If desired, serve over hot cooked couscous. Makes 4 servings.

Nutrition facts per serving: 203 calories, 9 g total fat (2 g saturated fat), 38 mg cholesterol, 318 mg sodium, 19 g carbohydrate, 2 g fiber, 14 g protein
Exchanges: 1½ Lean Meat, 1 Vegetable, 1 Fruit, 1 Fat

260 calories

Preparation time: 50 minutes

pork and broccoli stir-fry

Sweet and piquant, hoisin sauce adds a sweet-spicy flavor to this stir-fry. Hoisin sauce, also called Peking sauce, is available in most grocery stores. Look for it in a jar next to the soy sauce.

8 ounces lean boneless pork
¾ cup reduced-sodium chicken broth
3 tablespoons hoisin sauce
1 tablespoon cornstarch
1 tablespoon dry sherry (optional)
⅛ teaspoon crushed red pepper
  Nonstick spray coating
1 medium onion, sliced
1 10-ounce package frozen cut broccoli,
  thawed and well drained
1 clove garlic, minced
½ teaspoon grated fresh gingerroot
1 teaspoon cooking oil
½ cup sliced water chestnuts
2 cups hot cooked rice

1 Partially freeze meat (about 30 minutes). Thinly slice across the grain into bite-size strips.

2 Meanwhile, stir together broth, hoisin sauce, cornstarch, sherry (if using), and red pepper.

3 Spray an unheated wok or large skillet with nonstick coating. Preheat over medium-high heat. Add onion, broccoli, garlic, and gingerroot. Stir-fry for 3 minutes or until vegetables are crisp-tender. Remove vegetable mixture from wok.

4 Add the oil to hot wok. Add pork. Stir-fry for 2 to 3 minutes or until no pink remains. Push pork from center of wok.

5 Stir sauce and pour into the center of wok. Cook and stir until thickened and bubbly.

6 Return vegetables to wok. Stir in water chestnuts. Cook and stir for 2 minutes more. Serve with hot cooked rice. Makes 4 servings.

Nutrition facts per serving: 260 calories, 6 g total fat (2 g saturated fat), 26 mg cholesterol, 394 mg sodium, 38 g carbohydrate, 2 g fiber, 13 g protein
Exchanges: 1½ Starch, 1 Lean Meat, 2 Vegetable

304 calories

Preparation time: 30 minutes ● **Cooking time:** 10 minutes

fruited pork stew

Prunes or dried apples lend a sweetness to this perfect autumn stew. Cardamom, an aromatic spice related to ginger, adds a pungent sweet-spicy flavor.

Nonstick spray coating
12 **ounces lean boneless pork, cut into**
   ½-inch cubes
1 **medium onion, cut into thin wedges**
1 **clove garlic, minced**
½ **cup pitted prunes or dried apples, halved**
1 **cup water**
¼ **to ½ teaspoon ground cardamom**
   (optional)
¼ **teaspoon salt**
¼ **teaspoon ground cinnamon**
1 **18-ounce can sweet potatoes, cut up**
¾ **cup apple juice**
1 **tablespoon cornstarch**

1 Spray an unheated large skillet with nonstick coating. Preheat over medium-high heat. Add pork cubes, onion, and garlic. Cook, stirring frequently, until pork is brown on all sides. Drain off fat.

2 Stir in prunes or apples, water, cardamom (if desired), salt, and cinnamon. Bring to boiling; reduce heat. Simmer, covered, for 10 to 15 minutes or until pork is tender and no pink remains. Stir in sweet potatoes.

3 Stir together apple juice and cornstarch. Stir into skillet; cook and stir until thickened and bubbly. Cook and stir for 2 minutes more. Makes 4 servings.

Nutrition facts per serving: 304 calories, 6 g total fat (2 g saturated fat), 38 mg cholesterol, 235 mg sodium, 49 g carbohydrate, 5 g fiber, 15 g protein
Exchanges: 1 Starch, 2 Lean Meat, 2 Fruit

262 calories

Preparation time: 1 hour

creole-style pork

*Although this saucy dish has the the taste of New Orleans, it is stir-fried Oriental style,
which makes it easy to cook and quick to clean up.*

12 **ounces lean boneless pork**
 1 **cup tomato juice**
 1 **tablespoon cornstarch**
 1 **teaspoon chili powder**
 1 **teaspoon lemon juice**
 ½ **teaspoon sugar**
 ⅛ **to ¼ teaspoon ground red pepper**
    Nonstick spray coating
 2 **cups fresh green beans cut into 1-inch**
    pieces, or one 9-ounce package frozen
    cut green beans, thawed
 1 **cup sliced celery**
 1 **medium green or red sweet pepper,**
    cut into ½-inch squares
 1 **to 2 teaspoons cooking oil (optional)**
 2 **cups hot cooked rice**

1 Partially freeze meat about 30 minutes. Thinly slice across the grain into bite-size strips. For sauce, stir together ¼ cup *water,* tomato juice, cornstarch, chili powder, lemon juice, sugar, and red pepper.

2 Spray an unheated wok or 12-inch skillet with nonstick coating. Preheat over medium-high heat. Add fresh green beans (if using). Stir-fry for 3 minutes. Add celery. Stir-fry for 2 minutes. Add sweet pepper and thawed frozen beans (if using). Stir-fry about 1½ minutes more or until vegetables are crisp-tender. Remove from wok.

3 If necessary, add oil to hot wok. Add pork. Stir-fry for 2 to 3 minutes or until no pink remains. Push pork from center of wok.

4 Stir sauce; add to center of wok. Cook and stir until thickened and bubbly. Return vegetables to wok; stir to coat. Cook and stir for 2 minutes more. Serve with hot cooked rice. Makes 4 servings.

Nutrition facts per serving: 262 calories, 6 g total fat (2 g saturated fat), 38 mg cholesterol, 282 mg sodium, 36 g carbohydrate, 3 g fiber, 16 g protein
Exchanges: 1½ Starch, 2 Lean Meat, 2 Vegetable

346 calories

Preparation time: 18 minutes ● **Cooking time:** 15 minutes

barbecued pork sandwiches

*Spiked with a chili powder, these saucy pork sandwiches come together
in no time. For ease, use leftover pork roast.*

½ **cup chopped onion**
½ **cup chopped carrot**
⅓ **cup water**
¼ **cup catsup**
2 **tablespoons vinegar**
1 **tablespoon Worcestershire sauce**
1 **teaspoon brown sugar**
1 **teaspoon chili powder**
⅛ **teaspoon pepper**
12 **ounces lean cooked pork, cut into bite-size
   strips (about 2 cups)**
½ **cup sliced celery**
1 **tablespoon cold water**
1½ **teaspoons cornstarch**
4 **whole wheat hamburger buns, split and
   toasted**

1 In a 2-quart saucepan stir together the onion, carrot, the ⅓ cup water, catsup, vinegar, Worcestershire sauce, brown sugar, chili powder, and pepper.

2 Bring mixture to boiling; reduce heat. Simmer, covered, for 10 minutes.

3 Stir in pork and celery. Simmer, covered, for 5 minutes more or until heated through; stir once.

4 Stir together the 1 tablespoon cold water and the cornstarch. Stir into meat mixture. Cook and stir until thickened and bubbly. Cook and stir for 2 minutes more. To serve, spoon into hamburger buns. Makes 4 servings.

Nutrition facts per serving: 346 calories, 10 g total fat (3 g saturated fat), 84 mg cholesterol, 575 mg sodium, 33 g carbohydrate, 4 g fiber, 32 g protein
Exchanges: 2 Starch, 3½ Lean Meat

213 calories

Preparation time: 35 minutes ● **Cooking time:** 50 minutes

country-style pork stew

Chock-full of vegetables, this richly flavored stew is a complete meal in a bowl.

12 ounces boneless pork shoulder, trimmed of
  separable fat
  Nonstick spray coating
1¼ cups water
1¼ teaspoons instant chicken bouillon
  granules
  1 14½-ounce can tomatoes, undrained and
  cut up
  2 small onions, cut into wedges
  ½ cup sliced celery
  1 teaspoon dried oregano, crushed
  1 teaspoon ground cumin
  2 cloves garlic, minced
  1 bay leaf
  1 cup yellow summer squash or zucchini cut
  into ½-inch-thick slices
  1 9-ounce package frozen cut green beans
  1 tablespoon cold water
  1 tablespoon cornstarch

1 Cut meat into 1-inch cubes. Spray an unheated Dutch oven or large saucepan with nonstick coating. Preheat over medium-high heat. Add pork; cook, stirring frequently, until browned on all sides. Drain off fat.

2 Add the 1¼ cups water and the bouillon granules. Stir in the undrained tomatoes, onions, celery, oregano, cumin, garlic, and bay leaf. Bring to boiling; reduce heat. Simmer, covered, for 45 to 60 minutes or until pork is tender and no pink remains. Discard bay leaf.

3 Stir in squash and green beans. Return to boiling; reduce heat. Simmer, covered, for 5 minutes more. Stir together the 1 tablespoon cold water and the cornstarch. Stir into pork mixture. Cook and stir until thickened and bubbly. Cook and stir for 2 minutes more. Makes 4 servings.

Nutrition facts per serving: 213 calories, 10 g total fat (3 g saturated fat), 56 mg cholesterol, 508 mg sodium, 15 g carbohydrate, 2 g fiber, 18 g protein
Exchanges: 2 Medium-Fat Meat, 3 Vegetable

166 calories

Preparation time: 15 minutes ● **Roasting time:** 25 minutes ● **Standing time:** 15 minutes

roast pork and cabbage

Dillseed refers to the small, hard, dried seeds of the dill plant. Compared to the leaves from the plant, the seeds have a stronger, slightly pungent flavor.

12 ounces pork tenderloin, trimmed of separable fat
⅛ teaspoon pepper
6 cups shredded cabbage
1 large onion, sliced
⅔ cup shredded carrot
⅓ cup water
2 tablespoons vinegar
1 teaspoon dillseed, crushed
¼ teaspoon salt
⅛ teaspoon pepper

1 Sprinkle pork with the ⅛ teaspoon pepper. Place pork on a rack in a shallow roasting pan and insert a meat thermometer. Roast, uncovered, in a 425° oven for 25 to 35 minutes or until the thermometer registers 160°. Cover pork with foil; let stand for 15 minutes before carving (the temperature will rise 5° during standing).

2 Meanwhile, in a large saucepan combine cabbage, onion, carrot, water, vinegar, dillseed, salt, and ⅛ teaspoon pepper. Bring to boiling; reduce heat. Simmer, covered, for 8 to 10 minutes or until vegetables are just tender.

3 Slice pork and serve with vegetables. Makes 4 servings.

Nutrition facts per serving: 166 calories, 4 g total fat (1 g saturated fat), 60 mg cholesterol, 224 mg sodium, 14 g carbohydrate, 7 g fiber, 21 g protein
Exchanges: 2 Lean Meat, 3 Vegetable

174 calories

Preparation time: 30 minutes

peach-sauced pork

Serve the tender slices of pork and plump peach slices over rice for an extra-special dinner. Steamed broccoli or asparagus adds a pretty contrast of green to the yellow peaches.

12 **ounces pork tenderloin, trimmed of
     separable fat
     Nonstick spray coating**
 1 **16-ounce can peach slices in light syrup**
 ¼ **cup cold water**
1½ **teaspoons cornstarch**
 ¼ **teaspoon salt**
 ⅛ **teaspoon ground allspice
     Hot cooked rice (optional)**

1 Cut pork crosswise into about sixteen ½-inch-thick slices. Place 1 slice of pork between 2 pieces of plastic wrap. Working from the center to the edges, pound lightly with flat side of a meat mallet to ¼-inch thickness. Remove plastic wrap. Repeat with remaining pork slices.

2 Spray an unheated large skillet with nonstick coating. Preheat skillet over medium heat. Add half of the pork and cook about 4 minutes or until tender and juices run clear, turning once. Remove pork from skillet; keep warm. Repeat with remaining pork. Carefully wipe skillet with a paper towel.

3 Meanwhile, drain peaches, reserving ½ cup syrup. Set peaches aside. In a small bowl stir together the reserved syrup, the water, cornstarch, salt, and allspice. Add mixture to skillet. Cook and stir until thickened and bubbly. Cook and stir for 2 minutes more. Add the pork and peaches to skillet; heat through. If desired, serve with rice. Makes 4 servings.

Nutrition facts per serving: 174 calories, 3 g total fat (1 g saturated fat), 60 mg cholesterol, 183 mg sodium, 17 g carbohydrate, 1 g fiber, 19 g protein
Exchanges: 2 Lean Meat, 1 Fruit

156 calories

Preparation time: 40 minutes

pork with tarragon vegetables

Thin strips of carrot and celery combine well with the distinctive, anise- or licorice-like flavor of the tarragon, which complements the pork perfectly.

12 **ounces pork tenderloin, trimmed of**
    separable fat
1 **large onion, cut into thin wedges**
1 **cup celery cut into thin bite-size strips**
1 **cup carrot cut into thin bite-size strips**
1 **cup water**
2 **cloves garlic, minced**
2 **teaspoons instant chicken bouillon**
    granules
¾ **teaspoon snipped fresh tarragon**
    or ¼ teaspoon dried tarragon, crushed
1 **tablespoon cornstarch**
1 **tablespoon cold water**
    Nonstick spray coating

1 Cut pork crosswise into sixteen ½-inch-thick slices. Place 1 slice between 2 pieces of plastic wrap. Working from center to edges, pound lightly with flat side of a meat mallet to ¼-inch thickness. Remove plastic wrap. Repeat with remaining pork.

2 In a medium saucepan combine onion, celery, carrot, the 1 cup water, garlic, bouillon granules, tarragon, and dash *pepper*. Bring to boiling; reduce heat. Simmer, covered, for 8 to 10 minutes or until vegetables are crisp-tender.

3 Mix cornstarch and the 1 tablespoon water. Stir into vegetable mixture. Cook and stir until thickened and bubbly. Cook and stir for 2 minutes more.

4 Meanwhile, spray unheated large skillet with nonstick coating. Preheat over medium heat. Add half the pork; cook about 4 minutes or until tender and juices run clear, turning once. Remove from skillet; keep warm. Repeat with remaining pork.

5 To serve, spoon vegetable mixture onto a serving platter. Place pork slices on top of vegetables. Makes 4 servings.

Nutrition facts per serving: 156 calories, 4 g total fat (1 g saturated fat), 61 mg cholesterol, 530 mg sodium, 10 g carbohydrate, 2 g fiber, 20 g protein
Exchanges: 2 Lean Meat, 2 Vegetable

199 calories

Preparation time: 15 minutes ● **Roasting time:** 1¼ hours ● **Standing time:** 15 minutes

pork roast with pineapple chutney

To cook meat to perfection, always use a meat thermometer. When the thermometer reaches the correct temperature, push it in a little farther. If the temperature drops, continue cooking. If it stays the same, the roast is done.

1 **2-pound boneless pork loin roast (single loin), trimmed of separable fat**
¼ **teaspoon black pepper**
1 **20-ounce can crushed pineapple (juice-packed), undrained**
½ **cup chopped onion**
2 **tablespoons raisins**
2 **tablespoons brown sugar**
2 **tablespoons vinegar**
2 **teaspoons grated fresh gingerroot or ½ teaspoon ground ginger**
½ **teaspoon ground cinnamon**
⅛ **teaspoon crushed red pepper (optional)**

1 Rub pork with the black pepper. Place pork on a rack in a shallow roasting pan. Insert a meat thermometer. Roast, uncovered, in a 325° oven about 1¼ hours or until thermometer registers 155°. Cover; let stand 15 minutes (meat temperature will rise 5° during standing).

2 Meanwhile, for chutney, in a medium saucepan combine undrained pineapple, onion, raisins, brown sugar, vinegar, gingerroot or ginger, cinnamon, and crushed red pepper (if using). Bring to boiling; reduce heat. Simmer, uncovered, about 30 minutes or until liquid is syrupy. Serve warm with roast. Makes 8 servings.

Nutrition facts per serving: 199 calories, 7 g total fat (3 g saturated fat), 51 mg cholesterol, 42 mg sodium, 17 g carbohydrate, 1 g fiber, 17 g protein
Exchanges: 2 Lean Meat, 1 Fruit

200 calories

Preparation time: 35 minutes ● **Baking time:** 30 minutes

spicy pork-stuffed peppers

Raisins give just a hint of sweetness to the pleasantly spiced ground pork and rice filling. Try other colored peppers—red, yellow, or orange—for variety and eye appeal.

4 **medium green, red, yellow, or orange**
  sweet peppers
12 **ounces lean ground pork, lean ground**
  beef, or lean ground turkey
1 **clove garlic, minced**
½ **cup chopped onion**
½ **cup chopped carrot**
1 **8-ounce can tomato sauce**
½ **cup cooked rice**
¼ **cup raisins**
1 **to 1½ teaspoons chili powder**
⅛ **teaspoon salt**
⅛ **teaspoon ground allspice**
  Few dashes bottled hot pepper sauce

1 Cut tops from sweet peppers; discard seeds and membranes. If necessary, trim bottoms just slightly so peppers can stand upright. Chop enough of the tops to make ½ cup; set aside.

2 Immerse the whole sweet peppers in *boiling water* for 4 to 5 minutes or just until crisp-tender. Invert to drain; set aside.

3 In a skillet cook ground pork, beef, or turkey with garlic just until brown. Drain off any fat. Transfer meat to large mixing bowl. Add onion, carrot, and the chopped sweet pepper to skillet along with a small amount of *water*. Cook, covered, for 4 to 5 minutes or just until tender. Drain vegetables and add to meat in bowl.

4 Stir in tomato sauce, cooked rice, raisins, chili powder, salt, allspice, and hot pepper sauce. Spoon into whole sweet peppers. Place filled peppers in a 2-quart square baking dish. Cover with foil.

5 Bake in a 350° oven about 30 minutes or until heated through. Makes 4 servings.

Nutrition facts per serving: 200 calories, 7 g total fat (3 g saturated fat), 40 mg cholesterol, 464 mg sodium, 23 g carbohydrate, 2 g fiber, 13 g protein
Exchanges: 2 Lean Meat, 2 Vegetable, ½ Fruit

248 calories

Preparation time: 25 minutes ● **Baking time:** 1 hour 5 minutes

stuffed acorn squash

Acorn squash, with its bright orange flesh and slightly sweet flavor, makes a great serving "dish" for the apple-cinnamon pork stuffing.

Nonstick spray coating
2 small acorn squash (about 2 pounds total)
12 ounces lean ground pork or lean ground turkey
½ cup chopped celery
½ cup chopped onion
½ teaspoon salt
½ teaspoon curry powder
⅛ teaspoon ground cinnamon
1 cup unsweetened applesauce
2 slices raisin or whole wheat bread, cubed (1½ cups)

1 Spray a shallow baking pan with nonstick coating. Wash and halve squash; discard seeds. Place squash, cut sides down, in prepared baking pan. Bake, uncovered, in a 350° oven for 45 minutes or until tender.

2 Meanwhile, for stuffing, in a large skillet cook ground pork or turkey, celery, and onion until meat is brown and vegetables are tender. Drain off fat. Stir in salt, curry powder, and cinnamon; cook 1 minute more. Stir in applesauce and bread cubes.

3 Turn squash cut sides up in pan. Spoon stuffing into squash halves. Bake, uncovered, for 20 minutes more. Makes 4 servings.

Nutrition facts per serving: 248 calories, 7 g total fat (3 g saturated fat), 40 mg cholesterol, 373 mg sodium, 36 g carbohydrate, 6 g fiber, 14 g protein
Exchanges: 2 Starch, 2 Lean Meat, ½ Fruit

345 calories

Preparation time: 50 minutes

sweet-and-sour ham balls

While the meatballs bake, cook the vegetables, pineapple, and sauce on top of the stove. Use a gentle hand when stirring the ham balls into the sauce so they retain their shape.

  1 **beaten egg**
  1 **cup bran flakes**
 ⅓ **cup skim milk**
  1 **teaspoon grated fresh gingerroot
        or ¼ teaspoon ground ginger**
  8 **ounces ground veal or lean ground beef**
  8 **ounces ground cooked ham**
  1 **15¼-ounce can pineapple chunks
        (juice-packed)**
1½ **cups thinly sliced carrots**
 ½ **cup reduced-sodium chicken broth**
 ¼ **cup red wine vinegar**
  2 **tablespoons cornstarch**
  2 **tablespoons honey**
  2 **tablespoons reduced-sodium soy sauce**
  1 **cup fresh or frozen pea pods**
  3 **cups hot cooked rice**

1 In a large bowl combine egg, bran flakes, milk, and gingerroot. Let stand 5 minutes. Add veal or beef and ham; mix well. Shape into 24 meatballs.

2 Arrange meatballs in a 2-quart rectangular baking dish. Bake, uncovered, in a 350° oven for 30 minutes. Spoon off fat.

3 Meanwhile, for sauce, drain pineapple, reserving juice. Set both aside. In a large covered saucepan cook carrots in broth for 5 minutes or just until tender. Do not drain.

4 Combine vinegar, cornstarch, honey, and soy sauce. Stir into carrot mixture. Stir in reserved pineapple juice. Cook and stir until thickened and bubbly. Stir in pea pods; cook 2 minutes more. Stir in pineapple; heat through. Add meatballs; stir gently to coat. Serve with rice. Makes 6 servings.

Nutrition facts per serving: 345 calories, 5 g total fat (2 g saturated fat), 86 mg cholesterol, 819 mg sodium, 54 g carbohydrate, 4 g fiber, 23 g protein
Exchanges: 2 Starch, 2 Lean Meat, 1 Vegetable, 1 Fruit

269 calories

Preparation time: 35 minutes

pork lo mein

*If you prefer, use lean boneless pork, thinly sliced into bite-sized strips, instead
of the ground pork.* Boneless loin chops work well.*

12 ounces lean ground pork
 2 cups sliced fresh mushrooms
 1 cup shredded or biased-sliced carrot
 ½ cup red and/or green sweet pepper cut into
    bite-size pieces
 2 cloves garlic, minced
 1 tablespoon cornstarch
 1 cup reduced-sodium chicken broth
 1 tablespoon reduced-sodium soy sauce
 1 teaspoon grated fresh gingerroot
 ¼ teaspoon crushed red pepper
 ¼ teaspoon curry powder
 4 ounces packaged dried thin spaghetti,
    broken, or linguine, cooked, and drained
    (2 cups cooked)
 1 cup fresh bean sprouts
 ½ cup sliced green onions
    Sliced green onion (optional)

1 In a large skillet cook pork, mushrooms,
carrot, sweet pepper, and garlic until meat is brown
and vegetables are tender. Drain off fat.

2 Stir cornstarch into meat mixture. Stir in broth,
soy sauce, gingerroot, crushed red pepper, and curry
powder. Cook and stir until thickened and bubbly.
Cook and stir for 2 minutes more.

3 Stir in cooked pasta, bean sprouts, and ½ cup
green onions; heat through. If desired, garnish with
additional green onion. Makes 4 servings.

*Note: To cook boneless pork, heat 1 teaspoon
cooking oil in the large skillet. Add pork strips.
Stir-fry for 2 to 3 minutes or until no longer pink.
Remove pork from skillet. Cook mushrooms, carrot,
sweet pepper, and garlic as directed. Return pork to
skillet and continue as directed.

Nutrition facts per serving: 269 calories, 7 g total fat
(0 g saturated fat), 40 mg cholesterol, 350 mg sodium,
34 g carbohydrate, 3 g fiber, 17 g protein
Exchanges: 1 Starch, 2 Meat, 3 Vegetable

290 calories

Preparation time: 30 minutes ● **Marinating time:** 6 to 12 hours ● **Broiling time:** 12 minutes

herbed pork kabobs

A nice small size for kabobs, boiling onions range from about the size of a quarter to a half dollar. Eight ounces of boiling onions yields about 10 to 12 onions. Peel them before cooking, as you would for regular onions.

- 1 **teaspoon finely shredded orange peel**
- ⅓ **cup orange juice**
- 2 **teaspoons olive or cooking oil**
- ¾ **teaspoon snipped fresh rosemary
   or ¼ teaspoon dried rosemary, crushed**
- ¾ **teaspoon snipped fresh sage
   or ¼ teaspoon dried sage, crushed**
- 1 **clove garlic, minced**
- 12 **ounces lean boneless pork, cut into 1-inch
   pieces**
- 8 **ounces boiling onions**
- 2 **medium carrots, cut into 1-inch pieces**
- 1 **medium green sweet pepper, cut
   into 1-inch pieces**
- 1 **small orange, cut into 4 wedges and halved
   Hot cooked couscous (optional)**

1 For marinade, combine orange peel, juice, oil, herbs, garlic, ¼ teaspoon *salt,* and ¼ teaspoon *black pepper.* Place meat in a plastic bag set in a deep bowl. Pour marinade over meat; close bag. Marinate in the refrigerator for 6 to 12 hours.

2 In a medium covered saucepan cook onions and carrots in small amount of lightly *salted water* for 10 to 15 minutes or until nearly tender. Drain.

3 Drain pork, reserving marinade. On eight 12-inch skewers alternately thread pork, onions, carrots, and sweet pepper, leaving ¼ inch between pieces. Thread a piece of orange onto each skewer.

4 Place the skewers on the unheated rack of a broiler pan. Broil 4 inches from the heat for 12 to 15 minutes or until pork is slightly pink in center and juices run clear, turning and brushing twice with reserved marinade. If desired, serve kabobs with hot cooked couscous. Makes 4 servings.

Nutrition facts per serving: 290 calories, 8 g total fat (2 g saturated fat), 38 mg cholesterol, 59 mg sodium, 37 g carbohydrate, 7 g fiber, 17 g protein
Exchanges: 2½ Starch, 2 Lean Meat, 1 Vegetable

138 calories

Preparation time: 30 minutes ● **Cooking time:** 10 minutes

pork and eggplant stew

If you sprinkle bowls of this Mediterranean-style stew with the optional feta cheese, add only 19 calories and 2 grams fat to the nutrition facts per serving. The small addition is worth it.

Nonstick spray coating
8 **ounces lean boneless pork, cut into ¾-inch cubes**
1 **large onion, sliced and separated into rings**
1 **clove garlic, minced**
1 **small eggplant, peeled and cubed (4 cups)**
1 **14½-ounce can low-sodium tomatoes, undrained and cut up**
1 **medium green sweet pepper, cut into strips**
1 **5½-ounce can low-sodium vegetable juice**
1 **teaspoon dried oregano, crushed**
1 **teaspoon dried basil, crushed**
¼ **teaspoon salt**
¼ **teaspoon black pepper**
2 **tablespoons snipped fresh parsley**
¼ **cup crumbled feta cheese (optional)**

1 Spray a Dutch oven with nonstick coating. Add pork, onion, and garlic; cook over medium heat until pork is brown and onion is tender.

2 Stir in eggplant, undrained tomatoes, sweet pepper, vegetable juice, oregano, basil, salt, and black pepper.

3 Bring to boiling; reduce heat. Simmer, covered, for 10 to 15 minutes or until vegetables are tender. Stir in parsley.

4 Divide the stew among 4 soup bowls. If desired, sprinkle with the feta cheese. Makes 4 servings.

Nutrition facts per serving: 138 calories, 4 g total fat (1 g saturated fat), 26 mg cholesterol, 180 mg sodium, 15 g carbohydrate, 4 g fiber, 10 g protein
Exchanges: 1 Lean Meat, 3 Vegetable

254 calories

Preparation time: 20 minutes ● **Cooking time:** 15 minutes

ham and potato skillet

Fat-free sour cream makes a creamy, rich-tasting sauce in this family-style dish. For the best herb flavor, always use fresh herbs when you can. Any fresh herb you like can be substituted for the dill.

1 pound small potatoes
1 cup water
8 ounces fresh green beans, cut into 1-inch pieces, or one 9-ounce package frozen cut green beans
1 8-ounce carton fat-free dairy sour cream
2 tablespoons all-purpose flour
2 teaspoons prepared mustard
¾ teaspoon snipped fresh dill or ¼ teaspoon dried dillweed
⅛ teaspoon pepper
1½ cups cubed lower-fat, lower-sodium cooked ham (about 8 ounces)
Tomato slices (optional)
Fresh dill (optional)

1 Scrub and slice potatoes; halve any large slices.

2 In a large skillet bring the water to boiling. Add potatoes and fresh green beans (if using). Cover and cook about 15 minutes or until potatoes and beans are tender. (If using frozen beans, cook potatoes 10 minutes; add beans. Return to boil. Cook 5 minutes more.) Drain well; return to skillet.

3 Meanwhile, in a small saucepan stir together sour cream, flour, mustard, the fresh dill or dried dillweed, and the pepper. Cook and stir until thickened and bubbly. Pour over vegetables in skillet. Stir in ham. Heat through. If desired, garnish with tomato slices and additional fresh dill. Makes 4 servings.

Nutrition facts per serving: 254 calories, 2 g total fat (1 g saturated fat), 24 mg cholesterol, 698 mg sodium, 41 g carbohydrate, 3 g fiber, 18 g protein
Exchanges: 2 Starch, 2 Lean Meat, 1 Vegetable

215 calories

Preparation time: 30 minutes

ham and vegetables with penne

Penne pasta are straight tubes of pasta similar to mostaccioli. The slender shape is perfect in this creamy dish.

4 ounces packaged dried penne pasta
   (about 1½ cups)
2 cups sliced zucchini
½ cup sliced green onions
⅓ cup water
4 teaspoons cornstarch
2 teaspoons snipped fresh basil
   or ½ teaspoon dried basil, crushed
½ teaspoon snipped fresh marjoram
   or ¼ teaspoon dried marjoram, crushed
⅛ teaspoon pepper
1 cup evaporated skim milk
¼ cup water
1 cup lower-fat, lower-sodium cooked ham
   cut into bite-size strips (about 5 ounces)
   Fresh basil leaves (optional)

1 Cook pasta according to package directions, except omit any oil and salt; drain well. Set aside.

2 In a large saucepan combine zucchini, green onions, and the ⅓ cup water. Bring to boiling; reduce heat. Simmer, covered, for 4 to 5 minutes or until vegetables are crisp-tender; drain well in colander. Return vegetables to saucepan; cover and set aside.

3 Meanwhile, for sauce, in a small saucepan combine cornstarch, basil, marjoram, and pepper. Gradually stir in evaporated milk and the ¼ cup water; add ham. Cook and stir until thickened and bubbly. Cook and stir for 2 minutes more. Add the ham mixture and the drained pasta to the vegetables in the large saucepan. Heat through. If desired, garnish with fresh basil leaves. Makes 4 servings.

Nutrition facts per serving: 215 calories, 2 g total fat (0 g saturated fat), 17 mg cholesterol, 465 mg sodium, 34 g carbohydrate, 1 g fiber, 15 g protein
Exchanges: 2 Starch, 1 Lean Meat, 1 Vegetable

241 calories

Preparation time: 40 minutes ● **Baking time:** 30 minutes ● **Standing time:** 10 minutes

spinach and ham lasagna

Deviate from the traditional red-sauced lasagna. This luscious lasagna is layered with spinach, ham, cheese, and a lightened "cream" sauce. Ham adds a tasty smoky flavor.

 6 packaged dried lasagna noodles (4 ounces)
 1 10-ounce package frozen chopped spinach
 2 cups skim milk
 ¼ cup chopped onion
 3 tablespoons cornstarch
1½ cups diced lower-fat, lower-sodium cooked ham (about 8 ounces)
 ½ teaspoon dried Italian seasoning, crushed
 1 cup low-fat cottage cheese
 1 cup shredded mozzarella cheese (4 ounces)

1 Cook lasagna noodles according to package directions except omit oil. Drain. Rinse with cold water; drain again. Set aside.

2 Meanwhile, cook spinach according to package directions; drain well. Set aside. For sauce, in a medium saucepan combine milk, onion, and cornstarch. Cook and stir until thickened and bubbly. Cook and stir for 2 minutes more.

3 Spread 2 tablespoons of the sauce evenly on the bottom of a 2-quart rectangular baking dish. Stir ham and Italian seasoning into remaining sauce. Arrange 3 lasagna noodles in the dish. Spread with one-third of the remaining sauce. Layer the spinach on top. Layer another one-third of the sauce, the cottage cheese, and half of the mozzarella cheese over the spinach. Place remaining noodles on top. Top with the remaining sauce and mozzarella. Bake, uncovered, in a 375° oven for 30 to 35 minutes or until heated through. Let stand 10 minutes before serving. Makes 6 servings.

Nutrition facts per serving: 241 calories, 5 g total fat (2 g saturated fat), 30 mg cholesterol, 724 mg sodium, 26 g carbohydrate, 0 g fiber, 22 g protein
Exchanges: 1 Starch, 2 Lean Meat, 1 Vegetable, ½ Milk

282 calories

Preparation time: 25 minutes ● **Baking time:** 30 minutes

ham and cheese macaroni

Diet margarines generally contain a lot of water and will make the topping soggy. Use regular margarine or butter.

1   **cup packaged dried elbow macaroni**
2   **cups broccoli flowerets, or one 10-ounce package frozen cut broccoli, cooked and drained**
1   **cup cubed lower-fat, lower-sodium cooked ham or turkey ham (5 ounces)**
1   **medium red or green sweet pepper, cut into ¾-inch squares**
1   **cup skim milk**
1   **tablespoon cornstarch**
⅛   **teaspoon black pepper**
1   **cup cubed American cheese (4 ounces)**
¾   **cup soft bread crumbs (1 slice)**
1   **tablespoon margarine or butter, melted**

1 Cook macaroni according to package directions, except omit any oil and salt. Drain.

2 In a large mixing bowl combine macaroni, broccoli, ham, and sweet pepper. Set aside.

3 For sauce, in a small saucepan stir together the milk, cornstarch, and pepper. Cook and stir until thickened and bubbly. Add cheese; stir until melted. Stir sauce into broccoli mixture. Transfer to a 2-quart casserole. Combine bread crumbs and margarine or butter; sprinkle over mixture in casserole.

4 Bake, uncovered, in 350° oven for 30 minutes or until bubbly and bread crumbs are lightly browned. Makes 5 servings.

Microwave Directions: Prepare as above, except use a microwave-safe casserole and do not sprinkle bread crumbs over macaroni mixture before cooking. Cover macaroni mixture and microwave on 100% power (high) for 6 to 8 minutes or until heated through, stirring once. Sprinkle with bread crumb mixture. Cook, uncovered, on high for 1 minute more.

Nutrition facts per serving: 282 calories, 11 g total fat (5 g saturated fat), 34 mg cholesterol, 736 mg sodium, 29 g carbohydrate, 3 g fiber, 17 g protein
Exchanges: 1½ Starch, 2 Medium-Fat Meat, 1 Vegetable

365 calories

Preparation time: 25 minutes

fettuccine with creamy ham sauce

To keep the fat low, but the flavor high, we used evaporated skim milk in the sauce.
A little Swiss cheese boosts the flavor even more.

6 ounces packaged dried fettuccine
2 cups broccoli or cauliflower flowerets
1 cup sliced fresh mushrooms
1 cup evaporated skim milk
2 teaspoons cornstarch
½ teaspoon dry mustard
⅛ teaspoon salt
⅛ teaspoon pepper
¾ cup shredded Swiss cheese (3 ounces)
1 cup sliced lower-fat, lower-sodium cooked
   ham cut into thin strips (about 5 ounces)

1 Cook fettuccine according to package directions, except omit any oil and salt. Drain.

2 Meanwhile, in a medium covered saucepan cook broccoli or cauliflower and mushrooms in a small amount of *boiling water* for 7 to 8 minutes or until vegetables are tender. Drain.

3 In the same saucepan stir together evaporated skim milk, cornstarch, dry mustard, salt, and pepper. Cook and stir over medium heat until thickened and bubbly. Add cheese; heat and stir until melted. Stir in ham and cooked vegetables; heat through. Pour over hot pasta. Makes 4 servings.

Nutrition facts per serving: 365 calories, 8 g total fat (4 g saturated fat), 36 mg cholesterol, 603 mg sodium, 48 g carbohydrate, 3 g fiber, 25 g protein
Exchanges: 2 Starch, 2 Lean Meat, 2 Vegetable, ½ Milk

194 calories

Preparation time: 20 minutes ● **Baking time:** 30 minutes

savory ham and rice

Keep the ingredients on hand for this saucy casserole. Put it together in about 20 minutes, then just sit back and relax while it bakes. To round out the meal, add breadsticks and fresh fruit.

1 **cup chopped carrot**
¾ **cup water**
½ **cup chopped onion**
½ **cup chopped green or red sweet pepper**
1 **10¾-ounce can reduced-fat and reduced-sodium condensed cream of celery soup**
1 **cup quick-cooking rice**
6 **ounces lower-fat, lower-sodium cooked ham, cut into bite-size pieces (about 1 cup)**
1½ **teaspoons snipped fresh sage or ¼ teaspoon ground sage**
⅛ **teaspoon black pepper**
 Paprika (optional)

1 In a medium saucepan combine carrot, water, onion, and sweet pepper. Bring to boiling; reduce heat. Simmer, covered, for 4 to 5 minutes or until crisp-tender. Do not drain.

2 Stir in soup, uncooked rice, ham, sage, and black pepper. Spoon into a 1-quart casserole. If desired, sprinkle with paprika. Bake, covered, in a 350° oven for 30 to 35 minutes or until rice is tender and mixture is heated through. Makes 4 servings.

Nutrition facts per serving: 194 calories, 3 g total fat (1 g saturated fat), 19 mg cholesterol, 784 mg sodium, 31 g carbohydrate, 1 g fiber, 11 g protein
Exchanges: 1½ Starch, 1 Lean Meat, 1 Vegetable

159 calories

Preparation time: 25 minutes ● **Standing time:** 1 hour ● **Cooking time:** 1 hour 33 minutes

vegetable bean with ham soup

Look for packaged spinach at your supermarket that has already been washed. If you buy spinach in bunches that have not been cleaned, discard stems and rinse leaves several times in cold water to remove the sand.

¾ **cup dry navy beans (5 ounces)**
9 **cups water**
1 **cup sliced carrot**
1 **cup chopped onion**
½ **cup sliced celery**
2 **teaspoons instant chicken bouillon granules**
1 **teaspoon dried basil, crushed**
½ **teaspoon dried thyme, crushed**
¼ **teaspoon pepper**
2 **bay leaves**
1 **clove garlic, minced**
6 **ounces lower-fat, lower-sodium cooked ham, diced (about 1 cup)**
1½ **cups coarsely shredded fresh spinach or cabbage**

1 Rinse beans. In a large saucepan or Dutch oven combine beans and 4 cups of the water. Bring to boiling; reduce heat. Simmer, uncovered, for 2 minutes. Remove from heat; cover and let stand 1 hour. (Or, combine the beans and 4 cups water; cover and soak overnight in the refrigerator.)

2 Drain and rinse beans. Return beans to pan. Add the remaining 5 cups water, carrot, onion, celery, bouillon granules, basil, thyme, pepper, bay leaves, and garlic. Bring to boiling; reduce heat. Simmer, covered, for 1½ to 2 hours or until beans are tender. Stir in the ham and spinach or cabbage. Simmer for 3 to 5 minutes more. Discard bay leaves. Makes 5 servings.

Nutrition facts per serving: 159 calories, 2 g total fat (1 g saturated fat), 14 mg cholesterol, 768 mg sodium, 24 g carbohydrate, 2 g fiber, 13 g protein
Exchanges: 1 Starch, 1 Lean Meat, 1 Vegetable

111 calories

Preparation time: 20 minutes ● **Cooking time:** 10 minutes

oriental ham soup

Bok choy, a variety of Chinese cabbage, more closely resembles celery than cabbage.
Its sweet, mild flavor pairs well with ham in this delicious soup.

  4 cups water
1½ cups chopped bok choy
  ¾ cup carrot cut into thin strips
  ¾ cup chopped onion
  2 tablespoons reduced-sodium soy sauce
  2 tablespoons dry sherry (optional)
    Dash pepper
  8 ounces lower-fat, lower-sodium cooked ham, cut into thin strips (about 1½ cups)
  ½ cup packaged dried regular or spinach noodles

1 In a large saucepan or Dutch oven combine the water, bok choy, carrot, onion, soy sauce, dry sherry (if using), and pepper. Bring to boiling. Add ham and noodles. Simmer, uncovered, about 10 minutes or until noodles are tender and vegetables are crisp-tender. Makes 4 servings.

Nutrition facts per serving: 111 calories, 2 g total fat (1 g saturated fat), 30 mg cholesterol, 911 mg sodium, 11 g carbohydrate, 2 g fiber, 12 g protein
Exchanges: ½ Starch, 1 Lean Meat, 1 Vegetable

238 calories

Preparation time: 20 minutes ● **Cooking time:** 5 minutes

cabbage and ham hash

To slim down hash, we cut the margarine by more than half leaving just enough to lightly brown the potatoes. Another time, use leftover lean roast beef or pork in place of the ham.

½ **cup chopped onion**
2 **cups chopped cabbage**
¾ **cup shredded carrot**
1 **tablespoon margarine or butter**
10 **ounces lower-fat, lower-sodium cooked ham, diced (about 2 cups)**
2 **cups cubed cooked potatoes**
1 **teaspoon Worcestershire sauce**
⅛ **teaspoon pepper**

1 In a large skillet cook the onion, cabbage, and carrot in hot margarine or butter until the vegetables are tender.

2 Stir in the ham, potatoes, Worcestershire sauce, and pepper. Spread mixture evenly in skillet. Cook over medium heat for 5 minutes, turning occasionally with spatula. Makes 4 servings.

Nutrition facts per serving: 238 calories, 6 g total fat (1 g saturated fat), 30 mg cholesterol, 842 mg sodium, 33 g carbohydrate, 5 g fiber, 16 g protein
Exchanges: 1 Starch, 2 Lean Meat, 2 Vegetable

266 calories

Preparation time: 30 minutes ● **Baking time:** 25 minutes

ham with sweet potatoes and apples

Although it's hard to beat fresh vegetables of any kind, canned vegetables help out in a pinch. By using the canned sweet potatoes, you'll cut your preparation time to just 10 minutes.

4 medium sweet potatoes or one 18-ounce can sweet potatoes, drained
2 ½-inch-thick slices lower-fat, lower-sodium cooked ham, trimmed of separable fat (about 12 ounces)
2 medium apples
1 teaspoon finely shredded orange peel
¾ cup orange juice
2 teaspoons cornstarch
1 teaspoon reduced-sodium soy sauce
1 teaspoon grated fresh gingerroot
1 clove garlic, minced
Snipped fresh parsley (optional)

1 Peel and quarter fresh sweet potatoes. In a large covered saucepan cook potatoes in a small amount of *boiling water* for 15 minutes or until almost tender. Drain.

2 Cut each ham slice in half. Core apples and cut each apple into 8 wedges. Arrange drained sweet potatoes and apple wedges in a 2-quart rectangular baking dish. Arrange ham slices on top of sweet potatoes and apples.

3 In a small saucepan combine orange peel, orange juice, cornstarch, soy sauce, gingerroot, and garlic. Cook and stir until thickened and bubbly. Pour over ham in dish.

4 Bake, covered, in a 375° oven for 15 minutes. Uncover and bake about 10 minutes more or until potatoes and apples are just tender. If desired, sprinkle with fresh parsley. Makes 4 servings.

Nutrition facts per serving: 266 calories, 3 g total fat (1 g saturated fat), 36 mg cholesterol, 986 mg sodium, 44 g carbohydrate, 6 g fiber, 18 g protein
Exchanges: 1 Starch, 2 Lean Meat, 2 Fruit

Lamb

chapter index

185 calories

Preparation time: 25 minutes ● **Baking time:** 50 minutes

lamb chops with lemon vegetables

Today, lamb is leaner, milder in flavor, and more tender than ever. When purchasing lamb, look for pale pink meat. It will be more tender than darker red meat.

4 **lamb shoulder chops, cut ¾ inch thick and trimmed of separable fat (about 1¾ pounds total)**
1 **large onion, cut into thin wedges**
1 **medium carrot, cut into thin bite-size strips**
1 **medium turnip, cut into thin bite-size strips (about ¾ cup)**
1 **stalk celery, thinly sliced**
1 **teaspoon snipped fresh thyme or ¼ teaspoon dried thyme, crushed**
¼ **teaspoon garlic salt**
⅛ **teaspoon pepper**
4 **thin slices lemon**

1 Cut four 12-inch squares of heavy foil. (Or, cut eight squares of regular foil.)

2 Place a lamb chop on the center of each piece of heavy foil or on a double layer of regular foil. Divide vegetables and place on top of lamb chops.

3 Stir together the thyme, garlic salt, and pepper. Sprinkle evenly over vegetables and chops. Top each serving with a lemon slice. Bring up 2 opposite edges of foil and seal with a double fold. Fold remaining ends to completely enclose. Place foil packets on a baking sheet.

4 Bake in a 350° oven about 50 minutes or until chops and vegetables are tender. Discard lemon slices before serving. Makes 4 servings.

Nutrition facts per serving: 185 calories, 8 g total fat (3 g saturated fat), 66 mg cholesterol, 219 mg sodium, 7 g carbohydrate, 2 g fiber, 20 g protein
Exchanges: 3 Lean Meat, 1 Vegetable

208 calories

Preparation time: 30 minutes

lamb pepper chops

The secret ingredient in the sauce is marmalade. It adds a tangy sweetness mellowed with a little hoisin sauce. If you serve this dish with ½ cup of rice, you'll add about 100 calories (1 Starch) per serving.

3 **tablespoons reduced-calorie orange**
  marmalade or apricot preserves
2 **tablespoons hoisin sauce**
1 **tablespoon water**
  Nonstick spray coating
4 **lamb leg sirloin chops, cut ¾ inch thick**
  and trimmed of separable fat (about
  1½ pounds total)
1 **medium red sweet pepper, cut into strips**
1 **medium green sweet pepper, cut into strips**
2 **teaspoons cold water**
1 **teaspoon cornstarch**
  Hot cooked rice (optional)

1 In a mixing bowl stir together the orange marmalade or apricot preserves, hoisin sauce, and the 1 tablespoon water. Set aside.

2 Spray an unheated large skillet with nonstick coating. Preheat over medium heat. Add chops. Cook for 7 minutes. Turn and top with sweet pepper strips. Pour marmalade mixture evenly over meat and vegetables.

3 Bring mixture to boiling; reduce heat. Simmer, covered, for 5 to 8 minutes or until chops are of desired doneness.

4 Remove lamb and peppers to a serving platter; keep warm. Stir together the 2 teaspoons cold water and the cornstarch. Add to liquid in skillet. Cook and stir until thickened and bubbly. Cook and stir for 2 minutes more. Serve sauce over lamb and peppers. If desired, serve with hot cooked rice. Makes 4 servings.

Nutrition facts per serving: 208 calories, 7 g total fat (2 g saturated fat), 69 mg cholesterol, 212 mg sodium, 12 g carbohydrate, 0 g fiber, 22 g protein
Exchanges: ½ Starch, 3 Lean Meat, 1 Vegetable

182 calories

Preparation time: 12 minutes

sweet-and-sour lamb chops

*The lamb chops also can be grilled directly over medium coals. Grill for 10 to 14 minutes
for medium rare or 14 to 16 minutes for medium doneness.*

**4 lamb loin chops, trimmed of separable fat
(about 12 ounces total)**
1 medium onion, thinly sliced
**1 medium red and/or yellow sweet pepper,
sliced**
2 cloves garlic, minced
**2 tablespoons snipped fresh herbs (such as
basil, oregano, thyme, and/or marjoram)
or 1 teaspoon dried herb or mixture of
herbs, crushed**
2 teaspoons cooking oil
2 tablespoons red or white wine vinegar
**4 teaspoons brown sugar
Fresh herb (optional)**

1 Place lamb chops on the unheated rack of a
broiler pan. Broil 3 to 4 inches from heat for 7 to
11 minutes, turning once.

2 Meanwhile, in a covered large skillet cook
onion, sweet pepper, garlic, and dried herb (if
using) in hot oil until vegetables are just tender,
stirring once. Stir in vinegar, brown sugar, and
the 2 tablespoons fresh herb (if using); heat through.
To serve, spoon onion mixture over lamb chops.
If desired, garnish with additional fresh herb.
Makes 4 servings.

Nutrition facts per serving: 182 calories, 10 g total fat
(3 g saturated fat), 52 mg cholesterol, 51 mg sodium,
7 g carbohydrate, 0 g fiber, 16 g protein
Exchanges: 2 Lean Meat, 1 Vegetable, ½ Fat

301 calories

Preparation time: 10 minutes ● **Broiling time:** 12 minutes

honey-mustard lamb chops

A simple blend of Dijon-style mustard and honey accented with the bold, piny flavor of rosemary glazes the chops and the zucchini. Special, yet easy this meal takes less than 25 minutes to make.

4 small lamb loin chops, trimmed of separable fat (about 12 ounces total)
2 small zucchini, halved lengthwise
1 tablespoon Dijon-style mustard
1 tablespoon honey
1½ teaspoons snipped fresh rosemary or ½ teaspoon dried rosemary, crushed

1 Arrange lamb chops and zucchini, cut sides up, on the unheated rack of a broiler pan.

2 In a small bowl stir together mustard, honey, and rosemary. Spread some of the mustard mixture on top of the chops.

3 Broil chops and zucchini 3 inches from the heat for 6 minutes. Turn chops and zucchini over; spread more of the mustard mixture on the chops. Broil chops and zucchini 6 to 9 minutes more or until lamb is of desired doneness and the zucchinni is tender, spreading the remaining mustard mixutre on the zucchini the last 3 minutes of broiling. Makes 2 servings.

Nutrition facts per serving: 301 calories, 12 g total fat (4 g saturated fat), 107 mg cholesterol, 287 mg sodium, 13 g carbohydrate, 1 g fiber, 35 g protein
Exchanges: 4 Lean Meat, 3 Vegetable

243 calories

Preparation time: 20 minutes ● **Cooking time:** 55 minutes

lamb and bean stew

To pack the most punch into this stew, use Hungarian paprika. It is lighter in color than other paprikas but more pungent in flavor. Look for either sweet or hot Hungarian paprika in specialty food stores.

12 **ounces lean boneless lamb sirloin or shoulder, trimmed of separable fat**
2 **teaspoons cooking oil**
1 **cup chopped onion**
1 **tablespoon Hungarian paprika or paprika**
1 **14½-ounce can reduced-sodium chicken broth**
½ **cup dry white wine or water**
2 **cups cubed potato**
1 **cup sliced carrot**
1 **cup sliced celery**
1 **15-ounce can white kidney beans or great northern beans, rinsed and drained**
 Fat-free dairy sour cream (optional)
 Hungarian paprika or paprika (optional)

1 Cut meat into ¾-inch cubes.

2 Heat oil in large saucepan over medium heat; add meat, onion, and the 1 tablespoon paprika. Cook and stir until meat is browned and onion is tender. Carefully add broth and wine or water. Heat to boiling; reduce heat. Simmer, covered, for 30 minutes or until meat is nearly tender.

3 Add potato, carrot, and celery to meat mixture. Cook, covered, for 25 to 30 minutes more or until meat and vegetables are tender. Stir in beans; heat through. Mash mixture slightly to thicken. Ladle stew into serving bowls. If desired, top each serving with sour cream and sprinkle with additional paprika. Makes 6 servings.

Nutrition facts per serving: 243 calories, 9 g total fat (3 g saturated fat), 32 mg cholesterol, 365 mg sodium, 27 g carbohydrate, 5 g fiber, 15 g protein
Exchanges: 1½ Starch, 1 Medium-Fat Meat, 1 Vegetable, ½ Fat

251 calories

Preparation time: 30 minutes ● **Baking time:** 1¼ hours

rosemary lamb stew

What could be easier than an oven stew? Simply combine the meat and vegetables in a large Dutch oven and bake. The slow cooking allows a sensational flavor to develop.

1½	**pounds lean boneless lamb, trimmed of separable fat**
1	**14½-ounce can tomatoes, undrained and cut up**
¾	**cup water**
½	**cup dry white wine or water**
2½	**cups peeled parsnips cut into ½-inch-thick slices (1 pound) or 3 medium potatoes, peeled and cubed (1 pound)**
2	**cups fresh or frozen cut green beans**
1	**cup carrot cut into ½-inch-thick slices**
½	**cup chopped onion**
½	**teaspoon salt**
½	**teaspoon dried rosemary, crushed**
⅛	**teaspoon pepper**
2	**cloves garlic, minced**
¼	**cup cold water**
2	**tablespoons cornstarch**
⅓	**cup plain low-fat yogurt**

1 Cut meat into 1-inch cubes. In a large ovenproof Dutch oven combine meat, undrained tomatoes, the ¾ cup water, and the wine or water. Stir in parsnips or potatoes, green beans, carrot, onion, salt, rosemary, pepper, and garlic. Bake, covered, in a 350° oven for 1¼ to 1½ hours or until meat is tender. Remove Dutch oven from the oven; place on the range top.

2 Combine the ¼ cup cold water and the cornstarch. Stir into meat mixture. Cook and stir until thickened and bubbly. Cook and stir 2 minutes more. To serve, spoon some of the yogurt on top of each serving. Makes 6 servings.

Nutrition facts per serving: 251 calories, 7 g total fat (3 g saturated fat), 56 mg cholesterol, 369 mg sodium, 25 g carbohydrate, 5 g fiber, 20 g protein
Exchanges: 1 Starch, 2 Lean Meat, 2 Vegetable

214 calories

Preparation time: 25 minutes ● **Cooking time:** 1 hour

lamb and lentil soup

Browning meat adds flavor, seals in juices, and helps develop a rich color. Here, as in other recipes that call for a pound or more of meat, the lamb is browned in two batches so it cooks evenly without stewing.

1	**pound lean boneless lamb, trimmed of separable fat**
	Nonstick spray coating
1	**medium onion, chopped**
3½	**cups water**
1	**14½-ounce can tomatoes, undrained and cut up**
1	**cup coarsely chopped carrot**
1	**cup sliced celery**
1½	**teaspoons snipped fresh thyme or ½ teaspoon dried thyme, crushed**
½	**teaspoon salt**
¼	**teaspoon pepper**
1	**clove garlic, minced**
1	**bay leaf**
¾	**cup dry lentils**

1 Cut meat into ¾-inch pieces.

2 Spray an unheated large Dutch oven with nonstick coating. Preheat over medium heat. Add half of the meat; cook until browned. Remove meat from Dutch oven. Brown the remaining meat with the onion. Return all the meat to the pan.

3 Add the water, undrained tomatoes, carrot, celery, thyme, salt, pepper, garlic, and bay leaf. Bring to boiling; reduce heat. Simmer, covered, for 30 minutes.

4 Rinse lentils; add to meat mixture. Return to boiling; reduce heat. Simmer, covered, for 30 minutes more or until meat and lentils are tender. Discard bay leaf. Makes 6 servings.

Nutrition facts per serving: 214 calories, 5 g total fat (2 g saturated fat), 37 mg cholesterol, 358 mg sodium, 24 g carbohydrate, 3 g fiber, 20 g protein
Exchanges: 1 Starch, 2 Lean Meat, 1 Vegetable

381 calories

Preparation time: 30 minutes ● **Baking time:** 1¼ hours

curried lamb with apricot rice

Different brands of curry powder use varying proportions of as many as 20 ground spices, making some hotter than others. Experiment with different brands to see which you like best.

1 **pound lean boneless lamb, trimmed of separable fat**
1 **tablespoon cooking oil**
1 **medium onion, chopped**
1 **stalk celery, sliced**
1 **clove garlic, minced**
2 **to 3 teaspoons curry powder**
1 **14½-ounce can reduced-sodium chicken broth**
½ **cup water**
1 **cup brown rice**
⅓ **cup snipped dried apricots**
½ **teaspoon sugar**
⅛ **teaspoon ground cloves**

1 Cut meat into ¾-inch cubes.

2 In large saucepan brown half the meat in the hot oil. Remove from saucepan. Brown remaining meat with the onion, celery, and garlic until onion is tender. Return all meat to saucepan; stir in curry powder. Cook 1 minute more. Remove from heat.

3 In a 2-quart casserole combine chicken broth and water. Stir in rice, apricots, sugar, and cloves. Add browned meat mixture. Bake, covered, in a 350° oven for 1¼ to 1½ hours or until meat is tender and rice is done. Makes 4 servings.

Nutrition facts per serving: 381 calories, 12 g total fat (3 g saturated fat), 55 mg cholesterol, 352 mg sodium, 47 g carbohydrate, 4 g fiber, 22 g protein
Exchanges: 2 Starch, 2 Medium-Fat Meat, 1 Fruit

228 calories

Preparation time: 50 minutes

lamb and sweet pepper stir-fry

If you prefer, don't toast the pita bread and serve this stir-fry as a sandwich. Spoon the mixture and the yogurt into the pockets of halved pita bread rounds. Tuck some cucumber slices and radishes in on the sides.

12 ounces lean boneless lamb or beef top
  round steak, trimmed of separable fat
¼ cup sliced green onions
¼ cup snipped fresh parsley
1 tablespoon lemon juice
1½ teaspoons snipped fresh thyme
  or ½ teaspoon dried thyme, crushed,
  or 1 teaspoon snipped fresh mint or
  ¼ teaspoon dried mint, crushed
⅛ teaspoon black pepper
  Nonstick spray coating
1 medium red or green sweet pepper, cut
  into bite-size strips
1 clove garlic, minced
1 tablespoon cooking oil
¼ cup plain low-fat yogurt
2 6-inch pita bread rounds, split horizontally,
  quartered, and toasted

1 Partially freeze meat about 30 minutes. Thinly slice meat across the grain into bite-size strips.

2 In a medium mixing bowl combine green onions, parsley, lemon juice, thyme or mint, and black pepper. Stir in meat.

3 Spray an unheated wok or large skillet with nonstick coating. Preheat over medium-high heat. Add sweet pepper and garlic; stir-fry for 2 minutes or until sweet pepper is crisp-tender. Remove sweet pepper from wok.

4 Add oil to hot wok. Add meat mixture; stir-fry for 2 to 3 minutes more or until done. Return sweet pepper to wok. Heat through.

5 To serve, spoon each serving with yogurt. Serve with toasted pita wedges. Makes 4 servings.

Nutrition facts per serving: 228 calories, 9 g total fat (2 g saturated fat), 42 mg cholesterol, 205 mg sodium, 20 g carbohydrate, 0 g fiber, 17 g protein
Exchanges: 1 Starch, 2 Lean Meat, 1 Vegetable, ½ Fat

260 calories

Preparation time: 55 minutes ● **Marinating time:** 2 to 24 hours ● **Broiling time:** 6 minutes

minted lamb kabobs

Divide the preparation over two days by marinating the lamb overnight. You'll simplify the final steps needed for preparing the meal on the second day.

**1 pound boneless lean leg of lamb, cut 1 inch
      thick and trimmed of separable fat**
⅓ cup water
2 tablespoons lemon juice
**2 tablespoons snipped fresh mint
      or 1 teaspoon dried mint, crushed**
1 tablespoon Dijon-style mustard
1 tablespoon cooking oil
1 clove garlic, minced
2 small zucchini, cut into ½-inch-thick slices
**1 cup pearl onions or 1 cup frozen small
      whole onions, thawed**
5 cherry tomatoes
2½ cups hot cooked brown rice

1 Partially freeze meat about 30 minutes. Cut into ¼-inch-thick strips about 3 inches long and 1 inch wide. Place in a plastic bag set in a bowl.

2 For marinade, stir together the water, lemon juice, mint, mustard, oil, and garlic. Pour over meat.

Close bag. Marinate in the refrigerator for at least 2 hours or up to 24 hours, turning occasionally. Drain meat, reserving marinade.

3 In a small covered saucepan cook the zucchini and onions in a small amount of *boiling water* for 3 minutes. Drain.

4 On five 12- to 15-inch-long skewers, thread meat, accordion-style, alternately with onions and zucchini. Place skewers on the unheated rack of a broiler pan; brush with reserved marinade. Broil 3 inches from the heat for 6 to 8 minutes or to desired doneness, turning occasionally and brushing with marinade during the first half of broiling time.

5 Add a cherry tomato to the end of each skewer for the last 1 minute of broiling. Serve with hot rice. Makes 5 servings.

Nutrition facts per serving: 260 calories, 8 g total fat (2 g saturated fat), 46 mg cholesterol, 117 mg sodium, 28 g carbohydrate, 3 g fiber, 18 g protein
Exchanges: 1 Starch, 2 Lean Meat, 2 Vegetable

175 calories

Preparation time: 20 minutes ● **Marinating time:** 6 to 24 hours ● **Grilling time:** 16 minutes

herbed lamb with apples

Grill the apple rings in a foil packet alongside the lamb. Be sure to turn the packet often so the apples cook evenly.
To keep the apples from losing their shape and to add color, leave the peel on the apples.

1 cup apple juice or apple cider
¼ teaspoon finely shredded lemon peel
2 tablespoons lemon juice
1 tablespoon honey
1 teaspoon dried rosemary, crushed
1 clove garlic, minced
½ teaspoon salt
¼ teaspoon pepper
2 pounds boneless leg of lamb, cut crosswise
  into 1-inch-thick slices and trimmed of
  separable fat
4 small apples, cored and sliced crosswise
  into ½-inch-thick rings
3 tablespoons apple juice or apple cider

1 For marinade, stir together the 1 cup apple juice, the lemon peel, lemon juice, honey, rosemary, garlic, salt, and pepper. Place meat in a plastic bag set in a deep bowl. Pour marinade over meat. Close bag. Marinate in the refrigerator for at least 6 hours or up to 24 hours. Drain meat; reserve marinade.

2 Place apple slices on an 18×18-inch piece of heavy foil. Sprinkle with the 3 tablespoons apple juice or cider. Bring up long edges of foil and, leaving a little space for steam expansion, seal tightly with a double fold. Fold short ends to seal.

3 In a covered grill arrange medium-hot coals around the outside edges of the grill, then test for medium heat (see note, page 181) above the center of grill (not over coals). Place meat slices and the apple packet on the grill rack, not over the coals. Cover the grill; grill for 16 to 18 minutes for medium-rare or 18 to 20 minutes for medium, brushing meat occasionally with reserved marinade up until the last 5 minutes of grilling time. Grill apple slices for 16 to 18 minutes or just until tender. Serve meat with apples. Makes 8 servings.

Nutrition facts per serving: 175 calories, 5 g total fat (2 g saturated fat), 57 mg cholesterol, 212 mg sodium, 13 g carbohydrate, 1 g fiber, 18 g protein
Exchanges: 2 Lean Meat, 1 Fruit

293 calories

Preparation time: 1 hour ● **Marinating time:** 2 to 24 hours

lamb with green beans and noodles

Toss strips of stir-fried lamb with noodles and green beans for an easy one-dish meal.
If you like, substitute lean pork for the lamb.

12 **ounces lean boneless leg of lamb**
 1 **cup apple juice or apple cider**
 1 **tablespoon snipped fresh rosemary**
    or ½ teaspoon dried rosemary, crushed
 6 **cups egg-free medium noodles (8 ounces)**
 1 **9-ounce package frozen French-cut green**
    beans
 ½ **cup reduced-sodium chicken broth**
 1 **tablespoon cornstarch**
 2 **teaspoons cooking oil**
    Fresh rosemary (optional)

1 Partially freeze meat about 30 minutes. Thinly slice across the grain into bite-size strips. Place in a plastic bag set in a deep bowl. Add apple juice or cider and the 1 tablespoon fresh rosemary or the dried rosemary. Close bag. Marinate in the refrigerator for at least 2 hours or up to 24 hours, turning occasionally.

2 Cook noodles according to package directions, adding green beans the last 6 minutes of cooking time. Drain. Keep warm.

3 Meanwhile, drain meat, reserving marinade. Stir chicken broth and cornstarch into reserved marinade until thoroughly combined. Set aside.

4 In wok or large skillet heat oil over medium-high heat for 1 minute. Add meat. Cook and stir for 2 to 3 minutes or until meat is done. Stir in reserved marinade. Cook and stir until thickened and bubbly. Cook and stir for 2 minutes more. Stir in noodle mixture. Serve immediately. If desired, garnish with additional fresh rosemary. Makes 5 servings.

Nutrition facts per serving: 293 calories, 7 g total fat (2 g saturated fat), 74 mg cholesterol, 107 mg sodium, 40 g carbohydrate, 1 g fiber, 18 g protein
Exchanges: 2 Starch, 1 Lean Meat, 2 Vegetable

Poultry

chapter index

258 calories

Preparation time: 25 minutes ● **Baking time:** 15 minutes

baked chimichangas

Use leftover roasted chicken or turkey or roast beef or pork for this Mexican favorite.
Freeze any extra chimichangas for another meal (see directions, below).

8 ounces cooked chicken, turkey, pork,
    or beef (1½ cups)
1 8-ounce jar salsa
1 16-ounce can fat-free refried beans
1 4½-ounce can diced green chili peppers,
    drained
3 tablespoons thinly sliced green onions
4 ounces reduced-fat Monterey Jack
    or cheddar cheese, shredded (1 cup)
8 8- to 9-inch flour tortillas
    Fat-free dairy sour cream (optional)
    Salsa (optional)
    Thinly sliced green onion (optional)

1 Using 2 forks, shred cooked poultry, pork, or beef. In a large skillet combine poultry or meat, the salsa, beans, chili peppers, and the green onions. Cook and stir over medium heat until heated through. Stir in cheese.

2 Meanwhile, wrap tortillas in foil; warm in a 350° oven for 10 minutes. For each chimichanga, spoon about ½ cup meat mixture on a tortilla, near 1 edge. Fold in sides; roll up.

3 Place in a 13×9×2-inch baking pan. Bake, uncovered, in a 350° oven for 15 to 20 minutes or until heated through and tortillas are crisp and brown. If desired, serve with sour cream, additional salsa, and/or green onion. Makes 8 servings.

Freezing Directions: Place the unbaked chimichangas in freezer containers. Seal, label, and freeze for up to 6 months. To prepare, wrap the frozen chimichangas individually in foil. Bake in a 350° oven for 50 minutes. (Or, thaw chimichangas in refrigerator overnight. Wrap each in foil and bake about 30 minutes.) Remove the foil. Bake for 10 minutes more or until tortilla is crisp and brown.

Nutrition facts per serving: 258 calories, 9 g total fat (3 g saturated fat), 37 mg cholesterol, 685 mg sodium, 28 g carbohydrate, 3 g fiber, 18 g protein
Exchanges: 1½ Starch, 2 Lean Meat, 1 Vegetable

276 calories

Preparation time: 30 minutes

chicken tacos

These tasty tacos only take 30 minutes to make. If you don't have any leftover chicken to use, buy frozen chopped cooked chicken at your supermarket.

Nonstick spray coating
- **1 cup chopped onion**
- **1 clove garlic, minced**
- **2 cups chopped cooked chicken**
- **1 8-ounce can tomato sauce**
- **1 4½-ounce can diced green chili peppers, drained**
- **12 taco shells**
- **2 cups shredded lettuce**
- **1 medium tomato, seeded and chopped**
- **½ cup finely shredded reduced-fat cheddar cheese and/or Monterey Jack cheese (2 ounces)**

1 Spray an unheated large skillet with nonstick coating. Preheat over medium heat. Add onion and garlic; cook until tender.

2 Stir in chicken, tomato sauce, and chili peppers. Heat through.

3 Divide chicken mixture among taco shells. Top with lettuce, tomato, and cheese. Makes 6 servings.

Nutrition facts per serving: 276 calories, 12 g total fat (3 g saturated fat), 52 mg cholesterol, 502 mg sodium, 23 g carbohydrate, 2 g fiber, 21 g protein
Exchanges: 1 Starch, 2 Lean Meat, 2 Vegetable, 1 Fat

183 calories

Preparation time: 30 minutes

chicken with peppers and potatoes

This dish is packed with the flavor of fresh herbs and roasted sweet peppers. If you like, substitute Greek kalamata olives packed in vinegar, not oil, for the ripe olives.

12 ounces skinless, boneless chicken breast halves, cut into 1-inch chunks
   Nonstick spray coating
2 cups diced potatoes
1 7-ounce jar roasted red sweet peppers, drained and diced
½ cup reduced-sodium chicken broth
4½ teaspoons snipped fresh basil
   or 1½ teaspoons dried basil, crushed
4½ teaspoons snipped fresh oregano
   or 1½ teaspoons dried oregano, crushed
⅛ teaspoon salt
⅛ teaspoon black pepper
2 tablespoons sliced pitted ripe olives
   Fresh oregano (optional)

1 Rinse chicken; pat dry with paper towels. Spray an unheated large skillet with nonstick coating. Preheat over medium-high heat. Add chicken. Cook and stir for 4 to 5 minutes or until tender and no longer pink. Remove. Set aside.

2 Add uncooked potatoes, sweet peppers, chicken broth, basil, oregano, salt, and black pepper to the skillet. Bring to boiling; reduce heat. Simmer, covered, about 7 minutes or until potatoes are just tender. Stir in chicken and olives. Heat through. If desired, garnish with additional fresh oregano. Makes 4 servings.

Nutrition facts per serving: 183 calories, 4 g total fat (1 g saturated fat), 45 mg cholesterol, 213 mg sodium, 20 g carbohydrate, 2 g fiber, 19 g protein
Exchanges: 1 Starch, 2 Lean Meat, 1 Vegetable

330 calories

Preparation time: 25 minutes

chicken and penne with basil sauce

If fresh basil is unavailable, do not substitute dried basil. Use another fresh herb instead, such as tarragon, thyme, or sage. Dried herbs just can't compare to the flavor of fresh herbs used here.

1¼ **cups reduced-sodium chicken broth**
4 **teaspoons cornstarch**
⅛ **teaspoon black pepper**
2 **cups packaged dried penne pasta**
   Nonstick spray coating
1 **medium red sweet pepper, cut into thin strips**
1 **medium yellow or green sweet pepper, cut into thin strips**
3 **cloves garlic, minced**
1 **tablespoon cooking oil**
12 **ounces skinless, boneless chicken breast halves, cut into 1-inch cubes**
¼ **cup lightly packed fresh basil leaves, cut into thin shreds**
2 **tablespoons finely shredded Parmesan cheese**
   Fresh basil (optional)

1 Stir together chicken broth, cornstarch, and black pepper. Set aside.

2 Cook pasta according to package directions, omitting any oil and salt. Drain. Cover; keep warm.

3 Meanwhile, spray an unheated large skillet with nonstick coating. Preheat over medium heat. Add sweet peppers and garlic. Stir-fry for 2 to 3 minutes or until sweet peppers are crisp-tender. Remove from skillet. Add the oil to skillet; increase heat to medium-high. Add chicken; stir-fry for 3 to 4 minutes or until chicken is no longer pink. Stir broth mixture; add to skillet. Cook and stir until thickened and bubbly. Return sweet peppers to skillet; add the ¼ cup basil shreds. Cook and stir for 2 minutes more. Toss with hot pasta. Sprinkle with Parmesan cheese. If desired, garnish with additional basil. Makes 4 servings.

Nutrition facts per serving: 330 calories, 8 g total fat (1 g saturated fat), 47 mg cholesterol, 282 mg sodium, 39 g carbohydrate, 1 g fiber, 24 g protein
Exchanges: 2 Starch, 2 Lean Meat, 2 Vegetable

low-fat flavor boosters

To cook low-fat, yet full-flavored, dishes, stock your pantry and refrigerator with some of these low-fat flavor boosters. The next time your food needs perking up, you'll be ready for action. Experiment by adding a small amount of the ingredient first, then season to taste.

- **Lemon, lime, and orange juices.** Great for fish and beef dishes, pasta, and salad dressings.
- **Low-sodium soy sauce and teriyaki sauce.** Add to marinades for meat and poultry, savory sauces, and vegetable dishes.
- **Red and green onions, leeks, and shallots.** Sauté and add to main dishes and soups or slice raw and add to pizza and salads.
- **Salsas.** Spice up soups, gravies, and sauces with a spoonful; spread on a pizza shell instead of pizza sauce; toss with pasta.
- **Chutneys** (such as mango, peach, and pear). Serve alongside grilled and broiled meats and with rice dishes.
- **Asian ingredients** (such as cilantro, chili paste, and hoisin sauce). Experiment by adding to broth soups, pasta, and stir-fry dishes.
- **Fresh and dried herbs.** Add to salad dressings, marinades, and soups. Sprinkle atop pizzas, entrées (as a garnish), and salads. As a rule of thumb, use one-third more snipped fresh herb than dry herb.
- **Dried herb mixtures.** Save money and time and experience unique flavor combinations with herb mixtures such as fines herbes, Cajun seasoning, lemon-dill, Beau Monde seasoning, five-spice powder, and Jamaican Jerk seasoning.
- **Bottled hot pepper sauces.** Shake a few drops into dishes that could use a little heat.

- **Flavored pepper seasonings.** Great for grilling, these include lemon pepper, garlic pepper, and herb pepper.
- **Flavored vinegars.** Look for herbed, balsamic, champagne, fruit, and wine vinegars. Flavored vinegars add a real flavor boost to salad dressings and most other recipes that call for vinegar.
- **Roasted garlic.** To roast a head of garlic, cut off the pointed top and place cut side up in a baking dish. Drizzle with a little olive oil and bake, covered, in a 400° oven about 25 minutes or until soft. Use the cloves as a bread spread or add to main dishes and cooked vegetables. The flavor will be mild and smooth.
- **Fresh grated gingerroot.** Peel and grate this root then add to both sweet and savory foods, starting with ½ teaspoon or so and adding more to taste.
- **Fresh grated citrus peel** (such as lemon, lime, and orange). Add to vegetables, baked goods, salad dressings, and whole-grain dishes.
- **Mustard.** Choose from the many mustards, including honey, spicy, course-grain brown, herb, peppercorn, sweet-hot, and Chinese.
- **Roasted red peppers.** These come bottled for convenience and add a smoky, sweet pepper taste. Try them in appetizer spreads, main dishes, and salads.
- **Full-flavored oils.** Just a quick drizzle of chili, sesame, hazelnut, walnut, or virgin olive oil offers plenty of rich flavor.
- **Pungent cheeses.** Aged Parmesan, blue cheese, sharp cheddar, goat cheese, and feta cheese have bold enough flavors that a little goes a long way.

258 calories

Preparation time: 35 minutes ● **Marinating time:** 30 minutes

chicken and sweet pepper stir-fry

Dress up this simple stir-fry by using a variety of exotic mushrooms. Many kinds are available in larger grocery stores. Try chanterelle, shiitake (use only the caps), or straw mushrooms.

12 **ounces skinless, boneless chicken breast halves, cut into ½-inch pieces**
3 **tablespoons reduced-sodium soy sauce**
1 **tablespoon dry sherry**
 Nonstick spray coating
1 **medium onion, cut into wedges**
1 **medium green sweet pepper, thinly sliced**
1 **medium red sweet pepper, thinly sliced**
1½ **cups sliced fresh mushrooms**
2 **teaspoons cooking oil**
1 **teaspoon grated fresh gingerroot**
½ **of an 8-ounce can bamboo shoots, drained (about ½ cup)**
¼ **cup reduced-sodium chicken broth**
1 **teaspoon cornstarch**
¼ **teaspoon black pepper**
2 **cups hot cooked brown rice**

1 Place chicken pieces in a bowl; stir in soy sauce and sherry. Cover and marinate at room temperature for 30 minutes. Spray an unheated nonstick wok or large skillet with nonstick coating. Preheat over medium-high heat. Add onion; stir-fry for 2 minutes. Add sweet peppers; stir-fry for 2 minutes more. Add the mushrooms; stir-fry about 2 minutes more or until vegetables are crisp-tender. Remove vegetables from wok.

2 Drain chicken, reserving the marinade. Add oil to wok. Add gingerroot; stir-fry for 15 seconds. Add the chicken; stir-fry for 3 to 4 minutes or until chicken is no longer pink. Add the cooked vegetables and the bamboo shoots to wok; push from center of wok. Stir broth, cornstarch, and black pepper into reserved marinade; add to wok. Cook and stir until slightly thickened; toss gently to coat chicken mixture. Cook for 2 minutes more. Serve with hot cooked rice. Makes 4 servings.

Nutrition facts per serving: 258 calories, 5 g total fat (1 g saturated fat), 45 mg cholesterol, 480 mg sodium, 30 g carbohydrate, 1 g fiber, 21 g protein
Exchanges: 1½ Starch, 2 Lean Meat, 2 Vegetable

255 calories

Preparation time: 40 minutes

fiesta chicken

Tomato sauces subtly sweetened with raisins are often found in Mexican cooking. This dish features tender chicken and raisins in a chili-spiced sauce that gets a boost of citrus flavor from orange juice.

1   8-ounce can tomato sauce
½   cup orange juice
½   cup finely chopped onion
2   tablespoons raisins
2   tablespoons chopped pimiento
1½ teaspoons snipped fresh oregano
     or ½ teaspoon dried oregano, crushed
½   teaspoon chili powder
1   clove garlic, minced
     Several dashes bottled hot pepper sauce
12 ounces skinless, boneless chicken breast
     halves, cut into 2-inch pieces
1   tablespoon cold water
2   teaspoons cornstarch
¼   cup snipped fresh parsley
2   cups hot cooked rice

1 In a large skillet combine tomato sauce, orange juice, onion, raisins, pimiento, oregano, chili powder, garlic, and hot pepper sauce. Bring to boiling; reduce heat. Simmer, covered, for 5 minutes.

2 Stir chicken pieces into skillet; return to boiling. Simmer, covered, for 12 to 15 minutes more or until chicken is tender and no longer pink.

3 Meanwhile, stir together cold water and cornstarch. Stir into mixture in skillet. Cook and stir until thickened and bubbly. Cook and stir for 2 minutes more.

4 Toss parsley with rice. Serve chicken mixture over rice. Makes 4 servings.

Nutrition facts per serving: 255 calories, 3 g total fat (1 g saturated fat), 45 mg cholesterol, 392 mg sodium, 37 g carbohydrate, 2 g fiber, 20 g protein
Exchanges: 1½ Starch, 2 Lean Meat, 1 Vegetable, ½ Fruit

269 calories

Preparation time: 15 minutes ● **Baking time:** 27 minutes

southwestern chicken corn pudding

Added chicken makes simple corn pudding into a delicious main dish. Chili peppers and salsa gives it the southwestern touch. The result—a family-pleasing main dish.

Nonstick spray coating
1 cup cubed cooked chicken or turkey
1 cup frozen whole kernel corn
1 4½-ounce can diced green chili peppers,
    drained
2 beaten eggs
⅔ cup skim milk
¾ cup all-purpose flour
¼ teaspoon salt
⅛ teaspoon pepper
¼ cup finely shredded cheddar cheese
    (2 ounces)
Salsa (optional)
Light dairy sour cream (optional)
Fresh cilantro (optional)

1 Spray a 9-inch pie plate with nonstick coating. Set aside.

2 In a medium mixing bowl stir together chicken or turkey, corn, and chili peppers. Spread mixture in prepared pie plate.

3 In the same bowl stir together the eggs and milk. Beat in flour, salt, and pepper. Pour over chicken mixture.

4 Bake, uncovered, in a 400° oven for 25 to 30 minutes or until top is set and lightly browned. Sprinkle with cheese and bake for 2 to 3 minutes more or until cheese melts. If desired, serve with salsa and sour cream. If desired, garnish with cilantro. Makes 4 servings.

Nutrition facts per serving: 269 calories, 9 g total fat (3 g saturated fat), 148 mg cholesterol, 343 mg sodium, 27 g carbohydrate, 1 g fiber, 21 g protein
Exchanges: 2 Starch, 2 Lean Meat

307 calories

Preparation time: 25 minutes

chicken fajitas

We've kept this version of fajitas light but flavorful by using lean chicken breasts. For dessert,
serve Flan (see recipe, page 39), another favorite from Mexico.

8 7- to 8-inch flour tortillas
  Nonstick spray coating
1 **small onion, sliced and separated into rings**
2 **cloves garlic, minced**
1 **medium red or green sweet pepper, cut**
  into bite-size strips
1 **tablespoon cooking oil**
9 **ounces skinless, boneless chicken breast**
  halves, cut into bite-size strips
⅓ **cup salsa**
2 **cups shredded lettuce**
¼ **cup plain low-fat yogurt or light dairy sour**
  cream
1 **green onion, thinly sliced**

1 Wrap tortillas in foil. Heat in a 350° oven for
10 minutes.

2 Meanwhile, spray an unheated large skillet
with nonstick coating. Preheat over medium-high
heat. Add the onion rings and garlic; stir-fry for
2 minutes. Add the sweet pepper; stir-fry for 1 to
2 minutes more or until vegetables are crisp-tender.
Remove from skillet. Add oil to skillet. Add chicken;
stir-fry for 3 to 5 minutes or until chicken is tender
and no longer pink. Return vegetables to skillet. Add
salsa. Cook and stir until heated through.

3 To serve, divide chicken mixture evenly among
tortillas. Top with shredded lettuce. Spoon yogurt on
top and sprinkle with green onion. Roll up tortillas.
Makes 4 servings.

Nutrition facts per serving: 307 calories, 11 g total fat
(2 g saturated fat), 34 mg cholesterol, 357 mg sodium,
35 g carbohydrate, 2 g fiber, 18 g protein
Exchanges: 2 Starch, 1 Lean Meat, 2 Vegetable, 1 Fat

308 calories

Preparation time: 25 minutes

stroganoff-style chicken

Chicken replaces the usual beef in this rich-tasting dish. Named after a 19th-century Russian diplomat, traditional stroganoff contains butter and sour cream. Here, low-fat sour cream helps pare down the fat and calories.

Nonstick spray coating
2 **cups sliced fresh mushrooms**
½ **cup chopped onion**
2 **teaspoons cooking oil (optional)**
12 **ounces skinless, boneless chicken breast halves, cut into 1-inch cubes**
1 **8-ounce carton light dairy sour cream**
2 **tablespoons all-purpose flour**
1 **teaspoon paprika**
¼ **teaspoon salt**
½ **cup reduced-sodium chicken broth**
3¾ **cups hot cooked noodles**

1 Spray an unheated large skillet with nonstick coating. Preheat over medium heat. Add mushrooms and onion and cook until onion is nearly tender.

2 If needed, add oil to skillet. Add chicken cubes and cook for 3 to 4 minutes or until chicken is tender and no longer pink.

3 In a small bowl stir together the sour cream, flour, paprika, and salt; stir in chicken broth. Add to skillet. Cook and stir until slightly thickened and bubbly. Cook and stir for 1 minute more. Serve over hot cooked noodles. Makes 5 servings.

Nutrition facts per serving: 308 calories, 7 g total fat (2 g saturated fat), 79 mg cholesterol, 257 mg sodium, 39 g carbohydrate, 3 g fiber, 23 g protein
Exchanges: 2 Starch, 2 Lean Meat, 1 Vegetable

208 calories

Preparation time: 25 minutes ● **Marinating time:** 1 to 2 hours

moo shu chicken

Flour tortillas make an easy substitute for the pancake wrappers traditionally used in this Chinese-style burrito. If you like, use hoisin sauce in place of the duck sauce.

12 ounces skinless, boneless chicken breast halves, cut into bite-size strips
¼ cup orange juice
2 tablespoons reduced-sodium soy sauce
2 teaspoons rice vinegar
1 teaspoon ground ginger
1 teaspoon toasted sesame oil
⅛ teaspoon crushed red pepper
6 8-inch flour tortillas
2 small carrots, cut into bite-size strips
1 cup sliced fresh mushrooms
½ cup thinly sliced green onions
½ cup sliced bamboo shoots
1 to 2 teaspoons cooking oil
2 teaspoons cornstarch
2 cups shredded leaf lettuce
¼ cup sweet and sour duck sauce

1 Place chicken strips in a plastic bag set in deep bowl. Combine orange juice, soy sauce, vinegar, ginger, sesame oil, and red pepper; pour over chicken. Close bag; turn to coat. Marinate in refrigerator at least 1 hour or up to 2 hours, turning often. Drain, reserving marinade.

2 Wrap tortillas in foil. Heat in a 350° oven for 10 minutes. Meanwhile, spray an unheated large nonstick skillet with *nonstick spray coating*. Preheat over medium-high heat. Add carrots, mushrooms, onions, and bamboo shoots; stir-fry 2 minutes. Remove. Add oil to wok. Add chicken; stir-fry for 2 to 3 minutes or until no longer pink. Push to side. Stir cornstarch into reserved marinade; add to skillet. Cook and stir until bubbly. Return vegetables to skillet. Stir in the shredded lettuce; heat through.

3 Spread duck sauce on tortillas; top with chicken mixture. Fold tortillas over filling. Makes 6 servings.

Nutrition facts per serving: 208 calories, 6 g total fat (1 g saturated fat), 30 mg cholesterol, 371 mg sodium, 25 g carbohydrate, 2 g fiber, 14 g protein
Exchanges: 1 Starch, 1 Lean Meat, 2 Vegetable, ½ Fat

157 calories

Preparation time: 10 minutes • **Cooking time:** 18 minutes

chicken with olives and leeks

Don't shy away from using kalamata olives, also known as Greek olives, in this dish. Their salty flavor, combined with the leeks and vermouth, is what makes this dish so good.

4 small skinless, boneless chicken breast halves (12 ounces total)
Salt
Pepper
Nonstick spray coating
1½ cups sliced leeks (about 3 medium)
½ cup water
¼ cup dry vermouth, dry white wine, or chicken broth
⅛ teaspoon pepper
1 cup seeded coarsely chopped tomato
8 pitted kalamata olives or pitted ripe olives, quartered
Hot cooked linguine (optional)

1 Rinse chicken; pat dry with paper towels. Lightly sprinkle chicken with salt and pepper. Spray an unheated large skillet with nonstick coating. Preheat over medium heat. Add chicken. Cook for 8 to 10 minutes or until chicken is tender and no longer pink, turning to brown evenly. Remove from skillet; keep warm.

2 Add leeks, water, vermouth, and the ⅛ teaspoon pepper to skillet. Bring to boiling; reduce heat to medium-low. Cook, uncovered, for 10 minutes, stirring occasionally. Stir in tomato and olives; heat through. Serve leek mixture over chicken. If desired, serve with linguine. Makes 4 servings.

Nutrition facts per serving: 157 calories, 4 g total fat (1 g saturated fat), 45 mg cholesterol, 195 mg sodium, 10 g carbohydrate, 4 g fiber, 18 g protein
Exchanges: 2 Lean Meat, 2 Vegetable

217 calories

Preparation time: 12 minutes ● **Cooking time:** 5 minutes

curried chicken soup

This spiced chicken noodle soup can be ready in less than 15 minutes. It's a good way to use any leftover chicken. Or, if you don't have any, buy a roasted chicken from your supermarket's deli.

5 cups water
1 3-ounce package Oriental noodles with chicken flavor
2 to 3 teaspoons curry powder
1 cup sliced fresh mushrooms
2 cups cubed cooked chicken
1 medium apple, cored and coarsely chopped
½ cup sliced water chestnuts

1 In a large saucepan combine the water, the flavoring packet from noodles, and curry powder. Bring to boiling. Break up noodles and add to mixture in saucepan along with the mushrooms; reduce heat. Simmer, uncovered, for 3 minutes. Stir in chicken, apple, and water chestnuts. Heat through. Makes 5 servings.

Nutrition facts per serving: 217 calories, 8 g total fat (1 g saturated fat), 54 mg cholesterol, 449 mg sodium, 17 g carbohydrate, 1 g fiber, 20 g protein
Exchanges: 1 Starch, 2 Lean Meat, 1 Vegetable

183 calories

Preparation time: 25 minutes ● **Baking time:** 25 minutes

cheesy chicken rolls

As you roll up the chicken breasts, fold the sides in slightly. This helps to keep the cheese and mushroom filling enclosed inside the chicken as it bakes.

½ **cup shredded reduced-fat mozzarella cheese (2 ounces)**
1 **2½-ounce jar sliced mushrooms, drained**
¼ **cup plain low-fat yogurt**
1 **tablespoon snipped fresh chives and/or parsley**
1 **tablespoon chopped pimiento**
4 **medium skinless, boneless chicken breast halves (1 pound total)**
  Salt
  Pepper
1 **tablespoon fine dry bread crumbs**
⅛ **teaspoon paprika**
1 **tablespoon plain low-fat yogurt**

1 For filling, in a small bowl combine cheese, mushrooms, the ¼ cup yogurt, chives and/or parsley, and pimiento.

2 Rinse chicken; pat dry with paper towels. Place 1 chicken breast half, boned side up, between 2 pieces plastic wrap. Working from the center to the edges, pound lightly with flat side of a meat mallet to ⅛ inch thickness. Remove plastic wrap. Repeat with remaining chicken. Sprinkle lightly with salt and pepper.

3 Spoon one-fourth of cheese mixture onto the small end of each chicken breast. Fold in the sides and roll up. Arrange rolls, seam sides down, in a 2-quart square baking dish.

4 Combine bread crumbs and paprika. Brush chicken with the 1 tablespoon yogurt; sprinkle with the crumb mixture. Bake, uncovered, in a 350° oven about 25 minutes or until chicken is tender and no longer pink. Makes 4 servings.

Nutrition facts per serving: 183 calories, 6 g total fat (3 g saturated fat), 68 mg cholesterol, 288 mg sodium, 4 g carbohydrate, 1 g fiber, 27 g protein
Exchanges: 3 Lean Meat, 1 Vegetable

184 calories

Preparation time: 15 minutes ● **Baking time:** 45 minutes

garlic-clove chicken

The garlic in this dish mellows in flavor as it bakes. For ease, you can leave the skins on the garlic cloves.
To enjoy the buttery soft garlic, cut the skin and remove the clove with the tip of a knife.

1½ **to 2 pounds meaty chicken pieces (breasts,**
  thighs, and drumsticks), skinned
  Nonstick spray coating
25 **cloves garlic (about ½ cup or 2 to 3 bulbs)**
  ¼ **cup dry white wine**
  ¼ **cup reduced-sodium chicken broth**
  Salt
  Ground red pepper

1 Rinse chicken; pat dry with paper towels.
Spray an unheated large skillet with nonstick
coating. Preheat over medium heat. Add chicken
and cook for 10 minutes, turning to brown evenly.

2 Place chicken in a 2-quart square baking dish.
Add unpeeled garlic cloves.

3 In a small bowl combine wine and chicken
broth; pour over chicken. Lightly sprinkle chicken
with salt and ground red pepper.

4 Bake, covered, in a 325° oven for 45 to
50 minutes or until chicken is tender and no longer
pink. Makes 4 servings.

Nutrition facts per serving: 184 calories, 6 g total fat
(2 g saturated fat), 69 mg cholesterol, 140 mg sodium,
6 g carbohydrate, 0 g fiber, 23 g protein
Exchanges: 3 Lean Meat, 1 Vegetable

134 calories

Preparation time: 25 minutes ● **Cooking time:** 20 minutes

chicken cacciatore

Cacciatore is Italian for "hunter" and usually contains mushrooms, onions, tomatoes, and herbs. If you like, replace the ¼ cup water with red wine, an optional ingredient often used in this classic dish.

4 small skinless, boneless chicken breast halves (12 ounces total)
   Nonstick spray coating
1 14½-ounce can stewed tomatoes
1 medium green sweet pepper, cut into thin strips
½ cup sliced fresh mushrooms
¼ cup chopped onion
¼ cup water or red wine
2 teaspoons dried Italian seasoning, crushed
⅛ teaspoon black pepper

1 Rinse chicken; pat dry with paper towels. Spray an unheated large skillet with nonstick coating. Preheat over medium heat. Add chicken and cook about 6 minutes or until lightly browned, turning to brown evenly.

2 Stir in stewed tomatoes, sweet pepper, mushrooms, onion, water, Italian seasoning, and black pepper. Bring to boiling; reduce heat. Simmer, covered, about 15 minutes or until chicken is tender and no longer pink. Remove chicken from skillet; cover chicken to keep warm. Simmer tomato mixture, uncovered, about 5 minutes or to desired consistency. Makes 4 servings.

Nutrition facts per serving: 134 calories, 3 g total fat (1 g saturated fat), 45 mg cholesterol, 309 mg sodium, 10 g carbohydrate, 3 g fiber, 18 g protein
Exchanges: 2 Lean Meat, 2 Vegetable

124 calories

Preparation time: 30 minutes

chicken with garlic greens

*Don't be alarmed by the amount of fresh greens in this dish; they cook down
to an amount that is just right for four servings.*

**4 small skinless, boneless chicken breast
halves (12 ounces total)**
¼ teaspoon coarsely ground black pepper
⅛ teaspoon salt
Nonstick spray coating
⅔ cup reduced-sodium chicken broth
6 to 8 cloves garlic, minced
¼ teaspoon crushed red pepper
¼ teaspoon coarsely ground black pepper
**1 pound fresh greens (such as mustard
greens, beet greens, kohlrabi greens,
kale, collard greens, and/or turnip
greens), torn (about 16 cups)**
Balsamic vinegar (optional)
Red sweet pepper slices (optional)

1 Rinse chicken; pat dry with paper towels.
Sprinkle with ¼ teaspoon black pepper and the salt.
Spray an unheated large skillet with nonstick

coating. Preheat over medium heat. Add chicken.
Brown chicken quickly on both sides. Reduce heat
slightly. Cover and cook for 10 to 12 minutes or
until chicken is tender and no longer pink.

2 Meanwhile, in a very large saucepan or Dutch
oven combine broth, garlic, the crushed red pepper,
and remaining ¼ teaspoon black pepper. Bring to
boiling. Add greens; reduce heat. Cook, covered, for
9 to 12 minutes or until greens are just tender,
stirring once or twice.

3 Remove chicken breasts from skillet and slice.
Spoon greens and their juices onto 4 dinner plates.
Place chicken breast slices on top of greens. If
desired, drizzle lightly with the balsamic vinegar
and garnish with red sweet pepper slices. Makes
4 servings.

Nutrition facts per serving: 124 calories, 3 g total fat
(1 g saturated fat), 45 mg cholesterol, 238 mg sodium,
5 g carbohydrate, 3 g fiber, 20 g protein
Exchanges: 2 Lean Meat, 1 Vegetable

154 calories

Preparation time: 35 minutes ● **Cooking time:** 30 minutes

stuffed chicken spirals

Chopped fresh vegetables seasoned with lemon and thyme make a colorful and flavorful stuffing for these chicken spirals. Serve with spinach fettuccine if you like.

1½ **cups sliced fresh mushrooms**
2 **tablespoons shredded carrot**
2 **tablespoons sliced green onion**
2 **tablespoons finely chopped celery**
1 **medium tomato, peeled, seeded, and chopped**
2½ **teaspoons lemon juice**
½ **teaspoon dried thyme, crushed**
4 **medium skinless, boneless chicken breast halves (1 pound total)**
1 **teaspoon instant chicken bouillon granules**
¼ **cup skim milk**
1 **tablespoon cornstarch**

1 In covered saucepan cook first 4 ingredients in small amount *boiling water* about 5 minutes or until tender. Drain. Stir in tomato, *1½ teaspoons* of the juice, *half* of the thyme, and ⅛ teaspoon *pepper*.

2 Rinse chicken; pat dry with paper towels. Place 1 breast half, boned side up, between 2 pieces of plastic wrap. Pound lightly to ⅛ inch thickness.

Remove plastic wrap. Repeat with remaining chicken. Spoon one-fourth of the carrot mixture onto each chicken piece. Fold in sides; roll up. Secure with wooden toothpicks. Sprinkle with ⅛ teaspoon *salt* and few dashes *pepper*.

3 Spray an unheated skillet with *nonstick spray coating*. Preheat over medium heat. Add chicken; cook 8 to 10 minutes, turning to brown evenly. Add remaining lemon juice and thyme, bouillon granules, and ½ cup *water*. Bring to boiling; reduce heat. Simmer, covered, about 15 minutes or until chicken is no longer pink. Remove from skillet; keep warm.

4 If desired, strain cooking liquid; return to skillet. Mix milk and cornstarch. Add to skillet. Cook and stir until bubbly. Cook and stir 2 minutes more. Remove picks. Serve chicken with sauce. Serves 4.

Nutrition facts per serving: 154 calories, 4 g total fat (1 g saturated fat), 60 mg cholesterol, 354 mg sodium, 7 g carbohydrate, 1 g fiber, 23 g protein
Exchanges: 2½ Lean Meat, 1 Vegetable

117 calories

Preparation time: 20 minutes

chicken marsala

Accompany this dish with a colorful squash and sweet pepper combo. Cook cut-up summer squash and sweet pepper strips in a small amount of boiling water for 3 to 5 minutes or until just tender.

4 small skinless, boneless chicken breast halves (12 ounces total)
Nonstick spray coating
1½ cups sliced fresh mushrooms
2 tablespoons sliced green onion
2 tablespoons water
¼ teaspoon salt
¼ cup dry Marsala or dry sherry

1 Rinse chicken; pat dry with paper towels. Place 1 piece of chicken, boned side up, between 2 pieces of plastic wrap. Working from the center to the edges, pound lightly with flat side of a meat mallet to about ¼ inch thickness. Remove plastic wrap. Repeat with remaining chicken.

2 Spray an unheated large skillet with nonstick coating. Preheat skillet over medium heat. Add chicken. Cook for 4 to 6 minutes or until tender and no longer pink, turning to brown evenly. Remove from skillet; keep warm.

3 Add mushrooms, green onion, water, and salt to skillet. Cook over medium heat about 3 minutes or until mushrooms are tender and most of the liquid has evaporated. Add Marsala or sherry. Heat through. Spoon vegetables and liquid over chicken. Makes 4 servings.

Nutrition facts per serving: 117 calories, 3 g total fat (1 g saturated fat), 45 mg cholesterol, 175 mg sodium, 2 g carbohydrate, 0 g fiber, 17 g protein
Exchanges: 2 Lean Meat, 1 Vegetable

143 calories

Preparation time: 20 minutes

chicken with grapes

For a delicious dinner entrée, begin with fruit juice plus a few simple ingredients.
Red and green grapes add a light sweetness and a pretty color too.

**4 small skinless, boneless chicken breast
   halves (12 ounces total)**
   Nonstick spray coating
**½ cup white grape juice, apple juice, or
   apple cider**
1 teaspoon instant chicken bouillon granules
1 teaspoon cornstarch
**1 cup seedless green and/or red grapes,
   halved**
   Hot cooked linguine (optional)
   **Fresh herb, such as oregano or thyme
   (optional)**

1 Rinse chicken; pat dry with paper towels. Spray an unheated large skillet with nonstick coating. Preheat skillet over medium to medium-high heat. Add chicken. Cook for 8 to 10 minutes or until tender and no longer pink, turning to brown evenly. Remove from skillet; keep warm.

2 Meanwhile, combine grape or apple juice or cider, bouillon granules, and cornstarch. Add to skillet. Cook and stir until thickened and bubbly. Cook and stir 2 minutes more. Stir in grapes; heat through. Serve over chicken. If desired, serve with linguine and garnish with herb. Makes 4 servings.

Nutrition facts per serving: 143 calories, 3 g total fat (1 g saturated fat), 45 mg cholesterol, 258 mg sodium, 13 g carbohydrate, 0 g fiber, 17 g protein
Exchanges: 2 Lean Meat, 1 Fruit

202 calories

Preparation time: 10 minutes ● **Standing time:** 30 minutes ● **Grilling time:** 12 minutes

grilled chicken with black bean salsa

The combination of black beans, yellow corn, and red tomatoes makes a colorful topper. The salsa also can be served over grilled fish or flank steak or as a snack with tortilla chips.

4 small skinless, boneless chicken breast halves (12 ounces total)
3 tablespoons lime juice
1 tablespoon honey
1 teaspoon paprika
½ teaspoon ground turmeric
⅛ teaspoon garlic powder
Dash ground red pepper
1 15-ounce can black beans, rinsed and drained
½ cup frozen whole kernel corn, cooked and drained
1 small tomato, chopped
1 jalapeño pepper, seeded and finely chopped*
2 tablespoons snipped fresh cilantro
Tomato wedges (optional)

1 Rinse chicken; pat dry with paper towels. Combine *1 tablespoon* of the lime juice, the honey, paprika, turmeric, garlic powder, red pepper, and a dash *salt*. Brush over both sides of chicken breasts. Let stand 30 minutes. Grill directly over medium coals for 12 to 15 minutes or until tender and no longer pink, turning once.

2 Meanwhile, in a medium bowl combine the beans, corn, chopped tomato, jalapeño pepper, the remaining 2 tablespoons lime juice, and the cilantro. Serve with the chicken. If desired, garnish with tomato wedges. Makes 4 servings.

*****Note:** Because chili peppers, such as jalapeños, contain volatile oils that can burn your skin and eyes, avoid direct contact with them as much as possible. When working with chili peppers, wear plastic gloves. If your bare hands touch the chili peppers, wash your hands well with soap and water.

Nutrition facts per serving: 202 calories, 3 g total fat (1 g saturated fat), 45 mg cholesterol, 340 mg sodium, 25 g carbohydrate, 5 g fiber, 24 g protein
Exchanges: 1½ Starch, 2 Lean Meat, 1 Vegetable

127 calories

Preparation time: 10 minutes ● **Baking time:** 18 minutes

honey-ginger crusted chicken

*Honey, orange juice, and ginger gives "fried" chicken an updated flavor. Best of all, the chicken
has the crisp, crunchy texture of fried chicken, but without all the calories and fat.*

**4 small skinless, boneless chicken breast
   halves (12 ounces total)**
   Nonstick spray coating
1 tablespoon honey
1 tablespoon orange juice
¼ teaspoon ground ginger
¼ teaspoon black pepper
   Dash ground red pepper (optional)
¾ cup cornflakes, crushed (about ⅓ cup)
½ teaspoon dried parsley flakes

1 Rinse chicken; pat dry with paper towels.
Spray a shallow baking pan with nonstick coating.
Place chicken breasts in baking pan. In a small
bowl combine honey, orange juice, ginger, black
pepper, and red pepper (if desired). Brush honey
mixture over chicken. Combine cornflakes and
parsley flakes. Sprinkle cornflake mixture over
chicken to coat.

2 Bake, uncovered, in a 350° oven for 18 to
20 minutes or until chicken is tender and no longer
pink. Makes 4 servings.

Nutrition facts per serving: 127 calories, 3 g total fat
(1 g saturated fat), 45 mg cholesterol, 94 mg sodium,
8 g carbohydrate, 0 g fiber, 17 g protein
Exchanges: ½ Starch, 2 Lean Meat

288 calories

Preparation time: 20 minutes

ginger and peach chicken

If you can find fresh pea pods at your supermarket, use them instead of frozen pea pods. Remove the tips and strings and cook in a small amount of boiling water for 2 to 4 minutes or until crisp-tender.

4 small skinless, boneless chicken breast halves (12 ounces total)
Nonstick spray coating
1 15-ounce can peach slices (in light syrup)
1 tablespoon reduced-sodium soy sauce
2 teaspoons cornstarch
1 teaspoon grated fresh gingerroot
or ¼ teaspoon ground ginger
Dash ground red pepper
½ of an 8-ounce can (½ cup) sliced water chestnuts, drained
2 cups hot cooked rice
1 6-ounce package frozen pea pods, cooked and drained

1 Rinse chicken; pat dry with paper towels. Spray an unheated large nonstick skillet with nonstick coating. Preheat over medium heat. Add chicken. Cook for 8 to 10 minutes or until tender and no longer pink, turning to brown evenly. Remove from skillet; keep warm.

2 Meanwhile, drain peaches, reserving syrup. Add enough *water* to syrup to equal 1 cup liquid. Stir in the soy sauce, cornstarch, gingerroot, and ground red pepper. Add to skillet. Cook and stir until thickened and bubbly. Cook and stir for 1 minute more. Gently stir in peaches and water chestnuts; heat through.

3 On a serving platter or 4 individual plates arrange rice, pea pods, and chicken. Spoon peach mixture over chicken. Makes 4 servings.

Nutrition facts per serving: 288 calories, 3 g total fat (1 g saturated fat), 45 mg cholesterol, 182 mg sodium, 45 g carbohydrate, 2 g fiber, 21 g protein
Exchanges: 1½ Starch, 2 Lean Meat, 1 Vegetable, 1 Fruit

223 calories

Preparation time: 20 minutes

lime-sauced chicken

For the lime peel garnish, use a vegetable peeler to remove the peel from a lime. Scrape off as much of the white membrane from the peel as you can. Then with a sharp knife, cut the peel into very thin strips.

4 **small skinless, boneless chicken breast halves (12 ounces total)**
Nonstick spray coating
½ **of a medium lime**
¾ **cup apple juice or apple cider**
2 **teaspoons cornstarch**
½ **teaspoon instant chicken bouillon granules**
2 **cups hot cooked rice**
Lime slices (optional)

1 Rinse chicken; pat dry with paper towels. Spray an unheated large skillet with nonstick coating. Preheat over medium heat. Add chicken. Cook for 8 to 10 minutes or until tender and no longer pink, turning to brown evenly. Remove from skillet; keep warm.

2 Meanwhile, if desired, remove strips of peel from the lime, using a vegetable peeler. Cut peel into very thin strips; set aside. Squeeze 1 tablespoon juice from lime.

3 For sauce, combine lime juice, apple juice or cider, cornstarch, and bouillon granules; carefully add to skillet. Cook and stir until thickened and bubbly. Cook and stir for 2 minutes more.

4 To serve, cut each chicken breast half diagonally into 1-inch-thick pieces; arrange on top of rice. Spoon some of the sauce over each serving. If desired, garnish with lime strips and lime slices. Pass remaining sauce. Makes 4 servings.

Nutrition facts per serving: 223 calories, 3 g total fat (1 g saturated fat), 45 mg cholesterol, 152 mg sodium, 29 g carbohydrate, 0 g fiber, 18 g protein
Exchanges: 2 Starch, 2 Lean Meat

128 calories

Preparation time: 15 minutes ● **Cooking time:** 15 minutes

tarragon chicken and apples

Tarragon, one of the more assertive herbs, blends pleasantly with the mild flavor of chicken. Here, just a little perks up a light apple glaze.

4 small skinless, boneless chicken breast
  halves (12 ounces total)
½ cup apple juice
¾ teaspoon snipped fresh tarragon
  or ¼ teaspoon dried tarragon, crushed
½ teaspoon instant chicken bouillon granules
1 clove garlic, minced
  Dash pepper
1 medium apple, cored and sliced
¼ cup sliced green onions
1 tablespoon cold water
1½ teaspoons cornstarch
  Green onions (optional)

1 Rinse chicken; pat dry with paper towels. In a large skillet combine the apple juice, tarragon, bouillon granules, garlic, and pepper. Bring to boiling. Add chicken breasts; reduce heat. Simmer, covered, for 7 minutes.

2 Turn chicken over; add apple slices and sliced green onions. Simmer, covered, for 4 to 5 minutes more or until chicken is tender and no longer pink.

3 With a slotted spoon, remove chicken and apples; keep warm. Reserve cooking liquid.

4 In a small bowl stir together the cold water and cornstarch. Stir into cooking liquid in skillet. Cook and stir until thickened and bubbly. Cook and stir for 2 minutes more. Spoon over chicken and apples. If desired, garnish with additional green onions. Makes 4 servings.

Nutrition facts per serving: 128 calories, 3 g total fat (1 g saturated fat), 45 mg cholesterol, 150 mg sodium, 9 g carbohydrate, 1 g fiber, 16 g protein
Exchanges: 2 Lean Meat, ½ Fruit

151 calories

Preparation time: 15 minutes ● **Grilling time:** 35 minutes

chicken with papaya - mustard salsa

You can either cook the chicken directly over the coals or indirectly over a drip pan. Indirect grilling reduces flare-ups, excess smoke, and charring because the meat juices do not drip into the coals.

- **4 medium chicken breast halves (1½ pounds)**
- **1½ teaspoons cooking oil**
- **2 teaspoons finely chopped green onion**
- **¼ teaspoon dried thyme, crushed**
- **⅛ teaspoon garlic salt**
- **1 medium papaya**
- **1 tablespoon honey mustard**
- **1 tablespoon light mayonnaise dressing or salad dressing**
- **½ cup finely chopped zucchini or yellow summer squash**
- **2 tablespoons finely chopped red onion**
- **4 small red cabbage or radicchio leaves**
   Fresh thyme (optional)

1 Skin chicken breasts. Rinse chicken; pat dry. Combine oil, green onion, thyme, and garlic salt. Brush on skinned side of chicken breasts.

2 Grill chicken, bone sides up, on the rack of an uncovered grill directly over medium coals for 20 minutes. Turn and grill for 15 to 25 minutes more or until tender and no longer pink. (Or, in a covered grill, arrange medium-hot coals around a drip pan; test for medium heat above the pan [see note, page 285]. Place chicken, bone sides down, on grill rack directly over drip pan, not over coals. Cover and grill for 50 to 60 minutes or until tender and no longer pink.)

3 Meanwhile, peel and seed the papaya. Slice half of the papaya; finely chop remaining papaya (should have about ½ cup). Set aside. For salsa, in a medium bowl stir together mustard and mayonnaise dressing. Stir in chopped papaya, zucchini or summer squash, and red onion. (Salsa tends to water out on standing; use immediately.)

4 To serve, spoon salsa in cabbage leaves; place on plates with papaya slices. Add grilled chicken. If desired, garnish with fresh thyme. Makes 4 servings.

Nutrition facts per serving: 151 calories, 6 g total fat (1 g saturated fat), 45 mg cholesterol, 159 mg sodium, 8 g carbohydrate, 1 g fiber, 17 g protein
Exchanges: 2 Lean Meat, ½ Fruit

144 calories

Preparation time: 15 minutes ● **Marinating time:** 4 to 24 hours ● **Grilling time:** 12 minutes

grilled jerk chicken

Jamaican jerk seasoning is a dry blend of chilies, thyme, and spices (such as cinnamon, ginger, cloves, and allspice). Use as a rub or combined with a liquid for a marinade, as it is here.

4 **medium skinless, boneless chicken breast halves (about 1 pound)**
1 **large onion, quartered**
1 to 2 **jalapeño peppers, seeded and cut up***
1 **tablespoon snipped fresh thyme or 1 teaspoon dried thyme, crushed**
½ **teaspoon ground allspice**
¼ **teaspoon ground nutmeg Dash ground cloves**
¼ **cup orange juice Torn mixed greens (optional) Pineapple wedges (optional) Orange slices, quartered (optional)**

1 Rinse chicken; pat dry with paper towels. Place chicken in a plastic bag set in a shallow dish.

2 In a food processor bowl or blender container combine onion, jalapeño peppers, thyme, allspice, nutmeg, cloves, and ¼ teaspoon *salt*. Cover; process or blend until almost smooth. With food processor or blender running, add the orange juice. Blend or process until almost smooth. Pour over chicken. Close bag. Marinate in the refrigerator for at least 4 hours or up to 24 hours, turning occasionally.

3 Drain chicken; discard marinade. Grill chicken on the rack of an uncovered grill directly over medium coals for 12 to 15 minutes or until tender and no longer pink, turning once. If desired, place greens on plates with pineapple and oranges. Add chicken. If desired, drizzle with additional *orange juice*. Makes 4 servings.

*Note: Because chili peppers, such as jalapeños, contain volatile oils that can burn your skin and eyes, avoid direct contact with them as much as possible. When working with chili peppers, wear plastic gloves. If your bare hands touch the chili peppers, wash your hands well with soap and water.

Nutrition facts per serving: 144 calories, 3 g total fat (1 g saturated fat), 59 mg cholesterol, 189 mg sodium, 5 g carbohydrate, 1 g fiber, 22 g protein
Exchanges: 3 Lean Meat

219 calories

Preparation time: 20 minutes ● **Baking time:** 1 hour ● **Standing time:** 10 minutes

chicken and barley bake

Replace your high-fat chicken noodle casserole with this updated one-dish meal. It's low in calories and fat and it's economical, too. Barley supplies more fiber than noodles or rice.

4 chicken thighs, skinned (1½ pounds total)
Nonstick spray coating
1 cup chopped onion
¾ cup chopped carrot
¾ cup water
½ cup pearl barley
1 teaspoon instant chicken bouillon granules
½ teaspoon poultry seasoning
1 clove garlic, minced
2 tablespoons snipped fresh parsley

1 Rinse chicken; pat dry with paper towels. Spray an unheated large skillet with nonstick coating. Preheat over medium heat. Add chicken and cook for 10 minutes, turning to brown evenly. Remove from skillet.

2 In same skillet combine the onion, carrot, water, barley, bouillon granules, poultry seasoning, and garlic. Bring to boiling.

3 Pour hot mixture into a 1½-quart casserole. Arrange chicken thighs on top of mixture.

4 Bake, covered, in a 350° oven about 1 hour or until barley and chicken are tender and chicken is no longer pink. Let stand, covered, for 10 minutes before serving. Sprinkle with parsley. Makes 4 servings.

Nutrition facts per serving: 219 calories, 7 g total fat (2 g saturated fat), 49 mg cholesterol, 284 mg sodium, 23 g carbohydrate, 5 g fiber, 17 g protein
Exchanges: 1 Starch, 2 Lean Meat, 1 Vegetable

293 calories

Preparation time: 20 minutes ● **Roasting time:** 1¼ hours

herb roasted chicken

The best way to cut back on fat and calories with poultry is to remove the skin. However, leaving the skin on during roasting helps keep the meat moist. Simply remove the skin when carving or leave it on your plate.

¼ **cup snipped fresh herbs (such as basil,**
    rosemary, marjoram, or sage) or
    4 teaspoons dried mixed herbs, crushed
¼ **teaspoon salt**
¼ **teaspoon pepper**
1 **3-pound whole broiler-fryer chicken**
2 **cups ½-inch-long carrot pieces**
1 **cup pearl onions, peeled**
2 **teaspoons olive oil**
1 **10-ounce package frozen peas, thawed**
    Fresh rosemary (optional)

1 For herb rub, combine the ¼ cup fresh herbs or the dried herbs, salt, and pepper. Rinse chicken; pat dry with paper towels. Loosen skin on chicken breast. Using your fingers, carefully spread *half* of the herb rub under the skin. Skewer neck skin to back; tie legs to tail. Twist wings under back. Place chicken, breast side up, on a rack in a shallow roasting pan. If desired, insert a meat thermometer into center of an inside thigh muscle. Roast, uncovered, in a 375° oven for 30 minutes.

2 Combine carrots and onions in a 1½-quart casserole. Toss with the remaining herb rub and the olive oil. Cover; add to oven. Roast about 45 minutes more or until chicken is no longer pink and juices run clear (the meat thermometer, if using, should register 180° to 185°) and vegetables are tender, adding peas to the vegetable casserole for the last 15 minutes of roasting. If desired, garnish with additional fresh rosemary. Makes 6 servings.

Nutrition facts per serving: 293 calories, 14 g total fat (4 g saturated fat), 79 mg cholesterol, 230 mg sodium, 13 g carbohydrate, 4 g fiber, 27 g protein
Exchanges: ½ Starch, 3 Lean Meat, 1 Vegetable, ½ Fat

184 calories

Preparation time: 30 minutes ● **Cooking time:** 35 minutes

basil chicken with wine sauce

If you must use dried herbs rather than fresh, use the freshest possible, as they lose flavor the longer they sit in your pantry. Buy small quantities, rather than bulk, of dried herbs so you use them up quickly.

2 pounds meaty chicken pieces (breasts, thighs, and drumsticks), skinned
Nonstick spray coating
2 cups sliced fresh mushrooms
1 small onion, chopped
2 tablespoons snipped fresh basil
or 2 teaspoons dried basil, crushed
1 clove garlic, minced
⅓ cup reduced-sodium chicken broth
⅓ cup dry white wine
¼ teaspoon salt
¼ teaspoon pepper
1 tablespoon cornstarch
1 tablespoon cold water

1 Rinse chicken; pat dry with paper towels. Set aside.

2 Spray an unheated large skillet with nonstick coating. Preheat over medium heat. Add sliced mushrooms, onion, dried basil (if using), and garlic. Cook over medium heat until onion is tender.

3 Stir in fresh basil (if using), chicken broth, wine, salt, and pepper. Arrange chicken in skillet. Bring to boiling; reduce heat. Simmer, covered, about 30 minutes or until chicken is tender and no longer pink. Transfer chicken and vegetables to a serving platter. Keep warm.

4 For sauce, measure the cooking liquid. If necessary, add enough *water* to measure 1 cup total liquid. Pour into skillet.

5 Combine the cornstarch and the 1 tablespoon water. Stir into cooking liquid in skillet. Cook and stir until thickened and bubbly. Cook and stir for 2 minutes more. Serve sauce over chicken. Makes 5 servings.

Nutrition facts per serving: 184 calories, 6 g total fat (2 g saturated fat), 74 mg cholesterol, 217 mg sodium, 4 g carbohydrate, 1 g fiber, 25 g protein
Exchanges: 3 Lean Meat, 1 Vegetable

194 calories

Preparation time: 1 hour

mediterranean-style chicken

Olives added to the robust sauce impart a characteristic briny or salty flavor. You can use either full-flavored pimiento-stuffed green olives or the smooth, mellow tasting black variety.

1½ to 2 pounds meaty chicken pieces (breasts, thighs, and drumsticks), skinned
   Nonstick spray coating
1 14½-ounce can tomatoes, undrained and cut up
¼ cup dry red wine
1 tablespoon snipped fresh basil or 1 teaspoon dried basil, crushed
1 teaspoon sugar
1 clove garlic, minced
1 bay leaf
1 tablespoon cold water
2 teaspoons cornstarch
   Hot cooked spaghetti (optional)
¼ cup sliced pimiento-stuffed green olives or pitted ripe olives

1 Rinse chicken; pat dry with paper towels.

2 Spray an unheated large skillet with nonstick coating. Preheat over medium heat. Add chicken; cook for 10 to 15 minutes, turning to brown evenly.

3 Add undrained tomatoes, wine, basil, sugar, garlic, and bay leaf. Bring to boiling; reduce heat. Simmer, covered, about 35 minutes or until chicken is tender and no longer pink. Remove chicken from skillet; cover and keep warm. Discard bay leaf.

4 In a small bowl stir together cold water and cornstarch. Stir into tomato mixture in skillet. Cook and stir until thickened and bubbly. Cook and stir for 2 minutes more.

5 If desired, serve chicken and tomato mixture over hot cooked spaghetti. Sprinkle with the olives. Makes 4 servings.

Nutrition facts per serving: 194 calories, 7 g total fat (2 g saturated fat), 69 mg cholesterol, 401 mg sodium, 8 g carbohydrate, 1 g fiber, 23 g protein
Exchanges: 3 Lean Meat, 1 Vegetable

274 calories

Preparation time: 30 minutes ● **Cooking time:** 35 minutes

paella

Paella (pi-AY-yuh) hails from Spain and boasts a saffron-spiced rice. Saffron, an integral ingredient in traditional paella, is costly, but a little goes a long way. Saffron is harvested from the purple crocus flower.

8 ounces fresh or frozen medium shrimp
1½ pounds meaty chicken pieces (breasts, thighs, and drumsticks)
Nonstick spray coating
1 cup chopped onion
1 clove garlic, minced
1 14½-ounce can reduced-sodium chicken broth
1 7½-ounce can tomatoes, undrained and cut up
1 teaspoon snipped fresh thyme or ¼ teaspoon dried thyme, crushed
¼ teaspoon ground saffron
⅛ to ¼ teaspoon ground red pepper
1 cup long grain rice
1 medium red or green sweet pepper, coarsely chopped
1 cup frozen peas

1 Thaw shrimp, if frozen. Peel and devein shrimp. Rinse shrimp and chicken; pat dry with paper towels. Cover and refrigerate until needed.

2 Spray an unheated Dutch oven with nonstick coating. Preheat over medium heat. Add onion and garlic. Cook until onion is tender.

3 Add chicken pieces, chicken broth, undrained tomatoes, thyme, saffron, and ground red pepper. Bring to boiling; reduce heat. Simmer, covered, for 15 minutes.

4 Stir in uncooked rice. Simmer, covered, about 15 minutes more or until rice is nearly tender.

5 Stir sweet pepper, shrimp, and peas into the rice mixture. Simmer, covered, about 5 minutes more or until rice and chicken are tender and shrimp are opaque. Makes 6 servings.

Nutrition facts per serving: 274 calories, 5 g total fat (1 g saturated fat), 90 mg cholesterol, 363 mg sodium, 33 g carbohydrate, 2 g fiber, 24 g protein
Exchanges: 1½ Starch, 2 Lean Meat, 2 Vegetable

271 calories

Preparation time: 25 minutes ● **Cooking time:** 35 minutes

caraway chicken and noodles

Use a mortar and pestle to crush the caraway seed, releasing a burst of flavor and aroma. This utensil is good to keep on hand to use any time a recipe calls for crushed seeds or spices.

1½ **pounds meaty chicken pieces (breasts, thighs, and drumsticks), skinned**
　　Nonstick spray coating
　¾ **cup water**
　1 **teaspoon caraway seed, slightly crushed**
　1 **teaspoon instant chicken bouillon granules**
　⅛ **teaspoon pepper**
　⅔ **cup skim milk**
　1 **tablespoon cornstarch**
　½ **cup sliced green onions**
　2 **cups hot cooked noodles**

1 Rinse chicken; pat dry with paper towels.

2 Spray an unheated large skillet with nonstick coating. Preheat over medium heat. Add chicken and cook for 10 minutes, turning to brown evenly.

3 Carefully add the water, caraway seed, bouillon granules, and pepper. Bring to boiling; reduce heat. Simmer, covered, for 30 to 35 minutes or until chicken is tender and no longer pink. Remove chicken; cover and keep warm.

4 Stir together milk and cornstarch. Stir into skillet along with the green onions. Cook and stir until thickened and bubbly. Cook and stir for 2 minutes more. Serve over hot cooked noodles and chicken. Makes 4 servings.

Nutrition facts per serving: 271 calories, 7 g total fat (2 g saturated fat), 95 mg cholesterol, 303 mg sodium, 23 g carbohydrate, 2 g fiber, 27 g protein
Exchanges: 1½ Starch, 3 Lean Meat

142 calories

Preparation time: 25 minutes

orange-and-honey-sauced chicken

*A simple orange and honey sauce makes this a flavorful dish with no added fat. Use a fresh orange
for the optimal orange flavor. You'll need about 2 medium oranges for ½ cup of juice.*

**4 small skinless, boneless chicken breast
halves (12 ounces total)**
Nonstick spray coating
1 small onion, finely chopped
1 clove garlic, minced
½ cup reduced-sodium chicken broth
½ teaspoon finely shredded orange peel
½ cup orange juice
1 tablespoon honey
4 teaspoons cornstarch
2 teaspoons reduced-sodium soy sauce
Hot cooked rice (optional)
Orange slices (optional)
Fresh parsley (optional)

1 Rinse chicken; pat dry with paper towels.
Spray an unheated large skillet with nonstick
coating. Preheat over medium heat. Add chicken.
Cook for 8 to 10 minutes or until tender and no
longer pink, turning to brown evenly. Remove from
skillet; keep warm.

2 Add the onion and garlic to skillet; cook until
onion is tender. Stir together chicken broth, orange
peel, orange juice, honey, cornstarch, and soy sauce;
add to skillet. Cook and stir until thickened and
bubbly. Cook and stir for 2 minutes more.

3 To serve, spoon some of the sauce over each
serving. If desired, serve with rice and garnish with
orange slices and parsley. Makes 4 servings.

Nutrition facts per serving: 142 calories, 3 g total fat
(1 g saturated fat), 45 mg cholesterol, 209 mg sodium,
12 g carbohydrate, 1 g fiber, 17 g protein
Exchanges: 2½ Lean Meat, 1 Fruit

268 calories

Preparation time: 30 minutes ● **Baking time:** 30 minutes

turkey and rice bake

To make ahead, assemble this family-style casserole the day before and chill it overnight. To serve, bake in a 350° oven for 45 to 50 minutes or until heated through. Sprinkle with cheese as directed.

2½ **cups water**
2 **teaspoons instant chicken bouillon granules**
¾ **teaspoon poultry seasoning**
1 **cup long grain rice**
1 **large onion, chopped**
1 **large carrot, chopped**
1 **stalk celery, sliced**
2 **cups cubed cooked turkey or chicken**
1 **10-ounce package frozen chopped spinach, thawed and drained**
½ **cup shredded reduced-fat cheddar cheese (2 ounces)**

1 In a large saucepan combine the water, bouillon granules, and poultry seasoning; bring to boiling. Stir in the rice, onion, carrot, and celery. Return to boiling; reduce heat. Simmer, covered, about 15 minutes or until rice is tender. Stir in turkey and spinach. Transfer to a 2-quart square baking dish. Bake, covered, in a 350° oven about 30 minutes or until heated through. Sprinkle with cheddar cheese; let stand until cheese is melted. Makes 6 servings.

Nutrition facts per serving: 268 calories, 6 g total fat (2 g saturated fat), 52 mg cholesterol, 448 mg sodium, 31 g carbohydrate, 1 g fiber, 21 g protein
Exchanges: 1½ Starch, 2 Lean Meat, 2 Vegetable

246 calories

Preparation time: 25 minutes ● **Baking time:** 20 minutes

biscuit-topped turkey casserole

Reduced-fat biscuit mix takes the place of the typical high fat pastry dough, often used for pot pies. Substitute any frozen vegetable mixture you prefer for the peas and carrots.

1 cup reduced-sodium chicken broth
½ cup finely chopped onion
½ cup finely chopped celery
1½ cups frozen peas and carrots
⅓ cup reduced-sodium chicken broth
3 tablespoons all-purpose flour
2 cups cubed cooked turkey breast
1 cup evaporated skim milk
1½ teaspoons snipped fresh sage
    or ½ teaspoon dried sage, crushed
⅛ teaspoon pepper
1¼ cups reduced-fat packaged biscuit mix
½ cup skim milk
2 tablespoons snipped fresh parsley

1 In a medium saucepan combine the 1 cup broth, the onion, and celery; cook, covered, for 5 minutes. Add peas and carrots; bring to boiling.

2 Stir the ⅓ cup broth into the flour until well mixed; stir into vegetable mixture in saucepan. Cook and stir until thickened and bubbly. Stir in turkey, evaporated milk, sage, and pepper. Pour into a 2-quart casserole.

3 In a small bowl stir together the biscuit mix, skim milk, and parsley. Stir with a fork just until moistened. Drop into 6 mounds on top of the hot turkey mixture. Bake, uncovered, in a 425° oven for 20 to 25 minutes or until biscuits are golden brown. Makes 6 servings.

Nutrition facts per serving: 246 calories, 4 g total fat (1 g saturated fat), 34 mg cholesterol, 548 mg sodium, 30 g carbohydrate, 2 g fiber, 22 g protein
Exchanges: 2 Starch, 2 Lean Meat

255 calories

Preparation time: 25 minutes

turkey and chili pepper stir-fry

Anaheim peppers are larger in size and milder in flavor than jalapeño peppers. Both are readily available in most supermarkets. Anaheims are mild while jalapeños range from hot to very hot.

⅓ cup water
2 tablespoons reduced-sodium soy sauce
2 teaspoons cornstarch
Nonstick spray coating
4 cups chopped bok choy
1 medium red or green sweet pepper, cut into thin strips
¼ cup finely chopped seeded Anaheim pepper or 1 tablespoon finely chopped seeded jalapeño pepper*
1½ cups cooked turkey breast, cut into bite-size strips (about 8 ounces)
¼ cup sliced water chestnuts
2 cups hot cooked rice

1 For sauce, in a small bowl combine water, soy sauce, and cornstarch. Set aside.

2 Spray an unheated wok or large skillet with nonstick coating. Preheat over medium-high heat. Add bok choy, sweet pepper, and Anaheim or jalapeño pepper; stir-fry for 2½ to 3 minutes or until peppers are crisp-tender. Remove from wok.

3 Add turkey to wok; stir-fry about 2 minutes or until heated through. Push turkey from center of wok. Stir sauce mixture; add to center of wok. Cook and stir until thickened and bubbly.

4 Return vegetables to wok; add water chestnuts. Stir to coat all ingredients; cook about 1 minute more or until heated through. Serve with hot cooked rice. Makes 4 servings.

*Note: Because chili peppers, such as jalapeños, contain volatile oils that can burn your skin and eyes, avoid direct contact with them as much as possible. When working with chili peppers, wear plastic gloves. If your bare hands touch the chili peppers, wash your hands well with soap and water.

Nutrition facts per serving: 255 calories, 6 g total fat (2 g saturated fat), 54 mg cholesterol, 312 mg sodium, 30 g carbohydrate, 1 g fiber, 20 g protein
Exchanges: 1½ Starch, 2 Lean Meat, 2 Vegetable

156 calories

Preparation time: 20 minutes ● **Grilling time:** 1¼ hours

turkey with tomatillo guacamole

A tomatillo, often called the Mexican green tomato, resembles a small tomato with a parchment-like skin. It's available canned and fresh. Here it replaces part of the avocado—which is high in fat—in the guacamole.

1 2- to 3-pound fresh or frozen turkey breast portion
2 teaspoons ground coriander
½ teaspoon onion powder
¼ teaspoon chili powder
Dash ground red pepper
1 tablespoon margarine or butter
1 tablespoon lemon juice
1 recipe Tomatillo Guacamole
Tomato wedges (optional)
Lime peel strips (optional)

1 Thaw turkey, if frozen. Rinse turkey; pat dry. Remove skin and excess fat from turkey. In a small saucepan cook coriander, onion powder, chili powder, and red pepper in margarine or butter for 1 minute. Remove from heat; stir in lemon juice. Spread spice mixture on all sides of turkey.

2 In a covered grill arrange medium-hot coals around a drip pan. Test for medium heat above the pan (see note, page 285). Insert a meat thermometer into the thickest part of turkey breast, but not touching the bone (if present). Place turkey breast on grill rack over drip pan but not over coals. Cover and grill for 1¼ to 1¾ hours or until thermometer registers 170°. Add more coals as needed. Serve turkey with Tomatillo Guacamole. If desired, garnish with tomatoes and lime strips. Makes 8 servings.

Tomatillo Guacamole: In a small mixing bowl stir together 2 *canned tomatillos,* rinsed, drained, and finely chopped (¼ cup); 1 *Roma tomato,* chopped; ½ of a small *avocado,* peeled, seeded, and chopped (about ½ cup); 1 tablespoon *canned diced green chili peppers;* 2 teaspoons *lemon juice;* and ⅛ teaspoon *garlic salt.*

Nutrition facts per serving: 156 calories, 6 g total fat (1 g saturated fat), 50 mg cholesterol, 157 mg sodium, 3 g carbohydrate, 0 g fiber, 22 g protein
Exchanges: 3 Lean Meat

154 calories

Preparation time: 20 minutes ● **Roasting time:** 2½ hours ● **Standing time:** 15 minutes

turkey with cranberry sauce

Want to enjoy this classic combination any day of the week? Use turkey tenderloin steaks instead of the turkey breast half. Broil steaks 4 to 5 inches from the heat for 8 to 10 minutes, turning once.

1 **2½- to 3-pound fresh or frozen turkey breast half with bone**
1½ **cups cranberries**
½ **cup coarsely shredded carrot**
½ **teaspoon finely shredded orange peel**
½ **cup orange juice**
2 **tablespoons raisins**
2 **tablespoons sugar**
    Dash ground cloves
1 **tablespoon cold water**
2 **teaspoons cornstarch**
    Fresh parsley (optional)

1 Thaw turkey, if frozen. Rinse turkey; pat dry with paper towels. Remove skin and excess fat from turkey breast. Place turkey breast, bone side down, on a rack in a shallow roasting pan. Insert a meat thermometer into the thickest portion of the breast, making sure the bulb does not touch the bone. Cover breast loosely with foil.

2 Roast in a 325° oven for 2½ to 3 hours or until thermometer registers 165°. Remove foil for the last 30 minutes of roasting. Let turkey stand, covered, for 15 minutes before slicing.

3 Meanwhile, for sauce, in a small saucepan combine the cranberries, carrot, orange peel, orange juice, raisins, sugar, and cloves. Bring to boiling; reduce heat. Simmer, uncovered, for 3 to 4 minutes or until cranberry skins pop.

4 In a small bowl combine the cold water and cornstarch. Stir into cranberry mixture in saucepan. Cook and stir until thickened and bubbly. Cook and stir for 2 minutes more.

5 Serve turkey with cranberry sauce. If desired, garnish with parsley. Makes 8 servings.

Nutrition facts per serving: 154 calories, 2 g total fat (1 g saturated fat), 50 mg cholesterol, 49 mg sodium, 11 g carbohydrate, 1 g fiber, 22 g protein
Exchanges: 3 Lean Meat, ½ Fruit

105 calories

Preparation time: 1 hour ● **Grilling time:** 1½ to 2 hours ● **Standing time:** 10 minutes

chipotle - rubbed smoked turkey

Chipotle peppers, commonly used in southwestern cooking, have a unique, smoky flavor, enhancing the smoked flavor of the meat.

1 **2- to 2½-pound fresh or frozen turkey breast half with bone**
3 **cups hickory or mesquite wood chips**
1 **teaspoon ground coriander**
½ **teaspoon paprika**
¼ **to ½ teaspoon black pepper**
1 **small dried chipotle pepper, seeded and crushed, or ⅛ to ¼ teaspoon ground red pepper**
2 **teaspoons cooking oil**
Hot cooked rice (optional)
Fresh cilantro (optional)
Fresh chili peppers (optional)

1 Thaw turkey, if frozen. At least 1 hour before grilling, soak wood chips in enough water to cover. Meanwhile, in a small bowl combine coriander, paprika, black pepper, and chipotle pepper.

2 Rinse turkey; pat dry with paper towels. Remove skin and excess fat from turkey breast. Brush skinned surface of turkey with the oil. Rub with the spice mixture. Insert a meat thermometer into the thickest part of the turkey, making sure the bulb does not touch the bone.

3 Drain wood chips. In a covered grill arrange medium-hot coals around the outside edges of grill. Sprinkle *half* of the wood chips over coals, then test for medium heat (see note, page 285) above the center of grill (not over coals). Place turkey, bone side down, in a roasting pan (not over coals) on the grill rack. Cover and grill for 45 minutes.

4 Sprinkle coals with remaining chips. Cover and grill for 45 minutes to 1¼ hours more or until meat thermometer registers 170°. Add more coals as needed. Remove turkey from grill. Loosely cover with foil; let stand for 10 minutes before slicing. If desired, serve with rice and garnish with cilantro and fresh chili peppers. Serves 8 to 10.

Nutrition facts per serving: 105 calories, 3 g total fat (1 g saturated fat), 41 mg cholesterol, 38 mg sodium, 0 g carbohydrate, 0 g fiber, 18 g protein
Exchanges: 2 Lean Meat

285 calories

Preparation time: 25 minutes ● **Roasting time:** 2¾ hours ● **Standing time:** 15 minutes

turkey with fruit sauce

A simple sauce made with dried fruit, marmalade, and ginger makes ordinary turkey a company-special dish.
To keep fat and calories low, remove the skin from the turkey before serving.

1 10- to 12-pound fresh or frozen turkey
1 onion, quartered
1 apple, quartered
1 cup reduced-sodium chicken broth
½ cup dried cranberries, cherries, or apricots
1 cup low-calorie orange marmalade spread
2 teaspoons cornstarch
1 teaspoon grated fresh gingerroot
    or ¼ teaspoon ground ginger
    Orange slices, halved (optional)

1 Thaw turkey, if frozen. Rinse turkey; pat dry with paper towels. Place the onion and apple in the body cavity. Pull neck skin to back and fasten with a skewer. If a band of skin crosses tail, tuck drumsticks under band. If there is no band, tie drumsticks to tail. Twist wing tips under the back.

2 Place bird, breast side up, on a rack in a shallow roasting pan. Insert a meat thermometer into center of an inside thigh muscle, making sure bulb does not touch bone. Cover loosely with foil. Press

foil lightly at ends of drumsticks and neck. Roast in a 325° oven for 2¾ to 3 hours or until thermometer registers 180°, or drumsticks move easily in their sockets and meat is no longer pink. (After 2 hours of roasting, remove foil; cut band of skin or string between drumsticks.) When done, remove from oven; cover with foil. Let stand 15 to 20 minutes before carving. Discard apple and onion.

3 Meanwhile, for sauce, in small saucepan combine the broth and dried fruit. Bring to boiling; reduce heat. Simmer, covered, for 10 minutes. Stir together the marmalade spread, cornstarch, and gingerroot or ginger; stir into broth mixture. Cook and stir until slightly thickened and bubbly. Cook and stir for 2 minutes more. Pass sauce with turkey. If desired, garnish with orange slices. Serves 12.

Nutrition facts per serving: 285 calories, 11 g total fat (3 g saturated fat), 108 mg cholesterol, 131 mg sodium, 13 g carbohydrate, 0 g fiber, 32 g protein
Exchanges: 4 Lean Meat, 1 Fruit

184 calories

Preparation time: 5 minutes ● **Cooking time:** 8 minutes

turkey with curried peanut sauce

Another time, pair the zesty peanut sauce with broiled or grilled pork chops. Top each serving with a few crushed roasted peanuts, if desired.

1   **pound turkey breast tenderloin steaks**
    Nonstick spray coating
2   **tablespoons reduced-fat peanut butter**
2   **tablespoons low-calorie apricot spread**
1   **teaspoon curry powder**
½   **cup skim milk**
    Snipped fresh chives (optional)

1 Rinse turkey; pat dry with paper towels. Spray an unheated large skillet with nonstick coating. Preheat over medium heat. Add turkey; cook for 6 to 8 minutes or until tender and no longer pink, turning once. Transfer turkey to a serving plate; cover and keep warm.

2 In a small mixing bowl stir together the peanut butter, apricot spread, and curry powder. Stir in milk. Pour mixture into skillet; heat to boiling. Pour over turkey steaks. If desired, garnish with snipped chives. Makes 4 servings.

Nutrition facts per serving: 184 calories, 6 g total fat (1 g saturated fat), 50 mg cholesterol, 105 mg sodium, 9 g carbohydrate, 1 g fiber, 25 g protein
Exchanges: 3 Lean Meat, ½ Fruit

146 calories

Preparation time: 20 minutes ● **Marinating time:** 30 minutes to 2 hours ● **Grilling time:** 12 minutes

orange-sesame turkey kabobs

Kabobs are a perfect plan-ahead meal. Cut up your vegetables ahead of time, place them in a sealable plastic bag, and store them in the refrigerator. When it's time to cook, all you have left to do is skewer and grill.

12 **ounces turkey breast tenderloin, cut into 1-inch pieces**
¼ **cup frozen orange juice concentrate, thawed**
2 **teaspoons sesame seed**
1½ **teaspoons snipped fresh thyme or ½ teaspoon dried thyme, crushed**
1 **teaspoon toasted sesame oil**
¼ **teaspoon salt**
2 **cups desired fresh vegetables (such as 1-inch pieces red and/or green sweet pepper, whole mushrooms, 1-inch-thick half-slices zucchini or yellow summer squash, and whole cherry tomatoes)**
Nonstick spray coating
Hot cooked linguine (optional)
Orange wedges (optional)

1 Rinse turkey; pat dry with paper towels.

2 In a shallow dish combine orange juice concentrate, sesame seed, thyme, sesame oil, and salt. Add turkey, stirring to coat. Cover; marinate at room temperature for 30 minutes or in the refrigerator for up to 2 hours. Drain, reserving marinade. Alternately thread turkey and vegetables onto long skewers. (If using tomatoes, add to end of skewers for the last 1 minute of grilling.) Brush with remaining marinade.

3 Spray an unheated grill rack with nonstick coating. Grill kabobs on prepared rack directly over medium coals for 12 to 14 minutes or until turkey is tender and no longer pink, turning occasionally to cook evenly. If desired, serve over linguine and garnish with orange wedges. Makes 4 servings.

Nutrition facts per serving: 146 calories, 4 g total fat (1 g saturated fat), 37 mg cholesterol, 171 mg sodium, 10 g carbohydrate, 1 g fiber, 18 g protein
Exchanges: 2 Lean Meat, 1 Vegetable, ½ Fruit

345 calories

Preparation time: 25 minutes ● **Cooking time:** 20 minutes

spanish turkey and rice

A small amount of green olives goes a long way in providing a distinctive, Spanish flavor to this one-dish meal.
For the best flavor, use fresh oregano rather than dried. Fresh herb flavor just can't be beat.

Nonstick spray coating
12 **ounces turkey breast tenderloin, cut into**
    ¾-inch pieces
2 **teaspoons olive oil or cooking oil**
1 **cup coarsely chopped green sweet pepper**
½ **cup chopped onion**
¼ **cup coarsely chopped pitted green olives**
2 **tablespoons snipped fresh oregano**
    or 2 teaspoons dried oregano, crushed
3 **garlic cloves, minced**
¼ **teaspoon black pepper**
1 **cup long grain rice**
1 **14½-ounce can reduced-sodium chicken**
    broth
¼ **cup water**
1 **cup chopped peeled tomato**
1 **cup frozen peas**
2 **tablespoons snipped fresh parsley**

1 Spray an unheated 3-quart saucepan with nonstick coating. Preheat over medium-high heat. Add turkey pieces; cook and stir for 3 to 4 minutes or until browned. Remove from saucepan.

2 Add oil to saucepan. Add sweet pepper, onion, olives, oregano, garlic, and black pepper. Cook over low heat until vegetables are tender. Increase heat to medium-high; stir in *uncooked* rice and the turkey. Add broth and water. Bring to boiling; reduce heat. Simmer, covered, about 15 minutes or until liquid is absorbed and rice is tender. Stir in tomato and peas; heat through. Stir in parsley. Makes 4 servings.

Nutrition facts per serving: 345 calories, 6 g total fat (1 g saturated fat), 37 mg cholesterol, 522 mg sodium, 49 g carbohydrate, 3 g fiber, 23 g protein
Exchanges: 3 Starch, 2 Lean Meat, 1 Vegetable

151 calories

Preparation time: 25 minutes ● **Marinating time:** 30 minutes to 2 hours ● **Cooking time:** 15 minutes

turkey mushroom marsala

Shiitake mushrooms impart a rich earthy flavor to this delicate wine glaze. Discard the stems and use only the caps. Serve the turkey with linguine, if you like (a ¾-cup serving has about 105 calories or 1½ starches).

4 **4-ounce turkey breast tenderloin steaks**
1 **cup sliced shiitake mushrooms**
⅓ **cup dry Marsala**
1½ **teaspoons snipped fresh thyme**
  or ½ teaspoon dried thyme, crushed
1 **teaspoon snipped fresh rosemary**
  or ¼ teaspoon dried rosemary, crushed
⅛ **teaspoon salt**
⅛ **teaspoon pepper**
2 **teaspoons olive oil or cooking oil**
2 **teaspoons cold water**
1 **teaspoon cornstarch**
  Hot cooked linguine (optional)
  Fresh rosemary (optional)

1 Rinse turkey; pat dry with paper towels. Set turkey aside.

2 Place turkey in a plastic bag set in a shallow dish. For marinade, combine ⅓ cup *water,* the mushrooms, Marsala, thyme, rosemary, salt, and pepper. Pour over turkey. Close bag. Marinate in refrigerator for at least 30 minutes or up to 2 hours, turning bag occasionally.

3 Remove turkey from marinade, reserving marinade; pat dry. In a large skillet heat oil over medium heat. Cook turkey in hot oil for 8 to 10 minutes or until tender and no longer pink, turning once. Remove turkey; cover and keep warm. Add marinade to skillet. Bring to boiling; reduce heat. Simmer, covered, for 2 minutes.

4 Stir together the 2 teaspoons cold water and the cornstarch; stir into mixture in skillet. Cook and stir until thickened and bubbly. Cook and stir for 2 minutes more. If desired, serve turkey and mushroom mixture over linguine and garnish with additional fresh rosemary. Makes 4 servings.

Nutrition facts per serving: 151 calories, 5 g total fat (1 g saturated fat), 50 mg cholesterol, 114 mg sodium, 1 g carbohydrate, 0 g fiber, 22 g protein
Exchanges: 3 Lean Meat

234 calories

Preparation time: 25 minutes

turkey with mixed dried fruit

A mixture of dried fruits, such as apricots, pears, and apples, lend a slightly sweet flavor to this dish. The dried fruit also makes this dish easy—the fruit is already cut up for you.

- **12 ounces turkey breast tenderloin steaks**
- **Nonstick spray coating**
- **1 cup apple juice or apple cider**
- **1 cup mixed dried fruit bits**
- **½ cup chopped onion**
- **1½ teaspoons snipped fresh thyme**
  or ½ teaspoon dried thyme, crushed
- **2 cloves garlic, minced**
- **½ cup apple juice or apple cider**
- **1 tablespoon cornstarch**
- **Hot cooked orzo or rice (optional)**
- **Apple slices (optional)**
- **Fresh thyme (optional)**

1 Rinse turkey; pat dry with paper towels. Spray an unheated large skillet with nonstick coating. Preheat over medium-high heat. Add turkey; cook for 8 to 10 minutes or until tender and no longer pink, turning once. Remove from skillet.

2 For sauce, in same skillet combine the 1 cup apple juice, dried fruit bits, onion, thyme, and garlic. Bring to boiling; reduce heat. Simmer, covered, for 2 to 4 minutes or just until fruit bits are tender.

3 Stir together the ½ cup apple juice and the cornstarch. Add to mixture in skillet. Cook and stir until thickened and bubbly. Cook and stir for 2 minutes more. Return turkey to skillet; heat through. If desired, serve turkey and sauce with orzo or rice and garnish with apple slices and additional fresh thyme. Makes 4 servings.

Nutrition facts per serving: 234 calories, 2 g total fat (1 g saturated fat), 37 mg cholesterol, 60 mg sodium, 39 g carbohydrate, 0 g fiber, 18 g protein
Exchanges: 2 Lean Meat, 2½ Fruit

143 calories

Preparation time: 15 minutes ● **Marinating time:** 8 to 24 hours ● **Grilling time:** 15 minutes

tandoori turkey

Tandoori-style dishes typically use yogurt as the marinade base, and are seasoned with cumin, coriander, and turmeric, all spices common to Indian cuisine.

4 **4-ounce turkey breast tenderloin steaks**
½ **cup chopped onion**
2 **tablespoons lime juice**
1 **tablespoon cooking oil**
1 **teaspoon ground cumin**
1 **teaspoon coriander seed**
½ **teaspoon salt**
½ **teaspoon ground ginger**
½ **teaspoon ground turmeric**
¼ **teaspoon crushed red pepper**
½ **cup plain fat-free yogurt**
   Nonstick spray coating
   Hot cooked couscous (optional)

1 Rinse turkey; pat dry with paper towels. Set turkey aside.

2 For marinade, in a food processor bowl or blender container combine onion, lime juice, oil, cumin, coriander seed, salt, ginger, turmeric, and crushed red pepper. Cover and process or blend until mixture is nearly smooth. Pour mixture into a shallow nonmetal dish or pan; stir in yogurt.

3 Cut small slits in both sides of the tenderloin steaks. Place steaks in the yogurt mixture, turning to coat both sides. Cover; marinate in the refrigerator for at least 8 hours or up to 24 hours, turning steaks occasionally. Remove the steaks from marinade; discard marinade.

4 Spray an unheated grill rack with nonstick coating. Grill turkey on prepared rack directly over medium coals for 15 to 18 minutes or until tender and no longer pink, turning once. (Or, spray the unheated rack of a broiler pan with nonstick coating. Place turkey on prepared rack; broil 4 to 5 inches from the heat for 8 to 10 minutes or until tender and no longer pick, turning once.) If desired, serve over hot cooked couscous. Makes 4 servings.

Nutrition facts per serving: 143 calories, 4 g total fat (1 g saturated fat), 50 mg cholesterol, 192 mg sodium, 3 g carbohydrate, 0 g fiber, 22 g protein
Exchanges: 3 Lean Meat

164 calories

Preparation time: 20 minutes ● **Baking time:** 30 minutes

turkey with tomato relish

The crumb coating on these turkey tenderloins is made from salsa-flavored crackers. Of course, you can try any type of reduced-fat crackers you like. An easy stir-together relish adds the finishing touch.

4 turkey breast tenderloin steaks (about 12 ounces total)
Nonstick spray coating
½ cup finely crushed reduced-fat salsa-flavored or reduced-fat cheese-flavored crackers
¼ teaspoon ground cumin
¼ teaspoon celery seed
1 tablespoon margarine or butter, melted
1 14½-ounce can diced tomatoes, drained
1 4½-ounce can diced green chili peppers, drained
½ cup finely chopped onion
2 to 4 tablespoons snipped fresh cilantro
1 tablespoon vinegar
1 teaspoon sugar
⅛ teaspoon salt
Fresh cilantro (optional)

1 Rinse turkey; pat dry with paper towels. Spray a 2-quart rectangular baking dish with nonstick coating. Set aside.

2 In a shallow dish combine crushed crackers, cumin, and celery seed. Coat turkey breast with crushed cracker mixture. Place in the prepared dish. Drizzle with the melted margarine or butter. Bake, uncovered, in a 375° oven about 30 minutes or until turkey is tender and no longer pink.

3 Meanwhile, for relish, in a medium mixing bowl combine the drained tomatoes, chili peppers, onion, and the snipped cilantro. Stir in the vinegar, sugar, and salt. Cover and refrigerate until serving time. Serve turkey with the relish. If desired, garnish with additional fresh cilantro. Makes 4 servings.

Nutrition facts per serving: 164 calories, 6 g total fat (1 g saturated fat), 37 mg cholesterol, 490 mg sodium, 11 g carbohydrate, 1 g fiber, 18 g protein
Exchanges: 2 Lean Meat, 2 Vegetable

110 calories

Preparation time: 15 minutes ● **Cooking time:** 8 minutes

turkey piccata

Serve this lemon-flavored turkey dish with spinach linguine if you like. It adds color to your plate and fills you up, too. A ¾- cup serving adds about 105 calories (1½ Starch exchanges) to your total per serving.

- **4 2¾- to 3-ounce turkey breast cutlets or slices**
- **¼ teaspoon salt**
- **¼ teaspoon coarsely ground black pepper**
    Nonstick spray coating
- **1 teaspoon olive oil**
- **2 to 3 cloves garlic, minced**
- **¾ cup reduced-sodium chicken broth**
- **1 tablespoon all-purpose flour**
- **2 tablespoons snipped fresh parsley**
- **4 teaspoons lemon juice**
    Hot cooked spinach linguine or noodles (optional)
    Lemon wedges (optional)

1 Rinse turkey; pat dry with paper towels. Place 1 turkey breast between 2 pieces of heavy plastic wrap. Working from the center to the edges, pound lightly with flat side of a meat mallet to ⅛ inch thickness. Remove plastic wrap. Repeat with remaining steaks. Sprinkle turkey with the salt and pepper. Spray an unheated large nonstick skillet with nonstick coating. Preheat over medium-high heat. Add 2 of the turkey pieces; cook for 2 to 3 minutes or until lightly browned and centers are no longer pink, turning once. Transfer to serving platter; cover and keep warm. Add the oil to skillet. Repeat with remaining turkey pieces. Remove to platter, reserving drippings in skillet.

2 For sauce, add garlic to skillet; cook 30 seconds. In a screw-top jar combine chicken broth and flour. Cover and shake well. Add to skillet; cook and stir until thickened and bubbly. Cook and stir for 1 minute more. Stir in parsley and lemon juice; heat through. To serve, spoon sauce over turkey. If desired, serve with hot cooked pasta and garnish with lemon wedges. Makes 4 servings.

Nutrition facts per serving: 110 calories, 3 g total fat (1 g saturated fat), 37 mg cholesterol, 289 mg sodium, 3 g carbohydrate, 0 g fiber, 17 g protein
Exchanges: 2 Lean Meat

268 calories

Preparation time: 25 minutes ● **Grilling time:** 12 minutes

grilled turkey with cherry sauce

Three different cherry sources give this dish an ultra-rich cherry flavor. For a family dinner, substitute orange juice for the liqueur. (A ½-cup serving of long grain and wild rice adds 150 calories and 2 starches.)

½ cup cherry jelly or jam
⅓ cup dried tart cherries, cut up
2 tablespoons cherry liqueur or orange juice
1 tablespoon lemon juice
¼ teaspoon salt
⅛ teaspoon coarsely ground black pepper
4 4-ounce turkey breast tenderloin steaks
Hot cooked long grain and wild rice mix (optional)

1 For sauce, in a small saucepan combine the jelly or jam, dried cherries, liqueur or orange juice, lemon juice, salt, and pepper. Cook over low heat about 15 minutes or until jelly is melted and sauce is slightly thickened, stirring occasionally.

2 Grill turkey directly over medium coals* for 6 minutes. Turn and brush with some of the sauce. Grill 6 to 9 minutes more or until turkey is tender and no longer pink.

3 To serve, bring remaining sauce to boiling; spoon over turkey. If desired, serve with rice. Makes 4 servings.

Broiling Directions: Place turkey on unheated rack of a broiler pan. Broil 4 to 5 inches from heat for 3 minutes. Turn and brush with some of the sauce. Broil 3 to 5 minutes more or until no longer pink. To serve, bring remaining sauce to boiling; spoon over turkey.

Nutrition facts per serving: 268 calories, 2 g total fat (1 g saturated fat), 50 mg cholesterol, 185 mg sodium, 37 g carbohydrate, 1 g fiber, 22 g protein
Exchanges: 3 Lean Meat, 2½ Fruit

*Note: To check for medium heat, hold your hand, palm side down, over where the meat will cook and at about the same height of the meat. The heat is right when you can hold your hand there for only 3 seconds.

251 calories

Preparation time: 20 minutes ● **Grilling time:** 14 minutes

basil turkey burgers

What a treat this burger is from regular burgers. The dried tomato mayonnaise adds a special touch to the basil-infused burgers. If possible, use fresh basil leaves for the best flavor.

¼ **cup skim milk**
2 **tablespoons finely chopped onion**
1 **tablespoon fine dry bread crumbs**
1 **tablespoon snipped fresh basil**
   or 1 teaspoon dried basil, crushed
⅛ **teaspoon salt**
⅛ **teaspoon pepper**
12 **ounces ground raw turkey**
4 **lettuce leaves**
4 **hamburger buns, split and toasted**
¼ **cup Dried Tomato Mayonnaise**

1 In a medium mixing bowl combine the milk, onion, bread crumbs, basil, salt, and pepper. Add ground turkey; mix well. Shape mixture into four ¾-inch-thick patties.

2 Grill patties on the grill rack of an uncovered grill directly over medium coals for 14 to 18 minutes or until no longer pink, turning once. (Or, place patties on the unheated rack of a broiler pan. Broil 4 inches from the heat for 12 to 14 minutes or until no longer pink, turning once.)

3 To serve, place a lettuce leaf on the bottom half of each bun and top with 1 of the patties. Spoon 1 tablespoon of the Dried Tomato Mayonnaise on top of each patty. Place bun tops on top of the burgers. Makes 4 servings.

Dried Tomato Mayonnaise: In a small mixing bowl pour enough *boiling water* over 2 tablespoons snipped *dried tomatoes (not oil-pack)* to cover. Let stand about 10 minutes or until tomatoes are pliable. Drain well. Stir tomatoes into ⅓ cup *fat-free mayonnaise dressing* or *light mayonnaise dressing*. Cover and store leftovers in the refrigerator. Makes about ½ cup.

Nutrition facts per serving with 2 tablespoons Dried Tomato Mayonnaise: 251 calories, 9 g total fat (2 g saturated fat), 32 mg cholesterol, 488 mg sodium, 27 g carbohydrate, 1 g fiber, 16 g protein
Exchanges: 2 Starch, 1½ Lean Meat, ½ Fat

333 calories

Preparation time: 30 minutes ● **Baking time:** 30 minutes

turkey meatballs in wine sauce

If you like, make the meatballs up to 24 hours before you plan to serve them. Prepare the recipe through step 2; cover and refrigerate the meatballs. Just before serving, continue with step 3.

 1 **egg white**
 1 **cup soft bread crumbs**
 ½ **cup finely chopped onion**
 2 **tablespoons skim milk**
 ¾ **teaspoon snipped fresh thyme**
     or ¼ teaspoon dried thyme, crushed
 ¼ **teaspoon salt**
 1 **pound ground raw turkey**
     Nonstick spray coating
 2 **cups sliced fresh mushrooms**
 2 **tablespoons cornstarch**
 1 **teaspoon instant chicken bouillon granules**
 ⅓ **cup dry white wine**
 2 **tablespoons snipped fresh parsley**
3¾ **cups hot cooked noodles**
     Carrot curls (optional)

1 In a medium mixing bowl stir together the egg white, soft bread crumbs, *half* of the onion, the milk, thyme, salt, and dash *pepper.* Add turkey; mix well. Shape mixture into 1-inch meatballs.

2 Spray a 13×9×2-inch baking pan with nonstick coating. Place meatballs in the baking pan. Bake, uncovered, in a 350° oven for 30 to 35 minutes or until meatballs are no longer pink. Drain off any juices; cool meatballs slightly.

3 Spray an unheated large skillet with nonstick coating. Add mushrooms and remaining onion. Cook until onion is tender. Stir together 1 cup *cold water,* cornstarch, and bouillon granules. Stir cornstarch mixture into mushroom mixture. Cook and stir until thickened and bubbly. Stir in meatballs and wine; heat through. Stir in parsley. Serve over hot cooked noodles. If desired, garnish with carrot curls. Makes 5 servings.

Nutrition facts per serving: 333 calories, 9 g total fat (2 g saturated fat), 72 mg cholesterol, 389 mg sodium, 39 g carbohydrate, 3 g fiber, 20 g protein
Exchanges: 2½ Starch, 2 Lean Meat, 1 Vegetable

316 calories

Preparation time: 25 minutes ● **Baking time:** 25 minutes ● **Standing time:** 10 minutes

spicy pasta pie

Vermicelli is thinner than thin spaghetti but thicker than angel hair pasta. In this pasta dish, it creates the crust to hold a spicy sausage sauce.

4 ounces packaged dried vermicelli, broken
1 beaten egg white
  Nonstick spray coating
1 cup shredded mozzarella cheese (4 ounces)
1 pound turkey breakfast sausage
1 cup sliced fresh mushrooms
½ cup chopped onion
1 clove garlic, minced
1 7½-ounce can low-sodium tomatoes,
  undrained and cut up
½ of a 6-ounce can (⅓ cup) tomato paste
1 teaspoon dried Italian seasoning, crushed
⅛ teaspoon crushed red pepper
2 tablespoons grated Parmesan cheese or
  Romano cheese
  Celery leaves (optional)

1 Cook vermicelli according to package directions, except omit any oil and salt. Drain well. Toss with the egg white. Spray a 9-inch quiche dish or 9-inch pie plate with nonstick coating. Press vermicelli mixture into bottom of prepared dish. Sprinkle with mozzarella cheese. Set aside.

2 Meanwhile, in a large skillet cook the turkey sausage, mushrooms, onion, and garlic until sausage is no longer pink and onion is tender. Drain off fat. Stir in the *undrained* tomatoes, tomato paste, Italian seasoning, and crushed red pepper. Pour sausage mixture over cheese layer.

3 Cover dish loosely with foil. Bake in a 350° oven for 25 to 30 minutes or until heated through. Sprinkle with the Parmesan or Romano cheese. Let stand 10 minutes. If desired, garnish with the celery leaves. Cut pie into wedges to serve. Makes 6 servings.

Nutrition facts per serving: 316 calories, 14 g total fat (6 g saturated fat), 41 mg cholesterol, 732 mg sodium, 22 g carbohydrate, 1 g fiber, 26 g protein
Exchanges: 1 Starch, 3 Medium-Fat Meat, 1 Vegetable

315 calories

Preparation time: 20 minutes ● **Cooking time:** 1 hour 20 minutes

cassoulet

The calories and fat of this simplified version of the classic French dish has been pared down substantially from traditional cassoulet. To reduce the sodium, replace the canned beans with cooked dried beans.*

Nonstick spray coating
4 ounces smoked turkey sausage, cut into bite-size pieces
4 ounces lean boneless pork, cubed
1 cup chopped onion
1 cup chopped carrot
1 cup sliced celery
2 cloves garlic, minced
1 14½-ounce can reduced-sodium chicken broth
1 8-ounce can low-sodium tomato sauce
½ teaspoon dried thyme, crushed
1 bay leaf
2 15-ounce cans navy beans, rinsed and drained

1 Spray an unheated large saucepan with nonstick coating. Preheat over medium heat. Add the turkey sausage, pork, onion, carrot, celery, and garlic. Cook and stir until pork is browned on all sides and vegetables are nearly tender.

2 Stir in the chicken broth, tomato sauce, thyme, and bay leaf. Bring to boiling; reduce heat. Simmer, covered, about 1 hour or until pork is tender, stirring occasionally.

3 Stir in beans. Simmer, uncovered, for 20 to 30 minutes more or until of desired consistency. Discard bay leaf. Makes 5 servings.

Nutrition facts per serving: 315 calories, 5 g total fat (1 g saturated fat), 25 mg cholesterol, 1,266 mg sodium, 47 g carbohydrate, 3 g fiber, 23 g protein
Exchanges: 2½ Starch, 2 Lean Meat, 2 Vegetable

*Note: To cook dried beans, rinse 8 ounces of navy beans. In a large Dutch oven combine the beans and 4 cups cold water. Bring to boiling; reduce heat. Simmer for 2 minutes. Remove from heat. Cover and let stand for 1 hour. Drain and rinse. In same pan combine beans and 4 cups fresh water. Bring to boiling; reduce heat. Simmer, covered, for 1 to 1½ hours or until beans are tender.

156 calories

Preparation time: 20 minutes ● **Baking time:** 55 minutes

southwestern stuffed squash

For a more exciting way to serve chili, spoon it in a squash "bowl." If you can't find butternut squash at the supermarket, simply use baked potatoes, omitting steps for squash.

3 1½- to 2-pound butternut squash
8 ounces ground raw turkey or chicken
2 green onions, sliced
1 to 2 teaspoons chili powder
½ teaspoon dried oregano, crushed
1 15-ounce can black beans or pinto beans, rinsed and drained
1 8-ounce can tomato sauce
¼ cup sliced pitted ripe olives (optional)
1 jalapeño pepper, seeded and chopped*
   Light dairy sour cream (optional)
   Green onion tops (optional)

1 Cut off the blossom end of each squash. From one side of each squash, cut off a shallow lengthwise slice. Finely chop enough of the slices to equal ½ cup; set aside. Remove and discard seeds from the cavities of the squash. Hollow out squash, leaving ½-inch-thick shells. Invert squash on a shallow baking pan. Bake, uncovered, in a 350° oven about 40 minutes or until squash are tender.

2 Meanwhile, in a large skillet cook turkey or chicken and chopped squash until meat is browned. Stir in onions, chili powder, and oregano. Cook and stir 2 minutes more. Stir in beans, tomato sauce, olives (if desired), and jalapeño pepper. Bring to boiling. Spoon bean mixture into hollows of baked squash. Bake, uncovered, about 15 minutes or until heated through. If desired, serve with sour cream; garnish with green onion. Makes 6 servings.

Nutrition facts per serving: 156 calories, 3 g total fat (1 g saturated fat), 14 mg cholesterol, 430 mg sodium, 26 g carbohydrate, 7 g fiber, 11 g protein
Exchanges: 1½ Starch, 1 Lean Meat

*Note: Because chili peppers, such as jalapeños, contain volatile oils that can burn your skin and eyes, avoid direct contact with them as much as possible. When working with chili peppers, wear plastic gloves. If your bare hands touch the chili peppers, wash your hands well with soap and water.

200 calories

Preparation time: 20 minutes ● **Baking time:** 55 minutes ● **Standing time:** 5 minutes

ginger turkey meat loaf

To make sure you're buying lean ground turkey, read the label to be certain that it does not contain any skin. Otherwise, ask your butcher to grind turkey breast for you without added skin.

Nonstick spray coating
1 egg
1 egg white
1 cup soft whole wheat bread crumbs (about 1⅓ slices bread)
½ cup finely chopped green onions
1 2-ounce jar diced pimiento, drained
2 tablespoons reduced-sodium soy sauce
1 tablespoon milk or water
¼ teaspoon pepper
1½ pounds ground raw turkey
2 tablespoons apricot preserves
¼ teaspoon ground ginger
Fresh tomato wedges (optional)
Fresh sage (optional)

1 Spray a 9×5×3-inch loaf pan with nonstick coating. Set aside.

2 In a large bowl combine the egg, egg white, bread crumbs, green onions, pimento, soy sauce, milk or water, and pepper. Add the ground turkey; mix well. Press mixture into the prepared pan, patting to smooth the top. Bake, uncovered, in a 350° oven for 45 minutes.

3 Meanwhile, in a small bowl stir together the apricot preserves and ginger; brush over surface of loaf. Bake 10 to 15 minutes more or until no longer pink. Remove from oven; pour off any drippings. Let stand for 5 minutes; invert onto a plate. Turn right side up for slicing. If desired, garnish with tomato wedges and fresh sage. Makes 6 servings.

Nutrition facts per serving: 200 calories, 10 g total fat (3 g saturated fat), 78 mg cholesterol, 289 mg sodium, 10 g carbohydrate, 0 g fiber, 18 g protein
Exchanges: 3 Lean Meat, ½ Fruit

Fish

chapter index

114 calories

Preparation time: 20 minutes

cod with lemon cream sauce

Fish is great for dieters. It's generally low in fat and calories. Here, spinach noodles make both a colorful backdrop and filling accompaniment (a ¾-cup serving has 158 calories or 2 Starch exchanges).

1 **pound fresh or frozen cod or other fish**
    fillets, ½ to ¾ inch thick
1½ **cups water**
1 **tablespoon lemon juice**
½ **cup finely chopped carrot**
½ **cup finely chopped onion**
½ **cup skim milk**
1 **teaspoon cornstarch**
½ **teaspoon instant chicken bouillon granules**
1 **teaspoon snipped fresh dill**
    or ¼ teaspoon dried dillweed
    Hot cooked spinach noodles or other
    desired hot cooked noodles (optional)

1 Thaw fish, if frozen. Rinse fish; pat dry with paper towels. Turn under any thin edges of fish.

2 In a 12-inch skillet combine water and lemon juice. Bring to boiling. Add fish. Simmer, covered, for 6 to 8 minutes or until fish flakes easily when tested with a fork. Remove fish from skillet and keep warm.

3 Meanwhile, in a small covered saucepan cook carrot and onion in a small amount of *boiling water* about 3 minutes or until crisp-tender. Drain well. Stir together milk, cornstarch, bouillon granules, and dill. Stir into vegetables in saucepan. Cook and stir until thickened and bubbly. Cook and stir for 2 minutes more.

4 Serve vegetable sauce over fish. If desired, serve with hot cooked noodles. Makes 4 servings.

Nutrition facts per serving: 114 calories, 1 g total fat (0 g saturated fat), 45 mg cholesterol, 199 mg sodium, 5 g carbohydrate, 1 g fiber, 20 g protein
Exchanges: 3 Very Lean Meat, 1 Vegetable

116 calories

Preparation time: 28 minutes ● **Cooking time:** 4 minutes per ½-inch thickness of fish

fish and sweet peppers

To thaw fish, remove it from the freezer the night before you serve it. Place, unopened, in a container in the refrigerator—it should be thawed by the next evening. Never thaw fish at room temperature.

4 4-ounce fresh or frozen cod or other fish fillets
¾ cup chicken broth
1 medium onion, sliced and separated into rings
2¼ teaspoons snipped fresh oregano or marjoram or ¾ teaspoon dried oregano or marjoram, crushed
½ teaspoon finely shredded lemon peel
1 tablespoon lemon juice
1 clove garlic, minced
1½ cups bite-size strips green and/or red sweet peppers (2 small)
1 tablespoon cold water
1½ teaspoons cornstarch
1 lemon, halved and sliced (optional)

1 Thaw fish, if frozen. Rinse fish; pat dry with paper towels. Measure thickness of fish. Set aside.

2 In a large skillet combine broth, onion, oregano or marjoram, lemon peel, lemon juice, and garlic. Bring to boiling; reduce heat. Simmer, covered, about 3 minutes or until onion is tender.

3 Arrange fish fillets in onion mixture. Add sweet peppers. Cook, covered, over medium heat for 4 to 6 minutes for each ½-inch thickness of fish or until fish flakes easily when tested with a fork. Using a slotted spoon, remove fish and vegetable mixture to a serving platter. Keep warm.

4 Combine cold water and cornstarch. Add to pan juices. Cook and stir until thickened and bubbly. Cook and stir for 2 minutes more. Spoon over fish and vegetables. If desired, garnish with lemon. Makes 4 servings.

Nutrition facts per serving: 116 calories, 1 g total fat (0 g saturated fat), 45 mg cholesterol, 211 mg sodium, 6 g carbohydrate, 1 g fiber, 20 g protein
Exchanges: 3 Very Lean Meat, 1 Vegetable

161 calories

Preparation time: 15 minutes ● **Baking time:** 6 minutes per ½-inch thickness of fish

oven-fried fish

For a fish sandwich, tuck this crispy coated fish into a whole wheat hamburger bun. Top with sliced tomatoes and fat-free mayonnaise dressing (see Calorie Tally, page 464 for added calories).

4 **4-ounce fresh or frozen cod or other fish fillets**
   Nonstick spray coating
3 **tablespoons seasoned fine dry bread crumbs**
3 **tablespoons cornmeal**
¼ **teaspoon lemon-pepper seasoning**
1 **tablespoon cooking oil**
1 **slightly beaten egg white**
   Tomato slices (optional)
   Fresh parsley (optional)

1 Thaw fish, if frozen. Rinse fish; pat dry with paper towels. Measure thickness of fish. Spray a shallow baking pan with nonstick coating. Set aside.

2 Stir together the bread crumbs, cornmeal, and lemon-pepper seasoning. Add oil, tossing to combine. Brush 1 side of each fish fillet with the egg white, then dip in bread crumb mixture. Place fish fillets, crumb sides up, in prepared pan.

3 Bake, uncovered, in a 500° oven for 6 to 8 minutes for each ½-inch thickness of fish or until fish flakes easily when tested with a fork. If desired, serve with tomato slices and garnish with fresh parsley. Makes 4 servings.

Nutrition facts per serving: 161 calories, 5 g total fat (1 g saturated fat), 43 mg cholesterol, 283 mg sodium, 9 g carbohydrate, 0 g fiber, 20 g protein
Exchanges: ½ Starch, 3 Very Lean Meat, ½ Fat

136 calories

Preparation time: 25 minutes

chilled cod with gazpacho sauce

All you need are five ingredients for this lazy-day summertime salad.
Choose from both eat-now or eat-later chilling options.

8 ounces fresh or frozen cod, cusk, flounder, or orange roughy fillets, ½ inch thick
1 lemon, halved and sliced
¼ cup deli marinated cucumber salad or mixed vegetable salad, drained
¼ cup chunky salsa
2 cups torn mixed greens

1 Thaw fish, if frozen. Rinse fish; pat dry with paper towels. In a large skillet or saucepan place a large open steamer basket over ½ inch of *water.* Bring water to boiling; reduce heat. Carefully place the fish fillets in the steamer basket. (If necessary, cut the fish into 2 pieces to fit.) Top with half of the lemon slices. Cover and steam fish about 6 minutes or until fish flakes easily when tested with a fork. Discard lemon slices.

2 Remove fish from steamer basket. Carefully immerse the fish in a bowl of *ice water.* Let the fish stand in the ice water about 5 minutes or until thoroughly chilled. Remove fish from water; drain on paper towels. (Or, cover and refrigerate for 2 to 4 hours or until chilled.)

3 Meanwhile, for sauce, cut up any large pieces of cucumber or mixed vegetable salad. Stir together the salad and the salsa.

4 Arrange mixed greens on 2 dinner plates. Place half of the chilled fish on top of each plate of greens. Spoon salsa mixture over fish. Garnish with remaining lemon slices. Makes 2 servings.

Nutrition facts per serving: 136 calories, 5 g total fat (1 g saturated fat), 43 mg cholesterol, 234 mg sodium, 4 g carbohydrate, 1 g fiber, 19 g protein
Exchanges: 2 Lean Meat, 1 Vegetable

179 calories

Preparation time: 20 minutes ● **Marinating time:** 45 minutes ● **Grilling time:** 6 minutes

citrus-tarragon salmon steaks

Unlike meat and poultry, fish needs only a short time to marinate. In fact, acidic ingredients, such as citrus juices and vinegars, will cause fish to become tough and chewy with long marinating.

4 fresh or frozen salmon steaks, cut ¾ inch thick (about 1 pound)
1 teaspoon finely shredded orange peel
¼ cup orange juice
¼ cup lime juice
1 tablespoon champagne vinegar or white wine vinegar
1 tablespoon snipped fresh tarragon or ½ teaspoon dried tarragon, crushed
1 teaspoon olive oil or salad oil
¼ teaspoon salt
⅛ teaspoon pepper
  Nonstick spray coating

1 Thaw fish, if frozen. Rinse fish; pat dry with paper towels. For the marinade, stir together the orange peel, orange juice, lime juice, vinegar, tarragon, oil, salt, and pepper.

2 Place fish in a shallow nonmetal baking dish. Pour marinade over fish. Cover and marinate in the refrigerator for 45 minutes, turning the fish once. Drain fish, reserving the marinade.

3 Spray an unheated grill rack with nonstick coating. Grill fish on prepared rack over medium coals for 6 to 9 minutes or until fish just begins to flake easily when tested with a fork; turn the fish halfway through the grilling time and brush with reserved marinade. Makes 4 servings.

Nutrition facts per serving: 179 calories, 8 g total fat (1 g saturated fat), 42 mg cholesterol, 184 mg sodium, 4 g carbohydrate, 0 g fiber, 24 g protein
Exchanges: 3 Lean Meat

294 calories

Preparation time: 30 minutes

sweet-and-sour fish

Oriental-style sweet and sour dishes are usually fried, but this version uses poached lean fish.
Although we trimmed the calories and fat, we kept the great flavor.

1 **pound fresh or frozen fish steaks (such as halibut, swordfish, or tuna)**
2 **tablespoons brown sugar**
2 **tablespoons vinegar**
2 **tablespoons reduced-sodium soy sauce**
4 **teaspoons cornstarch**
⅔ **cup reduced-sodium chicken broth**
1 **medium green or red sweet pepper, cut into 1-inch squares**
1 **medium carrot, thinly bias sliced**
½ **cup seedless grapes, halved**
2 **cups hot cooked rice**

1 Thaw fish, if frozen. Rinse fish; pat dry with paper towels. Cut into 1-inch pieces. In a large covered saucepan cook fish pieces in *boiling water* about 5 minutes or until fish flakes easily when tested with a fork. Drain. Keep warm.

2 In a small bowl combine brown sugar, vinegar, soy sauce, and cornstarch. Set aside.

3 In a medium saucepan combine chicken broth, sweet pepper, and carrot. Bring to boiling; reduce heat. Simmer, covered, about 3 minutes or until vegetables are crisp-tender.

4 Stir brown sugar mixture into vegetable mixture. Cook and stir until thickened and bubbly. Cook and stir for 2 minutes more. Gently stir in fish and grapes. Cook about 1 minute more or until heated through. Serve over hot cooked rice. Makes 4 servings.

Nutrition facts per serving: 294 calories, 3 g total fat (1 g saturated fat), 36 mg cholesterol, 446 mg sodium, 38 g carbohydrate, 1 g fiber, 27 g protein
Exchanges: 2 Starch, 3 Very Lean Meat, 1 Vegetable

148 calories

Preparation time: 30 minutes ● **Baking time:** 25 minutes

sweet-pepper-stuffed sole

Fines herbes transforms a simple wine sauce from ordinary to delicious. This herb mix usually contains chervil, parsley, chives, and tarragon. Look for it with the other dried herbs in your grocery store.

4 **4-ounce fresh or frozen sole or flounder fillets, ¼ to ½ inch thick**
2 **small red, yellow, and/or green sweet peppers, cut into thin bite-size strips**
4 **green onions, halved lengthwise and cut into 3-inch-long pieces**
2 **teaspoons margarine or butter**
⅓ **cup dry white wine or chicken broth**
¼ **teaspoon dried fines herbes, crushed**
⅛ **teaspoon salt (optional)**
⅛ **teaspoon black pepper**
1 **tablespoon cold water**
2 **teaspoons cornstarch**
   Hot cooked wild rice and/or brown rice (optional)

1 Thaw fish, if frozen. In a medium covered saucepan cook sweet peppers and onions in a small amount of *boiling water* for 3 minutes. Drain.

2 Rinse fish; pat dry. Dot each fillet with ½ teaspoon of the margarine or butter. Place one-fourth of the pepper mixture across the center of each fillet. Roll up fillets from short sides. Secure with wooden picks. Place fish, seam sides down, in a shallow baking dish. Stir together wine or broth, fines herbes, salt (omit if using broth), and black pepper; drizzle over fish.

3 Bake, covered, in a 350° oven for 25 to 30 minutes or until fish flakes easily when tested with a fork. Transfer fish to a platter; keep warm.

4 For sauce, measure pan juices; add enough *water* to measure ¾ cup. In a saucepan combine the 1 tablespoon cold water and the cornstarch; stir in pan juices. Cook and stir over medium heat until thickened and bubbly. Cook and stir for 2 minutes more. If desired, serve fish on bed of rice. Spoon sauce over fish. Makes 4 servings.

Nutrition facts per serving: 148 calories, 3 g total fat (1 g saturated fat), 60 mg cholesterol, 184 mg sodium, 4 g carbohydrate, 0 g fiber, 22 g protein
Exchanges: 3 Very Lean Meat, 1 Vegetable

166 calories

Preparation time: 30 minutes

vegetable-fish soup

Serve this flavorful vegetable-filled soup in just 30 minutes. Watch the soup carefully once you add the fish.
Cook it just until it flakes when tested with a fork. Overcooked fish will be tough and chewy.

8 ounces fresh or frozen fish fillets
2 cups water
1 14½-ounce can tomatoes, undrained and
   cut up
2 cups frozen mixed vegetables
1 cup thinly sliced celery
¾ cup chopped onion
4 teaspoons snipped fresh oregano
   or 1 teaspoon dried oregano, crushed
1½ teaspoons instant chicken bouillon
   granules
1 clove garlic, minced
   Several dashes bottled hot pepper sauce

1 Thaw fish, if frozen. Rinse fish; pat dry with paper towels. Cut into 1-inch pieces.

2 In a large saucepan combine the water, undrained tomatoes, frozen vegetables, celery, onion, dried oregano (if using), bouillon granules, garlic, and hot pepper sauce. Bring to boiling; reduce heat. Simmer, covered, about 10 minutes or until vegetables are tender.

3 Stir in fish and fresh oregano (if using). Return just to boiling; reduce heat. Simmer gently, covered, for 3 to 5 minutes or until fish flakes easily when tested with a fork. Makes 4 servings.

Nutrition facts per serving: 166 calories, 2 g total fat (0 g saturated fat), 27 mg cholesterol, 623 mg sodium, 23 g carbohydrate, 4 g fiber, 15 g protein
Exchanges: 1 Lean Meat, 4 Vegetable

312 calories

Preparation time: 35 minutes

lime-sauced fish and linguine

For fish stir-fries, such as this one, select a firm fish. Swordfish, shark, sea bass, cod, or orange roughy all work well.

12 ounces fresh or frozen skinless, boneless fish
¼ cup dry white wine or chicken broth
¼ cup chicken broth
2 tablespoons lime juice
2 teaspoons cornstarch
1 teaspoon honey
¼ teaspoon ground ginger
¼ teaspoon ground coriander
Nonstick spray coating
1 medium cucumber, seeded and cut into 2×½-inch sticks
1 medium zucchini, cut into 2×½-inch sticks
1 medium red or green sweet pepper, cut into ¾-inch squares
1 teaspoon cooking oil
3 cups hot cooked linguine
Lime wedges (optional)

1 Thaw fish, if frozen. Rinse fish; pat dry with paper towels. Cut into ¾-inch pieces. Set aside.

2 For sauce, stir together wine, broth, lime juice, cornstarch, honey, ginger, coriander, and ⅛ teaspoon *black pepper*. Set aside.

3 Spray an unheated wok or large skillet with nonstick coating. Preheat over medium-high heat. Add cucumber and zucchini; stir-fry for 1½ minutes. Add sweet pepper; stir-fry about 1½ minutes more or until crisp-tender. Remove vegetables from wok.

4 Add oil to wok. Add fish; stir-fry for 2 to 3 minutes or until fish flakes easily when tested with a fork. Push fish from center of wok. Stir sauce; add to center of wok. Cook and stir until thickened and bubbly. Return vegetables to wok; stir to coat. Cook and stir for 2 minutes. Serve with linguine. If desired, garnish with lime wedges. Makes 4 servings.

Nutrition facts per serving: 312 calories, 6 g total fat (1 g saturated fat), 34 mg cholesterol, 130 mg sodium, 39 g carbohydrate, 3 g fiber, 23 g protein
Exchanges: 2 Starch, 2 Lean Meat, 2 Vegetable

157 calories

Preparation time: 20 minutes ● **Baking time:** 8 minutes

lake trout with corn salsa

Ask your butcher to skin the lake trout before you bring it home. If you opt to cook it with the skin on, then place the fish, skin side down, in the baking dish.

1 **pound fresh or frozen lake trout or walleye fillets, ½ inch thick**
1 **cup frozen whole kernel corn**
¼ **cup water**
½ **cup small cherry tomatoes, quartered**
½ **cup finely chopped, peeled jicama**
¼ **cup snipped fresh cilantro or parsley**
2 **tablespoons lime juice**
1 **small jalapeño pepper, seeded and finely chopped***
Dash salt
Nonstick spray coating
3 **tablespoons fat-free Italian salad dressing**
1 **teaspoon chili powder**

1 Thaw fish, if frozen. Rinse fish; pat dry with paper towels. Cut into 4 serving-size pieces. In a small saucepan combine the corn and the water. Bring to boiling; reduce heat. Simmer, covered, for 5 minutes. Drain.

2 For corn salsa, in a medium serving bowl combine the cooked corn, tomatoes, jicama, cilantro or parsley, lime juice, jalapeño pepper, and salt. Toss to combine. Set aside.

3 Spray a 2-quart rectangular baking dish with nonstick coating. Stir together the Italian salad dressing and chili powder; brush over fish. Place fish in the prepared baking dish. Bake, uncovered, in a 450° oven for 8 to 12 minutes or until fish flakes easily when tested with a fork. Serve fish with corn salsa. Makes 4 servings.

***Note:** Because chili peppers contain volatile oils that can burn your skin and eyes, avoid direct contact with them as much as possible by wearing plastic gloves. If your bare hands touch the chili peppers, wash your hands well with soap and water.

Nutrition facts per serving: 157 calories, 1 g total fat (0 g saturated fat), 45 mg cholesterol, 196 mg sodium, 13 g carbohydrate, 1 g fiber, 24 g protein
Exchanges: 1 Starch, 3 Very Lean Meat

160 calories

Preparation time: 15 minutes ● **Marinating time:** 20 minutes ● **Broiling time:** 10 minutes

spicy broiled shark steaks

To check for doneness of fish, stick the tines of a fork into the thickest portion of the fish at a 45-degree angle. Then gently twist the fork and pull up some of the flesh. If the fish flakes easily, it's done.

1 pound fresh or frozen shark or swordfish
steaks, cut ¾ inch thick
2 green onions, thinly sliced
2 tablespoons orange juice
2 tablespoons chili sauce
1 tablespoon snipped fresh basil
or 1 teaspoon dried basil, crushed
1 tablespoon finely chopped fresh gingerroot
1 tablespoon reduced-sodium soy sauce
Several dashes hot chili oil
Nonstick spray coating
Orange slices (optional)
Fresh chives (optional)

1 Thaw fish, if frozen. Rinse fish; pat dry with paper towels. Cut into serving-size pieces. For marinade, in a shallow bowl combine the green onions, orange juice, chili sauce, basil, gingerroot, soy sauce, and chili oil. Add the fish; turn to coat with marinade. Cover; marinate at room temperature for 20 minutes.

2 Spray the unheated rack of a broiler pan with nonstick coating. Drain fish, reserving marinade. Place fish on prepared rack. Broil 4 inches from the heat for 5 minutes. Using a wide spatula, carefully turn fish over. Brush with the reserved marinade. Broil for 5 to 7 minutes more or until fish flakes easily when tested with a fork. If desired, serve fish on top of orange slices and garnish with fresh chives. Makes 4 servings.

Nutrition facts per serving: 160 calories, 5 g total fat (1 g saturated fat), 45 mg cholesterol, 342 mg sodium, 3 g carbohydrate, 0 g fiber, 23 g protein
Exchanges: 3 Lean Meat

151 calories

Preparation time: 10 minutes ● **Grilling time:** 8 to 12 minutes

swordfish with cucumber sauce

Yogurt, cucumber, and snipped mint leaves team up as a garden-fresh sauce for grilled fish steaks.
A simple side dish of sautéed sweet peppers and onions keeps it light.

2 fresh or frozen swordfish or halibut steaks,
   cut ¾ inch thick (1 pound total)
⅓ cup plain low-fat yogurt
¼ cup finely chopped cucumber
1 teaspoon snipped fresh mint or dill
   or ¼ teaspoon dried mint, crushed, or
   dried dillweed
Dash pepper
Nonstick spray coating

1 Thaw fish, if frozen. Rinse fish; pat dry with paper towels. Cut each steak in half.

2 For sauce, in a small bowl stir together yogurt, cucumber, mint or dill, and pepper. Cover and refrigerate until serving time.

3 Spray an unheated grill rack with nonstick coating. Grill fish steaks on prepared rack over medium-hot coals for 6 to 9 minutes or until fish is lightly browned. Turn and grill 2 to 3 minutes more or until fish flakes easily when tested with a fork.

4 Serve the fish with the cucumber sauce. Makes 4 servings.

Broiling Directions: Spray the unheated rack of a broiler pan with nonstick coating. Place fish on rack. Broil 4 inches from the heat for 4 to 6 minutes or until fish is lightly browned. Turn and broil 2 to 3 minutes more or until fish flakes easily when tested with a fork.

Nutrition facts per serving: 151 calories, 5 g total fat (1 g saturated fat), 46 mg cholesterol, 115 mg sodium, 2 g carbohydrate, 0 g fiber, 23 g protein
Exchanges: 3 Lean Meat

299 calories

Preparation time: 25 minutes ● **Baking time:** 20 minutes

sole with feta and tomatoes

When baking fish fillets, fold under the thin ends so the fish is an even thickness. This prevents the ends from cooking too quickly and drying out before the rest of the fish is done.

1¼ **pounds fresh or frozen sole or other fish fillets, ½ to ¾ inch thick**
1 **14½-ounce can low-sodium tomatoes, undrained and cut up**
8 **green onions, thinly sliced**
2 **tablespoons lemon juice**
1 **teaspoon dried Italian seasoning, crushed**
¼ **teaspoon pepper**
  Nonstick spray coating
3 **cups hot cooked spinach fettuccine**
2 **tablespoons crumbled feta cheese**
  or 2 tablespoons sliced pitted ripe olives

1 Thaw fish, if frozen. Rinse fish; pat dry with paper towels. Cut into 4 serving-size portions.

2 For sauce, in a large skillet combine undrained tomatoes, green onions, lemon juice, Italian seasoning, and pepper. Bring to boiling; reduce heat. Simmer, uncovered, for 8 to 10 minutes or until nearly all the liquid has evaporated.

3 Spray a shallow 2-quart baking dish with nonstick coating. Arrange fish fillets in the dish, tucking under any thin edges for an even thickness. Spoon some of the sauce over each fillet. Bake, covered, in a 350° oven for 20 to 25 minutes or until fish flakes easily when tested with a fork. Serve fish and sauce on top of fettuccine. Sprinkle with feta cheese or olives. Makes 4 servings.

Nutrition facts per serving: 299 calories, 4 g total fat (2 g saturated fat), 74 mg cholesterol, 220 mg sodium, 34 g carbohydrate, 2 g fiber, 31 g protein
Exchanges: 1½ Starch, 3 Lean Meat, 2 Vegetable

169 calories

Preparation time: 15 minutes ● **Baking time:** 12 minutes

parmesan baked fish

Quick, easy, slimming, and delicious—what more can you ask of a recipe? Keep the meal simple by adding a vegetable, and for dessert, indulge in you favorite flavor of fat-free ice cream.

**4 4-ounce fresh or frozen skinless salmon
    fillets or other firm fish fillets, ¾ to
    1 inch thick**
    Nonstick spray coating
**¼ cup light mayonnaise dressing or salad
    dressing**
2 tablespoons grated Parmesan cheese
**1 tablespoon snipped fresh chives or sliced
    green onion**
**1 teaspoon white wine Worcestershire sauce
    Fresh chives (optional)**

1 Thaw fish, if frozen. Rinse fish; pat dry with paper towels. Spray a 2-quart square or rectangular baking dish with nonstick coating. Set aside.

2 In a small bowl stir together mayonnaise dressing or salad dressing, Parmesan cheese, the 1 tablespoon snipped chives or green onion, and the Worcestershire sauce. Spread mayonnaise mixture over fish fillets.

3 Bake, uncovered, in a 450° oven for 12 to 15 minutes or until fish flakes easily when tested with a fork. If desired, garnish with additional fresh chives. Makes 4 servings.

Nutrition facts per serving: 169 calories, 10 g total fat (2 g saturated fat), 23 mg cholesterol, 247 mg sodium, 1 g carbohydrate, 0 g fiber, 18 g protein
Exchanges: 3 Lean Meat

317 calories

Preparation time: 15 minutes ● **Baking time:** 19 minutes

crunchy-topped fish with potatoes

*This oven-fried version of fish and chips makes for great family dining. Stuffing mix
contributes the crunchy coating for the fish.*

4 **4-ounce fresh or frozen catfish or other
fish fillets, ½ to ¾ inch thick**
Nonstick spray coating
2 **medium baking potatoes (12 ounces total),
cut into 3×½×½-inch sticks**
2 **teaspoons cooking oil**
Garlic salt or seasoned pepper
¾ **cup herb-seasoned stuffing mix, crushed**
1 **tablespoon margarine or butter, melted**
1 **tablespoon water**

1 Thaw fish, if frozen. Rinse fish; pat dry with
paper towels. Set aside.

2 Line a large shallow baking pan with foil.
Spray foil with nonstick coating. Arrange potato
sticks in a single layer over half of the baking sheet.
Brush potatoes with the oil. Sprinkle with the garlic
salt or seasoned pepper. Bake in a 450° oven for
10 minutes.

3 Meanwhile, stir together the stuffing mix, the
melted margarine or butter, and the water. Place fish
on baking sheet next to potatoes, tucking under any
thin edges of the fish for an even thickness. Sprinkle
stuffing mix over fish. Return pan to oven and bake
for 9 to 12 minutes more or until fish flakes easily
when tested with a fork and potatoes are tender.
Makes 4 servings.

Nutrition facts per serving: 317 calories, 14 g total fat
(3 g saturated fat), 63 mg cholesterol, 358 mg sodium,
26 g carbohydrate, 1 g fiber, 22 g protein
Exchanges: 1½ Starch, 3 Lean Meat, ½ Fat

214 calories

Preparation time: 30 minutes ● **Soaking time:** 45 minutes ● **Cooking time:** 10 minutes

mixed seafood with pasta

Frozen scallops and shrimp work as well as fresh, but you'll need to use fresh clams. When buying clams, look for moist shells without cracks or chips and choose those that close when gently tapped.

6 **ounces fresh or frozen sea scallops**
8 **ounces fresh or frozen shelled shrimp**
12 **small clams**
1 **medium yellow sweet pepper, cut into ¾-inch pieces**
½ **cup chopped onion**
1 **tablespoon *each* snipped fresh basil and oregano or 1 teaspoon *each* dried basil and oregano, crushed**
2 **cloves garlic, minced**
½ **teaspoon instant chicken bouillon granules**
2 **tablespoons cornstarch**
2 **medium tomatoes, seeded and chopped**
3 **cups hot cooked spaghetti or linguine**
¼ **cup grated Parmesan cheese**
2 **tablespoons snipped fresh parsley**

1 Thaw scallops and shrimp, if frozen. Rinse scallops and shrimp; pat dry. Set aside. Scrub clams under cold running water. Cover clams with salted water, using 3 tablespoons *salt* to 8 cups *cold water*.

Soak for 15 minutes; drain and rinse. Discard water. Repeat twice. Meanwhile, halve any large scallops and devein shrimp.

2 In a large skillet combine clams, sweet pepper, onion, dried basil and dried oregano (if using), garlic, bouillon granules, 1 cup *water,* and ¼ teaspoon *black pepper.* Cook, covered, about 5 minutes or until onion is tender and clams have opened. Remove clams; discard any unopened ones.

3 Stir together cornstarch and 2 tablespoons *cold water;* stir into onion mixture. Cook and stir until bubbly. Stir in scallops, shrimp, and fresh herbs (if using). Cook 3 to 4 minutes more or until scallops and shrimp are opaque. Stir in tomatoes and clams; heat through. Serve with cooked pasta. Sprinkle with Parmesan cheese and parsley. Makes 6 servings.

Nutrition facts per serving: 214 calories, 3 g total fat (1 g saturated fat), 76 mg cholesterol, 285 mg sodium, 28 g carbohydrate, 1 g fiber, 19 g protein
Exchanges: 1 Starch, 2 Lean Meat, 2 Vegetable

264 calories

Preparation time: 25 minutes

scallops and broccoli pasta

*Sweet, succulent scallops step up a basic stir-fry to a dish of sophistication. Buy scallops
that are firm, sweet smelling, and moist, but not cloudy.*

**12 ounces fresh or frozen scallops or peeled
and deveined shrimp**
2 cups frozen cut broccoli
½ cup sliced green onions
4 teaspoons cornstarch
1 teaspoon dried fines herbes, crushed
¼ teaspoon garlic powder
⅛ teaspoon black pepper
¾ cup reduced-sodium chicken broth
**2 tablespoons dry white wine or reduced-
sodium chicken broth**
**¼ cup chopped roasted red sweet peppers or
pimientos**
3 cups hot cooked spaghetti or fettuccine

1 Thaw scallops or shrimp, if frozen. Rinse; pat
dry with paper towels. Cook broccoli according to
package directions, adding green onions for the last
minute of cooking. Drain. Set aside.

2 In a medium saucepan combine cornstarch,
fines herbes, garlic powder, and black pepper. Stir in
broth and wine. Cook and stir until thickened and
bubbly. Add scallops or shrimp; return to boiling.
Cook and stir for 1 to 3 minutes more or until
scallops or shrimp are opaque. Stir in broccoli-onion
mixture and roasted red peppers or pimientos. Cook
about 1 minute more or until heated through. Serve
over hot cooked pasta. Makes 4 servings.

Nutrition facts per serving: 264 calories, 2 g total fat
(0 g saturated fat), 25 mg cholesterol, 263 mg sodium,
42 g carbohydrate, 3 g fiber, 19 g protein
Exchanges: 2 Starch, 2 Lean Meat, 1 Vegetable

208 calories

Preparation time: 30 minutes

scallops and artichoke stir-fry

Accent this light and lemony stir-fry by serving it over couscous, a quick-cooking grain commonly used in North African cuisine. Look for couscous near the rice or pasta in your grocery store.

12 ounces fresh or frozen scallops
3 tablespoons lemon juice
1 tablespoon cornstarch
1 teaspoon sugar
1 teaspoon instant chicken bouillon granules
⅛ teaspoon black pepper
1 8- or 9-ounce package frozen artichoke hearts
Nonstick spray coating
2 medium green and/or red sweet peppers, cut into thin bite-size strips
2 cups sliced shiitake, oyster, or brown mushrooms
1 tablespoon cooking oil
2 cups hot cooked couscous

1 Thaw scallops, if frozen. Halve any large scallops. Rinse; pat dry with paper towels. Set aside.

2 For sauce, combine ¾ cup *water,* lemon juice, cornstarch, sugar, bouillon granules, and black pepper. Set aside.

3 Place artichokes in a colander. Run *cold water* over them until partially thawed; halve any large pieces. Set aside.

4 Spray an unheated nonstick wok or large skillet with nonstick coating. Preheat over medium-high heat. Add artichokes; stir-fry for 2 minutes. Add sweet peppers and mushrooms; stir-fry for 2 to 4 minutes or until peppers are crisp-tender. Remove vegetable mixture from wok.

5 Add oil to hot wok. Add scallops; stir-fry 2 to 3 minutes or until opaque. Push from center of wok.

6 Stir sauce; add to center of wok. Cook and stir until thickened and bubbly. Return vegetable mixture to wok. Cook and stir about 2 minutes or until heated through. Serve over hot couscous. Makes 4 servings.

Nutrition facts per serving: 208 calories, 5 g total fat (1 g saturated fat), 26 mg cholesterol, 409 mg sodium, 28 g carbohydrate, 8 g fiber, 17 g protein
Exchanges: 1 Starch, 1½ Lean Meat, 2 Vegetable

263 calories

Preparation time: 35 minutes

fettuccine with garlic scallops

*Dried tomatoes that are not packed in oil need to be rehydrated in boiling water. Their intensity
lend a wonderful flavor punch to this elegant dish.*

1 **pound fresh or frozen scallops**
6 **dried tomato halves (not oil-packed)**
⅓ **cup boiling water**
2 **teaspoons cooking oil**
3 **large cloves garlic, minced**
2 **cups sliced fresh mushrooms**
2 **tablespoons lemon juice**
2 **teaspoons cornstarch**
4 **green onions, sliced**
2 **tablespoons snipped fresh parsley**
½ **teaspoon finely shredded lemon peel**
3 **cups hot cooked spinach and/or plain
    fettuccine**
    Lemon wedges (optional)

1 Thaw scallops, if frozen. Rinse; pat dry with
paper towels. In a small bowl combine dried
tomatoes and boiling water. Let stand 10 minutes.
Drain tomatoes, reserving liquid. Cut tomatoes into
thin bite-size strips. Set aside.

2 Pour oil into a large nonstick skillet. Heat over
medium-high heat. Cook garlic in hot oil for
15 seconds. Add mushrooms. Cook and stir for
2 minutes. Add scallops and tomatoes. Cook and stir
for 2 to 3 minutes or until scallops are opaque.

3 Combine lemon juice and cornstarch. Add to
skillet along with reserved tomato liquid, green
onions, snipped parsley, and lemon peel. Cook and
stir until slightly thickened and bubbly. Cook and
stir for 2 minutes more.

4 Serve scallop mixture over hot pasta. If
desired, garnish with lemon wedges. Makes
4 servings.

Nutrition facts per serving: 263 calories, 4 g total fat
(0 g saturated fat), 34 mg cholesterol, 281 mg sodium,
36 g carbohydrate, 2 g fiber, 21 g protein
Exchanges: 2 Starch, 2 Lean Meat, 1 Vegetable

188 calories

Preparation time: 25 minutes ● **Baking time:** 8 minutes

cheesy crab and broccoli

Sharp cheddar cheese boosts the flavor of the rich-tasting sauce. Here we've used regular—not lower-fat—cheese. Lower-fat cheese may not work as well here. Prolonged or high-temperature cooking cause it to toughen.

2 **cups frozen cut broccoli**
6 **ounces refrigerated crab-flavored fish pieces or one 6-ounce can crabmeat, drained, flaked, and cartilage removed**
1 **tablespoon margarine or butter**
2 **cups sliced fresh mushrooms**
1 **clove garlic, minced**
2 **tablespoons all-purpose flour**
⅛ **teaspoon pepper**
1 **cup skim milk**
¼ **cup shredded sharp cheddar cheese (1 ounce)**
2 **tablespoons grated Parmesan cheese**
2 **tablespoons crushed rich round crackers (about 3 crackers)**

1 Cook the broccoli according to package directions; drain. In 4 individual 14- to 16-ounce au gratin dishes or oval casseroles arrange broccoli and crab-flavored fish pieces. Set dishes aside.

2 For sauce, in medium saucepan melt the margarine or butter over medium-high heat. Add mushrooms and garlic and cook about 4 minutes or until mushrooms are tender. Stir in flour and pepper. Stir in milk all at once. Cook and stir until thickened and bubbly; remove from heat. Stir in cheddar cheese until melted.

3 Spoon sauce over broccoli and fish in dishes. Cover dishes with foil. Bake in a 400° oven for 8 to 10 minutes or until bubbly. (If desired, refrigerate casseroles for 2 to 24 hours. To serve, bake, covered, in a 400° oven for 20 to 25 minutes or until bubbly.) Combine Parmesan cheese and crushed crackers; sprinkle over casseroles. Makes 4 servings.

Nutrition facts per serving: 188 calories, 8 g total fat (3 g saturated fat), 19 mg cholesterol, 565 mg sodium, 17 g carbohydrate, 3 g fiber, 14 g protein
Exchanges: 1 Lean Meat, 2 Vegetable, ½ Milk, ½ Fat

153 calories

Preparation time: 35 minutes ● **Baking time:** 10 minutes

crab and asparagus gratin

Crab legs are readily available precooked and frozen. Or, you can use 6 ounces of refrigerated or thawed, frozen crab-flavored fish pieces.

1 **pound fresh or frozen split crab legs**
1 **10-ounce package frozen cut asparagus**
1 **tablespoon margarine or butter**
1 **cup sliced fresh mushrooms**
¼ **cup finely chopped onion**
1 **tablespoon cornstarch**
⅛ **teaspoon salt**
⅛ **teaspoon ground nutmeg**
  Dash pepper
1 **cup skim milk**
2 **tablespoons chopped toasted almonds**
2 **tablespoons grated Parmesan cheese**

1 Thaw crab legs, if frozen. Remove meat from shells; cut meat into 1-inch pieces. Cook asparagus according to package directions; drain well. Set aside.

2 In a medium saucepan melt margarine or butter over medium heat. Add mushrooms and onion; cook until onion is tender. Stir in cornstarch, salt, nutmeg, and pepper. Add the milk all at once. Cook and stir until thickened and bubbly. Cook and stir for 2 minutes more. Stir in crab and asparagus.

3 Spoon the crab mixture into 4 individual 10- to 14-ounce au gratin dishes or oval casserole dishes.

4 In a small bowl stir together almonds and Parmesan cheese. Sprinkle over casseroles.

5 Bake in a 400° oven about 10 minutes or until mixture is heated through. Makes 4 servings.

Nutrition facts per serving: 153 calories, 7 g total fat (1 g saturated fat), 26 mg cholesterol, 649 mg sodium, 10 g carbohydrate, 2 g fiber, 15 g protein
Exchanges: 2 Lean Meat, 2 Vegetable

242 calories

Preparation time: 40 minutes

crab gumbo

To Cajuns, gumbo isn't gumbo without a dusting of filé powder. It thickens the gumbo and adds a woodsy, root beerlike flavor. Add it at the end of cooking. If it is boiled, filé powder becomes tough and stringy.

½ **cup chopped green sweet pepper**
½ **cup sliced green onions**
1 **clove garlic, minced**
1 **tablespoon cooking oil**
1 **14½-ounce can reduced-sodium chicken broth**
1 **cup water**
2 **medium tomatoes, peeled and chopped**
¾ **teaspoon snipped fresh thyme or ¼ teaspoon dried thyme, crushed**
⅛ to ¼ **teaspoon bottled hot pepper sauce**
1 **10-ounce package frozen sliced okra**
1 **6-ounce can crabmeat**
½ **cup diced turkey ham**
1 **tablespoon filé powder (optional)**
2 **cups hot cooked rice**

1 In a large saucepan cook sweet pepper, green onions, and garlic in hot oil until vegetables are tender. Stir in chicken broth, water, tomatoes, thyme, and hot pepper sauce. Bring to boiling. Stir in okra; reduce heat. Simmer, covered, about 1 minute or until okra is tender.

2 Meanwhile, drain, flake, and remove cartilage from crabmeat. Stir crabmeat and turkey ham into gumbo. Heat through. If desired, stir in filé powder.

3 To serve, divide gumbo among 4 soup bowls. Top gumbo with the rice. Makes 4 servings.

Nutrition facts per serving: 242 calories, 6 g total fat (1 g saturated fat), 41 mg cholesterol, 627 mg sodium, 33 g carbohydrate, 2 g fiber, 16 g protein
Exchanges: 1½ Starch, 1 Lean Meat, 2 Vegetable

169 calories

Preparation time: 35 minutes

clam chowder

This lightened version of clam chowder saves you about 220 calories and 18 grams of fat per serving over a traditional recipe made with cream.

2 6½-ounce cans minced clams
1½ cups cubed potatoes
½ cup chopped onion
½ cup chopped celery
1 tablespoon snipped fresh thyme
   or ½ teaspoon dried thyme, crushed
2½ cups skim milk
4 teaspoons cornstarch
⅓ cup shredded carrot
1 teaspoon instant chicken bouillon granules
2 slices turkey bacon, cooked and chopped
   (optional)
   Fresh thyme (optional)

1 Drain clams, reserving liquid. Set clams aside. Add enough *water* to clam liquid to equal 1 cup liquid. In a 2-quart saucepan combine clam liquid, potatoes, onion, celery, and snipped or dried thyme. Bring to boiling; reduce heat. Simmer, covered, about 10 minutes or until potatoes are just tender.

2 Meanwhile, gradually stir a little of the milk (about ¼ cup) into cornstarch. Add to mixture in saucepan along with remaining milk, the carrot, and bouillon granules. Cook and stir over medium heat until mixture is slightly thickened and bubbly. Reduce heat. Cook and stir for 2 minutes more. Stir in drained clams. Heat through. If desired, garnish with turkey bacon and additional fresh thyme. Makes 4 servings.

Nutrition facts per serving: 169 calories, 2 g total fat (0 g saturated fat), 60 mg cholesterol, 364 mg sodium, 27 g carbohydrate, 2 g fiber, 14 g protein
Exchanges: 1 Starch, 1 Lean Meat, 1 Vegetable, ½ Milk

209 calories

Preparation time: 15 minutes ● **Cooking time:** 15 minutes

linguine with clam sauce

Crushed red pepper perks up this classic combination of pasta, clams, and white wine. To brighten the sauce use half of a red sweet pepper and half of a green one.

- 2 6½-ounce cans minced clams
- 1 medium green or red sweet pepper, chopped
- 2 green onions, sliced
- 1 teaspoon snipped fresh basil or ¼ teaspoon dried basil, crushed
- ¼ teaspoon crushed red pepper
- 2 cloves garlic, minced
- ¼ cup dry white wine
- 4 teaspoons cornstarch
- 2 tablespoons snipped fresh parsley
- 2¼ cups hot cooked linguine or fettuccine
- 2 tablespoons grated Parmesan cheese

1 Drain clams, reserving liquid. In a medium saucepan combine reserved clam liquid, sweet pepper, green onions, basil, crushed red pepper, and garlic. Bring to boiling; reduce heat. Simmer, uncovered, about 5 minutes or until green onions are tender.

2 In a small bowl stir together the wine and cornstarch; stir into mixture in saucepan. Cook and stir until thickened and bubbly. Cook and stir for 2 minutes more.

3 Stir in clams and parsley; heat through.

4 Spoon clam mixture over linguine. Sprinkle with Parmesan cheese. Makes 3 servings.

Nutrition facts per serving: 209 calories, 2 g total fat (1 g saturated fat), 3 mg cholesterol, 348 mg sodium, 36 g carbohydrate, 2 g fiber, 8 g protein
Exchanges: 2 Starch, 1 Lean Meat

271 calories

Preparation time: 20 minutes

saucy shrimp and pasta

To remove the black vein that runs along the back of a shrimp, use a sharp knife to make a slit from the head to the tail end. Then hold the shrimp under cold water to rinse away the vein.

1 pound fresh or frozen shrimp in shells
1 14½-ounce can Italian-style stewed
    tomatoes, cut up
4 teaspoons cornstarch
1 tablespoon snipped fresh parsley
    or 1 teaspoon dried parsley flakes
½ teaspoon sugar
½ teaspoon dried Italian seasoning, crushed
    Dash ground red pepper
3 cups hot cooked spaghetti
    Fresh parsley (optional)

1 Thaw shrimp, if frozen. Peel and devein shrimp. Rinse; pat dry with paper towels. Set aside.

2 In a large saucepan stir together the tomatoes, cornstarch, parsley, sugar, Italian seasoning, and ground red pepper. Cook and stir until thickened and bubbly.

3 Stir in shrimp. Return to boiling; cook for 1 to 3 minutes more or until shrimp are opaque.

4 Serve shrimp mixture over hot cooked spaghetti. If desired, garnish with additional fresh parsley. Makes 4 servings.

Nutrition facts per serving: 271 calories, 1 g total fat (0 g saturated fat), 131 mg cholesterol, 545 mg sodium, 43 g carbohydrate, 1 g fiber, 21 g protein
Exchanges: 1½ Starch, 2 Lean Meat, 2 Vegetable

220 calories

Preparation time: 25 minutes

sautéed shrimp with peppers

Sauté technically means to cook in a small amount of fat. But you can get the same results, only with fewer calories and fat, by using nonstick spray coating. Invest in a nonstick pan for even better no-fat cooking.

8 ounces fresh or frozen shrimp in shells
  Nonstick spray coating
2 small red and/or green sweet peppers, cut
  into thin strips
¼ cup sliced green onions
1 clove garlic, minced
½ cup canned sliced water chestnuts
2 tablespoons apricot preserves
1 tablespoon light or regular soy sauce
  Several dashes bottled hot pepper sauce
1 teaspoon toasted sesame seeds
1 cup hot cooked rice or orzo

1 Thaw shrimp, if frozen. Peel and devein shrimp. Rinse; pat dry with paper towels. Set aside.

2 Spray an unheated medium skillet with nonstick coating. Preheat over medium heat. Add sweet peppers, green onions, and garlic; cook for 3 to 4 minutes or until tender.

3 Add shrimp and water chestnuts. Cook and stir for 3 to 4 minutes more or until shrimp are opaque. Remove from heat.

4 Stir in apricot preserves, soy sauce, and hot pepper sauce. Sprinkle with sesame seeds. Serve over hot cooked rice or orzo. Makes 2 servings.

Nutrition facts per serving: 220 calories, 2 g total fat (0 g saturated fat), 131 mg cholesterol, 436 mg sodium, 34 g carbohydrate, 1 g fiber, 17 g protein
Exchanges: 2 Starch, 1 Lean Meat, 1 Vegetable

232 calories

Preparation time: 30 minutes

szechwan shrimp

Szechwan peppers generally supply the heat in Szechwan cooking. In this recipe, convenient-to-use crushed red pepper steps in. If you like milder foods, reduce the red pepper to ¼ or even ⅛ teaspoon.

1 **pound fresh or frozen shrimp in shells**
3 **tablespoons water**
2 **tablespoons catsup**
1 **tablespoon reduced-sodium soy sauce**
1 **tablespoon rice wine, dry sherry, or water**
2 **teaspoons cornstarch**
1 **teaspoon honey**
½ **teaspoon crushed red pepper**
1 **teaspoon grated fresh gingerroot**
    or ¼ teaspoon ground ginger
1 **tablespoon peanut oil or cooking oil**
½ **cup sliced green onions**
4 **cloves garlic, minced**
2 **cups hot cooked rice**

1 Thaw shrimp, if frozen. Peel and devein shrimp; cut in half lengthwise. Rinse; pat dry with paper towels. Set aside.

2 For sauce, in a small mixing bowl stir together the 3 tablespoons water, the catsup, soy sauce, rice wine or dry sherry, cornstarch, honey, crushed red pepper, and ground ginger (if using). Set aside.

3 Pour oil into a large skillet or wok. Heat over medium-high heat. Add green onions, garlic, and fresh grated gingerroot (if using); stir-fry for 30 seconds.

4 Add shrimp. Stir-fry for 2 to 3 minutes or until shrimp are opaque; push to side of skillet or wok. Stir sauce; add to center of skillet. Cook and stir until thickened and bubbly. Cook and stir for 2 minutes more. Serve with hot cooked rice. Makes 4 servings.

Nutrition facts per serving: 232 calories, 4 g total fat (1 g saturated fat), 131 mg cholesterol, 387 mg sodium, 29 g carbohydrate, 0 g fiber, 17 g protein
Exchanges: 2 Starch, 2 Lean Meat

200 calories

Preparation time: 25 minutes

lemony shrimp and asparagus

If you buy shrimp in shells, allow about 1 pound. By the time you remove and discard the shells, the shrimp will weigh about 12 ounces.

- **12 ounces fresh or frozen peeled and deveined shrimp**
- **1 pound fresh asparagus, trimmed and cut into 2-inch pieces, or one 10-ounce package frozen cut asparagus**
- **1 medium red or green sweet pepper, cut into thin strips**
- **2 cloves garlic, minced**
- **⅔ cup water**
- **1 tablespoon reduced-sodium soy sauce**
- **2 teaspoons cornstarch**
- **1 teaspoon finely shredded lemon peel**
- **1 tablespoon lemon juice**
- **2 cups hot cooked rice**

1 Thaw shrimp, if frozen. In a medium covered saucepan cook asparagus in a small amount of *boiling water* for 3 minutes. Add shrimp, sweet pepper, and garlic. Return to boiling. Cook, covered, for 1 to 2 minutes more or until shrimp are opaque. Drain.

2 Meanwhile, in a large saucepan stir together the ⅔ cup water, the soy sauce, cornstarch, lemon peel, and lemon juice. Cook and stir until thickened and bubbly. Cook and stir for 2 minutes more. Stir in vegetable-shrimp mixture. Heat through. Serve with rice. Makes 4 servings.

Nutrition facts per serving: 200 calories, 1 g total fat (0 g saturated fat), 131 mg cholesterol, 287 mg sodium, 29 g carbohydrate, 2 g fiber, 19 g protein
Exchanges: 1 Starch, 2 Lean Meat, 2 Vegetable

231 calories

Preparation time: 35 minutes ● **Cooking time:** 11 minutes

shrimp creole

Shrimp are sold by the pound in a variety of sizes. Generally, the larger shrimp cost more with fewer per pound. Although we used large shrimp in this classic Louisiana dish, medium work fine, too.

12 ounces fresh or frozen peeled and deveined large shrimp
¾ cup chopped onion
¾ cup chopped green sweet pepper
½ cup chopped celery
1 14½-ounce can Cajun-style or Mexican-style stewed tomatoes, undrained and cut up
2 tablespoons snipped fresh thyme or 1 teaspoon dried thyme, crushed
1 teaspoon instant chicken bouillon granules
1 teaspoon sugar
2 cloves garlic, minced
Several dashes bottled hot pepper sauce (optional)
2 teaspoons cornstarch
2 cups hot cooked rice
¼ cup snipped fresh parsley or celery tops

1 In a large saucepan bring 4 cups *water* to boil; add shrimp. Return to boiling; reduce heat. Simmer, uncovered, for 1 to 3 minutes or until shrimp are opaque. Drain in colander. Set aside.

2 In same saucepan combine the onion, sweet pepper, celery, and ⅓ cup *water.* Bring to boiling; reduce heat. Simmer, covered, for 3 to 4 minutes or until vegetables are crisp-tender. Do not drain.

3 Stir in undrained tomatoes, thyme, bouillon granules, sugar, garlic, and hot pepper sauce (if using). Simmer, covered, for 8 minutes.

4 Combine cornstarch and 1 tablespoon *cold water;* stir into skillet. Cook and stir over medium heat until thickened and bubbly; reduce heat. Cook and stir for 2 minutes more. Add shrimp; heat through. Combine rice and parsley or celery tops. Serve shrimp mixture with rice. Makes 4 servings.

Nutrition facts per serving: 231 calories, 1 g total fat (0 g saturated fat), 131 mg cholesterol, 751 mg sodium, 37 g carbohydrate, 1 g fiber, 18 g protein
Exchanges: 1½ Starch, 1 Lean Meat, 2 Vegetable

155 calories

Preparation time: 35 minutes

gingered shrimp soup

Rice wine, gingerroot, and tofu mark the Asian influence on this soup. Follow it up with a scoop of Apricot Sherbet (see recipe, page 455) for a light, yet satisfying meal.

8 ounces fresh or frozen peeled and deveined shrimp
3 cups reduced-sodium chicken broth
1½ cups water
¼ cup rice wine or dry sherry
1 tablespoon reduced-sodium soy sauce
1 teaspoon grated fresh gingerroot
½ teaspoon toasted sesame oil
¼ teaspoon pepper
2 cloves garlic, minced
4 ounces firm tofu (fresh bean curd), cubed
1 cup fresh pea pods, halved crosswise, or ½ of a 6-ounce package frozen pea pods, halved crosswise
¾ cup thinly bias-sliced carrot
¼ cup thinly sliced green onions

1 Thaw shrimp, if frozen. Halve shrimp lengthwise. Rinse shrimp; pat dry with paper towels. Set aside.

2 In a large saucepan combine chicken broth, water, rice wine or sherry, soy sauce, gingerroot, sesame oil, pepper, and garlic. Bring to boiling. Add the shrimp, tofu, fresh pea pods (if using), carrot, and green onions. Return to boiling; reduce heat. Simmer, covered, about 3 minutes or until shrimp turn opaque. Stir in frozen pea pods (if using); heat through. Makes 4 servings.

Nutrition facts per serving: 155 calories, 4 g total fat (1 g saturated fat), 87 mg cholesterol, 736 mg sodium, 9 g carbohydrate, 2 g fiber, 17 g protein
Exchanges: 2 Lean Meat, 2 Vegetable

Meatless
MAIN DISHES

chapter index

214 calories

Preparation time: 35 minutes

Vegetable-stuffed tortillas

*Lentils pinch-hit for meat in this colorful filling. The more commonly found lentil is greenish brown in color.
If you opt for the faster-cooking red lentils, shave 15 minutes from the preparation time.*

⅓ **cup dry lentils or red lentils**
1 **medium onion, chopped**
1 **stalk celery, sliced**
1 **clove garlic, minced**
1 **teaspoon cumin seed**
2 **teaspoons cooking oil**
2 **cups thinly sliced zucchini and/or yellow**
   summer squash
2 **cups fresh or frozen whole kernel corn**
1 **cup red and/or green sweet pepper strips**
8 **7- or 8-inch flour tortillas**
1 **cup salsa**
1 **cup shredded reduced-fat cheddar cheese**
   (4 ounces)
   Shredded lettuce (optional)
   Salsa (optional)

1 Rinse the lentils with cold water. Combine the lentils and 1 cup *water*. Bring to boiling; reduce heat. Simmer, covered, about 20 minutes for dry

lentils or about 5 minutes for red lentils or until tender. Drain.

2 Meanwhile, in a large skillet cook the onion, celery, garlic, and cumin seed in the hot oil about 8 minutes or until onion and celery are very tender. Add the zucchini or summer squash, corn, sweet pepper, and cooked lentils. Cook and stir about 10 minutes more.

3 Wrap the tortillas in foil. Heat in a 350° oven for 10 minutes or until warm. Spoon about ½ cup of the hot mixture down center of each tortilla. Top each tortilla with about 2 tablespoons salsa and 2 tablespoons cheese. Fold the sides of the tortilla over the filling. If desired, serve on a bed of shredded lettuce and top with additional salsa. Makes 8 servings.

Nutrition facts per serving: 214 calories, 7 g total fat (2 g saturated fat), 10 mg cholesterol, 321 mg sodium, 31 g carbohydrate, 4 g fiber, 10 g protein
Exchanges: 1½ Starch, 1 Medium-Fat Meat, 1 Vegetable

352 calories

Preparation time: 25 minutes

pasta primavera

Serve this pasta to guests, if you like—no one will label this dish as "diet food." Reduced-fat cream cheese gives a richness and smoothness to the creamy sauce.

1 9-ounce package frozen French-cut green beans
2 cups sliced fresh mushrooms
½ cup coarsely chopped red or green sweet pepper
¼ cup water
1 clove garlic, minced
¼ teaspoon salt
¼ teaspoon black pepper
1 12-ounce can evaporated skim milk
4 teaspoons cornstarch
½ of an 8-ounce package reduced-fat cream cheese (Neufchâtel), cubed
3 cups hot cooked rotini or fettuccine
1 medium tomato, cut into wedges

1 For sauce, in a medium saucepan combine frozen green beans, mushrooms, sweet pepper, water, garlic, salt, and black pepper. Bring to boiling; reduce heat. Simmer, covered, about 4 minutes or until vegetables are almost tender, stirring occasionally. Do not drain.

2 Stir together the milk and cornstarch; stir into vegetable mixture. Cook and stir over medium heat until thickened and bubbly. Reduce heat. Cook and stir for 2 minutes more. Add the cream cheese, stirring until melted.

3 To serve, pour the sauce over hot cooked pasta. Serve with tomato wedges. Makes 4 servings.

Nutrition facts per serving: 352 calories, 8 g total fat (4 g saturated fat), 25 mg cholesterol, 359 mg sodium, 54 g carbohydrate, 1 g fiber, 17 g protein
Exchanges: 1½ Starch, 3 Vegetable, 1 Milk, ½ Fat

296 calories

Preparation time: 20 minutes ● **Baking time:** 30 minutes

bow ties and cheese

Pasta ranks high among dieters because it's very filling. Serve this dish with a simple vegetable, such as steamed broccoli or green beans, or a fresh tossed salad drizzled with low-calorie dressing.

1 **8-ounce package dried medium bow tie pasta**
¼ **cup finely chopped onion**
2 **teaspoons cooking oil**
2 **teaspoons all-purpose flour**
1 **teaspoon dry mustard**
⅓ **cup skim milk**
1 **cup fat-free cottage cheese**
⅔ **cup shredded reduced-fat cheddar cheese**
   Nonstick spray coating
1 **tablespoon toasted wheat germ or fine dry bread crumbs**
   Chopped tomato (optional)
   Sliced green onion (optional)

1 Cook pasta according to package directions, except omit any oil.

2 In a large saucepan cook onion in hot oil until tender. Stir in the flour and mustard. Add milk all at once. Cook and stir until thickened and bubbly. Stir in the cottage cheese and reduced-fat cheddar cheese. Cook and stir over low heat until cheddar cheese is melted. Stir in the drained pasta.

3 Spray a 1½-quart casserole with nonstick coating. Spoon pasta mixture into casserole. Bake, covered, in a 350° oven for 20 minutes. Uncover and sprinkle with wheat germ or bread crumbs. Bake, uncovered, for 10 to 15 minutes more or until heated through. If desired, garnish with tomato and green onion. Makes 5 servings.

Nutrition facts per serving: 296 calories, 6 g total fat (1 g saturated fat), 16 mg cholesterol, 301 mg sodium, 40 g carbohydrate, 0 g fiber, 19 g protein
Exchanges: 2½ Starch, 2 Lean Meat

212 calories

Preparation time: 40 minutes ● **Baking time:** 30 minutes

spinach lasagna rolls

Get a jump start on dinner. Up to 24 hours ahead, assemble the lasagna rolls and prepare the sauce. Cover and refrigerate. To serve, bake the rolls in a 375° oven for 35 to 40 minutes and reheat the sauce.

Nonstick spray coating
1 **10-ounce package frozen chopped spinach, cooked and well drained**
2 **cups low-fat cottage cheese**
½ **cup grated Parmesan cheese**
1 **beaten egg**
⅛ **teaspoon ground nutmeg**
8 **lasagna noodles, cooked and drained**
1 **large onion, chopped**
1 **medium green sweet pepper, chopped**
2 **cups sliced fresh mushrooms**
2 **cloves garlic, minced**
1 **14½-ounce can tomatoes, undrained and cut up**
2 **teaspoons snipped fresh basil or ½ teaspoon dried basil, crushed**
1 **8-ounce can tomato sauce**
½ **teaspoon sugar**

1 Spray a 2-quart rectangular baking dish with nonstick coating; set aside.

2 For filling, in a bowl stir together the spinach, cottage cheese, Parmesan cheese, egg, and nutmeg. Spread about ⅓ cup of the filling on each noodle. Roll up, jelly-roll style, beginning at a short end. Place rolls, seam sides down, in prepared dish.

3 Cover with foil. Bake rolls in a 375° oven about 30 minutes or until heated through.

4 Meanwhile, for the sauce, spray an unheated 2-quart saucepan with nonstick coating. Preheat over medium heat. Add onion, sweet pepper, mushrooms, and garlic. Cook until vegetables are tender. Stir in undrained tomatoes, basil, tomato sauce, sugar, and ¼ teaspoon *pepper*. Bring to boiling; reduce heat. Simmer, uncovered, for 5 to 10 minutes or until desired consistency. Serve sauce over lasagna rolls. Makes 8 servings.

Nutrition facts per serving: 212 calories, 4 g total fat (2 g saturated fat), 36 mg cholesterol, 637 mg sodium, 28 g carbohydrate, 2 g fiber, 16 g protein
Exchanges: 1 Starch, 1 Lean Meat, 3 Vegetable

227 calories

Preparation time: 45 minutes ● **Baking time:** 30 minutes ● **Standing time:** 10 minutes

vegetarian lasagna

Chockful of vegetables, you won't even miss the meat in this lighter lasagna. If you want variety, substitute 10 ounces of your favorite frozen vegetable or frozen mixed vegetables for the broccoli.

- 1 14½-ounce can low-sodium tomatoes, undrained and cut up
- 1 15-ounce can low-sodium tomato sauce
- 1 cup chopped celery
- 1 cup chopped onion
- 1 cup chopped green or red sweet pepper
- 1½ teaspoons dried basil or oregano, crushed
- 2 bay leaves
- ¼ teaspoon salt
- 1 clove garlic, minced
- 1 beaten egg
- 2 cups fat-free ricotta or cottage cheese
- ¼ cup grated Parmesan cheese
- 1 10-ounce package frozen chopped broccoli, cooked and drained
- 8 lasagna noodles, cooked and drained
- 1 cup shredded part-skim mozzarella cheese

1 For sauce, in a large saucepan stir together undrained tomatoes, tomato sauce, celery, onion, sweet pepper, basil or oregano, bay leaves, salt, and garlic. Bring to boiling; reduce heat. Simmer, uncovered, for 20 to 25 minutes or until sauce is thick, stirring occasionally. Discard bay leaves.

2 Meanwhile, for filling, in a bowl stir together the egg, ricotta cheese or cottage cheese, Parmesan cheese, and ¼ teaspoon *pepper*. Stir in broccoli.

3 Spread about ½ cup of the sauce in a 3-quart rectangular baking dish. Top with half of the lasagna noodles, half of the filling, and half of the remaining sauce. Repeat layers, ending with the sauce.

4 Bake, uncovered, in a 350° oven for 25 minutes; sprinkle with mozzarella cheese. Bake about 5 minutes more or until heated through. Let stand 10 minutes before serving. Makes 8 servings.

Nutrition facts per serving: 227 calories, 4 g total fat (2 g saturated fat), 43 mg cholesterol, 272 mg sodium, 31 g carbohydrate, 3 g fiber, 19 g protein
Exchanges: 1 Starch, 2 Lean Meat, 2 Vegetable

282 calories

Preparation time: 25 minutes ● **Marinating time:** 30 minutes

ginger tofu and vegetables

*By itself, tofu tastes mild, but it readily assumes the flavors of other ingredients. In this recipe, tofu marinates
in a flavorful blend of lime juice, molasses, ginger, curry, garlic, and soy sauce.*

2 **tablespoons reduced-sodium soy sauce**
2 **tablespoons lime juice**
1 **tablespoon molasses or honey**
2 **teaspoons grated fresh gingerroot**
   or ½ teaspoon ground ginger
½ **teaspoon curry powder**
1 **large clove garlic, minced**
   Dash ground red pepper
10 **ounces extra-firm tofu (fresh bean curd),**
   cubed
¾ **cup reduced-sodium chicken broth or**
   vegetable broth
1 **tablespoon cornstarch**
   Nonstick spray coating
½ **cup bias-sliced carrot**
¼ **cup bias-sliced green onions**
1 **6-ounce package frozen pea pods, thawed**
   and drained
3 **cups hot cooked linguine**

1 In a medium mixing bowl stir together the soy
sauce, lime juice, molasses or honey, gingerroot or
ginger, curry powder, garlic, and ground red pepper.
Add tofu, stirring gently to coat. Cover and marinate
at room temperature for 30 minutes, stirring gently
once or twice. Drain, reserving marinade. Stir broth
and cornstarch into reserved marinade.

2 Spray an unheated large skillet with nonstick
coating. Preheat over medium-high heat about
1 minute. Add carrot; stir-fry for 3 minutes. Add
green onions; stir-fry for 2 minutes. Stir broth
mixture; carefully add to skillet. Cook and stir until
thickened and bubbly. Reduce heat. Gently stir in
thawed pea pods and tofu; cook 1 to 2 minutes
more or until heated through. Spoon over hot
cooked linguine. Makes 4 servings.

Nutrition facts per serving: 282 calories, 3 g total fat
(0 g saturated fat), 0 mg cholesterol, 411 mg sodium,
50 g carbohydrate, 1 g fiber, 14 g protein
Exchanges: 2½ Starch, 1 Very Lean Meat, 2 Vegetable

305 calories

Preparation time: 30 minutes

tofu and vegetable stir-fry

*Tofu comes in soft, firm, and extra-firm styles. Use the extra-firm style for stir-fry recipes,
such as this one, because it retains its shape better than the softer styles.*

½ **cup water**
2 **tablespoons dry sherry (optional)**
1 **tablespoon cornstarch**
1 **tablespoon reduced-sodium soy sauce**
1 **teaspoon sugar**
½ **teaspoon instant chicken or vegetable
    bouillon granules**
  Nonstick spray coating
1 **cup thinly sliced carrots**
1 **clove garlic, minced**
1 **teaspoon grated fresh gingerroot**
3 **cups cut-up broccoli**
6 **ounces extra-firm tofu (fresh bean curd),
    cubed**
1 **cup hot cooked brown rice**
1 **tablespoon toasted sesame seeds (optional)**

1 For sauce, stir together the water, dry sherry (if
desired), cornstarch, soy sauce, sugar, and bouillon
granules. Set aside.

2 Spray an unheated wok or large skillet with
nonstick coating. Preheat over medium-high heat.
Add carrots, garlic, and gingerroot; stir-fry for
2 minutes. Add broccoli; stir-fry for 3 to 4 minutes
more or until all vegetables are crisp-tender. Push
vegetables from center of wok.

3 Stir sauce; add to center of wok. Cook and
stir until thickened and bubbly. Add tofu to wok.
Stir to coat all with sauce. Cook and stir for
2 minutes more or until heated through.

4 Serve over hot cooked brown rice. If desired,
sprinkle with sesame seeds. Makes 2 servings.

Nutrition facts per serving: 305 calories, 6 g total fat
(1 g saturated fat), 0 mg cholesterol, 584 mg sodium,
48 g carbohydrate, 10 g fiber, 16 g protein
Exchanges: 1½ Starch, 1 Lean Meat, 4 Vegetable

210 calories

Preparation time: 20 minutes • **Baking time:** 33 minutes

corn and tofu quiche

Instead of baking this quiche in a high-fat pastry shell, coat the pie plate with bread crumbs. Tofu, a nutritious, no-cholesterol food, replaces some of the eggs. The result—a great-tasting meal that is healthful, too.

 1 **teaspoon margarine or butter**
 2 **tablespoons fine dry bread crumbs**
 1 **10½-ounce package tofu (fresh bean curd), drained and cut up**
 2 **egg whites**
 1 **egg**
 ½ **cup shredded reduced-fat cheddar cheese (2 ounces)**
 ⅓ **cup skim milk**
 1½ **teaspoons snipped fresh oregano or ½ teaspoon dried oregano, crushed**
 ¼ **teaspoon black pepper**
 ⅛ **teaspoon garlic salt**
 ⅛ **teaspoon salt**
 1 **cup frozen whole kernel corn**
 ¼ **cup chopped roasted red sweet pepper**
 1 **tablespoon dried minced onion**
 ¼ **cup shredded reduced-fat cheddar cheese (1 ounce)**
 Snipped fresh chives (optional)

1 Use the margarine or butter to grease the bottom and sides of a 9-inch pie plate. Sprinkle with bread crumbs to coat the dish.

2 In a food processor bowl or blender container combine tofu, egg whites, whole egg, the ½ cup cheddar cheese, the milk, oregano, black pepper, garlic salt, and salt. Cover and process or blend until smooth. Stir in corn, roasted red sweet pepper, and dried onion. Pour into prepared pie plate.

3 Bake, uncovered, in a 350° oven for 30 to 35 minutes or until a knife inserted near the center comes out clean.

4 Sprinkle the ¼ cup cheddar cheese over quiche. Bake about 3 minutes more or until cheese is melted. If desired, garnish with fresh chives. Makes 4 servings.

Nutrition facts per serving: 210 calories, 10 g total fat (3 g saturated fat), 69 mg cholesterol, 383 mg sodium, 15 g carbohydrate, 0 g fiber, 18 g protein
Exchanges: 1 Starch, 2 Medium-Fat Meat

293 calories

Preparation time: 30 minutes

gingered cabbage stir-fry

Keep gingerroot on hand to add to dishes for a simple flavor boost. Wrap the root in paper towel and store in the refrigerator for up to a month.

1 **tablespoon cooking oil**
1 **medium red onion, cut into thin wedges**
1 **tablespoon grated fresh gingerroot**
1 **or 2 large cloves garlic, minced**
1 **medium red or yellow sweet pepper, cut into strips**
8 **ounces yellow wax, green, or Italian green beans, trimmed and cut into 1-inch pieces (about 1½ cups)**
4 **cups coarsely chopped Chinese cabbage**
1 **tablespoon rice vinegar or white wine vinegar**
1 **tablespoon reduced-sodium soy sauce**
½ **teaspoon toasted sesame oil**
4 **ounces lentil sprouts or bean sprouts (about 1 cup)**
2 **pita bread rounds, halved, or 2 cups hot cooked rice**

1 In wok or large skillet heat oil over high heat. Add red onion, gingerroot, and garlic. Reduce heat; stir-fry about 4 minutes or until onion is almost tender. Add sweet pepper and beans; cover and cook over medium-low heat about 3 minutes or until pepper is crisp-tender. Stir in cabbage; cover and cook about 4 minutes or until crisp-tender.

2 In small bowl combine vinegar, soy sauce, and sesame oil. Stir into vegetable mixture along with sprouts. Heat through. Serve with pita bread or rice. Makes 4 servings.

Nutrition facts per serving: 293 calories, 6 g total fat (1 g saturated fat), 0 mg cholesterol, 307 mg sodium, 49 g carbohydrate, 3 g fiber, 14 g protein
Exchanges: 2 Starch, 4 Vegetable, 1 Fat

261 calories

Preparation time: 55 minutes ● **Baking time:** 25 minutes

barley-stuffed cabbage rolls

A blend of fennel, wild rice, walnuts, and barley fills these rolls. Fennel imparts a light licorice flavor.
If you like, save the feathery leaves and use as a garnish.

⅓ **cup wild rice**
1 **cup vegetable broth or chicken broth**
½ **cup pearl barley**
½ **cup shredded carrot**
1 **small fennel bulb, chopped (about ¾ cup)**
1 **tablespoon snipped fresh thyme**
   or ½ teaspoon dried thyme, crushed
¼ **cup toasted chopped walnuts**
8 **large cabbage leaves**
2 **8-ounce cans low-sodium tomato sauce**
1 **tablespoon brown sugar**
   Few dashes bottled hot pepper sauce
   Grated Parmesan cheese (optional)
   Fresh thyme or fennel leaves (optional)

1 Rinse wild rice in cold water; drain.

2 In a saucepan heat 1¾ cups *water* and broth to boiling. Add barley and rice. Reduce heat; simmer, covered, 30 minutes. Stir in carrot, fennel, and thyme. Simmer, covered, 10 to 15 minutes or until barley and rice are tender. Drain; stir in walnuts.

3 Meanwhile, fill a large Dutch oven with *water*. Bring to boiling. Cut out center veins from cabbage leaves, keeping each leaf in 1 piece. Immerse leaves, 4 at a time, into the boiling water for 2 to 3 minutes or until leaves are limp. Drain well.

4 Place about ½ cup of the rice mixture on each cabbage leaf; fold in sides. Starting at an unfolded edge, carefully roll up each leaf. For sauce, stir together the tomato sauce, brown sugar, and hot pepper sauce. Spoon about ¾ cup of the sauce into a 2-quart square baking dish. Place cabbage rolls in dish. Spoon remaining sauce over cabbage rolls. Bake, covered, in a 400° oven about 25 minutes or until heated through. If desired, sprinkle cabbage rolls with Parmesan cheese and garnish with fresh thyme or fennel leaves. Makes 4 servings.

Nutrition facts per serving: 261 calories, 6 g total fat (1 g saturated fat), 0 mg cholesterol, 302 mg sodium, 47 g carbohydrate, 9 g fiber, 9 g protein
Exchanges: 2 Starch, 3 Vegetable, ½ Fat

255 calories

Preparation time: 15 minutes • **Cooking time:** 8 minutes

couscous cakes with black bean salsa

Like better-quality pastas, couscous is made from ground semolina. Here, couscous replaces some of the flour in these buttermilk cakes. Look for couscous with the rice or pasta products in your supermarket.

⅔ cup corn relish
½ of a 15-ounce can (about ¾ cup) black
    beans, rinsed and drained
2 small Roma tomatoes, chopped
1½ teaspoons lime juice
¼ teaspoon ground cumin
½ cup couscous
2 tablespoons whole wheat flour
½ teaspoon sugar
¼ teaspoon baking soda
⅛ teaspoon salt
¾ cup buttermilk or sour milk*
1 slightly beaten egg white
1 tablespoon cooking oil

1 For salsa, in medium mixing bowl combine the corn relish, beans, tomatoes, lime juice, and cumin. Set aside.

2 In another medium mixing bowl combine the *uncooked* couscous, whole wheat flour, sugar, baking soda, and salt. In a small bowl combine buttermilk, egg white, and oil; stir with a wire whisk until well mixed. Stir buttermilk mixture into flour mixture. For each cake, spoon about 2 tablespoons batter onto hot, lightly greased griddle or skillet. Cook for 4 to 6 minutes, turning to second side when bottoms are lightly browned and edges are slightly dry.

3 Serve cakes with the salsa mixture. Makes 4 servings.

***Note:** To sour milk, place 2 teaspoons lemon juice or vinegar in a glass measuring cup. Add enough milk to make ¾ cup total liquid; stir. Let the mixture stand for 5 minutes before using it in recipe.

Nutrition facts per serving: 255 calories, 4 g total fat (1 g saturated fat), 2 mg cholesterol, 516 mg sodium, 46 g carbohydrate, 7 g fiber, 10 g protein
Exchanges: 3 Starch

230 calories

Preparation time: 20 minutes ● **Cooking time:** 30 minutes

curried lentils and vegetables

Lentils serve as a meat substitute in many parts of the Middle East and India. Like meat, lentils contain iron and protein, but no saturated fat or cholesterol, making them a very healthful substitute.

2 cups dry lentils
2 14½-ounce cans reduced-sodium chicken broth or vegetable broth
1½ cups water
1½ cups chopped carrots
1½ cups chopped onion
1 cup sliced celery
2 to 3 teaspoons curry powder
1 clove garlic, minced
1 teaspoon grated fresh gingerroot or or ¼ teaspoon ground ginger
⅛ teaspoon pepper
1 8-ounce carton plain low-fat yogurt or light dairy sour cream
1 medium tomato, chopped
1 tablespoon snipped fresh parsley or cilantro (optional)
Pita wedges (optional)

1 Rinse lentils in cold water. Drain.

2 In a large saucepan combine the lentils, chicken or vegetable broth, water, carrots, onion, celery, curry powder, garlic, gingerroot or ginger, and pepper. Bring to boiling; reduce heat. Simmer, covered, about 30 minutes or just until the lentils are tender. Drain.

3 Meanwhile, in a medium mixing bowl stir together the yogurt or sour cream, tomato, and parsley or cilantro (if desired). Serve with the lentil mixture. If desired, serve lentil mixture with pita wedges. Makes 6 servings.

Nutrition facts per serving: 230 calories, 2 g total fat (0 g saturated fat), 2 mg cholesterol, 332 mg sodium, 39 g carbohydrate, 4 g fiber, 16 g protein
Exchanges: 2 Starch, 1 Lean Meat, 1 Vegetable

276 calories

Preparation time: 30 minutes • **Baking time:** 23 minutes

rice and beans with cheese

*Rely on canned beans as a convenient, low-fat protein source. Rinse and drain them before using
to significantly reduce the sodium or look for low-sodium varieties.*

1⅓ cups water
1 cup shredded carrot
⅔ cup long grain rice
½ cup sliced green onions
½ teaspoon instant chicken or vegetable
    bouillon granules
½ teaspoon ground coriander
    Dash bottled hot pepper sauce
1 15-ounce can pinto or navy beans, rinsed
    and drained
1 cup low-fat cottage cheese
1 8-ounce carton plain low-fat yogurt
1 tablespoon snipped fresh parsley
½ cup shredded reduced-fat cheddar cheese
    (2 ounces)
    Carrot curls (optional)

1 In a large saucepan combine the water,
shredded carrot, rice, green onions, bouillon
granules, coriander, and bottled hot pepper sauce.
Bring to boiling; reduce heat. Simmer, covered,
about 15 minutes or until rice is tender and the
water is absorbed.

2 Stir in the pinto or navy beans, cottage cheese,
yogurt, and parsley. Spoon into a 2-quart baking
dish. Bake, covered, in a 350° oven for 20 to
25 minutes or until heated through. (If desired,
spoon into individual oven-safe casserole dishes.)
Sprinkle with the cheddar cheese. Bake, uncovered,
for 3 to 5 minutes more or until cheese melts. If
desired, garnish with carrot curls. Makes 5 servings.

Nutrition facts per serving: 276 calories, 4 g total fat
(2 g saturated fat), 15 mg cholesterol, 704 mg sodium,
41 g carbohydrate, 6 g fiber, 18 g protein
Exchanges: 2 Starch, 1 Lean Meat, 1 Vegetable, ½ Milk

229 calories

Preparation time: 25 minutes

bulgur-rice pilaf with green beans

*Toasting enhances the flavor of nuts enabling just a few to perk up an entire dish. Here, just a few
toasted almonds supply a pleasant crunch to this lemon-scented pilaf.*

½ cup chopped onion
2 teaspoons cooking oil
1 14½-ounce can (1¾ cups) vegetable broth
⅔ cup quick-cooking brown rice
⅔ cup bulgur
1 9-ounce package frozen cut or French-cut
  green beans
¼ teaspoon finely shredded lemon peel
½ cup shredded reduced-fat cheddar cheese
  (2 ounces)
2 tablespoons toasted sliced almonds
  Spiral-cut or shredded carrot (optional)

1 In a large saucepan cook onion in hot oil
about 5 minutes or until onion is almost tender.
Carefully add broth, rice, bulgur, and frozen beans.
Bring to boiling; reduce heat. Simmer, covered,
about 15 minutes or until rice, bulgur, and beans are
tender. Stir in lemon peel. Sprinkle cheese and
almonds over rice mixture. If desired, garnish with
carrot. Makes 4 servings.

Nutrition facts per serving: 229 calories, 8 g total fat
(2 g saturated fat), 10 mg cholesterol, 534 mg sodium,
34 g carbohydrate, 7 g fiber, 10 g protein
Exchanges: 2 Starch, 1 Vegetable, 1 Fat

306 calories

Preparation time: 10 minutes ● **Cooking time:** 20 minutes

tex-mex chili with dumplings

For a family-style, meatless dinner, dish up steaming bowls of this saucy chili topped with fluffy cornmeal dumplings. Add a tossed salad to complete the meal.

⅓ **cup all-purpose flour**
⅓ **cup yellow cornmeal**
1 **teaspoon baking powder**
1 **beaten egg white**
¼ **cup skim milk**
2 **tablespoons cooking oil**
1 **cup chopped onion**
1 **clove garlic, minced**
1 **15-ounce can garbanzo beans, rinsed and drained**
1 **15-ounce can reduced-sodium red kidney beans, rinsed and drained**
2 **8-ounce cans low-sodium tomato sauce**
1 **4½-ounce can diced green chili peppers**
2 **teaspoons chili powder**
1½ **teaspoons cornstarch**
Reduced-fat cheddar cheese (optional)

1 In a medium bowl stir together the flour, cornmeal, baking powder, and ¼ teaspoon *salt*. In a small bowl combine egg white, milk, and oil.

2 In a skillet combine onion, garlic, and ¾ cup *water*. Bring to boiling; reduce heat. Simmer, covered, about 5 minutes or until tender. Stir in beans, tomato sauce, chili peppers, and chili powder. In a small bowl stir together cornstarch and 1 tablespoon *cold water*. Stir into bean mixture. Cook and stir until slightly thickened. Reduce heat.

3 For dumplings, add milk mixture to cornmeal mixture; stir just until combined. Drop batter from a tablespoon into 5 mounds on top of the bubbling bean mixture. Simmer, covered, for 10 to 12 minutes or until a toothpick inserted into the center of a dumpling comes out clean. (Do not lift cover while simmering.) If desired, sprinkle with cheese. Makes 5 servings.

Nutrition facts per serving: 306 calories, 8 g total fat (1 g saturated fat), 0 mg cholesterol, 685 mg sodium, 51 g carbohydrate, 10 g fiber, 13 g protein
Exchanges: 3 Starch, 1 Vegetable, 1 Fat

271 calories

Preparation time: 20 minutes ● **Cooking time:** 20 minutes

cajun-style beans and rice

Although traditionally made with sausage, this meatless version tastes just as good as the traditional Cajun classic. Canned beans turn it into a quick-to-fix supper.

½ cup chopped celery
½ cup chopped green sweet pepper
½ cup chopped onion
½ cup sliced okra
1 clove garlic, minced
1 tablespoon cooking oil
1 16-ounce can tomatoes, undrained and
    cut up
¼ cup dry red wine, beer, or water
1 tablespoon snipped fresh oregano
    or 1 teaspoon dried oregano, crushed
1 tablespoon snipped fresh thyme
    or 1 teaspoon dried thyme, crushed
1 teaspoon dried parsley flakes
1 teaspoon bottled hot pepper sauce
¼ teaspoon paprika
⅛ teaspoon black pepper
1 15- or 15½-ounce can small red beans or
    black beans, rinsed and drained
2 cups hot cooked white or brown rice
    Fresh oregano (optional)

1 In large saucepan cook celery, sweet pepper, onion, okra, and garlic in hot oil about 10 minutes or until tender, stirring occasionally.

2 Stir in ½ cup *water,* the undrained tomatoes, wine, snipped or dried oregano, thyme, parsley, hot pepper sauce, paprika, ¼ teaspoon *salt,* and the black pepper. Reduce heat. Simmer, uncovered, for 15 minutes, stirring frequently. Stir in beans; cook about 5 minutes more or until heated through. Serve over hot cooked rice. If desired, garnish with additional fresh oregano. Makes 4 servings.

Nutrition facts per serving: 271 calories, 4 g total fat (1 g saturated fat), 0 mg cholesterol, 459 mg sodium, 50 g carbohydrate, 8 g fiber, 12 g protein
Exchanges: 2½ Starch, 2 Vegetable, ½ Fat

193 calories

Preparation time: 20 minutes ● **Cooking time:** 20 minutes

minestrone

Check the nutrition labels on jars of "light" spaghetti sauces. Fat, calorie, and sodium content vary greatly among brands. Choose the one that best meets your health requirements and flavor preference.

3 **cups water**
1 **cup shredded cabbage**
1 **medium onion, chopped**
1 **medium carrot, chopped**
1 **stalk celery, sliced**
1 **16-ounce jar light tomato and herb-flavored spaghetti sauce**
1 **15-ounce can white kidney beans or great northern beans, rinsed and drained**
1 **small zucchini, halved lengthwise and sliced**
⅓ **cup packaged dried small shell pasta**
⅛ **teaspoon salt**
4 **teaspoons grated Parmesan cheese**

1 In a large saucepan or Dutch oven combine the water, cabbage, onion, carrot, and celery. Bring to boiling; reduce heat to medium. Cook, covered, for 10 to 15 minutes or until vegetables are tender.

2 Add spaghetti sauce, kidney or great northern beans, zucchini, uncooked pasta, and salt. Return to boiling; reduce heat. Simmer, covered, for 10 to 15 minutes more or until vegetables and pasta are tender. Sprinkle each serving with 1 teaspoon of the Parmesan cheese. Makes 4 servings.

Nutrition facts per serving: 193 calories, 2 g total fat (0 g saturated fat), 2 mg cholesterol, 342 mg sodium, 42 g carbohydrate, 9 g fiber, 11 g protein
Exchanges: 2 Starch, 3 Vegetable

217 calories

Preparation time: 15 minutes ● **Cooking time:** 5 minutes

garbanzo bean stew

Garbanzo beans have a rounded shape, buff color, and a nutty flavor. They are a common ingredient in Mediterranean cooking (as is feta cheese) and add an ethnic flavor to this stew.

1 **large onion, chopped**
1 **medium green sweet pepper, chopped**
3 **cloves garlic, minced**
2 **teaspoons cooking oil**
1½ **teaspoons ground cumin**
½ **teaspoon paprika**
⅛ **to ¼ teaspoon ground red pepper**
2 **cups reduced-sodium chicken broth or vegetable broth**
1 **10-ounce package (2 cups) frozen whole kernel corn**
2 **tablespoons snipped fresh parsley**
2 **tablespoons snipped fresh oregano or 2 teaspoons dried oregano, crushed**
1 **15-ounce can garbanzo beans, rinsed and drained**
1 **medium tomato, chopped**
2 **tablespoons lemon juice**
¼ **cup crumbled feta cheese (optional)**
2 **tablespoons thinly sliced green onion**

1 In a large covered saucepan cook onion, sweet pepper, and garlic in hot oil until onion is tender, stirring occasionally. Stir in cumin, paprika, and ground red pepper; cook 1 minute.

2 Carefully add 1½ cups *water,* the chicken or vegetable broth, frozen corn, parsley, and oregano. Bring to boiling; reduce heat. Simmer, covered, for 5 to 10 minutes or until corn is tender. Stir in beans, tomato, and lemon juice. Heat through. Ladle stew into serving bowls. Sprinkle each serving with feta cheese (if desired) and green onion. Makes 4 servings.

Nutrition facts per serving: 217 calories, 6 g total fat (1 g saturated fat), 0 mg cholesterol, 672 mg sodium, 38 g carbohydrate, 5 g fiber, 9 g protein
Exchanges: 2 Starch, 2 Vegetable, ½ Fat

188 calories

Preparation time: 25 minutes

mushroom and barley soup

Serve thick slices of crusty French bread with this flavorsome soup. If you like the flavor of a more earthy mushroom, use a combination of regular and wild mushroom, such as cèpe, shiitake, or chanterelle.

2 14½-ounce cans beef broth or vegetable
   broth
2½ cups water
¾ cup quick-cooking barley
½ cup chopped onion
2 cloves garlic, minced
1 tablespoon snipped fresh basil
   or 1 teaspoon dried basil, crushed
½ teaspoon Worcestershire sauce
⅛ teaspoon pepper
3 cups sliced fresh mushrooms
½ cup shredded carrot
2 tablespoons cornstarch
2 tablespoons cold water
1 tablespoon snipped fresh parsley

1 In a large saucepan bring beef or vegetable broth and the 2½ cups water to boiling. Stir in barley, onion, garlic, basil, Worcestershire sauce, and pepper. Simmer, covered, for 5 minutes. Stir in mushrooms and carrot. Simmer, covered, about 5 minutes more or until barley is tender.

2 Meanwhile, in a small bowl combine the cornstarch and the 2 tablespoons cold water; stir into saucepan. Cook and stir until thickened and bubbly. Cook and stir for 2 minutes more. Sprinkle with parsley. Makes 4 servings.

Nutrition facts per serving: 188 calories, 2 g total fat (0 g saturated fat), 0 mg cholesterol, 692 mg sodium, 37 g carbohydrate, 4 g fiber, 8 g protein
Exchanges: 1½ Starch, 2 Vegetable

377 calories

Preparation time: 20 minutes ● **Cooking time:** 15 minutes

vegetarian chili with rice

Brighten a rainy day with cumin-scented bowls of chili. Mix up a batch of Parmesan Corn Bread Puffs (see recipe, page 413) to serve with this colorful chili.

1 15½-ounce can red kidney beans, rinsed
    and drained
1 15-ounce can great northern beans, rinsed
    and drained
1 14½-ounce can low-sodium tomatoes,
    undrained and cut up
1 8-ounce can low-sodium tomato sauce
1 cup water
¾ cup chopped green sweet pepper
½ cup chopped onion
1 tablespoon chili powder
1 teaspoon sugar
1 teaspoon snipped fresh basil or ½ teaspoon
    dried basil, crushed
½ teaspoon ground cumin
¼ teaspoon salt
    Dash ground red pepper
2 cloves garlic, minced
2 cups hot cooked rice

1 In a large saucepan combine beans, undrained tomatoes, tomato sauce, water, sweet pepper, onion, chili powder, sugar, basil, cumin, salt, ground red pepper, and garlic. Bring to boiling; reduce heat. Simmer, covered, about 15 minutes, stirring occasionally.

2 Top each serving of chili with ½ cup of the hot cooked rice. Makes 4 servings.

Nutrition facts per serving: 377 calories, 2 g total fat (0 g saturated fat), 0 mg cholesterol, 365 mg sodium, 77 g carbohydrate, 9 g fiber, 20 g protein
Exchanges: 4 Starch, 3 Vegetable

267 calories

Preparation time: 40 minutes ● **Standing time:** 1 hour ● **Cooking time:** 1¼ hours

mixed bean soup

If you don't want to store extra beans, buy a package of mixed dried beans instead of the three different kinds. Prepare the recipe as directed using 1½ cups of the bean mix.

½ cup dry baby lima beans or garbanzo beans
½ cup dry pinto beans or kidney beans
½ cup dry navy beans or great northern beans
4 cups cold water
1 cup chopped celery
1 cup chopped onion
1 cup chopped carrot
3 cloves garlic, minced
1 tablespoon olive oil or cooking oil
3 cups water
1 14½-ounce can vegetable broth
1 teaspoon dried thyme, crushed
½ teaspoon dried marjoram, crushed
¼ teaspoon pepper
1 14½-ounce can diced tomatoes
1½ cups low-sodium vegetable juice
Fresh marjoram (optional)

1 Rinse beans; transfer to 4-quart Dutch oven and add the 4 cups water. Bring to boiling; reduce heat. Simmer for 2 minutes; remove from heat. Cover and let stand for 1 hour. (Or, omit simmering; soak beans in cold water overnight in a covered Dutch oven.) Drain and rinse beans in a colander.

2 In the same covered Dutch oven cook the celery, onion, carrot, and garlic in the hot oil until tender, stirring once or twice. Add beans. Stir in the 3 cups water, the vegetable broth, thyme, marjoram, and pepper. Bring to boiling; reduce heat. Simmer, covered, for 1¼ to 1½ hours or until beans are tender. Stir in the undrained tomatoes and vegetable juice. Heat through. If desired, garnish with fresh marjoram. Makes 5 servings.

Nutrition facts per serving: 267 calories, 4 g total fat (1 g saturated fat), 0 mg cholesterol, 594 mg sodium, 49 g carbohydrate, 5 g fiber, 14 g protein
Exchanges: 2 Starch, 3 Vegetable, ½ Fat

222 calories

Preparation time: 20 minutes ● **Baking time:** 10 minutes

succotash cups

For a meatless taco salad, top these veggie-filled tortilla cups with shredded lettuce in addition to the tomato. Serve with fat-free sour cream, if you like.

1 **10-ounce package frozen baby lima beans**
1 **10-ounce package frozen whole kernel corn**
⅓ **cup chopped onion**
1 **tablespoon margarine or butter**
¾ **cup salsa**
   Nonstick spray coating
6 **6-inch corn tortillas**
½ **cup shredded reduced-fat Monterey Jack or reduced-fat cheddar cheese (2 ounces)**
1 **small tomato, chopped**

1 In large covered saucepan cook beans in a small amount of *boiling water* for 8 minutes. Add corn and onion; cook 4 to 5 minutes more or until vegetables are tender. Drain well. Stir in the margarine or butter until melted. Stir in the salsa.

2 While vegetables are cooking, lightly spray six 10-ounce individual casseroles or custard cups with nonstick coating. Place on shallow baking pan.

3 To soften the tortillas, wrap tortillas in microwave-safe paper towels. Microwave on 100% power (high) for 15 to 20 seconds. (Or, wrap tortillas in foil and heat in a 350° oven for 10 minutes.) Gently press each tortilla into a prepared casserole or custard cup. Spoon about ⅔ cup of the vegetable mixture into each tortilla cup; sprinkle with cheese. Bake in a 400° oven about 10 minutes or until heated through. Top with chopped tomato. Makes 6 servings.

Nutrition facts per serving: 222 calories, 6 g total fat (2 g saturated fat), 7 mg cholesterol, 254 mg sodium, 37 g carbohydrate, 5 g fiber, 10 g protein
Exchanges: 2½ Starch, 1 Lean Meat

308 calories

Preparation time: 55 minutes

cheese-sauce-topped potatoes

Once relegated to humble side dishes, baked potatoes take center stage with this simple entrée. To save time, cook the potatoes in your microwave oven while you make the cheese sauce.

4 **medium baking potatoes (6 to 8 ounces each)**
1 **cup skim milk**
1 **tablespoon cornstarch**
½ **teaspoon dry mustard**
⅛ **teaspoon pepper**
¾ **cup shredded American cheese (3 ounces)**
2 **cups desired cooked vegetables or frozen mixed vegetables (such as broccoli, mushroom, onion, and red sweet pepper)**

1 To bake potatoes, scrub thoroughly and prick skim with a fork. Bake in a 425° oven for 40 to 60 minutes or until done. (Or, microwave on 100% power [high] for 10 to 15 minutes. Let stand for 5 minutes.)

2 Meanwhile, in a small saucepan stir together the milk, cornstarch, mustard, and pepper. Cook and stir until thickened and bubbly. Add the cheese, stirring until melted. Stir in the cooked vegetables and heat through.

3 Cut potatoes into quarters lengthwise. Spoon vegetable mixture over potatoes. Makes 4 servings.

Nutrition facts per serving: 308 calories, 7 g total fat (4 g saturated fat), 21 mg cholesterol, 372 mg sodium, 50 g carbohydrate, 1 g fiber, 12 g protein
Exchanges: 2½ Starch, 1 Medium-Fat Meat, 2 Vegetable

258 calories

Preparation time: 25 minutes ● **Baking time:** 20 minutes

cheese calzones

Thanks to reduced-fat products, dieters can indulge in these cheese-stuffed Italian turnovers.
Plan ahead and thaw the dough overnight in the refrigerator.

1 16-ounce loaf frozen bread dough, thawed
½ cup chopped onion
2 cloves garlic, minced
1 10-ounce package frozen chopped spinach,
   thawed and well-drained
1 teaspoon dried Italian seasoning, crushed
1 slightly beaten egg
1 15-ounce carton low-fat ricotta cheese
¾ cup shredded reduced-fat mozzarella
   cheese (3 ounces)
¼ cup grated Parmesan cheese
   Nonstick spray coating
1 8-ounce can low-sodium tomato sauce
½ teaspoon dried Italian seasoning, crushed
¼ teaspoon garlic salt

1 Divide bread dough into 8 equal pieces. Place on a floured surface and cover dough with a towel. Let dough rest while preparing filling.

2 In a small covered saucepan cook onion and garlic in a small amount of *boiling water* until onion is tender. Drain. Stir in spinach and the 1 teaspoon Italian seasoning. In a bowl stir together egg, ricotta cheese, mozzarella cheese, and Parmesan cheese.

3 Roll each piece of dough into a 6-inch circle. Spread 2 tablespoons of the spinach mixture over half of each circle, spreading to within ½ inch of edge. Top with ¼ cup of the cheese mixture. Moisten edges of dough with water. Fold each circle in half, pinching edges or pressing edges together with a fork. Prick tops with fork. Spray an extra large baking sheet with nonstick coating; place calzones on sheet.

4 Bake in a 375° oven for 20 to 25 minutes or until golden. Meanwhile, in a small saucepan stir together tomato sauce, the ½ teaspoon Italian seasoning, and the garlic salt. Heat through over medium heat. Serve with calzones. Makes 8 servings.

Nutrition facts per serving: 258 calories, 5 g total fat (2 g saturated fat), 44 mg cholesterol, 273 mg sodium, 31 g carbohydrate, 1 g fiber, 16 g protein
Exchanges: 1½ Starch, 2 Lean Meat, 1 Vegetable

372 calories

Preparation time: 25 minutes ● **Baking time:** 20 minutes

deep-dish vegetable pizza

There is no substitute for gluten flour in this pizza dough. Gluten flour is a must in breads made from flours that have little gluten, such as whole wheat flour. Gluten is a protein in flour that allows breads to rise.

- **1 tablespoon cornmeal**
- **1 recipe Pizza Dough**
- **1 medium onion, sliced**
- **2 cloves garlic, minced**
- **2 teaspoons olive oil or cooking oil**
- **2 cups chopped broccoli**
- **⅓ cup refrigerated light alfredo sauce**
- **¾ cup shredded reduced-fat cheddar cheese**
- **6 cherry tomatoes, quartered**

1 Lightly grease an 11×7×1½-inch or 9×9×2-inch baking pan. Sprinkle with cornmeal. Pat Pizza Dough onto bottom and halfway up sides of pan. Prick with a fork. Bake in a 400° oven 10 minutes.

2 Meanwhile, in a saucepan cook onion and garlic in hot oil for 5 minutes. Stir in broccoli. Cook 3 to 4 minutes more or until broccoli is crisp-tender. Stir in sauce. Sprinkle crust with ½ *cup* of the cheese. Top with onion mixture, tomatoes, and remaining cheese. Bake for 10 to 15 minutes more or until cheese is melted. Makes 4 servings.

Pizza Dough: In food processor bowl combine 1¼ cups *whole wheat flour;* ¼ cup *gluten flour;* 2 tablespoons grated *Parmesan cheese;* 1 teaspoon snipped *fresh oregano* or ¼ teaspoon *dried oregano,* crushed; ¼ teaspoon *salt;* and 1 package *fast-rising active dry yeast.* Cover; process with 3 or 4 on-off turns to mix. With machine running, slowly add 2 teaspoons *olive oil* or *cooking oil* and only as much *warm water* (120° to 130°) as necessary for dough to form a ball (½ to ⅔ cup warm water). Check dough. It should feel moist and sticky; if not, add a few drops of water. If too wet, add more whole wheat flour, 1 teaspoon at a time. Process dough 30 to 40 seconds. Let dough rest 10 minutes.

Nutrition facts per serving: 372 calories, 13 g total fat (5 g saturated fat), 27 mg cholesterol, 532 mg sodium, 45 g carbohydrate, 8 g fiber, 20 g protein
Exchanges: 2½ Starch, 1 Medium-Fat Meat, 2 Vegetable, 1 Fat

353 calories

Preparation time: 30 minutes • **Baking time:** 10 minutes

vegetable-barley pot pies

Vary the filling by replacing any of the listed vegetables with other vegetables you like, such as peas, corn, cut green beans, strips of sweet peppers, or sliced zucchini.

  1 **cup cauliflower flowerets**
  1 **cup broccoli flowerets**
  1 **cup potato cut into ½-inch cubes**
  1 **cup chopped onion**
  1 **cup shredded carrot**
 ⅓ **cup quick-cooking barley**
  1 **10¾-ounce can reduced-fat and reduced-
      sodium condensed cream of potato soup**
 ⅔ **cup skim milk**
 ½ **teaspoon dried thyme, crushed**
 ½ **cup all-purpose flour**
 ⅓ **cup cornmeal**
1½ **teaspoons baking powder**
  2 **tablespoons shortening**
 ⅓ **cup skim milk**

1 Spray four 10-ounce custard cups or individual casseroles or one 2-quart casserole with *nonstick coating*. Set in shallow baking pan. Set aside.

2 In a large saucepan heat 2 cups *water* to boiling. Add vegetables and barley. Cook for 8 to 10 minutes or until vegetables are crisp-tender. Drain. Return vegetables and barley to saucepan.

3 In small mixing bowl stir together soup, the ⅔ cup milk, thyme, and ⅛ teaspoon *pepper*. Stir into vegetables. Divide mixture among prepared custard cups or casseroles or spoon into the casserole.

4 In a bowl combine flour, cornmeal, baking powder, and ⅛ teaspoon *salt*. Using a pastry blender, cut in shortening until mixture resembles coarse crumbs. Make a well in the center; add the ⅓ cup milk. Stir with a fork just until moistened. Drop small spoonfuls of dough on top of each individual casserole or 8 mounds of dough onto large casserole. Bake, uncovered, in a 400° oven for 10 to 12 minutes for individual casseroles or about 18 minutes for large casserole or until topping is golden. Makes 4 servings.

Nutrition facts per serving: 353 calories, 9 g total fat (2 g saturated fat), 4 mg cholesterol, 585 mg sodium, 59 g carbohydrate, 6 g fiber, 10 g protein
Exchanges: 3 Starch, 2 Vegetable, 1 Fat

158 calories

Preparation time: 30 minutes

puffy oven pancake

*Who says pancakes must only grace the breakfast table? The savory vegetable filling
makes these puffed gems suitable for a satisfying supper meal.*

Nonstick spray coating
2 eggs
2 egg whites
½ cup skim milk
½ cup all-purpose flour
⅛ teaspoon salt
1 cup sliced fresh mushrooms
1 cup broccoli flowerets
½ cup chopped onion
1 medium tomato, chopped
2 tablespoons toasted wheat germ
2 teaspoons snipped fresh thyme or oregano
  or ¼ teaspoon dried thyme or oregano,
  crushed
1 tablespoon grated Parmesan cheese

1 Spray an 8-inch ovenproof skillet with nonstick coating. Place in a 450° oven for 2 minutes. Meanwhile, in a medium mixing bowl use a wire whisk or rotary beater to beat together the eggs and egg whites. Add the milk, flour, and salt. Beat until batter is smooth. Immediately pour the batter into the hot skillet. Bake for 18 to 20 minutes or until puffed and browned.

2 Meanwhile, spray an unheated medium saucepan with nonstick coating. Preheat over low to medium heat. Add mushrooms, broccoli, and onion; cook about 5 minutes or until tender, stirring occasionally. Remove from heat. Toss with tomato, wheat germ, and thyme or oregano.

3 To serve, cut pancake into wedges. Spoon vegetable mixture over wedges. Sprinkle with Parmesan cheese. Makes 4 servings.

Nutrition facts per serving: 158 calories, 4 g total fat (1 g saturated fat), 108 mg cholesterol, 184 mg sodium, 20 g carbohydrate, 3 g fiber, 11 g protein
Exchanges: ½ Starch, 1 Lean Meat, 2 Vegetable

169 calories

Preparation time: 25 minutes ● **Baking time:** 10 minutes

asparagus frittata

This frittata finishes cooking in the oven. It's best to use an iron skillet, if you have one. However, if the skillet you're using has a plastic handle, cover it with foil to make it oven-safe.

12 **ounces fresh asparagus spears or one**
    10-ounce package frozen cut asparagus
 6 **eggs**
¾ **cup low-fat cottage cheese**
 2 **teaspoons prepared mustard**
1½ **teaspoons snipped fresh thyme or tarragon**
    or ¼ teaspoon dried thyme or tarragon,
    crushed
⅛ **teaspoon salt**
    Dash pepper
    Nonstick spray coating
 1 **cup sliced fresh mushrooms**
¼ **cup chopped tomato**

1 In a large covered saucepan cook fresh asparagus in a small amount of *boiling water* for 8 to 10 minutes or until crisp-tender. Drain. Reserve 3 spears for garnish; cut remaining asparagus into 1-inch pieces. (Or, cook frozen asparagus according to package directions; drain.) Set aside.

2 Meanwhile, in a medium mixing bowl beat eggs until foamy. Beat in cottage cheese, mustard, thyme or tarragon, salt, and pepper. Set aside.

3 Spray an unheated large ovenproof skillet with nonstick coating. Preheat over medium heat. Add mushrooms and cook just until tender. Stir in asparagus pieces. Pour egg mixture over mushrooms and asparagus.

4 Cook over low heat about 5 minutes or until mixture bubbles slightly and begins to set around the edges. (If using fresh asparagus, arrange the 3 reserved spears on top.)

5 Bake, uncovered, in a 400° oven about 10 minutes or until set. Sprinkle with tomato. Makes 4 servings.

Nutrition facts per serving: 169 calories, 9 g total fat (3 g saturated fat), 321 mg cholesterol, 369 mg sodium, 7 g carbohydrate, 2 g fiber, 17 g protein
Exchanges: 2 Medium-Fat Meat, 1 Vegetable

169 calories

Preparation time: 35 minutes

oven omelets with pesto

Use any frozen stir-fry mixture or combination of frozen vegetables that you like. Prepare the pesto ahead of time and store it in an airtight container for up to 2 days. Bring to room temperature before using.

1 recipe Pesto
2 cups desired frozen vegetables
3 cups refrigerated or frozen egg product,
    thawed, or 12 eggs
    Fresh basil (optional)

1 Prepare Pesto. Set aside.

2 Cook frozen vegetables according to package directions. Drain. Cut up any large pieces. Stir in 3 tablespoons of the prepared pesto.

3 Meanwhile, spray a 15×10×1-inch baking pan with *nonstick coating;* set pan aside.

4 In a mixing bowl combine egg product or eggs, ¼ cup *water,* ¼ teaspoon *salt,* and ⅛ teaspoon *pepper.* Using a fork or rotary beater, beat until combined but not frothy. Place prepared pan on center oven rack. Pour egg mixture into pan. Bake, uncovered, in a 400° oven about 8 minutes or until mixture is set but still has a glossy surface.

5 Cut baked eggs into six 5-inch squares. Remove omelet squares from pan using a large spatula. Invert omelet squares onto warm serving plates. Spoon about ¼ cup of the cooked vegetables on half of each omelet; fold other half over, forming a triangle. If desired, garnish with basil. Serves 6.

Pesto: In a food processor bowl combine ½ cup packed torn *fresh spinach;* ¼ cup packed *fresh basil leaves;* 2 tablespoons *grated Parmesan cheese;* 2 tablespoons chopped *walnuts;* 1 small *clove garlic,* quartered; and dash *salt.* Cover and process with several on-off turns until a paste forms, stopping the machine several times and scraping sides. With machine running, gradually add 2 tablespoons *water* and 1 tablespoon *olive oil* or *cooking oil.* Process until the mixture is the consistency of soft butter.

Nutrition facts per serving: 169 calories, 9 g total fat (2 g saturated fat), 3 mg cholesterol, 385 mg sodium, 5 g carbohydrate, 0 g fiber, 17 g protein
Exchanges: 2 Lean Meat, 1 Vegetable, ½ Fat

193 calories

Preparation time: 25 minutes ● **Baking time:** 20 minutes

eggplant and orzo casserole

*Try something new in place of rice tonight. Orzo is simply a rice-shaped pasta.
Look for it in the pasta section of your supermarket.*

1 **small eggplant (about 12 ounces)**
  Nonstick spray coating
1 **cup chopped red sweet pepper**
½ **cup sliced onion**
1 **large clove garlic, minced**
2 **teaspoons snipped fresh thyme**
  or ½ teaspoon dried thyme, crushed
1 **tablespoon olive oil or cooking oil**
  (optional)
1 **slightly beaten egg**
1½ **cups cooked orzo (about ¾ cup uncooked)**
¼ **cup milk**
¼ **cup grated Parmesan cheese**
½ **cup plain low-fat yogurt**

1 Wash eggplant; peel, if desired. Chop eggplant (should have about 4 cups). Spray an unheated large skillet with nonstick coating. Preheat over medium-high heat. Add eggplant, sweet pepper, onion, garlic, and 1 teaspoon of the thyme; cook until vegetables are tender. (If necessary, add the oil to prevent sticking.) Remove from heat. Stir in the egg, orzo, milk, and Parmesan cheese. Spoon mixture into a 1½-quart casserole.

2 Bake, uncovered, in a 350° oven about 20 minutes or until heated through. Combine yogurt and remaining thyme. Spoon some of the yogurt mixture over each serving. Makes 4 servings.

Nutrition facts per serving: 193 calories, 8 g total fat (3 g saturated fat), 61 mg cholesterol, 163 mg sodium, 22 g carbohydrate, 3 g fiber, 9 g protein
Exchanges: 1 Starch, 1 Medium-Fat Meat, 1 Vegetable

Side
DISHES

chapter index

49 calories

Preparation time: 12 minutes

asparagus with orange mayonnaise

Dress up asparagus spears with a simple yogurt-mayonnaise dressing. It's a great match for a mildly seasoned fish entrée, such as Sweet-Pepper-Stuffed Sole (see recipe, page 300).

1 pound fresh asparagus spears
    or one 10-ounce package frozen
    asparagus spears
2 tablespoons plain fat-free yogurt
2 tablespoons light mayonnaise dressing or
    salad dressing
½ teaspoon finely shredded orange peel
    Dash ground red pepper
    Orange slices, halved (optional)

1 Snap off and discard woody bases from fresh asparagus. If desired, scrape off scales. In a medium covered saucepan cook fresh asparagus in a small amount of *boiling water* for 4 to 6 minutes or until crisp-tender. (Or, cook frozen asparagus according to package directions.) Drain; keep warm.

2 Meanwhile, in a small bowl combine the yogurt, mayonnaise dressing or salad dressing, orange peel, and ground red pepper. Spoon over hot asparagus. If desired, garnish with orange slices. Makes 4 servings.

Nutrition facts per serving: 49 calories, 3 g total fat (1 g saturated fat), 0 mg cholesterol, 64 mg sodium, 5 g carbohydrate, 2 g fiber, 2 g protein
Exchanges: 1 Vegetable, ½ Fat

105 calories

Preparation time: 12 minutes ● **Cooking time:** 18 minutes

lemony asparagus and new potatoes

Spring brings with it the abundance of asparagus and tiny new potatoes. The simplicity of the flavors of this dish makes it an appealing accompaniment to either grilled fish or shrimp.

12 ounces fresh asparagus spears
8 whole tiny new potatoes, cut into quarters (about 10 ounces)
2 teaspoons olive oil or cooking oil
**¾ teaspoon snipped fresh thyme
    or ¼ teaspoon dried thyme, crushed**
½ teaspoon finely shredded lemon peel
¼ teaspoon salt

1 Snap off and discard woody bases from fresh asparagus. If desired, scrape off scales. Cut into 2-inch pieces. Set aside.

2 In a 2-quart covered saucepan cook the quartered potatoes in a small amount of *boiling water* for 10 minutes. Add the asparagus. Cook, covered, about 8 minutes more or until asparagus is crisp-tender and potatoes are tender. Drain. Transfer to a serving bowl.

3 Meanwhile, for dressing, combine the oil, thyme, lemon peel, and salt. Add to the vegetables, tossing gently to coat. Serve warm. Makes 4 servings.

Nutrition facts per serving: 105 calories, 3 g total fat (0 g saturated fat), 0 mg cholesterol, 141 mg sodium, 19 g carbohydrate, 2 g fiber, 3 g protein
Exchanges: 1 Starch, 1 Vegetable

99 calories

Preparation time: 15 minutes ● **Roasting time:** 35 minutes

herbed roasted vegetables

*Toss sweet potatoes, carrots, red onion, and parsnip with a little oil and herbs for a luscious side dish.
Roast them alongside your meat entrée, such as chicken, pork loin, or eye of round beef roast.*

2 **medium sweet potatoes or white potatoes,
   cut into 1-inch cubes (about
   12 ounces)**
2 **carrots, cut into 1-inch chunks**
1 **medium parsnip, peeled and cut into
   1-inch pieces**
1 **medium red onion, quartered**
1 **tablespoon olive oil**
3 **cloves garlic, minced**
2 **teaspoons dried mixed herbs (such as
   marjoram, thyme, rosemary, and
   oregano), crushed**
¼ **teaspoon salt**
¼ **teaspoon pepper**

1 Place potatoes, carrots, parsnip, and red onion
in a 13×9×2-inch baking pan. Combine oil, garlic,
mixed herbs, salt, and pepper. Drizzle over
vegetables, tossing to coat.

2 Cover with foil. Bake in a 425° oven for
30 minutes. Remove foil; stir vegetables. Bake,
uncovered, for 5 to 10 minutes more or until
vegetables are tender. Makes 6 servings.

Nutrition facts per serving: 99 calories, 2 g total fat
(0 g saturated fat), 0 mg cholesterol, 111 mg sodium,
19 g carbohydrate, 4 g fiber, 2 g protein
Exchanges: 1 Starch, 1 Vegetable

31 calories

Preparation time: 20 minutes ● **Roasting time:** 25 minutes

roasted garlic and vegetables

*Roasting is not for meats only. It's a great low-fat cooking method
that brings out a full, well-developed flavor in vegetables, too.*

1 small eggplant (about 12 ounces)
1 medium zucchini
2 cloves garlic
1½ teaspoons olive oil
1 tablespoon capers, drained (optional)
⅛ teaspoon salt
⅛ teaspoon pepper
1 small tomato, cut into wedges

1 Cut eggplant into 1-inch cubes. Cut zucchini in half lengthwise, then crosswise into 1-inch-thick pieces. Spear unpeeled garlic cloves on wooden picks (for easy removal). Place eggplant cubes, zucchini slices, and garlic cloves in a 13×9×2-inch baking pan. Drizzle oil over vegetables; stir to coat. Bake, uncovered, in a 375° oven about 25 minutes or until vegetables are just tender, stirring every 10 minutes.

2 Remove garlic cloves. Cover pan of vegetables; keep warm. Remove garlic cloves from skin; mash garlic with flat side of knife or the back of a spoon. In a custard cup or small bowl stir together mashed garlic, capers (if desired), salt, and pepper. Add to vegetables in pan; stir gently to combine. Transfer vegetables to a serving bowl. Gently stir in tomato wedges. Makes 6 servings.

Nutrition facts per serving: 31 calories, 1 g total fat (0 g saturated fat), 0 mg cholesterol, 48 mg sodium, 5 g carbohydrate, 2 g fiber, 1 g protein
Exchanges: 1 Vegetable

38 calories

Preparation time: 15 minutes ● **Cooking time:** 8 minutes

lemon-tarragon vegetables

Pair the delicate flavors of this vegetable medley with grilled chicken, pork, or fish.

- **1 medium onion, cut into wedges**
- **8 ounces large whole fresh mushrooms, halved or quartered**
- **2 small yellow summer squash or zucchini, halved lengthwise and cut into ½-inch-thick slices**
- **¾ cup bias-sliced celery**
- **2 tablespoons chopped roasted red sweet pepper or pimiento**
- **½ teaspoon finely shredded lemon peel**
- **1 tablespoon lemon juice**
- **2 teaspoons snipped fresh tarragon or ¼ teaspoon dried tarragon, crushed**
- **⅛ teaspoon salt**

1 In a large covered saucepan cook onion, mushrooms, squash, and celery in a small amount of *boiling water* about 7 minutes or until tender. Drain.

2 Return vegetables to saucepan. Stir in roasted red sweet pepper or pimiento, lemon peel, lemon juice, tarragon, and salt. Cook and stir about 1 minute more or until heated through. Makes 4 servings.

Nutrition facts per serving: 38 calories, 0 g total fat, 0 mg cholesterol, 91 mg sodium, 8 g carbohydrate, 2 g fiber, 2 g protein
Exchanges: 1 Vegetable

82 calories

Preparation time: 15 minutes ● **Grilling time:** 15 minutes

grilled peppers and mushrooms

Portobello mushrooms are mature brown mushrooms with a hearty beef flavor. Their giant size makes them excellent for grilling. When buying, choose firm mushrooms that are not moist or bruised.

2 fresh portobello mushrooms
2 green sweet peppers, seeded and quartered
2 red sweet peppers, seeded and quartered
1 tablespoon olive oil
2 tablespoons snipped fresh basil
1 tablespoon balsamic vinegar

1 Remove stems from mushrooms and discard; cut mushroom caps in half. Brush sweet peppers and mushroom halves with the oil.

2 Lay peppers, skin sides down, and mushroom halves, top sides down, on grill rack directly over medium-low coals.* Grill about 15 minutes or until peppers are crisp-tender and lightly brown and mushrooms are fork tender, turning once. If desired, slice or quarter the mushrooms.

3 Place peppers and mushrooms in a large bowl. Add basil and balsamic vinegar. Toss well. Serve immediately or cool to room temperature. Makes 4 servings.

Nutrition facts per serving: 82 calories, 4 g total fat (1 g saturated fat), 0 mg cholesterol, 4 mg sodium, 12 g carbohydrate, 3 g fiber, 2 g protein
Exchanges: 2 Vegetable, ½ Fat

*__Note:__ To check for medium-low heat, hold your hand, palm side down, over where the food will cook and at about the same height of the food. The heat is right when you can hold your hand there for only 5 seconds.

71 calories

Preparation time: 20 minutes

indian-style cauliflower

A delightful blend of spices commonly used in Indian cooking transforms cauliflower from a humdrum vegetable into an exciting side dish. Use a nonstick skillet to reduce the need for much oil during cooking.

1 **head cauliflower (about 1½ pounds)**
½ **teaspoon dry mustard**
¼ **teaspoon ground turmeric**
¼ **teaspoon ground cumin**
⅛ **teaspoon ground coriander**
⅛ **teaspoon ground red pepper**
1 **tablespoon cooking oil**
4 **green onions, bias-sliced into 1-inch pieces**
1 **small red or green sweet pepper, cut into 1-inch pieces**
¼ **cup chicken broth**

1 Rinse the cauliflower; remove leaves and woody stem. Break cauliflower into flowerets, slicing any large pieces. (You should have about 4 cups.)

2 In a bowl combine the dry mustard, turmeric, cumin, coriander, and ground red pepper. Set aside.

3 Heat oil in a wok or large skillet over medium-high heat. (Add more oil as necessary.) Add cauliflower; stir-fry for 3 minutes. Add green onions and sweet pepper; stir-fry for 1 to 1½ minutes. Reduce heat to medium. Add mustard mixture. Cook and stir for 30 seconds. Carefully stir in broth. Cook and stir about 1 minute more or until heated through. Serve immediately. Makes 4 servings.

Nutrition facts per serving: 71 calories, 4 g total fat (1 g saturated fat), 0 mg cholesterol, 58 mg sodium, 7 g carbohydrate, 3 g fiber, 3 g protein
Exchanges: 2 Vegetable, ½ Fat

40 calories

Preparation time: 35 minutes

tomatoes and zucchini

Since Parmesan is a strong-tasting cheese, just a little bit zips up an entire dish. For more flavor punch, buy a wedge of fresh Parmesan (instead of the packaged grated product) and finely shred it over these saucy vegetables.

Nonstick spray coating
1 **medium onion, thinly sliced**
1 **clove garlic, minced**
1 **14½-ounce can tomatoes, undrained and cut up**
2 **medium zucchini, thinly sliced**
1 **medium yellow or green sweet pepper, chopped**
2 **teaspoons snipped fresh basil**
   or ½ teaspoon dried basil, crushed
⅛ **to ¼ teaspoon black pepper**
2 **tablespoons grated Parmesan cheese**

1 Spray an unheated large skillet with nonstick coating. Preheat over medium heat. Add the onion and garlic; cook until onion is tender, stirring occasionally.

2 Stir in the undrained tomatoes, zucchini, sweet pepper, basil, and black pepper. Cook, covered, about 5 minutes or until zucchini is crisp-tender, stirring occasionally. Uncover; cook about 5 minutes more or until most of the liquid evaporates and the zucchini is tender.

3 Transfer to 6 individual serving bowls. Sprinkle with Parmesan cheese. Makes 6 servings.

Nutrition facts per serving: 40 calories, 1 g total fat (0 g saturated fat), 2 mg cholesterol, 153 mg sodium, 7 g carbohydrate, 2 g fiber, 2 g protein
Exchanges: 2 Vegetable

57 calories

Preparation time: 40 minutes ● **Baking time:** 20 minutes

broccoli-stuffed artichokes

When buying artichokes, look for compact, firm globes that are heavy for their size. Artichokes should yield slightly to pressure and have large, tightly closed leaves.

3 artichokes
  Lemon juice
1½ cups coarsely chopped broccoli flowerets
  1 cup sliced fresh mushrooms
  ½ cup reduced-sodium chicken broth
  2 tablespoons finely chopped onion
  ⅛ teaspoon dried thyme, crushed
  ¼ cup dry white wine or reduced-sodium chicken broth
  2 teaspoons cornstarch
  1 2-ounce jar diced pimiento, drained
  2 tablespoons grated Parmesan cheese (optional)

1 Remove loose outer leaves of artichokes. Snip off sharp leaf tips. Cut off stems close to base. Brush cut edges with lemon juice.

2 In a 3-quart covered saucepan simmer artichokes in *boiling water* for 20 to 30 minutes or until a leaf pulls out easily. Drain upside down. Cut artichokes in half lengthwise; remove center leaves and chokes.

3 In a medium saucepan combine the broccoli, mushrooms, chicken broth, onion, and thyme. Bring to boiling; reduce heat. Simmer, covered, for 8 to 10 minutes or until vegetables are tender. Stir together the wine or broth and cornstarch; stir into vegetable mixture. Cook and stir until bubbly; add pimiento. Cook and stir for 2 minutes more.

4 Spoon mixture into the artichoke halves. Place in a 13×9×2-inch baking pan. Bake, uncovered, in a 350° oven for 20 to 25 minutes or until heated through. If desired, sprinkle with the Parmesan cheese. Makes 6 servings.

Nutrition facts per serving: 57 calories, 0 g total fat, 0 mg cholesterol, 120 mg sodium, 11 g carbohydrate, 5 g fiber, 4 g protein
Exchanges: 2 Vegetable

48 calories

Preparation time: 20 minutes

broccoli with mustard vinaigrette

Tired of the same vegetables at every meal? Try the broccoli raab option. This dark green vegetable has leafy stalks and buds that resemble broccoli. The sharp, bitter flavor pairs well with the mustard dressing.

12 **ounces broccoli or broccoli raab**
2 **cloves garlic, minced**
1 **tablespoon cider vinegar**
1 **tablespoon water**
2 **teaspoons olive oil**
2 **teaspoons coarse-grain brown mustard**
¼ **teaspoon salt**

1 Wash broccoli or broccoli raab. Cut broccoli lengthwise into spears or, if using broccoli raab, cut into 2-inch pieces. Cut any thick stem pieces in half lengthwise.

2 In a large covered saucepan cook broccoli or broccoli raab in a small amount of *boiling water* for 8 to 12 minutes or until crisp-tender. Drain.

3 Meanwhile, for vinaigrette, in a small screw-top jar combine the garlic, vinegar, water, oil, mustard, and salt. Cover and shake well. Drizzle vinaigrette over vegetables. Serve immediately. Makes 4 servings.

Nutrition facts per serving: 48 calories, 3 g total fat (0 g saturated fat), 0 mg cholesterol, 189 mg sodium, 5 g carbohydrate, 3 g fiber, 3 g protein
Exchanges: 1 Vegetable, ½ Fat

101 calories

Preparation time: 10 minutes • **Cooking time:** 7 minutes

mexican-style creamed corn

Chili peppers in cans are available in mild, medium, or hot. Pick the level according to your preference.

1 **10-ounce package frozen whole kernel corn**
½ **cup water**
½ **cup chopped red and/or green sweet pepper**
¼ **cup chopped celery**
¼ **of an 8-ounce tub reduced-fat cream cheese (about ¼ cup)**
½ **of a 4½-ounce can diced green chili peppers**
¼ **teaspoon salt**
Dash black pepper
1 **tablespoon skim milk (optional)**

1 In a medium saucepan combine the corn, water, sweet pepper, and celery. Bring to boiling; reduce heat. Simmer, covered, about 5 minutes or until corn is tender. Drain.

2 Stir in the cream cheese, chili peppers, salt, and black pepper. If necessary, stir in enough of the milk to make of desired consistency. Heat through. Makes 4 servings.

Nutrition facts per serving: 101 calories, 3 g total fat (2 g saturated fat), 7 mg cholesterol, 263 mg sodium, 18 g carbohydrate, 0 g fiber, 4 g protein
Exchanges: 1 Starch, ½ Fat

74 calories

Preparation time: 10 minutes

cream - sauced peas and onions

This updated version of creamed peas and onions is easier to make and kinder to the waistline. Reduced-fat cream cheese is the secret ingredient.

2 10-ounce packages frozen peas with pearl onions
¼ of an 8-ounce tub reduced-fat cream cheese (about ¼ cup)
1 tablespoon skim milk
⅛ teaspoon cracked black pepper
⅛ teaspoon garlic powder

1 Cook peas with pearl onions according to package directions. Drain well. Return peas and onions to the saucepan. Stir in the cream cheese, milk, pepper, and garlic powder. Cook and stir over medium heat until heated through. Makes 5 servings.

Microwave Directions: In a microwave-safe 1½-quart casserole combine frozen vegetables and 2 tablespoons *water*. Cover and cook on 100% power (high) for 7 to 9 minutes or just until tender. Drain well. Stir in the cream cheese, milk, pepper, and garlic powder.

Cover and cook on high for 2 to 3 minutes more or until heated through, stirring once.

Nutrition facts per serving: 74 calories, 2 g total fat (1 g saturated fat), 6 mg cholesterol, 105 mg sodium, 10 g carbohydrate, 3 g fiber, 4 g protein
Exchanges: 1 Starch

211 calories

Preparation time: 25 minutes

yams with pears

Yams meet with pears in this lightened version of candied yams or sweet potatoes.
Use canned pears if fresh ones aren't in season.

1 pound yams or sweet potatoes
4 teaspoons cornstarch
⅛ teaspoon salt
⅛ teaspoon ground allspice
1 cup apple juice or apple cider
¼ cup golden raisins and/or chopped dates
2 teaspoons lemon juice
2 ripe medium pears, cored and cut into
   ¾-inch pieces
   Fresh parsley (optional)

1 Wash and peel yams or sweet potatoes. Cut into 1-inch cubes. In a large covered saucepan cook yams or sweet potatoes in enough *boiling water* to cover about 10 minutes or until easily pierced with a fork. Drain.

2 Meanwhile, in a medium saucepan stir together the cornstarch, salt, and allspice. Stir in apple juice, raisins and/or dates, and lemon juice. Cook and stir until thickened and bubbly. Cook and stir for 2 minutes more. Gently stir in pears and cooked yams or sweet potatoes. Heat through. If desired, garnish with fresh parsley. Makes 4 servings.

Nutrition facts per serving: 211 calories, 1 g total fat (0 g saturated fat), 0 mg cholesterol, 79 mg sodium, 52 g carbohydrate, 6 g fiber, 2 g protein
Exchanges: 1 Starch, 2½ Fruit

156 calories

Preparation time: 40 minutes

roasted garlic mashed potatoes

Skip the gravy with these mashed potatoes—they don't need any. The roasted garlic, herb, and sour cream flavor them to delicious perfection.

  8 **to 10 cloves garlic**
  2 **pounds Yukon gold potatoes or other potatoes, cut up**
 ⅓ **cup light dairy sour cream**
 ¼ **cup skim milk**
  1 **tablespoon snipped fresh rosemary, thyme, or oregano**
 ½ **teaspoon salt**
 ¼ **teaspoon pepper**

1 To roast garlic, wrap unpeeled garlic cloves in aluminum foil. Bake in a 400° oven for 25 to 35 minutes or until cloves feel soft when pressed. When cool enough to handle, squeeze garlic paste from peels.

2 Meanwhile, in a covered kettle cook potatoes in a small amount of *boiling water* for 20 to 25 minutes or until tender. Drain; return to kettle.

3 Mash potatoes and garlic paste with a potato masher or an electric mixer on low speed. Add sour cream; milk; rosemary, thyme, or oregano; salt; and pepper. Beat until light and fluffy. Makes 6 servings.

Nutrition facts per serving: 156 calories, 1 g total fat (1 g saturated fat), 2 mg cholesterol, 207 mg sodium, 34 g carbohydrate, 2 g fiber, 4 g protein
Exchanges: 2 Starch

97 calories

Preparation time: 12 minutes ● **Baking time:** 55 minutes

twice-baked potatoes

Potatoes aren't fattening, unless you top them with regular sour cream and lots of butter. This rich-tasting version uses fat-free cream cheese, which only teases you into believing these potatoes are high in calories.

4 medium baking potatoes (about 6 ounces each)
¼ of an 8-ounce package fat-free cream cheese, cubed and softened
2 tablespoons snipped fresh chives or thinly sliced green onion tops
1 teaspoon snipped fresh dill or basil or ¼ teaspoon dried dillweed or basil, crushed
¼ teaspoon salt
⅛ teaspoon pepper
3 to 4 tablespoons skim milk
Paprika
Fresh dill (optional)

1 Prick potatoes with a fork. Bake potatoes in a 425° oven for 40 to 60 minutes or until tender. Cool slightly. Cut in half lengthwise. Gently scoop pulp from each potato half, leaving a thin shell.

2 Mash pulp with potato masher or electric mixer on low speed. Add cream cheese, chives or green onion, fresh or dried herb, salt, and pepper; beat until smooth. Add milk, 1 tablespoon at a time, beating until fluffy. (If necessary, add a little additional milk to get fluffy texture.) Pipe or spoon potato mixture into shells. Sprinkle with paprika. Place on baking sheet. Cover loosely with foil.

3 Bake in a 425° oven for 10 minutes. Uncover potatoes and bake 5 to 10 minutes more or until heated through. If desired, garnish with additional fresh dill. Makes 8 servings.

Microwave Directions: Microwave pricked potatoes on 100% power (high) for 9 to 12 minutes or until tender. Halve potatoes and prepare filling as above. Place filled potato shells on a 12-inch round microwave-safe platter. Cover loosely with vented plastic wrap. Cook on high for 1 to 2 minutes more or until heated through.

Nutrition facts per serving: 97 calories, 0 g total fat, 1 mg cholesterol, 76 mg sodium, 21 g carbohydrate, 1 g fiber, 3 g protein
Exchanges: 1 Starch

96 calories

Preparation time: 35 minutes ● **Standing time:** 30 minutes ● **Baking time:** 10 minutes

cheesy polenta squares

Polenta is a cornmeal mush that northern Italians eat in place of pasta. To prepare in advance, cool, cover, and chill the polenta overnight. Cut and bake it the next day.

Nonstick spray coating
1½ **cups skim milk**
½ **cup cornmeal**
½ **cup cold water**
¼ **teaspoon salt**
¼ **cup light dairy sour cream**
¼ **cup grated Parmesan cheese**
   Dash ground red pepper
   Canned pizza sauce, warmed (optional)

1 Spray an 8×8×2-inch baking pan with nonstick coating. Set aside. In a 2-quart saucepan heat milk to simmering.

2 Meanwhile, in a mixing bowl stir together the cornmeal, water, and salt. Gradually add cornmeal mixture to simmering milk, stirring constantly.

3 Cook and stir until mixture begins to simmer again; reduce heat. Cook, uncovered, over low heat about 10 minutes or until thick, stirring frequently.

4 Spread cornmeal mixture in prepared baking pan. Let stand, uncovered, for 30 to 40 minutes or until firm.

5 Meanwhile, in a small bowl stir together the sour cream, Parmesan cheese, and ground red pepper. Set aside.

6 Spray an oval baking dish or 15×10×1-inch baking pan with nonstick coating. Cut cornmeal mixture into 12 portions; place in prepared dish or pan. Spoon sour cream mixture over.

7 Bake, uncovered, in a 425° oven for 10 to 12 minutes or until heated through and tops are golden brown. If desired, serve with warm pizza sauce. Makes 6 servings.

Nutrition facts per serving: 96 calories, 2 g total fat (1 g saturated fat), 6 mg cholesterol, 211 mg sodium, 13 g carbohydrate, 1 g fiber, 5 g protein
Exchanges: 1 Starch

153 calories

Preparation time: 15 minutes ● **Standing time:** 5 minutes

herbed couscous and vegetables

Quick-cooking couscous makes a more interesting alternative to rice and pasta side dishes. Here it teams up with fresh mushrooms and tomatoes. For the most flavor, use fresh herbs.

1 **cup sliced fresh mushrooms**
1 **tablespoon margarine or butter**
1 **cup water**
1 **tablespoon snipped fresh parsley**
1½ **teaspoons snipped fresh basil**
    or ½ teaspoon dried basil, crushed
½ **teaspoon snipped fresh oregano**
    or ⅛ teaspoon dried oregano, crushed
¼ **teaspoon salt**
    Dash pepper
⅔ **cup quick-cooking couscous**
1 **medium tomato, chopped**
    Fresh parsley sprigs (optional)

1 In a medium saucepan cook mushrooms in hot margarine or butter until tender.

2 Carefully add water to saucepan. Stir in snipped parsley, basil, oregano, salt, and pepper. Bring to boiling. Stir in couscous. Remove from heat.

3 Cover and let stand about 5 minutes or until liquid has been absorbed. Stir in tomato. If desired, garnish with fresh parsley sprigs. Makes 4 servings.

Nutrition facts per serving: 153 calories, 3 g total fat (1 g saturated fat), 0 mg cholesterol, 175 mg sodium, 26 g carbohydrate, 5 g fiber, 5 g protein
Exchanges: 1½ Starch, 1 Vegetable

199 calories

Preparation time: 15 minutes

couscous with fruit and nuts

Couscous is a tiny, semolina grain that is an ideal alternative to potatoes or rice. Sweetened with citrus and dried fruit, this dish makes a great complement to roast chicken.

¼ **cup orange juice**
3 **tablespoons raisins**
3 **tablespoons snipped pitted dates**
1¼ **cups reduced-sodium chicken broth**
¾ **cup quick-cooking couscous**
4 **teaspoons chopped toasted almonds or walnuts**
   Orange slice, halved (optional)

1 In a small saucepan bring orange juice to boiling. Add raisins and dates. Remove from heat. Cover and let stand for 10 minutes.

2 Meanwhile, in another saucepan bring broth to boiling. Stir in couscous. Remove from heat. Cover and let stand about 5 minutes or until liquid has been absorbed. Stir in undrained raisin mixture and almonds or walnuts. If desired, garnish with orange slice. Makes 4 servings.

Nutrition facts per serving: 199 calories, 2 g total fat (0 g saturated fat), 0 mg cholesterol, 204 mg sodium, 41 g carbohydrate, 7 g fiber, 6 g protein
Exchanges: 2 Starch, 1 Fruit

144 calories

Preparation time: 25 minutes

creamy spaghetti with basil

To cut fat and calories, we skipped the pine nuts in this pesto-like pasta sauce and used cottage cheese.
A food processor works best to puree the cottage cheese, spinach, and basil.

1 10-ounce package frozen chopped spinach,
   thawed and well drained
½ **cup water**
⅓ **cup fat-free or low-fat cottage cheese**
⅓ **cup snipped fresh basil**
2 tablespoons grated Parmesan cheese
2 teaspoons olive oil or cooking oil
2 cloves garlic, minced
¼ **teaspoon salt**
4 cups hot cooked spaghetti or fusilli

1 For the sauce, in a food processor bowl combine the spinach, water, cottage cheese, basil, Parmesan cheese, oil, garlic, and salt. Cover and process until smooth.

2 Spoon basil sauce over the hot pasta. Toss to mix well. Serve immediately. Makes 8 servings.

Nutrition facts per serving: 144 calories, 2 g total fat (1 g saturated fat), 2 mg cholesterol, 157 mg sodium, 25 g carbohydrate, 0 g fiber, 6 g protein
Exchanges: 1½ Starch, 1 Vegetable

138 calories

Preparation time: 25 minutes

pasta with broccoli-onion sauce

Nutmeg and white wine flavor this creamy pasta and vegetable side dish. Serve it with broiled or grilled beef or chicken for a hearty meal.

3 ounces packaged dried linguine or
  fettuccine
1½ cups broccoli flowerets
  Nonstick spray coating
1 medium onion, thinly sliced and separated
  into rings
¾ cup skim milk
2 teaspoons cornstarch
1 teaspoon instant chicken bouillon granules
  Dash pepper
  Dash ground nutmeg
½ cup shredded part-skim mozzarella cheese
  (2 ounces)
1 tablespoon dry white wine (optional)

1 Cook linguine or fettuccine according to the package directions, adding the broccoli for the last 5 minutes of cooking. Drain well; return to pan.

2 Meanwhile, spray an unheated large skillet with nonstick coating. Preheat over medium-low heat. Add onion. Cook, covered, for 8 to 10 minutes or until tender, stirring occasionally.

3 In a small bowl stir together the milk, cornstarch, bouillon granules, pepper, and nutmeg. Add to onion in skillet. Cook and stir over medium heat until thickened and bubbly. Cook and stir for 2 minutes more. Stir in cheese and wine (if desired) until cheese is melted. Pour cheese mixture over pasta and broccoli; toss to coat. Makes 5 servings.

Nutrition facts per serving: 138 calories, 2 g total fat (1 g saturated fat), 7 mg cholesterol, 285 mg sodium, 20 g carbohydrate, 2 g fiber, 8 g protein
Exchanges: 1 Starch, 1 Vegetable, ½ Milk

66 calories

Preparation time: 20 minutes

wilted greens with pasta

This hybrid is a cross between pasta salad and spinach salad. The combination of pasta, spinach, and a light soy-honey dressing pairs well with grilled steak.

½ **cup packaged dried tiny ring macaroni (anelli) or tiny shell macaroni or other tiny pasta**
4 **cups torn fresh spinach or romaine**
¼ **cup sliced green onions**
2 **cloves garlic, minced**
2 **teaspoons cooking oil**
1 **tablespoon lemon juice**
1 **tablespoon soy sauce**
1 **tablespoon water**
1 **teaspoon honey**
   Dash ground red pepper
   Tomato slices (optional)

1 Cook pasta according to package directions. Drain well. Keep warm.

2 Meanwhile, in a large serving bowl combine the spinach and green onions.

3 For dressing, in a small skillet cook garlic in hot oil for 1 minute. Stir in the lemon juice, soy sauce, water, honey, and ground red pepper. Heat just to boiling.

4 Pour hot dressing over greens. Add hot pasta. Toss to mix well. If desired, garnish with tomato slices. Makes 6 servings.

Nutrition facts per serving: 66 calories, 2 g total fat (0 g saturated fat), 0 mg cholesterol, 202 mg sodium, 10 g carbohydrate, 1 g fiber, 3 g protein
Exchanges: ½ Starch, 1 Vegetable

114 calories

Preparation time: 20 minutes

caraway noodles with cabbage

Savor these creamy, German-style noodles with broiled pork chops or a pork roast. To keep the sauce velvety smooth, take care not to let the mixture boil once you add the fat-free sour cream.

6 cups water
¼ teaspoon salt
3 ounces packaged dried medium noodles (1½ cups)
¼ cup chopped onion
1 cup shredded cabbage
½ cup fat-free dairy sour cream
½ teaspoon caraway seed
Dash pepper

1 In a large saucepan bring the water and salt to boiling. Add the noodles and onion. Reduce heat slightly; boil gently, uncovered, for 5 minutes.

2 Add cabbage to boiling noodle mixture; cook for 3 to 5 minutes more or until noodles and cabbage are tender. Drain well. Return noodles and cabbage to saucepan.

3 Stir in sour cream, caraway seed, and pepper. Heat through, but do not boil. Makes 4 servings.

Nutrition facts per serving: 114 calories, 1 g total fat (0 g saturated fat), 18 mg cholesterol, 163 mg sodium, 21 g carbohydrate, 1 g fiber, 5 g protein
Exchanges: 1 Starch, 1 Vegetable

112 calories

Preparation time: 25 minutes ● **Chilling time:** 3 to 24 hours

asian-style pasta salad

Toasted sesame oil packs a lot of flavor into each drop. This aromatic, reddish brown oil is used more often to season foods than as a cooking oil. Look for it with other Oriental ingredients in your supermarket.

4　**ounces packaged dried cappellini or thin**
　　spaghetti, broken
2　**cups desired frozen mixed vegetables**
　　(½ of a 16-ounce package)
2　**tablespoons reduced-sodium soy sauce**
2　**tablespoons balsamic vinegar or wine**
　　vinegar
2　**tablespoons water**
1　**tablespoon honey**
1　**teaspoon grated fresh gingerroot**
　　or ¼ teaspoon ground ginger
1　**teaspoon toasted sesame oil**
1　**clove garlic, minced**
½　**teaspoon crushed red pepper (optional)**

1 Cook the pasta and frozen vegetables according to package directions. Drain.

2 Meanwhile, for dressing, in a small mixing bowl stir together the soy sauce, vinegar, water, honey, gingerroot or ground ginger, sesame oil, garlic, and crushed red pepper (if desired).

3 Transfer pasta and vegetables to a large bowl. Pour dressing over and toss lightly to coat.

4 Cover and refrigerate for at least 3 hours or up to 24 hours before serving, stirring occasionally. Makes 6 servings.

Nutrition facts per serving: 112 calories, 1 g total fat (0 g saturated fat), 0 mg cholesterol, 186 mg sodium, 21 g carbohydrate, 1 g fiber, 4 g protein
Exchanges: 1 Starch, 1 Vegetable

91 calories

Preparation time: 25 minutes ● **Chilling time:** 2 to 24 hours

vegetable and pasta toss

Double all of the ingredients and tote this simple pasta salad to your next potluck. No one will guess it's low in calories. Use any flavor of fat-free or reduced-calorie dressing you like.

¾ **cup packaged dried rotini (corkscrew) macaroni or elbow macaroni**
1 **cup broccoli flowerets**
1 **cup cauliflower flowerets**
1 **9-ounce package frozen artichoke hearts**
½ **cup thinly sliced carrot**
¼ **cup sliced green onions**
½ **cup reduced-calorie Italian salad dressing**
　Leaf lettuce (optional)

1 Cook pasta according to package directions omitting any oil, adding broccoli and cauliflower to boiling pasta for the last minute of cooking. Drain. Rinse with cold water; drain well.

2 Cook artichoke hearts according to package directions; drain. Rinse with cold water; drain well. Halve any large pieces.

3 In a large mixing bowl combine pasta mixture, artichoke hearts, carrot, and green onions.

4 Add the Italian dressing; toss to coat.

5 Cover and refrigerate for at least 2 hours or up to 24 hours. If desired, serve on lettuce-lined plates. Makes 6 servings.

Nutrition facts per serving: 91 calories, 2 g total fat (0 g saturated fat), 1 mg cholesterol, 208 mg sodium, 16 g carbohydrate, 4 g fiber, 4 g protein
Exchanges: ½ Starch, 1 Vegetable, ½ Fat

152 calories

Preparation time: 12 minutes ● **Cooking time:** 40 minutes ● **Standing time:** 5 minutes

wild rice and bulgur

Wild rice and bulgur join in this nutty-tasting side dish, great with almost any meat, poultry, or fish. Bulgur is tender yet chewy in texture.

½ **cup wild rice**
1 **14½-ounce can reduced-sodium chicken broth**
¾ **cup chopped onion**
¼ **cup water**
1 **teaspoon snipped fresh thyme or tarragon or ¼ teaspoon dried thyme or tarragon, crushed**
   Dash black pepper
½ **cup bulgur**
2 **tablespoons snipped fresh parsley**
   Yellow sweet pepper strips (optional)
   Fresh parsley sprigs (optional)

1 Place the uncooked wild rice in a strainer. Run cold water over the rice for 1 minute, lifting rice to rinse well.

2 In a medium saucepan combine the rinsed wild rice, chicken broth, onion, water, thyme or tarragon, and black pepper. Bring to boiling; reduce heat. Simmer, covered, for 40 to 45 minutes or until rice is just tender. Remove from heat. (Not all liquid will be absorbed.)

3 Stir in bulgur. Cover and let stand for 5 to 10 minutes or until bulgur is tender and all liquid is absorbed. Add the snipped parsley; fluff rice mixture with a fork. If desired, garnish with sweet pepper strips and fresh parsley sprigs. Makes 4 servings.

Nutrition facts per serving: 152 calories, 1 g total fat (0 g saturated fat), 0 mg cholesterol, 296 mg sodium, 31 g carbohydrate, 5 g fiber, 6 g protein
Exchanges: 2 Starch

113 calories

Preparation time: 12 minutes ● **Cooking time:** 17 minutes ● **Standing time:** 5 minutes

bulgur pilaf

Bulgur is a cracked wheat product that takes the place of rice in this fiber-rich pilaf.
If you can't find bulgur in your supermarket, try a health food store.

 1 14½-ounce can tomatoes, cut up
 ¼ cup sliced green onions
 1 teaspoon instant chicken bouillon granules
1½ teaspoons snipped fresh thyme
     or ½ teaspoon dried thyme, crushed
 1 cup bulgur
 ¼ cup raisins

1 Drain tomatoes, reserving juice. Set tomatoes aside. Add enough *water* to the juice to measure 2 cups liquid.

2 In a medium saucepan combine the tomato juice mixture, green onions, chicken bouillon granules, and thyme.

3 Bring to boiling; stir in bulgur. Cook, covered, for 12 minutes. Stir in tomatoes and raisins. Cook, covered, about 5 minutes more or until bulgur is tender. Let stand for 5 to 10 minutes or until liquid is absorbed. Makes 6 servings.

Nutrition facts per serving: 113 calories, 1 g total fat (0 g saturated fat), 0 mg cholesterol, 260 mg sodium, 26 g carbohydrate, 6 g fiber, 4 g protein
Exchanges: 1 Starch, 1 Vegetable

141 calories

Preparation time: 15 minutes • **Cooking time:** 18 minutes

curried barley

*Just a little curry powder perks up the flavor of this easy barley side dish.
It's a noteworthy replacement to rice.*

2 **cups water**
⅔ **cup quick-cooking barley**
½ **cup chopped carrot**
½ **cup chopped onion**
1½ **teaspoons instant chicken bouillon granules**
1 **teaspoon curry powder**
1 **tablespoon toasted sliced almonds**
1 **tablespoon snipped fresh parsley**
   Fresh parsley sprig (optional)

1 In a medium saucepan stir together the water, barley, carrot, onion, chicken bouillon granules, and curry powder.

2 Bring to boiling; reduce heat. Simmer, covered, about 15 minutes or until barley is tender. Uncover; cook for 3 to 5 minutes more or until desired consistency. Stir in almonds and snipped parsley. If desired, garnish with fresh parsley sprig. Makes 4 servings.

Nutrition facts per serving: 141 calories, 2 g total fat (0 g saturated fat), 0 mg cholesterol, 343 mg sodium, 28 g carbohydrate, 4 g fiber, 4 g protein
Exchanges: 1½ Starch

109 calories

Preparation time: 15 minutes ● **Cooking time:** 25 minutes

spanish rice

This rice side dish is as easy to make as a packaged rice mix and contains only a fraction of the sodium.
Pair it with baked or broiled pork chops, fish, or chicken.

  1 **cup water**
 ¾ **cup chopped green sweet pepper**
 ½ **cup chopped onion**
 ½ **cup chopped celery**
 ½ **teaspoon salt**
  1 **14½-ounce can tomatoes, cut up**
 ¾ **cup long grain rice**
  1 **teaspoon chili powder**
 ⅛ **teaspoon black pepper**
    Dash ground red pepper or bottled hot
      pepper sauce
    Fresh red serrano chili pepper (optional)
    Fresh cilantro (optional)

1 In a medium saucepan combine the water, sweet pepper, onion, celery, and salt. Bring to boiling; reduce heat. Simmer, covered, for 5 minutes.

2 Stir in undrained tomatoes, rice, chili powder, black pepper, and ground red pepper or hot pepper sauce. Return to boiling; reduce heat. Simmer, covered, about 20 minutes or until rice is tender and liquid is absorbed. If desired, garnish with serrano chili pepper and cilantro. Makes 6 servings.

Nutrition facts per serving: 109 calories, 0 g total fat, 0 mg cholesterol, 306 mg sodium, 24 g carbohydrate, 1 g fiber, 3 g protein
Exchanges: 1 Starch, 1 Vegetable

159 calories

Preparation time: 15 minutes ● **Cooking time:** 15 minutes

sausage rice

Just a small amount of turkey sausage boosts the flavor of this side dish. If you buy the sausage in a one pound package, add the remaining to a spaghetti sauce and toss with pasta for another meal.

4 ounces ground turkey sausage
½ cup shredded carrot
¼ cup thinly sliced celery
¼ cup chopped onion
1½ teaspoons snipped fresh oregano
**   or ½ teaspoon dried oregano, crushed**
½ teaspoon instant chicken bouillon granules
¼ teaspoon garlic powder
2 cups water
1 cup long grain rice

1 In a medium saucepan cook the sausage over medium-high heat until browned. Drain well. Stir the carrot, celery, onion, oregano, bouillon granules, and garlic powder into the sausage.

2 Add the water; heat to boiling. Stir in rice. Return to boiling; reduce heat. Simmer, covered, about 15 minutes or until liquid is absorbed and rice is tender. Makes 6 servings.

Nutrition facts per serving: 159 calories, 3 g total fat (1 g saturated fat), 7 mg cholesterol, 229 mg sodium, 27 g carbohydrate, 1 g fiber, 6 g protein
Exchanges: 1½ Starch, 1 Lean Meat

94 calories

Preparation time: 18 minutes ● **Standing time:** 5 minutes

broccoli rice

Fresh broccoli is economical and is available year round. Look for broccoli with firm stalks and green or purplish green heads that are tightly packed. Store in a plastic bag in the refrigerator for up to 4 days.

¾ **cup water**
1 **tablespoon snipped fresh basil**
   or 1 teaspoon dried basil, crushed
1 **teaspoon margarine or butter**
½ **teaspoon instant chicken or vegetable**
   bouillon granules
2 **cups coarsely chopped broccoli**
¼ **cup finely chopped onion**
¼ **cup chopped red or green sweet pepper**
⅔ **cup quick-cooking rice**

1 In a medium saucepan combine the water, basil, margarine or butter, and bouillon granules. Stir in the broccoli, onion, and sweet pepper.

2 Bring to boiling. Stir in rice. Cover and remove from heat. Let stand about 5 minutes or until all the water is absorbed. Makes 4 servings.

Nutrition facts per serving: 94 calories, 1 g total fat (0 g saturated fat), 0 mg cholesterol, 140 mg sodium, 18 g carbohydrate, 3 g fiber, 4 g protein
Exchanges: 1 Starch, 1 Vegetable

123 calories

Preparation time: 15 minutes ● **Cooking time:** 45 minutes ● **Standing time:** 5 minutes

lemony brown rice and vegetables

Grains of brown rice retain the bran layers that are removed when milling white rice. This results in a rice with a higher fiber content, a slightly chewier texture, and a longer cooking time.

1¼ **cups reduced-sodium chicken broth**
 ½ **cup brown rice***
 ¼ **teaspoon ground cumin**
 ⅛ **teaspoon salt**
 ⅛ **teaspoon black pepper**
 1 **small red or green sweet pepper, chopped**
 ¼ **cup sliced green onions**
 1 **cup frozen peas**
 1 **tablespoon snipped fresh parsley**
 ½ **teaspoon finely shredded lemon peel**

1 In a medium saucepan heat broth to boiling. Stir in rice, cumin, salt, and black pepper. Return to boiling; reduce heat. Simmer, covered, for 40 minutes. Stir in sweet pepper and green onions. Return to boiling; reduce heat. Simmer, covered, about 5 minutes more or until rice is tender and liquid is absorbed. Remove from heat. Stir in peas, parsley, and lemon peel; heat through. Cover and let stand for 5 minutes. Makes 4 servings.

*Note: If desired, substitute long grain rice for the brown rice. Cook rice, cumin, salt, and black pepper, covered, for 10 minutes. Add sweet pepper and green onions. Cook, covered, about 5 minutes more or until rice is tender. Continue as directed.

Nutrition facts per serving: 123 calories, 1 g total fat (0 g saturated fat), 0 mg cholesterol, 396 mg sodium, 24 g carbohydrate, 3 g fiber, 4 g protein
Exchanges: 1½ Starch

60 calories

Preparation time: 10 minutes ● **Cooking time:** 12 minutes ● **Standing time:** 5 minutes

brown rice pilaf

Shredded carrot adds a slight sweetness and a splash of color to this pilaf. Use wild mushrooms, such as shiitake, chanterelle, or portobello, for a more exotic dish.

1 **cup water**
1 **teaspoon instant chicken bouillon granules**
1 **cup sliced fresh mushrooms**
¾ **cup quick-cooking brown rice**
½ **cup shredded carrot**
¾ **teaspoon snipped fresh marjoram**
    or ¼ teaspoon dried marjoram, crushed
    Dash pepper
¼ **cup thinly sliced green onions**
1 **tablespoon snipped fresh parsley**
    Fresh marjoram sprig (optional)

1 In a medium saucepan stir together the water and bouillon granules. Bring to boiling. Stir in the mushrooms, rice, carrot, the snipped fresh or the dried marjoram, and the pepper. Return to boiling; reduce heat. Simmer, covered, for 12 minutes.

2 Remove from heat; let stand for 5 minutes. Add green onions and parsley; toss lightly with a fork. If desired, garnish with fresh marjoram sprig. Makes 4 servings.

Nutrition facts per serving: 60 calories, 1 g total fat (0 g saturated fat), 0 mg cholesterol, 230 mg sodium, 13 g carbohydrate, 2 g fiber, 2 g protein
Exchanges: ½ Starch, 1 Vegetable

101 calories

Preparation time: 15 minutes ● **Cooking time:** 45 minutes

white and wild rice

Plum tomatoes and snips of herb make ordinary rice taste fresh and flavorful. Top each serving with just a spoonful of yogurt for a refreshing tang.

2 cups water
¼ teaspoon salt
⅛ teaspoon pepper
1 clove garlic, minced
2 teaspoons snipped fresh oregano
    or ½ teaspoon dried oregano, crushed
2 teaspoons snipped fresh thyme
    or ½ teaspoon dried thyme, crushed
⅓ cup wild rice, rinsed and drained
½ cup long grain rice
4 medium plum tomatoes, coarsely chopped
    (about 1½ cups)
⅓ cup plain low-fat yogurt (optional)
    Fresh thyme sprig (optional)

1 In a medium saucepan combine the water, salt, pepper, garlic, dried oregano (if using), and dried thyme (if using); bring to boiling. Stir in the wild rice; reduce heat. Simmer, covered, for 30 minutes.

2 Stir in the long grain rice. Return to boiling; reduce heat. Simmer, covered, for 15 to 20 minutes more or until all rice is tender. Stir in the fresh oregano (if using), snipped fresh thyme (if using), and tomatoes. Heat through. If desired, serve with yogurt and garnish with fresh thyme sprig. Makes 6 servings.

Nutrition facts per serving: 101 calories, 0 g total fat, 0 mg cholesterol, 98 mg sodium, 22 g carbohydrate, 1 g fiber, 3 g protein
Exchanges: 1 Starch, 1 Vegetable

38 calories

Preparation time: 10 minutes

spicy citrus dressing

*Honey gives this reduced-fat dressing body as well as sweetness. Drizzle it over
a mixture of fruit and salad greens.*

¼ **cup lemon or lime juice**
2 **tablespoons honey**
1 **tablespoon salad oil**
¼ **teaspoon ground cinnamon, allspice, or
   cardamom**
⅛ **teaspoon paprika**

1 In a screw-top jar combine lemon or lime
juice; honey; oil; cinnamon, allspice, or cardamom;
and paprika. Cover and shake well.

2 Refrigerate the dressing until serving time.
Shake well before serving. Makes about ⅜ cup
(six 1-tablespoon servings).

Note: If desired, to vary the flavor, add any one
of the following to the dressing along with the
spices: ½ teaspoon *poppy seeds* or *sesame seeds*, dash
bottled *hot pepper sauce,* or 1 teaspoon finely
chopped *crystallized ginger.*

Nutrition facts per tablespoon: 38 calories, 2 g total fat
(0 g saturated fat), 0 mg cholesterol, 0 mg sodium,
6 g carbohydrate, 0 g fiber, 0 g protein
Exchanges: ½ Fruit, ½ Fat

19 calories

Preparation time: 10 minutes

creamy salad dressing

One tablespoon of this herbed dressing will coat ¾ cup coleslaw mix or cooked pasta. Somewhat akin to ranch-style dressings, it's also tasty over mixed salad greens.

¼ **cup plain low-fat yogurt**
2 **tablespoons light mayonnaise dressing or salad dressing**
2 **to 3 tablespoons skim milk**
1 **tablespoon snipped fresh parsley or chives**
Dash salt

1 In a small mixing bowl stir together yogurt, mayonnaise dressing or salad dressing, milk, parsley or chives, and salt. Makes about ½ cup (eight 1-tablespoon servings).

Note: If desired, to vary the flavor, add any of the following to the dressing along with the herbs: 1 tablespoon *white balsamic vinegar* or *balsamic vinegar,* 1 teaspoon *prepared horseradish,* or 1 teaspoon snipped fresh *dill.*

Nutrition facts per tablespoon: 19 calories, 1 g total fat (0 g saturated fat), 1 mg cholesterol, 51 mg sodium, 1 g carbohydrate, 0 g fiber, 1 g protein
Exchanges: Free Food

9 calories

Preparation time: 10 minutes ● **Chilling time:** 2 to 48 hours

creamy italian salad dressing

*Tofu adds the body to this buttermilk-based dressing. Be sure to buy soft tofu,
as it whips up better in this creamy dressing.*

 4 **ounces soft tofu (fresh bean curd), cubed**
⅓ **cup buttermilk or sour milk***
 2 **tablespoons vinegar**
½ **teaspoon dried Italian seasoning, crushed
    or 1 tablespoon snipped fresh basil**
¼ **teaspoon dry mustard**
 1 **small clove garlic, minced**
   Dash salt
   Dash pepper

1 In a food processor bowl or blender container combine tofu, buttermilk or sour milk, vinegar, Italian seasoning, dry mustard, garlic, salt, and pepper. Cover and process or blend until smooth.

2 Transfer dressing to a covered container. Refrigerate for at least 2 hours or up to 48 hours. Makes about 1 cup (sixteen 1-tablespoon servings).

*Note: To make ⅓ cup sour milk, place 1 teaspoon lemon juice or vinegar in a glass measuring cup. Add enough milk to make ⅓ cup total liquid. Let the mixture stand for 5 minutes before using.

Nutrition facts per tablespoon: 9 calories, 0 g total fat, 1 mg cholesterol, 15 mg sodium, 1 g carbohydrate, 0 g fiber, 1 g protein
Exchanges: Free Food

51 calories

Preparation time: 15 minutes

tomato and zucchini salad

Take advantage of your local farmer's market to pick the freshest vegetables for salads such as this one. While you're there, look for fresh basil, too.

1 large tomato, coarsely chopped
1 small zucchini, thinly sliced
2 tablespoons sliced green onion
1 teaspoon snipped fresh basil
  or ¼ teaspoon dried basil, crushed
2 tablespoons reduced-calorie or fat-free
  Italian salad dressing
  Leaf lettuce
2 tablespoons crumbled feta cheese or
  shredded part-skim mozzarella cheese

1 In a medium mixing bowl combine tomato, zucchini, green onion, basil, and Italian salad dressing. Toss lightly to mix.

2 Line 4 salad plates with lettuce. Divide tomato mixture between plates. Sprinkle each serving with some of the cheese. Makes 4 servings.

Nutrition facts per serving: 51 calories, 3 g total fat (1 g saturated fat), 8 mg cholesterol, 157 mg sodium, 5 g carbohydrate, 1 g fiber, 2 g protein
Exchanges: 1 Vegetable, ½ Fat

115 calories

Preparation time: 20 minutes ● **Cooking time:** 15 minutes ● **Chilling time:** 4 to 24 hours

new potato salad

New potatoes retain their shape after cooking, so they're ideal for salads. They are most available in spring and early summer. In a pinch, use regular red potatoes, peeled and cut into large chunks.

12 **ounces fresh green beans, cut into 1-inch pieces**
12 **ounces tiny whole new potatoes, quartered**
 3 **tablespoons light mayonnaise dressing or salad dressing**
 3 **tablespoons light dairy sour cream**
 3 **tablespoons skim milk**
 ¾ **teaspoon snipped fresh dill or ¼ teaspoon dried dillweed**
 ½ **teaspoon onion salt**
 1 **small tomato, coarsely chopped**

 1 In a large covered saucepan cook the beans and potatoes in a small amount of *boiling water* about 15 minutes or until tender. Drain.

 2 In a medium mixing bowl combine the mayonnaise dressing or salad dressing, sour cream, milk, dill, and onion salt. Add beans and potatoes,

gently tossing to coat. Cover and refrigerate for at least 4 hours or up to 24 hours. To serve, stir in chopped tomato. Makes 6 servings.

Microwave Directions: In a 2-quart microwave-safe casserole combine the beans and ½ cup *water.* Cover and microwave on 100% power (high) for 4 minutes. Stir in the potatoes. Cover and microwave on high for 8 to 10 minutes or until beans and potatoes are tender, stirring once. Drain in a colander; set aside.

In the same casserole stir together mayonnaise dressing or salad dressing, sour cream, milk, dill, and onion salt. Stir in beans and potatoes. Cover and refrigerate for at least 4 hours or up to 24 hours. To serve, stir in chopped tomato.

Nutrition facts per serving: 115 calories, 3 g total fat (1 g saturated fat), 1 mg cholesterol, 208 mg sodium, 19 g carbohydrate, 2 g fiber, 3 g protein
Exchanges: 1 Starch, 1 Vegetable

57 calories

Preparation time: 20 minutes ● **Chilling time:** 2 to 24 hours

white bean and pepper salad

A lemon-dill vinaigrette and colorful vegetables impart a garden freshness to a simple can of beans.

2 **tablespoons lemon juice**
1½ **teaspoons olive oil or salad oil**
½ **teaspoon sugar**
½ **teaspoon snipped fresh dill or ¼ teaspoon dried dillweed**
⅛ **teaspoon black pepper**
1 **clove garlic, minced**
1 **15-ounce can white kidney beans or navy beans, rinsed and drained**
½ **cup chopped red or green sweet pepper**
½ **cup chopped seeded cucumber**
¼ **cup sliced green onions**

1 In a medium mixing bowl stir together the lemon juice, oil, sugar, dill, black pepper, and garlic.

2 Add beans, sweet pepper, cucumber, and green onions. Toss to coat.

3 Cover and refrigerate for at least 2 hours or up to 24 hours. Makes 6 servings.

Nutrition facts per serving: 57 calories, 1 g total fat (0 g saturated fat), 0 mg cholesterol, 111 mg sodium, 11 g carbohydrate, 4 g fiber, 4 g protein
Exchanges: 1 Starch

49 calories

Preparation time: 15 minutes ● **Chilling time:** 2 to 24 hours

marinated cucumbers

Add the radishes just before serving so they don't turn the cucumbers and onion red.

¼ cup water
3 tablespoons vinegar
1 tablespoon sugar
2 teaspoons salad oil
1½ teaspoons snipped fresh basil
    or ½ teaspoon dried basil, crushed
⅛ teaspoon salt
⅛ teaspoon black pepper
    Several dashes bottled hot pepper sauce
2 medium cucumbers, sliced (about 3 cups)
1 small onion, thinly sliced
½ cup sliced radishes

1 In a medium mixing bowl stir together the water, vinegar, sugar, oil, basil, salt, black pepper, and hot pepper sauce.

2 Add cucumbers and onion; toss to coat. Cover and refrigerate for at least 2 hours or up to 24 hours.

3 Before serving, toss radishes with the cucumber and onion mixture. Makes 4 to 6 servings.

Nutrition facts per serving: 49 calories, 2 g total fat (0 g saturated fat), 0 mg cholesterol, 71 mg sodium, 7 g carbohydrate, 1 g fiber, 1 g protein
Exchanges: 1 Vegetable, ½ Fat

141 calories

Preparation time: 15 minutes ● **Chilling time:** 2 to 24 hours

mexican-style pasta salad

Toss whatever medium-sized pasta you may have on hand, such as shells, macaroni, or cavatelli.
To make 2 cups of cooked pasta, start with a generous ¾ cup of uncooked pasta.

1 medium tomato, chopped
½ cup seeded chopped cucumber
2 tablespoons chopped red onion
1 tablespoon olive oil or salad oil
1 tablespoon red wine vinegar
½ teaspoon ground cumin
1 jalapeño pepper, seeded and finely
　chopped*
¼ teaspoon salt
2 cups cooked rotini (corkscrew) or other
　medium pasta
　Bibb or Boston lettuce (optional)

1 In large bowl combine the tomato, cucumber, red onion, oil, vinegar, cumin, jalapeño pepper, and salt. Stir in cooked pasta. Cover and refrigerate for at least 2 hours or up to 24 hours. Stir before serving. If desired, serve in a lettuce-lined bowl. Makes 4 servings.

*Note: Because chili peppers, such as jalapeños, contain volatile oils that can burn your skin and eyes, avoid direct contact with them as much as possible. When working with chili peppers, wear plastic gloves. If your bare hands touch the chili peppers, wash your hands well with soap and water.

Nutrition facts per serving: 141 calories, 4 g total fat (1 g saturated fat), 0 mg cholesterol, 138 mg sodium, 23 g carbohydrate, 2 g fiber, 4 g protein
Exchanges: 1 Starch, 1 Vegetable, ½ Fat

126 calories

Preparation time: 15 minutes ● **Chilling time:** 2 to 24 hours

pear and pepper salad

Pears and peppers may sound like an unusual combination, but the texture contrast of crunchy peppers and soft pears works deliciously.

1 **tablespoon cider vinegar**
1 **tablespoon olive oil or salad oil**
1 **tablespoon water**
2 **to 3 teaspoons honey**
⅛ **teaspoon salt**
1 **cup finely chopped very ripe fresh pear**
1 **cup finely chopped red and/or green sweet pepper**
1 **cup cooked long grain or brown rice, chilled**
1 **tablespoon snipped fresh parsley**
   Lettuce leaves
   Pear slices (optional)

1 In a medium bowl stir together the vinegar, oil, water, honey, and salt.

2 Add the chopped pear, sweet pepper, rice, and parsley; toss gently. Cover and refrigerate for at least 2 hours or up to 24 hours. Serve on lettuce-lined plates. If desired, garnish with the pear slices. Makes 4 servings.

Nutrition facts per serving: 126 calories, 4 g total fat (1 g saturated fat), 0 mg cholesterol, 70 mg sodium, 23 g carbohydrate, 2 g fiber, 2 g protein
Exchanges: 1 Starch, ½ Fruit, ½ Fat

128 calories

Preparation time: 30 minutes

grilled tomato and mozzarella salad

When garden fresh tomatoes are at their peak, serve this salad as the beginning to a grilled summer meal. Use olive oil, which will give you more flavor punch than salad oil.

Nonstick spray coating
1 **medium yellow summer squash, cut into ¼-inch-thick lengthwise slices**
2 **large ripe firm tomatoes, cut into ¼-inch-thick slices**
1 **tablespoon balsamic vinegar or red wine vinegar**
1 **tablespoon olive oil or salad oil**
1 **tablespoon water**
⅛ **teaspoon salt**
⅛ **teaspoon pepper**
4 **ounces part-skim mozzarella cheese, thinly sliced and cut into triangles**
2 **tablespoons snipped fresh mixed herbs (such as oregano, basil, thyme, and sage)**
Fresh oregano sprigs (optional)

1 Spray an unheated grill rack with nonstick coating. Grill squash on the prepared rack directly over medium coals for 3 minutes. Turn and grill 2 to 3 minutes more or until crisp-tender. Add tomato slices to rack; grill 2 to 4 minutes more or until heated through and still slightly firm, turning once.

2 Meanwhile, for dressing, in a screw-top jar combine the vinegar, oil, water, salt, and pepper. Cover and shake well.

3 Cut squash slices in half. To assemble salad, alternate pieces of tomato, squash, and mozzarella cheese on a shallow plate. Drizzle dressing over vegetables. Sprinkle snipped fresh herbs over the salad. If desired, garnish with fresh oregano sprigs. Makes 4 servings.

Nutrition facts per serving: 128 calories, 8 g total fat (3 g saturated fat), 16 mg cholesterol, 206 mg sodium, 7 g carbohydrate, 1 g fiber, 8 g protein
Exchanges: 1 Lean Meat, 1 Vegetable, 1 Fat

87 calories

Preparation time: 25 minutes

tossed italian salad

No time to clean greens? Substitute 4 cups of packaged torn mixed salad greens for the spinach and leaf lettuce.

2 cups torn fresh spinach
2 cups torn red leaf lettuce
1 medium yellow or green sweet pepper, cut into strips
²⁄₃ cup thinly sliced radishes
1 small red onion, sliced and separated into rings
2 tablespoons red wine vinegar
4 teaspoons olive oil or salad oil
1 tablespoon water
1 teaspoon snipped fresh oregano
**   or ½ teaspoon dried oregano, crushed**
½ teaspoon garlic salt
2 tablespoons grated Parmesan cheese
**   Coarsely ground black pepper (optional)**

1 For salad, in a large bowl combine the spinach, lettuce, sweet pepper strips, radish slices, and red onion rings. Toss lightly.

2 For dressing, in a screw-top jar combine the vinegar, oil, water, oregano, and garlic salt. Cover and shake well.

3 Pour dressing over salad. Toss lightly to coat. Sprinkle Parmesan cheese over salad. Toss lightly. If desired, sprinkle with coarsely ground pepper. Makes 4 servings.

Nutrition facts per serving: 87 calories, 6 g total fat (1 g saturated fat), 2 mg cholesterol, 342 mg sodium, 8 g carbohydrate, 2 g fiber, 3 g protein
Exchanges: 2 Vegetable, 1 Fat

109 calories

Preparation time: 25 minutes

curried fruit salad

*It's not absolutely necessary to peel kiwifruit. If you choose to leave the peel on the fruit,
rub the skin with a clean cloth to remove the excess fuzz.*

⅓ **cup light dairy sour cream**
1 **tablespoon skim milk**
2 **teaspoons honey or sugar**
¼ **teaspoon curry powder**
   Leaf lettuce
1 **cup seedless grapes, halved**
1 **large orange, peeled and sectioned**
1 **medium red apple, sliced**
1 **medium kiwifruit, peeled and sliced**

1 For dressing, in a small mixing bowl stir together the sour cream, milk, honey or sugar, and curry powder. Line 4 salad plates with lettuce.

2 Arrange grapes, orange sections, apple slices, and kiwifruit on lettuce; drizzle with dressing. Makes 4 servings.

Nutrition facts per serving: 109 calories, 2 g total fat (1 g saturated fat), 3 mg cholesterol, 29 mg sodium, 23 g carbohydrate, 2 g fiber, 3 g protein
Exchanges: 1½ Fruit, ½ Fat

36 calories

Preparation time: 15 minutes ● **Chilling time:** 45 minutes; 3 hours

apple-cheese gelatin salad

To unmold this shimmering salad, set the mold into a bowl or sink filled with warm water for several seconds or until the salad edges separate from the mold.

1 **4-serving-size package sugar-free lemon-flavored gelatin**
1 **cup boiling water**
¾ **cup cold water**
⅔ **cup chopped red apple**
⅓ **cup shredded reduced-fat cheddar cheese**
¼ **cup chopped celery**
   Leaf lettuce (optional)
   Apple slices (optional)

1 In a medium mixing bowl dissolve the lemon-flavored gelatin in the boiling water. Stir in the cold water. Chill until partially set (the consistency of unbeaten egg whites), about 45 minutes.

2 Fold the chopped apple, cheddar cheese, and celery into the gelatin mixture.

3 Pour gelatin mixture into a 3-cup mold. (Or, pour gelatin mixture into 6 individual molds or 6-ounce custard cups.)

4 Cover and refrigerate for at least 3 hours or until firm. Unmold onto plate(s) lined with lettuce (if desired). If desired, garnish with apple slices. Makes 6 servings.

Nutrition facts per serving: 36 calories, 1 g total fat (1 g saturated fat), 5 mg cholesterol, 59 mg sodium, 2 g carbohydrate, 0 g fiber, 3 g protein
Exchanges: ½ Fruit

50 calories

Preparation time: 10 minutes ● **Cooking time:** 12 minutes

cannellini bean and spinach soup

Cannellini beans are actually large, white kidney beans and are available either dried or canned. If you can't find them canned in your supermarket, simply substitute another white bean, such as navy beans.

2 14½-ounce cans vegetable broth or
    reduced-sodium chicken broth
1½ cups water
¼ cup finely chopped onion
¼ cup snipped fresh basil or 2 teaspoons
    dried basil, crushed
3 cloves garlic, minced
1 bay leaf
1 15-ounce can white kidney beans or navy
    beans, rinsed and drained
2 cups coarsely chopped fresh spinach
    or ½ of a 10-ounce package frozen
    chopped spinach, thawed and
    well-drained
1 tablespoon diced pimiento
    Pepper

1 In a large saucepan combine the broth and water; bring to boiling. Stir in onion, basil, garlic, and bay leaf. Return to boiling; reduce heat. Simmer, covered, for 10 minutes.

2 Stir in beans, spinach, and pimiento; cook for 2 to 3 minutes more or until spinach is wilted. Discard bay leaf. Season to taste with pepper. Makes 6 servings.

Nutrition facts per serving: 50 calories, 1 g total fat (0 g saturated fat), 0 mg cholesterol, 687 mg sodium, 13 g carbohydrate, 4 g fiber, 5 g protein
Exchanges: ½ Starch, 1 Vegetable

122 calories

Preparation time: 25 minutes

corn chowder

Chowders are generally cream-based. This lightened version is based on evaporated skim milk, which is much lower in calories than cream. Evaporated milk also adds more flavor than regular milk.

1   14½-ounce can reduced-sodium chicken
     broth
1   10-ounce package frozen whole kernel corn
1   cup chopped onion
½   cup chopped red and/or green sweet
     pepper
⅛   teaspoon black pepper
1   12-ounce can evaporated skim milk
¼   cup all-purpose flour
1   tablespoon snipped fresh parsley
     (optional)

1 In a medium saucepan combine the broth, corn, onion, sweet pepper, and black pepper. Bring to boiling; reduce heat. Simmer, covered, about 5 minutes or until onion is tender.

2 In a small bowl stir together the evaporated milk and flour. Stir into broth mixture. Cook and stir until thickened and bubbly. Cook and stir for 1 minute more. If desired, sprinkle with fresh parsley. Makes 6 servings.

Nutrition facts per serving: 122 calories, 1 g total fat (0 g saturated fat), 2 mg cholesterol, 261 mg sodium, 23 g carbohydrate, 1 g fiber, 7 g protein
Exchanges: 1 Starch, ½ Milk

Chicken Corn Chowder: Prepare the chowder as directed except, at the end of cooking, stir in 1 cup chopped *cooked chicken*. Heat through. Makes 3 main-dish servings.

Nutrition facts per serving: 255 calories, 4 g total fat (1 g saturated fat), 36 mg cholesterol, 424 mg sodium, 35 g carbohydrate, 1 g fiber, 22 g protein
Exchanges: 1½ Starch, 2 Lean Meat, ½ Milk

53 calories

Preparation time: 20 minutes ● **Cooking time:** 10 minutes

curried squash soup

Deep yellow and orange vegetables, such as winter squash, are an excellent source of vitamin A.
Just a few simple ingredients combine with this delicious vegetable for an elegant soup.

 3 **cups peeled and cubed butternut, acorn,**
    and/or Hubbard squash
1¼ **cups reduced-sodium chicken broth**
 ½ **cup chopped onion**
 ½ **cup water**
 ½ **teaspoon curry powder**
 ¼ **teaspoon ground ginger**
 ¼ **teaspoon salt**
 4 **teaspoons snipped fresh thyme**
    or ½ teaspoon dried thyme, crushed
    Light dairy sour cream (optional)
    Fresh thyme sprigs (optional)

1 In a large saucepan combine squash, chicken broth, onion, water, curry powder, ginger, salt, and the dried thyme (if using). Bring to a boil; reduce heat. Simmer, covered, about 10 minutes or until squash is tender. Mash squash. Stir in the snipped fresh thyme (if using). If desired, garnish with sour cream and fresh thyme sprigs. Makes 4 servings.

Nutrition facts per serving: 53 calories, 1 g total fat (0 g saturated fat), 0 mg cholesterol, 338 mg sodium, 12 g carbohydrate, 2 g fiber, 2 g protein
Exchanges: 1 Starch

58 calories

Preparation time: 25 minutes ● **Cooking time:** 20 minutes

tri-mushroom soup

The flavor combination of three different mushrooms makes this taste exotic, but it's simple to prepare.
Use whatever mushrooms you like best or whatever you find at your supermarket.

1 tablespoon olive oil or cooking oil
8 ounces fresh mushrooms, sliced
2 ounces portobello mushroom, sliced into
  ½-inch-thick pieces
2 ounces shiitake, porcini, or other
  exotic mushrooms, sliced into
  ½-inch-thick pieces
3 cloves garlic, minced
⅓ cup dry sherry (optional)
3 14½-ounce cans reduced-sodium chicken
  broth
1 tablespoon snipped fresh thyme
  Fresh thyme sprigs (optional)

1 In a large saucepan heat oil. Add all 3 types of mushrooms and the garlic. Cook, stirring occasionally, about 10 minutes or until mushrooms have softened and most of the liquid has evaporated. Stir in sherry (if desired); cook for 2 minutes more.

2 Add broth. Bring to boiling; reduce heat. Simmer, covered, for 20 minutes. Stir in the snipped thyme. If desired, garnish with fresh thyme sprigs. Makes 6 servings.

Nutrition facts per serving: 58 calories, 4 g total fat (0 g saturated fat), 0 mg cholesterol, 580 mg sodium, 4 g carbohydrate, 1 g fiber, 3 g protein
Exchanges: 1 Vegetable, ½ Fat

110 calories

Preparation time: 15 minutes ● **Cooking time:** 18 minutes

italian tomato and rice soup

Bottled salsa helps provide some of the tomato flavor for this chunky vegetable soup. Use mild, medium, or hot salsa to suit the tastes of your family or guests.

2 cups water
1 12-ounce jar chunky salsa
1 cup low-sodium tomato juice
⅓ cup quick-cooking brown rice
1 tablespoon dried minced onion
1 teaspoon dried Italian seasoning, crushed
½ teaspoon instant chicken bouillon granules
⅛ teaspoon dried minced garlic
⅛ teaspoon pepper
1 16-ounce package loose-pack frozen zucchini, carrots, cauliflower, lima beans, and Italian green beans
⅓ cup finely shredded or grated Parmesan cheese (optional)

1 In a large saucepan combine the water, salsa, tomato juice, brown rice, dried onion, Italian seasoning, bouillon granules, dried garlic, and pepper. Bring to boiling; reduce heat. Simmer, covered, for 10 minutes.

2 Meanwhile, place the frozen vegetables in a colander. Run cold water over vegetables until thawed. Stir vegetables into the rice mixture. Return to boiling; reduce heat. Simmer, covered, for 5 to 10 minutes or until rice and vegetables are tender.

3 If desired, top each serving with some of the Parmesan cheese. Makes 6 to 8 servings.

Nutrition facts per serving: 110 calories, 1 g total fat (0 g saturated fat), 0 mg cholesterol, 389 mg sodium, 22 g carbohydrate, 4 g fiber, 6 g protein
Exchanges: ½ Starch, 3 Vegetable

113 calories

Preparation time: 15 minutes ● **Cooking time:** 5 minutes

tortellini soup

*Need a fast-fixing supper? Enjoy steaming bowls of this filling pasta soup
with simple turkey or ham sandwiches.*

  1 14½-ounce can diced tomatoes, undrained
1¼ cups water
  1 cup reduced-sodium chicken broth
  2 teaspoons snipped fresh basil
       or ½ teaspoon dried basil, crushed
  1 teaspoon snipped fresh oregano
       or ¼ teaspoon dried oregano, crushed
 ⅛ teaspoon pepper
  2 cups loose-pack frozen broccoli,
       cauliflower, and carrots (about ½ of a
       16-ounce package)
1¼ cups refrigerated cheese tortellini
       (about ½ of a 9-ounce package)
  1 tablespoon snipped fresh parsley

1 In a medium saucepan combine the undrained
tomatoes, water, chicken broth, basil, oregano,
and pepper. Bring to boiling. Stir in the frozen
vegetables and tortellini.

2 Return to boiling; reduce heat. Simmer,
uncovered, for 5 to 6 minutes or until tortellini are
tender. Stir in fresh parsley. Makes 5 servings.

Nutrition facts per serving: 113 calories, 2 g total fat
(1 g saturated fat), 12 mg cholesterol, 431 mg sodium,
18 g carbohydrate, 2 g fiber, 6 g protein
Exchanges: ½ Starch, 2 Vegetable

Baking

chapter index

41 calories

Preparation time: 40 minutes ● **Resting/Rising time:** 35 minutes ● **Baking time:** 10 minutes

bread knots

For variety in shape, make half of the dough as knots and half as rosettes. Serve these caraway-studded rolls with a main-dish soup, such as Beef-Barley Soup (see recipe, page 169).

1 to 1⅓ cups all-purpose flour
1 package fast-rising active dry yeast
1 teaspoon caraway seed or ½ to 1 teaspoon coarsely ground black pepper
½ teaspoon salt
¾ cup hot water (120° to 130°)
1 tablespoon cooking oil
1 cup whole wheat flour
   Nonstick spray coating
1 egg white
   Caraway seed (optional)

1 In a medium mixing bowl combine ¾ *cup* of the all-purpose flour, the yeast, the 1 teaspoon caraway seed or pepper, and the salt. Add the hot water and oil. Beat with electric mixer on low speed for 30 seconds, scraping bowl constantly. Beat on high speed 3 minutes. Stir in whole wheat flour and as much of the remaining all-purpose flour as you can. On a floured surface knead in enough of the remaining all-purpose flour to make a moderately

stiff dough that is smooth and elastic (6 to 8 minutes total). Shape into a ball. Cover; let rest 15 minutes.

2 Divide dough into 4 portions. Divide each portion into 6 pieces. Roll each piece into an 8- to 10-inch-long rope. Tie each rope into a loose knot, leaving 2 long ends. (For rosettes, tuck top end under roll. Bring bottom end up; tuck into center.)

3 Spray 2 baking sheets with nonstick coating. Place rolls 1 inch apart on prepared sheets. Cover; let rise until nearly double (about 20 minutes). Beat together egg white and 1 tablespoon *water*. Brush rolls lightly with egg mixture. If desired, sprinkle with additional caraway seed. Bake in a 375° oven for 10 to 12 minutes or until golden brown. Remove from sheets. Cool on wire rack. Makes 24 rolls.

Nutrition facts per roll: 41 calories, 1 g total fat (0 g saturated fat), 0 mg cholesterol, 47 mg sodium, 7 g carbohydrate, 1 g fiber, 1 g protein
Exchanges: ½ Starch

69 calories

Preparation time: 15 minutes ● **Baking time:** 10 minutes ● **Cooling time:** 5 minutes

parmesan corn bread puffs

These puffs are best served warm from the oven. If you want to make them a few days ahead, wrap them in foil and store them at room temperature. To serve, reheat in a 300° oven for 10 minutes.

Nonstick spray coating
½ **cup all-purpose flour**
⅓ **cup yellow cornmeal**
4 **teaspoons sugar**
1 **teaspoon baking powder**
Dash salt
1 **slightly beaten egg white**
⅓ **cup skim milk**
2 **tablespoons cooking oil**
2 **tablespoons grated Parmesan cheese**

1 Spray twelve 1¾-inch muffin cups with nonstick coating. Set aside.

2 In a large bowl stir together flour, cornmeal, sugar, baking powder, and salt. Stir together egg white, milk, and oil. Add egg white mixture to the dry mixture, stirring just until smooth. Spoon into prepared muffin cups, filling each about ¾ full.

3 Bake in a 425° oven for 10 to 12 minutes or until golden brown. Remove from pan. Cool on a wire rack for 5 minutes. Place cheese in a plastic bag. Add warm puffs, a few at a time; toss to coat with cheese. Serve warm. Makes 12 puffs.

Nutrition facts per puff: 69 calories, 3 g total fat (1 g saturated fat), 1 mg cholesterol, 40 mg sodium, 9 g carbohydrate, 0 g fiber, 2 g protein
Exchanges: ½ Starch, ½ Fat

82 calories

Preparation time: 30 minutes ● **Rising/Resting time:** 65 minutes ● **Baking time:** 15 minutes

dill batter rolls

Yeast breads rise best in a draft-free area that's 80 to 85 degrees. Your oven can be just the spot. Place the bowl of dough in the unheated oven and set a large pan of hot water on the oven's lower rack.

1½ **cups all-purpose flour**
1 **package active dry yeast**
1 **cup low-fat cottage cheese**
¼ **cup water**
1 **tablespoon sugar**
2 **teaspoons dillseed or caraway seed**
½ **teaspoon salt**
1 **egg**
Nonstick spray coating

1 In a large mixing bowl combine *1 cup* of the flour and the yeast. Set aside.

2 In a small saucepan heat and stir cottage cheese, water, sugar, dillseed or caraway seed, and salt just until warm (120° to 130°). Add cottage cheese mixture to dry mixture along with the egg. Beat with an electric mixer on low speed for 30 seconds, scraping side of bowl constantly. Beat on high speed for 3 minutes. Using a wooden spoon, stir in remaining flour until nearly smooth.

3 Cover batter and let rise in a warm place until double in size (about 45 minutes). Stir batter down with a wooden spoon. Let rest for 5 minutes.

4 Spray twelve 2½-inch muffin cups with nonstick coating. Spoon batter evenly into cups. Cover loosely with plastic wrap; let batter rise until nearly double in size (15 to 20 minutes).

5 Bake in a 375° oven for 15 to 18 minutes or until golden brown. Serve warm. Makes 12 rolls.

Freezing Directions: Place completely cooled rolls in a freezer bag or container or tightly wrap in heavy foil. Freeze for up to 3 months. To warm rolls, wrap in foil and heat in a 300° oven about 25 minutes.

Nutrition facts per roll: 82 calories, 1 g total fat (0 g saturated fat), 19 mg cholesterol, 171 mg sodium, 13 g carbohydrate, 1 g fiber, 5 g protein
Exchanges: 1 Starch

80 calories

Preparation time: 20 minutes ● **Baking time:** 9 minutes

pumpkin crescent rolls

These biscuit-like rolls will remind you of pumpkin pie. Freeze leftovers in a freezer container or bag up to 3 months. Thaw wrapped rolls at room temperature 2 hours; reheat in a 375° oven 3 to 5 minutes.

1¾ **cups all-purpose flour**
1 **teaspoon baking powder**
¼ **teaspoon baking soda**
¼ **teaspoon ground nutmeg**
⅛ **teaspoon salt**
¾ **cup canned pumpkin**
3 **tablespoons cooking oil**
2 **tablespoons brown sugar**
2 **teaspoons granulated sugar**
¼ **teaspoon ground cinnamon**

1 In a medium mixing bowl combine flour, baking powder, baking soda, nutmeg, and salt.

2 In a small mixing bowl combine the pumpkin, oil, and brown sugar. Add pumpkin mixture to dry mixture, stirring with a fork until combined. Form into a ball.

3 Line a large baking sheet with foil. Turn dough out onto a lightly floured surface. Knead dough gently for 10 to 12 strokes. Divide dough in half. Roll each half to a 10-inch circle. Cut each circle into 8 wedges. To shape, begin at the wide end of each wedge and loosely roll toward the point. Place point sides down, about 2 inches apart, on the prepared baking sheet. Curve ends of rolls slightly.

4 Combine the granulated sugar and cinnamon; sprinkle over crescents. Bake in a 400° oven for 9 to 11 minutes or until golden brown. Serve warm. Makes 16 rolls.

Nutrition facts per roll: 80 calories, 3 g total fat (0 g saturated fat), 0 mg cholesterol, 60 mg sodium, 13 g carbohydrate, 1 g fiber, 1 g protein
Exchanges: 1 Starch

75 calories

Preparation time: 45 minutes ● **Rising/Resting time:** 70 minutes ● **Baking time:** 25 minutes

cracked pepper focaccia

The cracked pepper gives this focaccia its bite. Purchase black pepper already cracked or crush whole peppercorns with a mortar and pestle or by placing in a plastic bag and striking with flat side of a meat mallet.

1½ **to 2 cups all-purpose flour**
 1 **package active dry yeast**
⅔ **cup warm water (120° to 130°)**
 4 **teaspoons olive oil**
¼ **teaspoon salt**
   Nonstick spray coating
 1 **tablespoon cornmeal**
 2 **tablespoons shredded Parmesan cheese**
 1 **teaspoon cracked black pepper**

1 In a large mixing bowl combine ⅔ *cup* of the flour and the yeast. Add the warm water, *2 teaspoons* of the oil, and the salt to the dry mixture. Beat with an electric mixer on low to medium speed for 30 seconds, scraping side of bowl constantly. Beat on high speed for 3 minutes. Using a wooden spoon, stir in as much of the remaining flour as you can. Turn dough out onto a lightly floured surface. Knead in enough of the remaining flour to make a stiff dough that is smooth and elastic (8 to 10 minutes total). Shape dough into a ball.

2 Spray a medium bowl with nonstick coating. Place dough in the prepared bowl; turn once. Cover; let dough rise in a warm place until double in size (about 1 hour).

3 Punch dough down; turn onto a floured surface. Shape dough into a ball. Cover; let dough rest 10 minutes. Spray a 12-inch pizza pan or baking sheet with nonstick coating. Sprinkle with cornmeal. Roll or pat dough to a 12-inch circle. Transfer to prepared pan. Make deep indentations in dough every 2 inches. Brush with remaining oil. Sprinkle with Parmesan cheese and cracked black pepper.

4 Bake in a 375° oven about 25 minutes or until golden brown. Remove from pan. Cool on wire rack. Serve warm or at room temperature. Cut into wedges to serve. Makes 12 servings.

Nutrition facts per serving: 75 calories, 2 g total fat (0 g saturated fat), 1 mg cholesterol, 59 mg sodium, 12 g carbohydrate, 1 g fiber, 2 g protein
Exchanges: 1 Starch

76 calories

Preparation time: 45 minutes ● **Rising/Resting time:** 1 hour 25 minutes ● **Baking time:** 15 minutes per round

onion flatbread

This savory bread has the same chewy texture as focaccia and is made from a similar stiff dough. Your dough is stiff when it kneads easily on a floured surface, is firm to the touch, and holds its shape.

1¼ cups water
¼ cup dried minced onion
2¾ to 3¼ cups all-purpose flour
1 package active dry yeast
½ teaspoon salt
1 tablespoon olive oil or cooking oil
   Nonstick spray coating
1 teaspoon poppy seed and/or sesame seed

1 In a small saucepan combine the water and dried onion; let stand 10 minutes. Heat just until warm (120° to 130°). In a large mixing bowl combine *1 cup* of the flour, the yeast, and salt. Add onion mixture and oil to dry mixture. Beat with electric mixer on low speed for 30 seconds, scraping sides of bowl constantly. Beat on high speed for 3 minutes. Using a wooden spoon, stir in as much of the remaining flour as you can.

2 On a lightly floured surface knead in enough of the remaining flour to make a stiff dough that is smooth and elastic (8 to 10 minutes total). Shape into a ball. Spray a large bowl with nonstick coating. Place dough in prepared bowl; turn once. Cover; let rise in warm place until double in size (45 to 60 minutes).

3 Punch dough down. On a lightly floured surface divide dough into thirds. Cover; let rest for 10 minutes. Spray 3 baking sheets with nonstick coating. Roll each portion of dough into a 10-inch circle. Wrap dough around rolling pin; unroll onto prepared sheet. Brush dough with *water* and sprinkle with poppy and/or sesame seed. Cover; let rise until nearly double in size (30 to 40 minutes).

4 Bake, 1 at a time, in a 400° oven about 15 minutes or until golden brown. (Refrigerate remaining rounds until ready to bake.) To serve, cut or tear into pieces. Makes 3 rounds (18 servings).

Nutrition facts per serving: 76 calories, 1 g total fat (0 g saturated fat), 0 mg cholesterol, 60 mg sodium, 15 g carbohydrate, 1 g fiber, 2 g protein
Exchanges: 1 Starch

89 calories

Preparation time: 10 minutes ● **Baking time:** 15 minutes

onion and cheese biscuits

Stir whole wheat flour and Parmesan cheese into reduced-fat packaged biscuit mix for a biscuit that tastes homemade. For a change in flavor, try snipped fresh sage or chives in place of the oregano or basil.

1½ **cups reduced-fat packaged biscuit mix**
 ½ **cup whole wheat or all-purpose flour**
 3 **tablespoons grated Parmesan cheese**
 1 **tablespoon dried minced onion**
 1 **tablespoon snipped fresh oregano or basil or 1 teaspoon dried oregano or basil, crushed**
 1 **slightly beaten egg white**
 ¾ **cup skim milk**
   Nonstick spray coating

1 In a medium mixing bowl stir together the biscuit mix, flour, Parmesan cheese, dried onion, and oregano or basil.

2 In a small bowl combine the egg white and milk. Add egg white mixture to dry mixture, stirring just until combined. (Do not overmix.)

3 Spray baking sheet with nonstick coating. Drop dough from a tablespoon onto prepared baking sheet, forming 12 mounds. Bake in a 400° oven for 15 to 20 minutes or until lightly browned. Serve warm. Makes 12 biscuits.

Nutrition facts per biscuit: 89 calories, 2 g total fat (1 g saturated fat), 1 mg cholesterol, 214 mg sodium, 15 g carbohydrate, 1 g fiber, 3 g protein
Exchanges: 1 Starch

88 calories

Preparation time: 18 minutes ● **Baking time:** 10 minutes

green onion and basil biscuits

Even though these biscuits have only a small amount of oil, they are still tender and delicious. To add an Italian flavor to them, use olive oil in place of the cooking oil.

1 cup all-purpose flour
1 green onion, thinly sliced
1½ teaspoons baking powder
1 teaspoon sugar
¾ teaspoon snipped fresh basil
　 or ¼ teaspoon dried basil, crushed
　 Dash salt
⅓ cup skim milk
2 tablespoons cooking oil
　 Fat-free cream cheese (optional)

1 In a medium bowl combine the flour, green onion, baking powder, sugar, basil, and salt.

2 In a small bowl stir together the milk and oil. Add the milk mixture to dry mixture, stirring just until combined.

3 Turn out onto a lightly floured surface. Knead gently for 10 to 12 strokes. Roll or pat dough to ½-inch thickness. Cut with a 2-inch biscuit cutter, dipping cutter into additional flour between cuts. Transfer biscuits to an ungreased baking sheet.

4 Bake in a 450° oven for 10 to 12 minutes or until golden brown. Serve warm. If desired, serve with cream cheese. Makes 8 biscuits.

Nutrition facts per biscuit: 88 calories, 4 g total fat (1 g saturated fat), 0 mg cholesterol, 90 mg sodium, 12 g carbohydrate, 0 g fiber, 2 g protein
Exchanges: 1 Starch

77 calories

Preparation time: 15 minutes ● **Baking time:** 30 minutes

irish soda bread

*"Soda" in the name of this traditional bread refers to the baking soda used to help leaven or raise the bread.
Also, try the Whole Wheat Raisin Soda Bread variation (shown in foreground of photo.)*

2 cups all-purpose flour
1 teaspoon baking powder
½ teaspoon baking soda
¼ teaspoon salt
3 tablespoons margarine or butter
1 slightly beaten egg white
¾ cup buttermilk or sour milk (see note, page 336)
Nonstick spray coating

1 In a medium mixing bowl stir together the flour, baking powder, soda, and salt. Cut in margarine or butter until mixture resembles coarse crumbs. Make a well in the center of the mixture.

2 In a small mixing bowl combine the egg white and buttermilk or sour milk. Add egg white mixture all at once to dry mixture, stirring just until moistened.

3 Turn dough out onto a lightly floured surface. Knead for 10 to 12 strokes or until nearly smooth. Shape into a 7-inch round loaf.

4 Spray a baking sheet with nonstick coating. Place loaf on baking sheet. With a sharp knife, make 2 slashes in the top to form an X.

5 Bake in a 375° oven about 30 minutes or until golden brown. Serve bread warm. Makes 1 loaf (16 servings).

Nutrition facts per serving: 77 calories, 2 g total fat (0 g saturated fat), 0 mg cholesterol, 136 mg sodium, 12 g carbohydrate, 0 g fiber, 2 g protein
Exchanges: 1 Starch

Whole Wheat Raisin Soda Bread: Prepare as above, except substitute 1 cup *whole wheat flour* for 1 cup of the all-purpose flour. Add ¼ cup *raisins* to the buttermilk mixture before adding to dry mixture.

Nutrition facts per serving: 83 calories, 3 g total fat (1 g saturated fat), 0 mg cholesterol, 137 mg sodium, 13 g carbohydrate, 1 g fiber, 2 g protein
Exchanges: 1 Starch

84 calories

Preparation time: 20 minutes ● **Rising/Resting time:** 1 hour 30 minutes ● **Baking time:** 30 minutes

wheat and oat bread

When making yeast breads, always check the temperature of the liquid with a thermometer before adding it to the yeast mixture. If it's too hot or too cold, the bread won't rise.

1¾ to 2¼ cups all-purpose flour
⅓ cup rolled oats
1 package active dry yeast
1 cup warm water (120° to 130°)
2 tablespoons honey or maple-flavored syrup
1½ teaspoons cooking oil
⅔ cup whole wheat flour
   Nonstick spray coating
   Skim milk
   Rolled oats

1 In a medium bowl combine *1¼ cups* of the all-purpose flour, the ⅓ cup oats, the yeast, and ½ teaspoon *salt*. Add the water, honey or syrup, and oil. Beat with an electric mixer on low speed for 30 seconds, scraping bowl constantly. Beat on high speed 3 minutes. Stir in whole wheat flour and as much of the remaining all-purpose flour as you can.

2 On a lightly floured surface knead in enough remaining all-purpose flour to make a moderately stiff dough that is smooth and elastic (6 to 8 minutes total). Shape into a ball. Spray a bowl with nonstick coating. Place dough in bowl; turn once. Cover; let rise in a warm place until double in size (50 to 60 minutes). Punch down. Turn out onto a lightly floured surface. Cover; let rest 10 minutes.

3 Spray an 8×4×2-inch loaf pan with nonstick coating. Shape dough into loaf; place in pan. Cover; let rise until nearly double (30 to 45 minutes). Brush with milk; sprinkle lightly with additional oats.

4 Bake in a 375° oven for 30 to 35 minutes or until bread sounds hollow when lightly tapped. Remove from pan. Cool on wire rack. Makes 1 loaf (16 servings).

Spiced Wheat and Oat Bread: Prepare as above, except add ½ teaspoon ground cinnamon and ⅛ teaspoon ground ginger to the flour mixture.

Nutrition facts per serving: 84 calories, 1 g total fat (0 g saturated fat), 0 mg cholesterol, 68 mg sodium, 17 g carbohydrate, 1 g fiber, 2 g protein
Exchanges: 1 Starch

71 calories

Preparation time: 25 minutes ● **Cooking time:** 1¼ hours ● **Cooling time:** 10 minutes

boston brown bread

Boston brown bread is steamed, which makes it very moist and tender. During steaming, check the water occasionally and add more water, if necessary. The water should just simmer or boil very gently.

½ **cup whole wheat or rye flour**
¼ **cup all-purpose flour**
¼ **cup cornmeal**
½ **teaspoon baking powder**
¼ **teaspoon baking soda**
½ **cup buttermilk**
¼ **cup molasses**
1 **beaten egg white**
1 **teaspoon cooking oil**
¼ **cup raisins**
  Nonstick spray coating

1 In a medium mixing bowl stir together the whole wheat or rye flour, all-purpose flour, cornmeal, baking powder, soda, and ¼ teaspoon *salt*. In a small bowl combine buttermilk, molasses, egg white, and oil. Add buttermilk mixture to dry mixture, stirring just until combined. Stir in raisins.

2 Spray a 4- or 4½-cup ovenproof mold or bowl or a 7½×3½×2-inch loaf pan with nonstick coating. Pour batter into mold or pan.* Cut piece of foil large enough to cover mold or pan; spray with nonstick coating. Cover mold or pan tightly with foil.

3 Place mold or pan on a rack set in a Dutch oven. Pour *hot water* into Dutch oven around the mold or pan to a depth of 1 inch.

4 Bring water to boiling; reduce heat. Simmer, covered, until a wooden toothpick inserted near the center of bread comes out clean. (Allow about 1¼ hours for mold or bowl or about 1 hour for the pan.) Add *boiling water* to Dutch oven as needed.

5 Remove mold or pan from Dutch oven. Cool 10 minutes on a wire rack. Remove bread from mold or pan. Serve warm. Makes l loaf (12 servings).

*Note: To bake the bread instead of steaming it, do not cover mold or pan with foil. Bake bread in a 350° oven for 45 to 50 minutes or until wooden toothpick inserted near center comes out clean.

Nutrition facts per serving: 71 calories, 1 g total fat (0 g saturated fat), 0 mg cholesterol, 103 mg sodium, 15 g carbohydrate, 1 g fiber, 2 g protein
Exchanges: 1 Starch

89 calories

Preparation time: 25 minutes ● **Rising/Resting time:** 1 hour 40 minutes ● **Baking:** 30 minutes

cornmeal and wheat germ braids

Spread slices of this bread with herbed cream cheese. Blend half of an 8-ounce tub of fat-free cream cheese with a tablespoon or two of milk. Stir in snipped fresh herb, such as dill, oregano, or basil, to taste.

3¾ to 4¼ cups all-purpose flour
2 packages active dry yeast
1¾ cups skim milk
3 tablespoons sugar
3 tablespoons cooking oil
½ teaspoon salt
¾ cup cornmeal
½ cup toasted wheat germ
Nonstick spray coating

1 In a large mixing bowl combine *2 cups* of the flour and the yeast. Set aside.

2 Heat milk, sugar, oil, and salt just until warm (120° to 130°). Add milk mixture to dry mixture. Beat with an electric mixer on low speed for 30 seconds, scraping side of bowl constantly. Beat on high speed for 3 minutes. Using a wooden spoon, stir in cornmeal and wheat germ. Stir in as much of the remaining flour as you can.

3 Turn dough out onto a lightly floured surface. Knead in enough of the remaining flour to make a moderately stiff dough that is smooth and elastic (6 to 8 minutes total). Shape into a ball. Spray a large bowl with nonstick coating. Place dough in bowl; turn once. Cover; let rise in a warm place until double in size (about 1 hour). Punch down; divide into 6 portions. Cover; let rest for 10 minutes. Roll each portion into a 10-inch-long rope.

4 For each loaf, braid 3 ropes together and tuck ends under. Spray two 8×4×2-inch loaf pans with nonstick coating. Place braids in prepared pans. Cover; let rise until nearly double in size (about 30 minutes). Bake in a 375° oven about 30 minutes or until bread sounds hollow when lightly tapped (if necessary, cover loosely with foil the last 5 minutes of baking to prevent overbrowning). Remove from pans. Cool on racks. Makes 2 braids (32 servings).

Nutrition facts per serving: 89 calories, 2 g total fat (0 g saturated fat), 0 mg cholesterol, 41 mg sodium, 16 g carbohydrate, 1 g fiber, 3 g protein
Exchanges: 1 Starch

128 calories

Preparation time: 20 minutes ● **Baking time:** 45 minutes ● **Cooling time:** 1 hour

banana bread

The secret to a great-tasting banana bread is to use fully ripe bananas. Let bananas ripen at room temperature until the fruit is soft and the skins are well flecked with brown.

1½ **cups all-purpose flour**
1¼ **teaspoons baking powder**
 ½ **teaspoon baking soda**
 ½ **teaspoon ground cinnamon**
 ⅛ **teaspoon salt**
 2 **slightly beaten egg whites**
 1 **cup mashed banana**
 ¾ **cup sugar**
 ¼ **cup cooking oil**
   Nonstick spray coating

1 In a medium mixing bowl stir together the flour, baking powder, baking soda, cinnamon, and salt. Set aside.

2 In a large mixing bowl stir together the egg whites, banana, sugar, and oil. Add dry mixture to banana mixture, stirring just until moistened.

3 Spray an 8×4×2-inch loaf pan with nonstick coating. Spread batter in prepared pan. Bake in a 350° oven for 45 to 50 minutes or until a wooden toothpick inserted near the center comes out clean.

4 Cool bread in the pan on wire rack for 10 minutes. Remove from pan; cool completely on rack. Wrap bread in foil or plastic wrap; store overnight. Makes 1 loaf (16 servings).

Nutrition facts per serving: 128 calories, 4 g total fat (1 g saturated fat), 0 mg cholesterol, 92 mg sodium, 23 g carbohydrate, 1 g fiber, 2 g protein
Exchanges: 1 Starch, ½ Fruit, ½ Fat

100 calories

Preparation time: 20 minutes ● **Baking time:** 40 minutes ● **Cooling time:** 1 hour

apple-spice loaf

Some foods are better when served a day after they're made. This bread is one of those foods. Before serving, wrap the bread and store it at least overnight to ensure optimal moistness.

1½ **cups all-purpose flour**
½ **teaspoon baking soda**
½ **teaspoon ground cinnamon**
¼ **teaspoon baking powder**
¼ **teaspoon ground nutmeg**
2 **slightly beaten egg whites**
¾ **cup packed brown sugar**
¾ **cup finely shredded peeled apple**
3 **tablespoons cooking oil**
½ **teaspoon finely shredded orange peel**
   Nonstick spray coating
   Fat-free cream cheese (optional)

1 In a small mixing bowl stir together the flour, baking soda, cinnamon, baking powder, and nutmeg. Set aside.

2 In a large mixing bowl stir together the egg whites, brown sugar, apple, oil, and orange peel. Add the dry mixture to apple mixture, stirring just until moistened.

3 Spray an 8×4×2-inch loaf pan with nonstick coating. Spread batter in prepared pan.

4 Bake in a 350° oven for 40 to 45 minutes or until a wooden toothpick inserted in center comes out clean. Cool bread in pan on a wire rack for 10 minutes. Remove from pan; cool completely on the wire rack. Wrap the bread in foil or plastic wrap and store overnight. If desired, serve with cream cheese. Makes 1 loaf (16 servings).

Nutrition facts per serving: 100 calories, 3 g total fat (0 g saturated fat), 0 mg cholesterol, 55 mg sodium, 18 g carbohydrate, 0 g fiber, 2 g protein
Exchanges: 1 Starch, ½ Fat

61 calories

Preparation time: 30 minutes ● **Rising time:** 40 minutes ● **Baking time:** 20 minutes

easy apricot bread

Frozen bread dough and a simple filling of low-calorie fruit spread and fresh fruit are all you need to make this impressive loaf. Varying the filling is as simple as changing the variety of spread and fruit.

Nonstick spray coating
1 16-ounce loaf frozen white or whole wheat bread dough, thawed (see note, page 431)
½ **cup low-calorie apricot, strawberry, or raspberry spread**
½ **cup chopped apricots; chopped, peeled peaches; blueberries; or raspberries**
1 recipe Powdered Sugar Icing

1 Spray 2 baking sheets with nonstick coating. Turn the dough out onto a lightly floured surface. Divide dough in half. Roll each half of the dough into a 12×7-inch rectangle. Carefully transfer each rectangle to a prepared baking sheet.

2 Cut up any large pieces of fruit in the fruit spread. For each loaf, spoon ¼ cup of the fruit spread down the center third of the dough rectangle to within 1 inch of the ends. Sprinkle ¼ cup of the fresh fruit over the spread. On the long sides, make 2-inch-long cuts from the edges toward the center at 1-inch intervals. Starting at 1 end, alternately fold opposite strips of dough, at an angle, across fruit filling. Slightly press the ends together in the center to seal. Cover and let rise until nearly double in size (about 40 minutes).

3 Bake in a 350° oven about 20 minutes or until golden brown. Remove from baking sheets; cool slightly on a wire rack. Drizzle with Powdered Sugar Icing. Serve warm. Makes 2 loaves (24 servings).

Powdered Sugar Icing: In a small bowl stir together ½ cup sifted *powdered sugar,* 1 teaspoon *lemon juice,* and 1 to 2 teaspoons *skim milk.* Stir in enough additional *skim milk,* 1 teaspoon at a time, to make of drizzling consistency.

Nutrition facts per serving: 61 calories, 0 g total fat, 0 mg cholesterol, 5 mg sodium, 13 g carbohydrate, 0 g fiber, 1 g protein
Exchanges: 1 Starch

174 calories

Preparation time: 15 minutes ● **Baking time:** 12 minutes

scones with currants

When baking, be sure to use a margarine or stick spread that contains at least 60-percent vegetable oil.
Do not use an extra-light spread that contains less oil.

2½ **cups all-purpose flour**
¼ **cup sugar**
2 **teaspoons baking powder**
⅛ **teaspoon ground nutmeg**
2 **tablespoons margarine or butter, chilled**
⅓ **cup dried currants or raisins**
⅔ **cup skim milk**
1 **beaten egg**
1 **egg white**
2 **teaspoons skim milk**
1 **recipe Strawberry Cream Cheese (optional)**

1 Spray a baking sheet with *nonstick coating*. In a bowl stir together flour, sugar, baking powder, and nutmeg. With a pastry blender, cut in margarine or butter until mixture resembles coarse crumbs. Stir in currants. Make well in center of dry mixture.

2 In a mixing bowl stir together ⅔ cup milk, egg, and egg white. Add milk mixture all at once to dry mixture. Using a fork, stir just until moistened. Turn dough out onto a lightly floured surface.

Knead for 10 to 12 strokes or until smooth. Pat into a 9-inch circle; cut into 10 wedges. Place wedges on prepared baking sheet. Brush with the 2 teaspoons milk. Bake in a 450° oven about 12 minutes or until light golden brown. Serve warm. If desired, serve with Strawberry Cream Cheese. Makes 10 scones.

Nutrition facts per scone: 174 calories, 3 g total fat (1 g saturated fat), 22 mg cholesterol, 121 mg sodium, 32 g carbohydrate, 1 g fiber, 5 g protein
Exchanges: 2 Starch

Strawberry Cream Cheese: In a food processor bowl or blender container combine half of an 8-ounce tub fat-free cream cheese and 3 tablespoons low-calorie strawberry spread. Cover; process or blend until smooth. Makes about ½ cup.

Nutrition facts per tablespoon: 19 calories, 0 g total fat, 2 mg cholesterol, 6 mg sodium, 3 g carbohydrate, 0 g fiber, 2 g protein
Exchanges: Free Food

118 calories

Preparation time: 15 minutes ● **Baking time:** 18 minutes

apple and oat bran muffins

Enjoy these moist, wholesome muffins for breakfast any day of the week. The batter keeps in the refrigerator for up to three days. Bake just the number you want at a time.

1¼ cups whole wheat flour
1 cup oat bran or wheat bran
⅓ cup packed brown sugar
2½ teaspoons baking powder
¼ teaspoon baking soda
¼ teaspoon salt
¼ teaspoon ground nutmeg
¼ teaspoon ground cinnamon
1 cup buttermilk or sour milk*
2 egg whites
2 tablespoons cooking oil
¾ cup shredded peeled apple
Nonstick spray coating

1 In a medium bowl stir together whole wheat flour, oat or wheat bran, brown sugar, baking powder, baking soda, salt, nutmeg, and cinnamon. Set aside.

2 In a small bowl combine buttermilk or sour milk, egg whites, and oil. Add buttermilk mixture to dry mixture, stirring just until moistened. Stir in shredded apple. If desired, tightly cover and store batter in the refrigerator for up to 3 days.

3 To bake, spray twelve 2½-inch muffin cups with nonstick coating. Spoon about ¼ cup batter into each muffin cup. Bake in a 400° oven for 18 to 20 minutes or until a wooden toothpick inserted near the center comes out clean. Serve warm. Makes 12 muffins.

*Note: To sour milk, place 1 tablespoon lemon juice or vinegar in a glass measuring cup. Add enough milk to make 1 cup total liquid; stir. Let the mixture stand for 5 minutes before using.

Nutrition facts per muffin: 118 calories, 3 g total fat (1 g saturated fat), 1 mg cholesterol, 179 mg sodium, 22 g carbohydrate, 3 g fiber, 4 g protein
Exchanges: 1½ Starch

35 calories

Preparation time: 15 minutes ● **Baking time:** 17 minutes

blueberry gems

Muffin batter should be lumpy. When adding the liquid ingredients to the dry ingredients, stir just until the dry ingredients are moistened. Overmixing will cause the baked muffins to be tough.

Nonstick spray coating
1½ **cups all-purpose flour**
¼ **cup sugar**
1½ **teaspoons baking powder**
¼ **teaspoon salt**
2 **egg whites**
⅔ **cup orange juice**
2 **tablespoons cooking oil**
1 **teaspoon vanilla**
1 **cup fresh or frozen blueberries**

1 Spray thirty-six 1¾-inch muffin cups with nonstick spray coating. In a medium mixing bowl stir together the flour, sugar, baking powder, and salt. Set aside.

2 In a small mixing bowl beat together the egg whites, orange juice, oil, and vanilla. Add egg white mixture to dry mixture, stirring just until moistened. Fold in blueberries. Spoon into prepared muffin cups, filling each about ½ full.

3 Bake in a 400° oven about 17 minutes or until golden brown. Remove from pan; cool slightly on wire rack. Serve warm. Makes 36 muffins.

Nutrition facts per muffin: 35 calories, 1 g total fat (0 g saturated fat), 0 mg cholesterol, 33 mg sodium, 6 g carbohydrate, 0 g fiber, 1 g protein
Exchanges: ½ Starch

134 calories

Preparation time: 12 minutes ● **Baking time:** 15 minutes

gingerbread cupcakes

Enjoy these crackly-topped cupcakes with a glass of skim milk or a cup of tea.
They're sweet enough to satisfy your craving for dessert.

1 **cup all-purpose flour**
½ **teaspoon baking powder**
½ **teaspoon ground ginger**
½ **teaspoon ground cinnamon**
¼ **teaspoon baking soda**
Dash salt
1 **slightly beaten egg white**
⅓ **cup molasses**
⅓ **cup water**
3 **tablespoons cooking oil**

1 Line eight 2½-inch muffin cups with paper bake cups. In a medium mixing bowl stir together the flour, baking powder, ginger, cinnamon, soda, and salt. Set aside.

2 In a small mixing bowl stir together the egg white, molasses, water, and oil. Add molasses mixture to dry mixture, stirring just until moistened. Spoon mixture evenly into prepared muffin cups.

3 Bake in a 350° oven for 15 to 20 minutes or until cupcakes spring back when pressed lightly in center. Remove from pan. Serve warm, or cool on a wire rack. Makes 8 cupcakes.

Nutrition facts per cupcake: 134 calories, 5 g total fat (1 g saturated fat), 0 mg cholesterol, 88 mg sodium, 20 g carbohydrate, 0 g fiber, 2 g protein
Exchanges: 1 Starch, 1 Fat

140 calories

Preparation time: 20 minutes ● **Rising time:** 15 minutes ● **Baking time:** 20 minutes

peach butter sweet rolls

Frozen sweet roll dough make these peach butter- or apple butter-filled rolls more convenient to make. Serve them along with fresh fruit for a satisfying weekend brunch.

   Nonstick spray coating
1 **16-ounce loaf frozen sweet roll dough, thawed***
⅓ **cup peach butter or apple butter**
2 **tablespoons dried currants or raisins**
⅓ **cup sifted powdered sugar**
½ **teaspoon finely shredded orange peel**
1 **to 2 teaspoons orange juice or apple juice**

1 Spray twelve 2½-inch muffin cups with nonstick coating. Set aside.

2 On a lightly floured surface roll thawed dough to a 12×8-inch rectangle. Spread peach or apple butter evenly over dough. Sprinkle with currants or raisins. Roll up, jelly-roll style, starting from a long side. Pinch seam to seal. Slice roll into 12 equal pieces. Place pieces, cut sides down, in prepared muffin cups. Cover and let rise in a warm place for 15 minutes.

3 Bake rolls in a 350° oven about 20 minutes or until golden brown. Remove from pan. Place on a wire rack.

4 For icing, in a small bowl stir together the powdered sugar, orange peel, and enough of the orange or apple juice to make drizzling consistency. Drizzle icing over rolls. Serve warm. Makes 12 rolls.

***Note:** To quick-thaw frozen bread dough in your microwave oven, remove from wrapper and place dough in a microwave-safe bowl. Cover; cook on 10% power (low) for 15 to 17 minutes or until thawed, rotating dough frequently.

Nutrition facts per roll: 140 calories, 3 g total fat (1 g saturated fat), 22 mg cholesterol, 68 mg sodium, 26 g carbohydrate, 1 g fiber, 3 g protein
Exchanges: 1½ Starch, ½ Fat

Dessert

chapter index

202 calories

Preparation time: 15 minutes ● **Baking time:** 20 minutes

cherry-peach cobbler

*We cut the calories and fat by using fat-free yogurt to tenderize the biscuit-like
topping on this traditional homespun cobbler.*

1 cup all-purpose flour
2 tablespoons sugar
1½ teaspoons baking powder
¼ teaspoon ground nutmeg
2 tablespoons butter or margarine
½ cup sugar
4 teaspoons cornstarch
3 cups fresh or frozen unsweetened sliced,
**   peeled peaches**
2 cups fresh or frozen unsweetened pitted
**   tart red cherries**
⅓ cup plain fat-free yogurt
¼ cup refrigerated or frozen egg product,
**   thawed**
**   Ground nutmeg (optional)**

1 For topping, in a mixing bowl stir together the
flour, the 2 tablespoons sugar, the baking powder,
and the ¼ teaspoon nutmeg. Using a pastry blender,
cut in the butter or margarine until mixture
resembles coarse crumbs. Set aside.

2 For filling, in a large saucepan stir together the
½ cup sugar and the cornstarch. Stir in ⅓ cup *water.*
Add the peach slices and cherries. Cook and stir
until thickened and bubbly. Keep filling hot while
finishing topping.

3 To finish topping, stir together the yogurt and
egg product. Add yogurt mixture to flour mixture,
stirring just to moisten.

4 Transfer filling to a 2-quart square baking dish.
Using a spoon, immediately drop topping into
8 mounds on top of hot filling. Bake in a 400° oven
about 20 minutes or until a wooden toothpick
inserted into topping comes out clean. Serve warm.
If desired, sprinkle with additional ground nutmeg.
Makes 8 servings.

Nutrition facts per serving: 202 calories, 3 g total fat
(2 g saturated fat), 8 mg cholesterol, 120 mg sodium,
41 g carbohydrate, 2 g fiber, 4 g protein
Exchanges: 1 Starch, 2 Fruit

138 calories

Preparation time: 12 minutes ● **Baking time:** 15 minutes

gingered peach and pear crisp

You get a double dose of ginger with each bite of this luscious dessert. Grated gingerroot flavors the fruit filling, and gingersnaps, combined with rolled oats, form the crumb topping.

1 **16-ounce can peach slices (juice-packed), drained**
1 **16-ounce can pear halves (juice-packed), drained and cut up**
1 **teaspoon grated fresh gingerroot**
½ **cup finely crushed gingersnaps**
½ **cup quick-cooking rolled oats**
2 **tablespoons brown sugar**

1 In an 8-inch quiche dish or 8×1½-inch round baking pan place the peaches, pears, and gingerroot. Toss to mix.

2 In a small mixing bowl stir together the gingersnaps, oats, and brown sugar. Sprinkle evenly over fruit. Bake in a 425° oven for 15 to 20 minutes or until heated through. Makes 6 servings.

Nutrition facts per serving: 138 calories, 1 g total fat (1 g saturated fat), 0 mg cholesterol, 48 mg sodium, 32 g carbohydrate, 2 g fiber, 2 g protein
Exchanges: ½ Starch, 1½ Fruit

93 calories

Preparation time: 10 minutes ● **Cooking time:** 15 minutes

sweet and spicy peaches

Frozen peaches let you enjoy this dessert year-round. Top with yogurt as suggested, or spoon over a scoop of light ice cream.

2 tablespoons brown sugar
1 tablespoon lime or lemon juice
½ teaspoon vanilla
¼ teaspoon ground allspice
1 pound peaches, peeled, pitted, and sliced (3 cups) or 3 cups frozen unsweetened peach slices
¼ cup vanilla low-fat yogurt or fat-free dairy sour cream
Lime peel strips (optional)

1 In a medium saucepan combine the brown sugar, lime or lemon juice, vanilla, and allspice. Stir in the peaches. Bring to boiling; reduce heat. Simmer, covered, about 10 minutes or until peaches are tender and hot. Serve warm topped with the yogurt. If desired, garnish with lime peel strips. Makes 4 servings.

Microwave Directions: In a 1-quart microwave-safe casserole combine the brown sugar, lime or lemon juice, vanilla, and allspice. Stir in the peaches.

Cover and microwave on 100% power (high) for 2 to 5 minutes (4 to 7 minutes if using frozen peaches) or until the peaches are tender and heated through, stirring once. Serve warm topped with the yogurt. If desired, garnish with lime peel.

Nutrition facts per serving: 93 calories, 0 g total fat, 1 mg cholesterol, 11 mg sodium, 23 g carbohydrate, 2 g fiber, 2 g protein
Exchanges: 1½ Fruit

147 calories

Preparation time: 35 minutes ● **Baking time:** 10 minutes ● **Chilling time:** 2 to 3 hours

nectarine tart

*A calorie-trimmed pastry, a fat-free cream cheese filling, and juicy nectarines create
a luscious dessert that will delight nondieters as well as dieters.*

1 cup all-purpose flour
¼ teaspoon salt
¼ cup margarine or butter
2 to 4 tablespoons cold water
**1 8-ounce package fat-free cream cheese,
    softened**
¼ cup sugar
1 teaspoon vanilla
**4 or 5 nectarines or peeled peaches, pitted
    and sliced, or one 16-ounce package
    frozen unsweetened peach slices, thawed
    and drained**
½ cup fresh blueberries
½ cup reduced-calorie apricot spread

1 For pastry, in a bowl combine flour and salt.
Using a pastry blender, cut in margarine or butter
until pieces are the size of small peas. Sprinkle
1 tablespoon of the cold water over a portion of the
mixture. Toss with a fork. Push to side of bowl.
Repeat until mixture is moistened. Form into a ball.

2 On a lightly floured surface roll pastry into a
12-inch circle. Ease into a 10½-inch tart pan with
removable bottom. Do not stretch. Press pastry
about ½ inch up the sides of pan. Prick bottom well
with tines of a fork. Bake in a 450° oven for 10 to
12 minutes or until golden. Cool on wire rack.

3 Meanwhile, in a small mixing bowl combine
the cream cheese, sugar, and vanilla; beat with an
electric mixer until smooth. Spread over cooled
crust. Arrange nectarine or peach slices over cheese
layer. (If using frozen peach slices, cut slices in half
lengthwise as needed.) Sprinkle with blueberries.

4 In a small saucepan heat apricot spread until
melted; cut up any large pieces. Spoon over fruit.
Refrigerate for at least 2 hours or up to 3 hours.
Makes 12 servings.

Nutrition facts per serving: 147 calories, 4 g total fat
(1 g saturated fat), 3 mg cholesterol, 101 mg sodium,
24 g carbohydrate, 1 g fiber, 4 g protein
Exchanges: ½ Starch, 1 Fruit, 1 Fat

159 calories

Preparation time: 40 minutes ● **Chilling time:** 4 to 24 hours

poached pears with raspberry sauce

The word elegant sums up this pear dessert. The contrast of the crimson-colored sauce against the ivory flesh of the pear is striking, and the flavor combination is superb.

2 **cups frozen lightly sweetened red raspberries, thawed**
⅓ **cup dry white wine or white grape juice**
4 **teaspoons sugar**
4 **medium pears, cored and peeled***
Lemon juice
3 **cups water**

1 For sauce, place berries in a food processor bowl or blender container. Cover and process or blend until smooth. Press berries through a sieve; discard seeds.

2 Place berries in a small saucepan; stir in wine or juice and sugar. Bring to boiling; reduce heat. Simmer, uncovered, for 15 to 20 minutes or until reduced to about ¾ cup, stirring occasionally. Refrigerate for at least 2 hours or up to 24 hours.

3 Meanwhile, cut a thin slice off the bottom of each pear so it stands upright; brush pears with lemon juice. In a large saucepan bring the water to boiling. Place pears in the boiling water on their sides. (If necessary, add additional water to cover pears. This prevents the pears from turning brown.) Return to boiling; reduce heat. Simmer, covered, for 6 to 10 minutes or until tender. Transfer pears and cooking liquid to bowl. Refrigerate, covered, for at least 4 hours or up to 24 hours.

4 To serve, spoon most of the raspberry sauce onto 4 dessert plates. Remove pears from cooking liquid; place upright in sauce. Spoon remaining sauce over pears. Makes 4 servings.

*Note: Wash pears; pat dry with paper towels. Using an apple corer, core the pears from the bottom, leaving the stems attached. Peel pears.

Nutrition facts per serving: 159 calories, 1 g total fat (0 g saturated fat), 0 mg cholesterol, 1 mg sodium, 37 g carbohydrate, 7 g fiber, 1 g protein
Exchanges: 2½ Fruit

157 calories

Preparation time: 40 minutes ● **Baking time:** 12 minutes ● **Cooling time:** 1 hour

fruit tart

Top this tart with any fruit combo you like. Try sliced, peeled peaches; sliced nectarines; sliced plums; blueberries; raspberries; cut-up pineapple; and/or sliced bananas.

⅓ **cup whole wheat flour**

⅓ **cup all-purpose flour**

1 **tablespoon sugar**

3 **tablespoons margarine or butter**

4 to 5 **teaspoons ice water**

2 **teaspoons sugar**

1 **teaspoon cornstarch**

¼ **teaspoon ground ginger**

½ **cup orange juice**

1 **kiwifruit, peeled and sliced**

½ **of a papaya, peeled, seeded, and thinly sliced**

1 **cup fresh berries, such as thinly sliced strawberries, blueberries, and/or raspberries**

1 For crust, combine the whole wheat flour, all-purpose flour, and the 1 tablespoon sugar. Using a pastry blender, cut in margarine or butter until mixture resembles coarse crumbs. Sprinkle with 4 teaspoons ice water; toss until crumbly, sprinkling with the remaining ice water if necessary. Form dough into a ball. Press dough into a circle on waxed paper; cover with another sheet of waxed paper. Roll into a 10-inch circle. Remove top sheet of waxed paper; invert dough onto an ungreased baking sheet. Remove remaining waxed paper. Crimp crust edge. Prick crust with a fork.

2 Bake crust in a 400° oven for 12 to 15 minutes or until lightly browned. Cool.

3 Meanwhile, for glaze, in a small saucepan combine the 2 teaspoons sugar, the cornstarch, and ginger. Stir in the orange juice. Cook and stir until thickened and bubbly. Cook and stir for 2 minutes more. Remove from heat. Cool.

4 Place crust on a serving plate. Arrange fruit on crust. Spoon glaze over fruit. Serve immediately or cover and refrigerate for up to 1 hour. Serves 6.

Nutrition facts per serving: 157 calories, 6 g total fat (1 g saturated fat), 0 mg cholesterol, 71 mg sodium, 24 g carbohydrate, 3 g fiber, 2 g protein
Exchanges: ½ Starch, 1 Fruit, 1 Fat

75 calories

Preparation time: 10 minutes

fresh fruit with creamy sauce

*Fresh fruit desserts can satisfy your sweet tooth yet supply important vitamins.
The best part—they're generally low in calories.*

½ **cup vanilla low-fat yogurt**
¼ **cup unsweetened applesauce**
1 **teaspoon honey**
1 **cup sliced nectarines; sliced, peeled peaches; orange sections; or sliced strawberries**
1 **cup sliced apple or pear**
1 **small banana, sliced**
½ **cup seedless grapes**
Ground cinnamon or ground nutmeg

1 For sauce, stir together the yogurt, applesauce, and honey.

2 In a medium bowl stir together the nectarines, peaches, oranges, or strawberries, the apple or pear, the banana, and grapes. Divide the fruit mixture among 6 dessert dishes. Spoon some of the sauce over each serving. Sprinkle with cinnamon or nutmeg. Makes 6 servings.

Nutrition facts per serving: 75 calories, 1 g total fat (0 g saturated fat), 1 mg cholesterol, 12 mg sodium, 17 g carbohydrate, 1 g fiber, 1 g protein
Exchanges: 1 Fruit

68 calories

Preparation time: 15 minutes ● **Chilling time:** 1 to 4 hours

spicy fruit cup

Use a sharp knife to remove the peels from the oranges, taking care to remove all of the bitter-tasting white membrane. Cut up the oranges over a bowl to catch any juice.

1 8-ounce can pineapple chunks (juice-packed), undrained
½ cup orange juice
2 tablespoons dry white wine (optional)
⅛ teaspoon ground cinnamon
Dash ground nutmeg
2 medium oranges, peeled and sectioned
1 medium pear, cored and sliced
1 cup fresh strawberries, halved

1 In a mixing bowl combine the undrained pineapple, orange juice, wine (if desired), cinnamon, and nutmeg. Carefully stir in the oranges, pear, and strawberries. Cover and refrigerate for at least 1 hour or up to 4 hours. Makes 6 servings.

Nutrition facts per serving: 68 calories, 0 g total fat, 0 mg cholesterol, 1 mg sodium, 17 g carbohydrate, 2 g fiber, 1 g protein
Exchanges: 1 Fruit

163 calories

Preparation time: 10 minutes

rum-sauced bananas

Shop for the best nutritional bargain when selecting low-fat or light ice cream. Compare the calorie content of several brands and choose the one that's lowest in calories and fat.

¼ **cup apple juice**
4 **teaspoons brown sugar**
1 **teaspoon margarine or butter**
   Dash ground nutmeg
2 **large bananas, sliced (about 1¾ cups)**
1 **tablespoon rum**
1 **cup vanilla or coffee low-fat or light ice cream or frozen yogurt**

1 In a medium saucepan combine the apple juice, brown sugar, margarine or butter, and nutmeg. Heat just to boiling.

2 Add sliced bananas; toss to coat. Heat through. Stir in the rum.

3 Serve banana mixture over the ice cream. Makes 4 servings.

Microwave Directions: In a 1-quart microwave-safe bowl combine the apple juice, brown sugar, margarine or butter, and nutmeg. Microwave, uncovered, on 100% power (high) for 1 minute.

Add the sliced bananas; toss to coat. Microwave on 100% power (high) for 1½ to 2 minutes or until the bananas are heated through; stir in the rum. Serve over the ice cream.

Nutrition facts per serving: 163 calories, 3 g total fat (1 g saturated fat), 5 mg cholesterol, 41 mg sodium, 33 g carbohydrate, 2 g fiber, 2 g protein
Exchanges: 1 Starch, 1 Fruit, ½ Fat

85 calories

Preparation time: 20 minutes ● **Cooling time:** 30 minutes ● **Chilling time:** 2 to 4 hours

saucy rhubarb and strawberries

*Eat as is or spoon the fruit sauce over light ice cream or slices of angel food cake,
topped with a light or fat-free whipped dessert topping.*

¼ **cup sugar**
¼ **cup orange juice**
2 **cups fresh rhubarb cut into ½-inch-thick
   slices or frozen sliced rhubarb**
1 **tablespoon cold water**
2 **teaspoons cornstarch**
1 **cup sliced fresh strawberries
   Fresh mint (optional)**

1 In a medium saucepan combine the sugar and orange juice. Bring to boiling; stir in the fresh or frozen rhubarb. Return to boiling; reduce heat. Simmer, covered, for 5 to 7 minutes more or until rhubarb is nearly tender. Drain the rhubarb, reserving syrup. Set drained rhubarb aside.

2 If necessary, add water to reserved syrup to measure ⅔ cup liquid. Return syrup to saucepan. Stir together the cold water and cornstarch; stir into syrup. Cook and stir until thickened and bubbly. Cook and stir for 2 minutes more. Remove saucepan from the heat.

3 Gently stir in rhubarb and strawberries. Cool at room temperature for 30 minutes. Cover and refrigerate for at least 2 hours or up to 4 hours. If desired, garnish with fresh mint. Makes 4 servings.

Nutrition facts per serving: 85 calories, 0 g total fat, 0 mg cholesterol, 3 mg sodium, 21 g carbohydrate, 2 g fiber, 1 g protein
Exchanges: 1½ Fruit

57 calories

Preparation time: 10 minutes

sweet-topped raspberries

Yogurt lends a livelier flavor to frozen dessert topping by adding just a slight tang. Top other desserts with this slimming combination instead of fat-laden whipped cream.

½ **teaspoon finely shredded orange peel**
2 **tablespoons orange juice**
2 **cups fresh raspberries, blueberries, or sliced strawberries**
½ **cup thawed frozen light or fat-free whipped dessert topping**
¼ **cup vanilla low-fat yogurt**
 Finely shredded orange peel (optional)

1 In a medium bowl stir together the ½ teaspoon orange peel and the orange juice. Add the berries; toss to coat.

2 For topping, in a small bowl stir together the dessert topping and yogurt.

3 Divide berry mixture among 4 dessert dishes. Spoon some of the topping over each serving. If desired, sprinkle with additional finely shredded orange peel. Serve immediately. Makes 4 servings.

Nutrition facts per serving: 57 calories, 1 g total fat (1 g saturated fat), 1 mg cholesterol, 12 mg sodium, 11 g carbohydrate, 3 g fiber, 1 g protein
Exchanges: 1 Fruit

89 calories

Preparation time: 30 minutes ● **Chilling time:** 5 hours

lemon dessert with raspberries

This tart dessert combines cubes of angel food cake with lemon-spiked gelatin. The cool smoothness of the lemony gelatin is a perfect contrast to the light texture of the angel food cake.

Nonstick spray coating
1 **4-serving-size package sugar-free lemon-flavored gelatin**
½ **cup boiling water**
1 **12-ounce can evaporated skim milk**
½ **of a 6-ounce can (⅓ cup) frozen lemonade concentrate, thawed**
2 **cups cubed angel food cake**
2 **cups fresh raspberries**
1 **tablespoon sugar**

1 Spray the bottom of an 8-inch springform pan with nonstick coating. Set aside.

2 In a large bowl dissolve the lemon gelatin in the boiling water. Stir in the evaporated skim milk and thawed lemonade concentrate. Cover and refrigerate until mixture mounds when spooned (1 to 1½ hours), stirring occasionally.

3 Beat the gelatin mixture with an electric mixer on medium to high speed for 5 to 6 minutes or until mixture is fluffy.

4 Arrange angel food cake cubes in the bottom of the springform pan. Pour gelatin mixture over cake cubes. Cover and refrigerate for at least 4 hours or until firm.

5 Meanwhile, in a small bowl stir together the raspberries and sugar. Cover and refrigerate for at least 2 hours.

6 To serve, remove sides of pan. Cut dessert into wedges; place on dessert plates. Top each serving with raspberries. Makes 12 servings.

Nutrition facts per serving: 89 calories, 0 g total fat, 1 mg cholesterol, 107 mg sodium, 18 g carbohydrate, 1 g fiber, 4 g protein
Exchanges: 1 Starch

83 calories

Preparation time: 25 minutes ● **Chilling time:** 1 to 24 hours

strawberries with custard sauce

*Crystallized ginger, sometimes called candied ginger, adds a spiciness to the reduced-calorie custard sauce.
Look for crystallized ginger in the spice section of the supermarket or at specialty food stores.*

⅓ **cup skim milk**
2 tablespoons sugar
1 tablespoon chopped crystallized ginger
1 beaten egg
⅓ **cup skim milk**
½ **teaspoon vanilla**
3 cups sliced fresh strawberries
2 tablespoons slivered almonds, toasted

1 In a blender container combine ⅓ cup milk, the sugar, and crystallized ginger. Cover and blend until mixture is smooth.

2 For custard sauce, in a heavy small saucepan combine the egg and ⅓ cup milk. Add blended mixture. Cook and stir over medium heat about 10 minutes or until mixture just coats a metal spoon. Remove saucepan from heat. Stir in vanilla.

3 Quickly cool custard sauce by placing the saucepan in a sink of ice water for 1 to 2 minutes, stirring constantly. Pour custard sauce into a bowl. Cover the surface with plastic wrap. Refrigerate for at least 1 hour or up to 24 hours.

4 Place strawberries in 6 dessert dishes. Spoon custard sauce over berries. Sprinkle with almonds. Makes 6 servings.

Nutrition facts per serving: 83 calories, 3 g total fat (0 g saturated fat), 36 mg cholesterol, 48 mg sodium, 13 g carbohydrate, 2 g fiber, 3 g protein
Exchanges: 1 Starch

111 calories

Preparation time: 12 minutes

pineapple-topped ice cream

This versatile dessert can be as flashy or as humble as you like. Ignite the rum and serve as a sensational flambé. Or, skip the rum and crown with fat-free whipped dessert topping and a maraschino cherry.

½ **teaspoon finely shredded orange peel**
¼ **cup orange juice**
2 **teaspoons cornstarch**
½ **teaspoon ground ginger**
1 **20-ounce can crushed pineapple (juice-packed), undrained**
2 **tablespoons light rum (optional)**
1½ **cups vanilla low-fat or light ice cream or frozen yogurt**

1 In a large skillet stir together the orange peel, orange juice, cornstarch, and ground ginger. Stir in the undrained pineapple. Cook and stir until slightly thickened and bubbly. Cook and stir for 2 minutes more.

2 If desired, in a small saucepan heat the rum over low heat just until warm. Using a long match, carefully ignite the rum. While it's still flaming, carefully pour rum over the pineapple mixture. When the flame dies, serve immediately over the ice cream or frozen yogurt. Makes 6 servings.

Nutrition facts per serving: 111 calories, 2 g total fat (1 g saturated fat), 5 mg cholesterol, 30 mg sodium, 24 g carbohydrate, 1 g fiber, 2 g protein
Exchanges: 1 Starch, ½ Fruit

73 calories

Preparation time: 10 minutes

bella melone

Bella melone means "beautiful melon," and the Italians do it best. The secret is in the vinegar, and not just any kind will do. Balsamic vinegar boasts a rich, mellow flavor that wakes up your taste buds.

2 cups chilled seeded watermelon balls
2 cups chilled seeded cantaloupe ovals or balls
1 to 2 teaspoons sugar
¼ cup balsamic vinegar
1 teaspoon freshly ground black pepper (optional)

1 Divide chilled watermelon and cantaloupe among 4 dessert dishes. Stir sugar into vinegar until dissolved. Drizzle some of the vinegar mixture over each serving. If desired, sprinkle with freshly ground pepper. Makes 4 servings.

Nutrition facts per serving: 73 calories, 1 g total fat (0 g saturated fat), 0 mg cholesterol, 11 mg sodium, 17 g carbohydrate, 1 g fiber, 1 g protein
Exchanges: 1 Fruit

116 calories

Preparation time: 15 minutes ● **Baking time:** 30 minutes

apricot custards

Baked custard, one of the ultimate comfort foods, is born again with the addition of tangy apricots.

**1 16-ounce can unpeeled apricot halves
       (water-packed), drained**
2 beaten eggs
1 cup skim milk
2 tablespoons sugar
½ teaspoon vanilla
**6 to 8 drops rum flavoring or almond extract
       Several dashes ground cardamom or
         ground nutmeg
       Fresh mint (optional)**

1 If desired, slice 4 apricot halves for garnish; set aside. Chop remaining apricot halves. Place chopped apricots on paper towels to drain thoroughly.

2 Place four 6-ounce custard cups or individual soufflé dishes in a shallow baking pan. Divide the chopped apricots among the custard cups or soufflé dishes.

3 In a small mixing bowl combine the eggs, milk, sugar, vanilla, and rum flavoring or almond extract. Pour the egg mixture over chopped apricots. Sprinkle with cardamom or nutmeg.

4 Place the baking pan containing the cups on oven rack. Pour *boiling water* around custard cups in baking pan to a depth of 1 inch.

5 Bake in a 325° oven for 30 to 35 minutes or until a knife inserted near the centers comes out clean. Remove custard cups from water. Serve warm. If desired, garnish with the reserved apricot slices and fresh mint. Makes 4 servings.

Nutrition facts per serving: 116 calories, 3 g total fat (1 g saturated fat), 108 mg cholesterol, 67 mg sodium, 17 g carbohydrate, 2 g fiber, 6 g protein
Exchanges: 1 Lean Meat, 1 Fruit

104 calories

Preparation time: 15 minutes ● **Baking time:** 40 minutes

pumpkin custards

Count your Thanksgiving (or daily) blessings with these petite crustless pumpkin pies. You save almost 200 calories a serving without the crust, but you don't sacrifice any flavor.

 2 **slightly beaten egg whites**
 1 **cup canned pumpkin**
 ¾ **cup evaporated skim milk**
 3 **tablespoons sugar**
 ½ **teaspoon ground cinnamon**
 ⅛ **teaspoon ground ginger**
 ⅛ **teaspoon ground allspice**
   Dash salt
   Light whipped dessert topping (optional)

1 In a medium mixing bowl combine the egg whites, pumpkin, evaporated milk, sugar, cinnamon, ginger, allspice, and salt.

2 Place four 6-ounce custard cups or ramekins in a shallow baking pan. Pour pumpkin mixture into the cups.

3 Place the baking pan containing the cups on oven rack. Pour *boiling water* around custard cups in baking pan to a depth of 1 inch.

4 Bake in a 325° oven about 40 minutes or until a knife inserted near the centers comes out clean. Remove custard cups from water. Serve custards warm or refrigerate until thoroughly chilled. If desired, garnish with whipped dessert topping. Makes 4 servings.

Nutrition facts per serving: 104 calories, 0 g total fat, 2 mg cholesterol, 120 mg sodium, 20 g carbohydrate, 2 g fiber, 6 g protein
Exchanges: 1 Starch, ½ Milk

142 calories

Preparation time: 25 minutes ● **Chilling time:** 4 to 24 hours

pumpkin cheesecake

A blend of low-fat ricotta cheese and fat-free cream cheese keeps this cheesecake within reach of dieters.

¾ **cup finely crushed graham crackers**
2 **tablespoons margarine or butter, melted**
1 **15-ounce carton low-fat ricotta cheese**
1 **8-ounce tub fat-free cream cheese**
1 **cup canned pumpkin**
½ **cup skim milk**
1 **envelope unflavored gelatin**
2 **teaspoons finely shredded orange peel (set aside)**
½ **cup orange juice**
⅓ **cup granulated sugar**
⅓ **cup packed brown sugar**
2 **teaspoons vanilla**
1 **teaspoon pumpkin pie spice**
  Light whipped dessert topping (optional)
  Pumpkin pie spice (optional)

1 For crust, in a medium mixing bowl stir together the crushed graham crackers and melted margarine or butter until crackers are moistened. Press mixture onto bottom of a 9-inch springform pan. Refrigerate while preparing the filling.

2 For filling, in a food processor bowl or blender container combine half of the ricotta cheese, half of the cream cheese, half of the pumpkin, and half of the milk. Cover and process or blend until smooth. Transfer to a large mixing bowl. Repeat with remaining ricotta, cream cheese, pumpkin, and milk.

3 In a small saucepan sprinkle the gelatin over orange juice; let stand 5 minutes. Cook and stir over low heat until gelatin is dissolved. Stir into pumpkin mixture. Stir in the orange peel, granulated sugar, brown sugar, vanilla, and the pumpkin pie spice. Pour mixture into chilled crust. Cover; refrigerate for at least 4 hours or until firm.

4 To serve, loosen crust from sides of pan; remove sides of pan. Cut into wedges. If desired, garnish with whipped topping and sprinkle with additional pumpkin pie spice. Makes 12 servings.

Nutrition facts per serving: 142 calories, 2 g total fat (0 g saturated fat), 7 mg cholesterol, 214 mg sodium, 23 g carbohydrate, 1 g fiber, 11 g protein
Exchanges: 1½ Starch, 1 Lean Meat

42 calories

Preparation time: 15 minutes ● **Freezing time:** 4 hours

coffee ice

Pair scoops of this delightful ice with Biscotti (see recipe, page 459). It's much lower in calories than ice creams (even light- or low-fat ice creams), which allows you to enjoy every bite.

¼ **cup sugar**
4 **teaspoons instant espresso coffee powder**
1½ **cups cold water**
 Whole fresh strawberries (optional)

1 In a medium bowl combine sugar and coffee powder. Add the cold water; stir until dissolved.

2 Pour mixture into a 9×5×3-inch loaf pan. Freeze about 2 hours or until firm.

3 Break frozen mixture into small chunks; place in a chilled medium mixing bowl. Beat with an electric mixer on low to medium speed until fluffy.

4 Return to pan. Freeze mixture about 2 hours or until firm.

5 To serve, scrape or scoop ice into small dessert dishes. If desired, garnish each serving with a strawberry. Makes 5 (½-cup) servings.

Nutrition facts per serving: 42 calories, 0 g total fat, 0 mg cholesterol, 3 mg sodium, 11 g carbohydrate, 0 g fiber, 0 g protein
Exchanges: ½ Starch

106 calories

Preparation time: 50 minutes ● **Chilling time:** 1 hour

mint-chocolate chip ice cream

Evaporated low-fat milk gives extra richness and creaminess to this ice milk. Use a small ice-cream scoop to make several tiny scoops for a dainty ice-cream dish. It will trick you into thinking you have a lot.

¾ **cup sugar**
1 **envelope unflavored gelatin**
1 **12-ounce can evaporated low-fat milk**
1 **egg white**
1 **egg**
2½ **cups skim milk**
1 **tablespoon white crème de menthe**
    or a few drops mint extract
2 **teaspoons vanilla**
    Several drops green food coloring
    (optional)
1½ **ounces semisweet chocolate, chopped**

1 In a large saucepan stir together the sugar and gelatin. Stir in evaporated milk. Cook and stir over medium heat until sugar and gelatin dissolve and mixture almost boils. Remove from heat.

2 In a small bowl slightly beat the egg white and egg. Stir about ½ cup of the hot gelatin mixture into the egg mixture; return all to saucepan.

3 Cook and stir over low heat for 2 minutes more. *Do not boil.*

4 Stir in the skim milk, crème de menthe or mint extract, and vanilla. Cover and refrigerate for 1 hour.

5 If mixture isn't smooth, strain mixture. If desired, stir food coloring into mixture. Stir in chopped chocolate.

6 Freeze mixture in a 4- or 5-quart ice-cream freezer according to manufacturer's directions. Makes 14 (½-cup) servings.

Nutrition facts per serving: 106 calories, 2 g total fat (0 g saturated fat), 20 mg cholesterol, 45 mg sodium, 18 g carbohydrate, 0 g fiber, 4 g protein
Exchanges: ½ Starch, ½ Milk

83 calories

Preparation time: 25 minutes ● **Freezing time:** 5 hours

watermelon sherbet

Many grocery stores sell packages of cut-up watermelon to save you some work. You'll still need to remove the seeds.

4 cups cubed seeded watermelon
½ cup sugar
1 envelope unflavored gelatin
⅓ cup cranberry juice cocktail
Thin watermelon wedges (optional)

1 Place watermelon cubes in a food processor bowl or blender container. Cover and process or blend until smooth. (There should be about 3 cups of the mixture.) Stir in the sugar.

2 In a small saucepan combine the gelatin and cranberry juice cocktail. Let stand for 5 minutes. Stir mixture over low heat until gelatin is dissolved.

3 Stir the gelatin mixture into the melon mixture. Pour into an 8×8×2-inch baking pan.

4 Cover and freeze about 2 hours or until firm.

5 Break frozen mixture into small chunks; place in a chilled mixing bowl. Beat with an electric mixer on low to medium speed until light and fluffy.

6 Return to pan. Cover and freeze about 3 hours or until firm.

7 To serve, scoop sherbet into small dessert dishes. If desired, garnish with watermelon wedges. Makes 8 (½-cup) servings.

Nutrition facts per servings: 83 calories, 0 g total fat, 0 mg cholesterol, 3 mg sodium, 20 g carbohydrate, 0 g fiber, 1 g protein
Exchanges: 1½ Fruit

107 calories

Preparation time: 50 minutes ● **Cooling time:** 2 hours

apricot sherbet

By changing the flavor of the fruit nectar, you can make apricot, peach, or papaya sherbet.
Shop for the papaya nectar at larger grocery stores or health-food stores.

⅔ **cup sugar**
 1 **envelope unflavored gelatin**
 3 **cups apricot nectar, peach nectar,**
      or papaya nectar
 1 **teaspoon finely shredded lemon peel**
 1 **tablespoon lemon juice**
 1 **cup buttermilk**
      Fresh mint (optional)

1 In a large saucepan stir together the sugar and gelatin. Stir in the nectar, lemon peel, and lemon juice. Cook and stir over medium heat until sugar and gelatin dissolve. Cool to room temperature (to avoid curdling buttermilk). Stir in buttermilk.

2 Freeze in a 4- or 5-quart ice-cream freezer according to manufacturer's directions.*

3 To serve, scoop sherbet into small dessert dishes. If desired, garnish with fresh mint. Makes about 10 (½-cup) servings.

*Note: If you don't have an ice-cream freezer, transfer mixture to a 9×9×2-inch baking pan. Cover; freeze 4 to 6 hours or until almost firm. Break mixture into small chunks; place in a chilled mixing bowl. Beat with an electric mixer on low to medium speed until smooth but not melted. Return to pan. Cover; freeze until firm.

Nutrition facts per serving: 107 calories, 0 g total fat, 1 mg cholesterol, 29 mg sodium, 26 g carbohydrate, 0 g fiber, 2 g protein

176 calories

Preparation time: 20 minutes ● **Freezing time:** 4 to 24 hours

frozen cranberry pie

To soften the ice cream, place it in a chilled bowl and stir with a wooden spoon just until it is soft enough to stir in the remaining ingredients. If the ice cream becomes too soft, the pie will be icy instead of creamy.

Nonstick spray coating
6 **chocolate wafer cookies, finely crushed (about ⅓ cup)**
1 **quart vanilla low-fat or light ice cream**
1 **cup whole-berry cranberry sauce**
1 **teaspoon finely shredded orange peel**
Sugared cranberries (optional)*

1 Spray a 9-inch pie plate with nonstick coating. Coat with the crushed cookies. Set aside.

2 In a chilled medium mixing bowl stir the ice cream with a wooden spoon just until softened. Fold in the cranberry sauce and orange peel until combined. Spoon mixture into prepared pie plate. Cover and freeze for at least 4 hours or until firm.

3 To serve, cut into wedges. If desired, garnish with sugared cranberries. Makes 8 servings.

*Note: To make sugared cranberries, roll frozen cranberries in sugar.

Nutrition facts per serving: 176 calories, 3 g total fat (1 g saturated fat), 11 mg cholesterol, 83 mg sodium, 36 g carbohydrate, 1 g fiber, 2 g protein
Exchanges: 1 Starch, 1 Fruit, ½ Fat

117 calories

Preparation time: 20 minutes ● **Cooking time:** 10 minutes

peachy cherry sauce

To remove the peel from a peach, dip the peach into boiling water for 20 seconds. Then use a paring knife to remove the skin. If the skin doesn't peel easily, return the peach to the boiling water for a few seconds.

¼ **cup low-calorie orange marmalade spread**
¼ **cup orange juice**
2 **teaspoons cornstarch**
1 **teaspoon margarine or butter**
¼ **teaspoon ground cardamom or ground cinnamon**
2 **cups sliced, peeled peaches or nectarines or frozen unsweetened peach slices**
1 **cup pitted dark sweet cherries or frozen unsweetened pitted dark sweet cherries**
½ **cup frozen yogurt or low-fat or light ice cream**

1 In a medium saucepan combine the marmalade spread, orange juice, cornstarch, margarine or butter, and cardamom or cinnamon. Cook and stir until thickened and bubbly. Stir in the peaches and cherries. Cover and cook over medium heat for 10 to 12 minutes or until fruits are just tender, stirring once. Cool slightly.

2 To serve, spoon sauce into dessert dishes. Top each serving with a small spoonful of the frozen yogurt. Makes 5 servings.

Nutrition facts per serving: 117 calories, 2 g total fat (1 g saturated fat), 2 mg cholesterol, 21 mg sodium, 24 g carbohydrate, 2 g fiber, 2 g protein
Exchanges: 1½ Fruit

136 calories

Preparation time: 30 minutes ● **Standing time:** 30 minutes

tropical fruit compote

Make a simple fruit compote extra special by garnishing with an edible flower, such as geranium, violet, pansy, or nasturtium. Use only those flowers that have not been treated with pesticides.

⅓ **cup unsweetened pineapple juice**
3 **tablespoons sugar**
1 **teaspoon finely shredded lime or lemon peel (set aside)**
3 **tablespoons lime or lemon juice**
3 **whole cloves**
3 **inches stick cinnamon, broken**
3 **cardamom pods, opened (optional)**
1 **papaya or mango, peeled, seeded, and thinly sliced**
1 **kiwifruit, peeled and sliced**
1 **carambola (star fruit), sliced**
1 **cup fresh pineapple chunks**
1 **banana, sliced**
  Lime peel strips (optional)
  Edible flowers (optional)

1 In a small saucepan stir together the pineapple juice, sugar, and lime or lemon juice. Add the cloves, cinnamon, and cardamom pods (if desired).

2 Bring to boiling, stirring until sugar dissolves; reduce heat. Simmer, covered, for 10 minutes. Remove from heat. Let stand about 10 minutes to cool slightly. Sieve to remove spices; discard spices. Stir shredded lime or lemon peel into liquid.

3 Meanwhile, in a large mixing bowl toss together the papaya or mango, kiwifruit, carambola, pineapple, and banana. Pour juice mixture over fruit; stir gently to coat. Cover and let stand about 30 minutes, stirring once or twice.

4 To serve, spoon fruit and juices into small dessert dishes. If desired, garnish with lime peel strips and edible flowers. Makes 4 servings.

Nutrition facts per serving: 136 calories, 1 g total fat (0 g saturated fat), 0 mg cholesterol, 3 mg sodium, 34 g carbohydrate, 2 g fiber, 1 g protein
Exchanges: 2 Fruit

38 calories

Preparation time: 25 minutes ● **Baking time:** 31 minutes ● **Cooling time:** 2 hours

biscotti

A specialty of coffeehouses, these twice-baked Italian cookies make a great snack. With fewer than 40 calories each, they can curb your sweet tooth without causing you pangs of guilt.

Nonstick spray coating
2 cups all-purpose flour
2 teaspoons baking powder
2 teaspoons anise seed, crushed
1 teaspoon finely shredded lemon peel
¼ cup margarine or butter
½ cup sugar
2 eggs

1 Spray a large cookie sheet with nonstick coating. Set aside.

2 In a medium mixing bowl stir together the flour, baking powder, anise seed, and lemon peel. Set aside.

3 In a small mixing bowl beat margarine or butter with an electric mixer on medium speed for 30 seconds. Add sugar; beat until combined. Add eggs; beat well. Stir in flour mixture.

4 On waxed paper shape dough into two 12-inch-long logs. Place logs on prepared cookie sheet; flatten logs slightly.

5 Bake in a 375° oven for 15 to 20 minutes or until lightly browned. Cool completely on wire racks (about 1 hour).

6 Cut each log into ½-inch-thick slices. Arrange slices, cut sides down, on the baking sheet.

7 Bake in a 325° oven for 8 minutes. Turn over. Bake 8 to 10 minutes more or until crisp and light brown. Transfer to wire rack and cool completely. Makes 48 cookies.

Nutrition facts per cookie: 38 calories, 1 g total fat (0 g saturated fat), 9 mg cholesterol, 29 mg sodium, 6 g carbohydrate, 0 g fiber, 1 g protein
Exchanges: ½ Starch

52 calories

Preparation time: 20 minutes ● **Baking time:** 7 minutes

brown sugar 'n' spice cookies

For an old-fashioned cookie in a reduced-calorie package, try these sugar-topped treats.

⅓ cup margarine or butter, softened
⅓ cup granulated sugar
⅓ cup packed brown sugar
¾ teaspoon baking powder
½ teaspoon ground cinnamon
½ teaspoon ground ginger
¼ teaspoon ground nutmeg
1 egg
1 teaspoon vanilla
1¼ cups all-purpose flour
⅓ cup whole wheat flour
1 tablespoon granulated sugar
⅛ teaspoon ground cinnamon

1 In a large mixing bowl beat margarine or butter with an electric mixer on medium to high speed for 30 seconds. Add the ⅓ cup granulated sugar, brown sugar, baking powder, the ½ teaspoon cinnamon, the ginger, and nutmeg. Beat until combined. Beat in egg and vanilla. Beat in as much of the all-purpose flour and whole wheat flour as you can. Using a wooden spoon, stir in any remaining flour.

2 In a small bowl combine the 1 tablespoon granulated sugar and the ⅛ teaspoon cinnamon. Shape dough into 1-inch balls. Place balls 2 inches apart on ungreased cookie sheet. Flatten each ball with the tines of a fork in crisscross fashion. Sprinkle cookies with the sugar-cinnamon mixture. Bake in a 350° oven for 7 to 9 minutes or until cookies are firm. Cool on cookie sheet for 1 minute. Transfer cookies to a wire rack; let cool. Makes about 36 cookies.

Nutrition facts per cookie: 52 calories, 2 g total fat (0 g saturated fat), 6 mg cholesterol, 23 mg sodium, 8 g carbohydrate, 0 g fiber, 1 g protein
Exchanges: ½ Starch

37 calories

Preparation time: 20 minutes ● **Baking time:** 20 minutes ● **Cooling/Standing time:** 1 hour

macaroons

Made from whipped egg whites, macaroons have long been a friend to dieters.
A simple chocolate drizzle updates these feather-light morsels.

Nonstick spray coating
3 egg whites
1 cup sugar
2 cups flaked coconut (about 5 ounces)
1 ounce semisweet chocolate
½ teaspoon shortening

1 Spray a large cookie sheet with nonstick coating. Set aside.

2 In a large mixing bowl beat the egg whites with an electric mixer on high speed until soft peaks form (tips curl). Gradually add the sugar, 1 tablespoon at a time, beating until stiff peaks form (tips stand straight). Fold in the coconut.

3 Drop by rounded teaspoons 2 inches apart onto the prepared cookie sheet. Bake in a 325° oven about 20 minutes or until edges are light brown. Transfer cookies to a wire rack; let cool (about 30 minutes).

4 To serve, in a small saucepan combine the chocolate and shortening; cook and stir over low heat until melted and smooth. Cool slightly. Transfer chocolate mixture to a self-sealing plastic bag; seal bag. Cut a small hole in a corner of the bag; pipe chocolate through hole over cookies. Let stand until chocolate is set (about 30 minutes). Store cookies in an airtight container. Makes about 45 cookies.

Nutrition facts per cookie: 37 calories, 1 g total fat (1 g saturated fat), 0 mg cholesterol, 4 mg sodium, 6 g carbohydrate, 0 g fiber, 0 g protein
Exchanges: ½ Starch

124 calories

Preparation time: 15 minutes ● **Baking time:** 35 minutes ● **Cooling time:** 20 minutes

bread pudding

If you like, top bowls of this homespun dessert with the ginger-scented custard sauce used in Strawberries with Custard Sauce (see recipe, page 446). The sauce adds 46 calories to each serving.

Nonstick spray coating
- 2 **eggs**
- 2 **egg whites**
- 1½ **cups skim milk**
- 2 **tablespoons honey**
- 1 **teaspoon vanilla**
- 3 **cups cubed raisin bread (4 to 5 slices)**
  Orange sections (optional)

1 Spray a 9-inch pie plate with nonstick coating. Set aside.

2 In a large mixing bowl beat together the eggs and egg whites until combined. Beat in the milk, honey, and vanilla. Stir in the bread cubes. Pour into the prepared pie plate.

3 Bake in a 325° oven for 35 to 40 minutes or until puffed and a knife inserted near the center comes out clean. Let stand at room temperature about 20 minutes to cool slightly before serving. If desired, garnish with orange sections. Makes 6 servings.

Nutrition facts per serving: 124 calories, 3 g total fat (1 g saturated fat), 72 mg cholesterol, 139 mg sodium, 18 g carbohydrate, 0 g fiber, 7 g protein
Exchanges: 1 Starch, ½ Milk

125 calories

Preparation time: 50 minutes ● **Baking time:** 40 minutes ● **Cooling time:** 3 hours

chocolate - cinnamon angel cake

A mild chocolate flavor accented with cinnamon sets this angel cake apart from others. However, it's still low in calories and fat-free. Chocolate purists can omit the cinnamon.

1½ **cups egg whites (10 to 12 large eggs)**
1½ **cups sifted powdered sugar**
 1 **cup sifted cake flour or sifted all-purpose flour**
 3 **tablespoons unsweetened cocoa powder**
 ¼ **teaspoon ground cinnamon**
1½ **teaspoons cream of tartar**
 1 **teaspoon vanilla**
 1 **cup granulated sugar**
   Chocolate-flavored syrup (optional)

1 Allow egg whites to stand at room temperature for 30 minutes.

2 Meanwhile, sift powdered sugar, flour, cocoa powder, and cinnamon together 3 times. Set aside.

3 In a large mixing bowl combine the egg whites, cream of tartar, and vanilla; beat with an electric mixer on medium speed until soft peaks form (tips curl).

4 Gradually add the granulated sugar, about 2 tablespoons at a time, beating on high speed until stiff peaks form (tips stand straight). If bowl is too full, transfer to a larger bowl.

5 Sift about one-fourth of the dry mixture over the beaten egg whites; fold in gently. Repeat, folding in the remaining dry mixture by fourths. Pour into an ungreased 10-inch tube pan. Using a narrow metal spatula or knife, gently cut through the batter to eliminate any air bubbles.

6 Bake on the lowest rack in a 350° oven for 40 to 45 minutes or until top springs back when lightly touched.

7 Immediately invert cake (leave in pan); cool completely. Loosen side of cake from pan; remove cake. If desired, serve cake slices drizzled with chocolate-flavored syrup. Makes 16 servings.

Nutrition facts per serving: 125 calories, 0 g total fat, 0 mg cholesterol, 35 mg sodium, 28 g carbohydrate, 0 g fiber, 3 g protein
Exchanges: 1½ Starch

calorie tally

A

Alfalfa sprouts, 1 cup	10
American cheese, processed, 1 ounce	106
Angel food cake, 1 piece	161
Animal crackers, 10	112
Apple juice, 8 ounces	116
Apples, 1 medium	81
Applesauce, sweetened, ½ cup	97
Applesauce, unsweetened, ½ cup	53
Apricots, 3 medium	51
Apricots, canned in light syrup, 3 halves	54
Apricots, dried, 10 halves	83
Artichoke hearts, cooked, ½ cup	37
Artichokes, 1 medium	60
Asparagus, cooked, ½ cup or 6 spears	22
Avocados, 1 medium	339

B

Bacon, Canadian-style, cooked, 2 slices	86
Bacon, cooked, 3 slices	109
Bagel, 1	163
Baked beans (canned), ½ cup	282
Bananas, 1 medium	105
Barbecue sauce, 1 tablespoon	12
Barley, cooked, 1 cup	193
Beans (dried), cooked, 1 cup	
Black	227
Garbanzo	269
Great northern	210
Kidney	225
Navy	259
Pinto	235
Beans, refried (canned), ½ cup	270
Beef, cooked, 3 ounces	
Flank steak, lean only	194
Ground beef, lean	240
Ground beef, regular	250
Pot roast, chuck, lean only	188
Rib roast, lean only	208
Round steak, lean only	162
Sirloin steak, lean only	171

Beef bouillon cubes, 1	14
Beef broth, 1 cup	16
Beer, 12 fluid ounces	
Light	99
Regular	146
Biscuits, 1	103
Blueberries, 1 cup	82
Blue cheese, 1 ounce	100
Bran raisin muffins, 1	142
Bread, 1 slice	
French	81
Italian	78
Pumpernickel	82
Raisin	70
Rye	66
White	64
Whole wheat	65
Breadsticks, 2	77
Broccoli	
Cooked, ½ cup	22
Raw, 1 cup	24
Brownie with nuts, 3×1 inches	97
Brussels sprouts, cooked, ½ cup	30
Bulgur, cooked, 1 cup	152
Butter, 1 tablespoon	108

C

Cabbage, raw, shredded, ½ cup	8
Candy, hard, 1 ounce	106
Candy corn, ¼ cup	182
Cantaloupe, 1 cup	57
Carambola (star fruit), 1 medium	42
Carrots	
Cooked, ½ cup	35
Raw, 1 medium	31
Catsup, 1 tablespoon	16
Cauliflower, cooked, ½ cup	15
Celery, raw, 1 stalk	6

Cheddar cheese, 1 ounce	
Fat-free	41
Reduced-fat	90
Regular-fat,	114
Cheesecake, ¹⁄₁₆ of pie	257
Cherries, sweet, 10	49
Chicken	
Breast, without skin, roasted, ½ breast	142
Dark meat, without skin, roasted, 3 ounces	176
Drumstick, without skin, roasted, 1	76
Light meat, without skin, roasted, 3 ounces	148
Chicken bouillon cubes, 1	9
Chicken broth, 1 cup	24
Chocolate	
Milk, 1.55 ounce bar	226
Semisweet, 1 ounce	134
Semisweet pieces, 6 ounces (1 cup)	812
Unsweetened, 1 ounce	148
Chocolate chip cookies, 1	46
Chocolate syrup, 2 tablespoons	82
Clams, cooked, 3 ounces	126
Club soda, 12 fluid ounces	0
Cocoa powder, unsweetened, 1 tablespoon	11
Coconut, flaked and sweetened, 1 tablespoon	22
Cola, 12 fluid ounces	
Low-calorie	
Regular	151
Colby cheese, 1 ounce	112
Corn, cream-style, cooked, ½ cup	110
Corn, whole kernel, cooked, ½ cup	67
Cornbread, 1 piece	198
Corn chips, 1 ounce	153
Cottage cheese, 1 cup	
Creamed	217
Dry curd	123
1% fat	164
2% fat	203
Couscous, ½ cup cooked	88
Crab, cooked, 3 ounces	82
Crab-flavored fish, 3 ounces	87
Cranberries, 1 cup	46
Cranberry juice cocktail, 6 ounces	108

Cream, half-and-half, 1 tablespoon	20
Cream, whipping, 1 tablespoon	52
Cream cheese, 1 ounce	
Fat-free	25
Reduced fat (Neufchâtel)	74
Regular	100
Cucumber, ½ cup slices	7
Cupcakes with icing	173

D-F

Danish pastries, 1 piece	161
Doughnuts, cake, 1	105
Doughnuts, yeast, 1	176
Edam cheese, 1 ounce	101
Eggplant, cooked, ½ cup	13
Eggs	
Fried, 1	91
Poached, 1	74
Raw, white, 1	17
Raw, whole, 1	75
Raw, yolk, 1	59
Scrambled, 1 egg with milk	101
Egg substitute, refrigerated or frozen, ¼ cup	25
English muffins, 1	135
Fennel, raw, 1 cup sliced	27
Feta cheese, 1 ounce	75
Fig bars, 1	53
Fish, cooked, 3 ounces	
Cod	89
Flounder/sole	99
Haddock	95
Halibut	119
Orange roughy	75
Salmon (canned)	130
Salmon (fresh)	183
Swordfish	132
Tuna (fresh)	157
Tuna, light (canned in oil), drained	169
Tuna, light (canned in water), drained	111
Fish sticks, frozen, 4×2 inches, 1	76
Flour, all-purpose, 1 cup	455
Flour, whole wheat, 1 cup	407

Frankfurters, 1	
Beef	180
Turkey	100
French toast, 1 slice	153
Fruit cocktail, canned (juice-packed), ½ cup	56

G

Gelatin, fruit-flavored, ½ cup	80
Gelatin, fruit-flavored, low-calorie, ½ cup	8
Ginger ale, 12 fluid ounces	124
Gingersnaps, 1 cookie	34
Goat cheese, soft, 1 ounce	76
Graham crackers, 2½-inch square	30
Grapefruit, ½ medium	37
Grapefruit juice, ½ cup	47
Grape juice, 8 ounces	155
Grapes, ½ cup	94
Green beans, cooked, ½ cup	22
Gruyère cheese, 1 ounce	117
Gumdrops, 10 small	135

H-L

Ham, fully cooked, lean only, 3 ounces	124
Hoisin sauce, 1 tablespoon	35
Honey, 1 tablespoon	64
Honeydew melons, 1 cup	60
Horseradish, prepared, 1 tablespoon	6
Ice cream, ½ cup	
Chocolate	143
Strawberry	127
Vanilla	132
Ice milk, vanilla, ½ cup	92
Jam, 1 tablespoon	48
Jelly, 1 tablespoon	52
Jelly beans, 10 large (1 ounce)	104
Kiwifruit, 1 medium	46
Ladyfingers, 2	79
Lamb, cooked	
Leg, lean only, 3 ounces	158
Loin chop, 1	91
Lemonade (from frozen concentrate), 8 ounces	100

Lemon-lime soda, 12 fluid ounces	149
Lemon or lime juice, 1 tablespoon	4
Lentils, cooked, 1 cup	231
Lettuce, iceberg, 1 leaf	3
Lettuce, leaf, ½ cup shredded	5
Lima beans, cooked, ½ cup	85
Lobster, cooked, 3 ounces	83

M

Macaroni, cooked, 1 cup	197
Macaroons, 2 cookies	181
Mandarin oranges, canned (juice-packed), ½ cup	46
Mangoes, 1 medium	135
Maple syrup, 1 tablespoon	52
Margarine, 1 tablespoon	100
Marshmallow cream, 1 ounce	88
Marshmallows, miniature, 1 cup	147
Marshmallows, 1 regular	23
Mayonnaise, 1 tablespoon	
Fat-free	12
Reduced-fat	50
Regular-fat	100
Milk, 8 ounces	
Skim	86
1% fat	102
2% fat	121
Whole	150
Molasses cookies, 1	137
Monterey Jack cheese, 1 ounce	106
Mozzarella cheese, part skim, 1 ounce	72
Muenster cheese, 1 ounce	104
Muffins, 1	
Blueberry	112
Bran	112
Corn	115
Mushrooms, raw, ½ cup pieces	9
Mussels, cooked, 3 ounces	147
Mustard, brown, 1 teaspoon	5
Mustard, yellow, 1 teaspoon	4

N-O

Nectarines, 1 medium	67
Noodles, 1 cup, cooked	212
Nuts, 1 ounce	
Almonds	167
Cashews	163
Hazelnuts	188
Peanuts	164
Pecans	187
Pine nuts	146
Walnuts	182
Oatmeal, regular or quick, cooked, 1 cup	145
Oatmeal cookies, 1	62
Oil, 1 tablespoon	
Cooking (corn oil)	120
Olive oil	119
Omelet, made from 1 egg	92
Onions, green, 1	4
Onions, raw, ½ cup chopped	30
Orange juice, ½ cup	56
Orange marmalade, 1 tablespoon	49
Oranges, 1 medium	65
Orange soda, 12 fluid ounces	177
Oysters, cooked, 3 ounces	117

P

Pancakes, 1	62
With 1 tablespoon reduced-calorie syrup	46
With 1 tablespoon regular syrup	57
Papayas, 1 medium,	117
Parmesan cheese, grated, 1 tablespoon	23
Parmesan cheese, 1 ounce	111
Parsnips, cooked, ½ cup	63
Peaches, canned (juice-packed), 1 cup	109
Peaches, 1 medium	37
Peanut brittle, 1 ounce	128
Peanut butter, 2 tablespoons	188
Peanut butter cookies, 1 cookie	50
Pears, canned (juice-packed) 1 cup	123
Pears, 1 medium	98
Peas, cooked, ½ cup	67

Peppers, hot chili, 1	18
Peppers, sweet, ½ cup chopped	13
Pesto, 1 ounce	155
Pickle relish, 1 tablespoon	19
Pickles, dill, 1 large	12
Pies, ⅛ of pie	
Apple	282
Blueberry	286
Cherry	308
Lemon meringue	350
Peach	301
Pecan	431
Pumpkin	241
Rhubarb	299
Pimientos, 1 tablespoon	3
Pineapple, canned (juice-packed), 1 cup	150
Pineapple, fresh, 1 cup	77
Pineapple juice, ½ cup	70
Pita bread, 1	106
Plums, 1 medium	36
Popcorn, air-popped, 3.5 cups (1 ounce)	108
Popcorn, oil-popped, 2.6 cups (1 ounce)	142
Pork, loin, cooked, 3 ounces	206
Potatoes	
Baked without skin, 1	145
Baked with skin, 1	220
Boiled without skin, 1	116
Mashed, ½ cup	111
Potato chips, 1 ounce	
Barbecue	139
Light	134
Regular	152
Pretzels, 1 ounce	108
Prunes, dried, 10	201
Pudding (regular mix prepared with low-fat milk), ½ cup	
Chocolate	150
Vanilla	141
Pumpkin, canned, ½ cup	41

R

Radishes, 10	7
Raisins, ⅔ cup	300
Raspberries, 1 cup	61
Rhubarb, 1 cup pieces	29
Rice, cooked, 1 cup	
Brown	216
White	264
Wild	166
Ricotta cheese, ½ cup	
Part skim	171
Whole	216
Rolls, 1	
Dinner	85
French	137
Hamburger	114
Hoagie	400
Hot dog	114
Whole wheat French	105
Root beer, 12 fluid ounces	152
Rye bread, 1 slice	66

S

Salad dressings (low-calorie), 1 tablespoon	
French	22
Italian	16
Mayonnaise-type	50
Thousand Island	24
Salad dressings (regular), 1 tablespoon	
Blue cheese	77
French	67
Italian	69
Mayonnaise-type	57
Thousand Island	59
Salsa, ½ cup	29
Saltine crackers, 2	26
Sauerkraut, canned, ½ cup	22
Sausage, pork, cooked, 1 link	48
Scallops, raw, 3 ounces	75
Sherbet, orange, ½ cup	132
Shortbread cookies, 1	42
Shortening, 1 tablespoon	106

Shrimp, cooked, 3 ounces	84
Soup, condensed (prepared with 2% milk), 1 cup	
Cheese	230
Cream of celery	165
Cream of chicken	191
Cream of mushroom	203
Tomato	160
Soup, condensed (prepared with water), 1 cup	
Chicken noodle	75
Split pea with ham	189
Tomato	86
Sour cream, ¼ cup	
Fat-free	60
Light	80
Regular-fat	123
Sour cream dip, 1 ounce	40
Soy sauce, 1 tablespoon	10
Soy sauce, light, 1 tablespoon	11
Spaghetti, cooked, 1 cup	197
Spaghetti sauce, 1 cup	272
Spinach, ½ cup chopped	
Boiled	21
Raw	6
Strawberries, 1 cup	45
Squash, ½ cup	
Acorn, baked	57
Butternut, cooked	41
Spaghetti squash, cooked	23
Yellow summer, raw	12
Zucchini, raw	9
Succotash, cooked, ½ cup	111
Sugar, 1 tablespoon	
Brown	52
Granulated	48
Powdered	31
Sugar cookies, 2	71
Sweet potatoes	
Baked with skin, 1	118
Mashed, ½ cup	172
Swiss cheese, 1 ounce	107

T

Toaster pastries, 1 pastry	195
Tomatoes, 1	26
Tomatoes, dried, ½ cup	70
Tomatoes, dried and packed in oil, ½ cup	118
Tomatoes, stewed, 1 cup	80
Tomato juice, ½ cup	21
Tomato paste, ½ cup	110
Tomato sauce, ½ cup	37
Tortilla chips, 1 ounce	142
Tortillas, corn, 1	58
Tortillas, flour, 1	104
Turkey	
Bacon, cooked, 2 slices	68
Dark meat, without skin, roasted, 3 ounces	160
Ground, cooked, 3 ounces	188
Light meat, without skin, roasted, 3 ounces	135

V-Y

Vanilla wafers, 5	92
Veal, round, cooked, 3 ounces	129
Vegetable juice cocktail, ½ cup	23
Waffles, 1	245
Watermelon, 1 cup pieces	50
Wheat germ, toasted, ¼ cup	108
Whipped dessert topping, frozen, 1 tablespoon	
Light	10
Regular	15
Whipped topping mix (prepared), 1 tablespoon	
Reduced-calorie	5
Regular	10
Whole-grain rye wafers, 2	45
Whole wheat crackers, 2	40
Wine, 3.5 fluid ounces	
Red	74
White	70
Worcestershire sauce, 1 tablespoon	11
Yogurt	
Frozen, soft-serve, ½ cup	115
Fruit-flavored, fat-free, 8 ounces	120
Fruit-flavored, low-fat, 8 ounces	225
Plain, low-fat, 8 ounces	144
Vanilla, low-fat, 8 ounces	194

fast foods

Burrito, bean	447
Chicken	
Breast, breaded and fried	283
6 boneless pieces, breaded and fried	290
Chicken fillet sandwich, plain	515
Cookies, animal crackers	
1 box	299
Eggs, scrambled	
1 serving	140
English muffin	
With egg, cheese, and Canadian bacon	383
Fish sandwich	
With tartar sauce	431
With tartar sauce and cheese	523
French fries	
Small	220
Large	400
Hamburger	
Regular size, with condiments	275
Regular size, with cheese and condiments	295
Ham sandwich, with cheese	352
Hot dog, plain	242
Ice milk	
Vanilla, soft-serve, with cone	164
Pizza, 1 slice	
With cheese	140
With cheese, meat, and vegetables	184
Roast beef sandwich, plain	346
Shake	
Chocolate (small)	318
Vanilla (small)	278
Sundae, strawberry	268
Taco, 1 small	369
Tostada	
With beans, beef, and cheese	333

index

METRIC COOKING HINTS

By making a few conversions, cooks in Australia, Canada, and the United Kingdom can use the recipes in *Better Homes and Gardens® New Dieter's Cookbook* with confidence. The charts on this page provide a guide for converting measurements from the U.S. customary system, which is used throughout this book, to the imperial and metric systems. There also is a conversion table for oven temperatures to accommodate the differences in oven calibrations.

Product Differences: Most of the ingredients called for in the recipes in this book are available in English-speaking countries. However, some are known by different names. Here are some common American ingredients and their possible counterparts:
■ Sugar is granulated or castor sugar.
■ Powdered sugar is icing sugar.
■ All-purpose flour is plain household flour or white flour. When self-rising flour is used in place of all-purpose flour in a recipe that calls for leavening, omit the leavening agent (baking soda or baking powder) and salt.
■ Light corn syrup is golden syrup.
■ Cornstarch is cornflour.
■ Baking soda is bicarbonate of soda.
■ Vanilla is vanilla essence.
■ Green, red, or yellow sweet peppers are capsicums.
■ Golden raisins are sultanas.

Volume and Weight: Americans traditionally use cup measures for liquid and solid ingredients. The chart, *top right,* shows the approximate imperial and metric equivalents. If you are accustomed to weighing solid ingredients, the following approximate equivalents will be helpful.
■ 1 cup butter, castor sugar, or rice = 8 ounces = about 250 grams
■ 1 cup flour = 4 ounces = about 125 grams
■ 1 cup icing sugar = 5 ounces = about 150 grams
   Spoon measures are used for smaller amounts of ingredients. Although the size of the tablespoon varies slightly in different countries, for practical purposes and for recipes in this book, a straight substitution is all that's necessary.
   Measurements made using cups or spoons always should be level unless stated otherwise.

EQUIVALENTS: U.S. = AUSTRALIA/U.K.

⅛ teaspoon = 0.5 ml
¼ teaspoon = 1 ml
½ teaspoon = 2 ml
1 teaspoon = 5 ml
1 tablespoon = 15 ml
¼ cup = 2 tablespoons = 2 fluid ounces = 60 ml
⅓ cup = 3 fluid ounces = 90 ml
½ cup = 4 fluid ounces = 120 ml
⅔ cup = 5 fluid ounces = 150 ml
¾ cup = 6 fluid ounces = 180 ml
1 cup = 8 fluid ounces = 240 ml
2 cups = 16 fluid ounces (1 pint) = 475 ml
1 quart = 32 fluid ounces (2 pints) = 1 litre
½ inch =1.27 cm
1 inch = 2.54 cm

BAKING PAN SIZES

American	Metric
8×1½-inch round baking pan	20×4-centimetre cake tin
9×1½-inch round baking pan	23×3.5-centimetre cake tin
11×7×1½-inch baking pan	28×18×4-centimetre baking tin
13×9×2-inch baking pan	30×20×3-centimetre baking tin
2-quart rectangular baking dish	30×20×3-centimetre baking tin
15×10×1-inch baking pan	30×25×2-centimetre baking tin (Swiss roll tin)
9-inch pie plate	22×4- or 23×4-centimetre pie plate
7- or 8-inch springform pan	18- or 20-centimetre springform or loose-bottom cake tin
9×5×3-inch loaf pan	23×13×7-centimetre or 2-pound narrow loaf tin or paté tin
1½-quart casserole	1.5-litre casserole
2-quart casserole	2-litre casserole

OVEN TEMPERATURE EQUIVALENTS

Fahrenheit Setting	Celsius Setting*	Gas Setting
300°F	150°C	Gas Mark 2 (slow)
325°F	160°C	Gas Mark 3 (moderately slow)
350°F	180°C	Gas Mark 4 (moderate)
375°F	190°C	Gas Mark 5 (moderately hot)
400°F	200°C	Gas Mark 6 (hot)
425°F	220°C	Gas Mark 7
450°F	230°C	Gas Mark 8 (very hot)
Broil		Grill

*Electric and gas ovens may be calibrated using Celsius. However, for an electric oven, increase the Celsius setting 10° to 20° when cooking above 160°C. For convection or forced-air ovens (gas or electric), lower the temperature setting 10°C when cooking at all heat levels.